Decentering the Nation

Music, Culture, and Identity in Latin America

Series Editors: Pablo Vila, Temple University, and Héctor Fernández L'Hoeste, Georgia State University

Music is one of the most distinctive cultural characteristics of Latin American countries. But, while many people in the United States and Europe are familiar with musical genres such as salsa, merengue, and reggaetón, the musical manifestations that people listen to in most Latin American countries are much more varied than these commercially successful ones that have entered the American and European markets. The Music, Culture, and Identity in Latin America series examines the ways in which music is used to advance identity claims in different Latin American countries and among Latinos in the U.S. The series sheds new light on the complex ways in which music provides people from Latin American countries with both enjoyment and tools for understanding who they are in terms of nationality, region, race, ethnicity, class, gender, age, sexuality, and migration status (among other identitarian markers). Music, Culture, and Identity in Latin America seeks to be truly interdisciplinary by including authors from all the social sciences and humanities: political science, sociology, psychology, musicology, cultural studies, literature, history, religious studies, and the like.

Recent Titles in This Series

Decentering the Nation: Music, Mexicanidad, and Globalization
    by Jesús A. Ramos-Kittrell
The Latin American Songbook in the Twentieth Century: From Folklore to Militancy
    by Tânia Costa Garcia
Thinking about Music from Latin America: Issues and Questions
    by Juan Pablo González, translated by Nancy Morris
Sound, Image, and National Imaginary in the Construction of Latin/o
    American Identities
    edited by Pablo Vila and Héctor Fernández L'Hoeste

Decentering the Nation

Music, Mexicanidad, and Globalization

Edited by Jesús A. Ramos-Kittrell

LEXINGTON BOOKS
Lanham • Boulder • New York • London

Published by Lexington Books
An imprint of The Rowman & Littlefield Publishing Group, Inc.
4501 Forbes Boulevard, Suite 200, Lanham, Maryland 20706
www.rowman.com

6 Tinworth Street, London SE11 5AL, United Kingdom

Copyright © 2020 The Rowman & Littlefield Publishing Group, Inc.

All rights reserved. No part of this book may be reproduced in any form or by any electronic or mechanical means, including information storage and retrieval systems, without written permission from the publisher, except by a reviewer who may quote passages in a review.

British Library Cataloguing in Publication Information Available

Library of Congress Control Number: 2019951229

ISBN 978-1-4985-7317-7 (cloth)
ISBN 978-1-4985-7318-4 (electronic)

Contents

List of Figures   vii

Acknowledgments   ix

Foreword   xi
by Chela Sandoval

Introduction: Post-Mexicanidad apropos of the Postnational   xix
by Jesús A. Ramos-Kittrell

1   Afrodiasporic Visual and Sonic Assemblages: Racialized Anxieties and the Disruption of Mexicanidad in *Cine de Rumberas*   1
by Laura G. Gutiérrez

2   The *Danza de Inditas* in the Mexican Huasteca Region: Decolonizing Nationalist Discourse   23
by Lizette Alegre González

3   Chavela's Frida: Decolonial Performativity of the Queer Llorona   47
by Ana R. Alonso-Minutti

4   Vaquero World: Queer Mexicanidad, Trans Performance, and the Undoing of Nation   77
by Nadine Hubbs

5   *Soy gallo de Sinaloa jugado en varios palenques*: Production and Consumption of Narco-music in a Transnational World   99
by César Burgos Dávila and Helena Simonett

6	*Yo lo digo sin tristezas* (I say it without lament): Transnational Migration, Postnational Voicings, and the Aural Politics of Nation by Alex E. Chávez	127
7	Reclaiming 'the Border' in Texas-Mexican Conjunto Heritage and Cultural Memory by Cathy Ragland	149
8	Sounding Cumbia: Past and Present in a Globalized Mexican Periphery by Jesús A. Ramos-Kittrell	169
9	Southern California Chicanx Music and Culture: Affective Strategies within a Browning Temporal System of Global Contradictions by Peter J. García	193
10	Listening from 'The Other Side': Music, Border Studies, and the Limits of Identity Politics by Alejandro L. Madrid	211

Index	231
About the Contributors	237

List of Figures

Figure 1.1	Lobby card of the film *Coqueta* (Azteca Films, Inc., 1949).	2
Figure 1.2	Lobby card of the film *Mulata* (Azteca Films, Inc., 1954).	8
Figure 2.1	Dance during the watch for the *Virgen de Guadalupe*. Atotomoc, municipality of Atlapexco, Hidalgo.	31
Figure 2.2	*Inditas* of the "Virgen Morena" group. Atotomoc, municipality of Atlapexco, Hidalgo.	33
Figure 3.1	Frida Kahlo and, allegedly, Chavela Vargas ca. 1945.	57
Figure 4.1	Tardeada Vaquera outside Chicago, August 2018.	85
Figure 5.1	Screen shot of singer-songwriter Chalino Sánchez from the music video "Ati mi grandola."	103
Figure 7.1	Mural depicting Narisco Martinez and Freddy Fender in downtown San Benito.	154
Figure 7.2	San Benito's water tower memorializing the image of Freddy Fender.	159
Figure 9.1	Mariachi procession celebrating the *Fiesta de Santa Cecilia* at Boyle Heights.	198
Figure 9.2	Mariachi performance during the *Misa de Santa Cecilia*.	199

Figure 10.1	Screen shot of Doris at the Sixth Street Bridge in the film *Del otro lado del puente* (1979).	214
Figure 10.2	Screen shot of the football choreography in the film *Del otro lado del puente* (1979).	216
Figure 10.3	*El México que se nos fue* (1995), cover of music album by Juan Gabriel.	221
Figure 10.4	Screen shot of Juan Gabriel talking to Juan, the fictional return migrant in the video of "Canción 187" (1995).	222

Acknowledgments

This volume benefitted greatly from the support of the following entities and individuals. The editor and contributors would first like to thank Suzanne Ryan for the generous time she unselfishly spent assisting with feedback during the initial stages of this project. Her comments and suggestions greatly helped to galvanize ideas and move production of the volume forward. We would also like to thank the Humanities Institute; the Women's Gender and Sexuality Studies Program; El Instituto: Institute of Latina/o, Caribbean, and Latin American Studies; and the Department of Music of the University of Connecticut for their sponsorship of the colloquium *Decentering the Nation: Music, Mexicanidad, and Globalization*. This two-day event brought the contributors to this book into a dialogue about the points of intersection between their case studies. The substance and development of ideas, and the organic coherence of the book was the result of this stimulating exchange. We would also like to thank dearly our supporters from Lexington Books—Pablo Vila and Héctor Fernández L'Hoeste, editors of the series Music, Culture, and Identity in Latin America—for fully endorsing this project; and our fantastic editor, Nicolette Amstutz, for seeing that its intellectual energy reaches fruition.

More personally, the authors would like to acknowledge the following people: Laura G. Gutiérrez would like to thank Licia Fiol-Matta, Viviana García Besné, Yolanda Montes "Tongolele," and the staff at the LLILAS Benson Latin American Collection of The University of Texas at Austin. Lizette Alegre González thanks the dance group "Virgen Morena" from Atotomoc in Atlapexco, state of Hidalgo (Mexico). Ana Alonso-Minutti is grateful for the feedback received from Susan Campos Fonseca, Silvia Martínez, Pepa Anastasio, Carlota Aguilar, Laura G. Gutiérrez, Marysol Quevedo, Amanda Petersen, Kency Cornejo, Hettie Malcomson, Henry Stobart, and Sergio de la Mora; and for the assistance of Lisa White, Tim Mallette, and

Aubrie Powell during the elaboration of her chapter. Nadine Hubbs is grateful to Cáel Keegan, Curtis Marez, Lorena Munoz, Nancy de los Santos, Barry Shank, Ruby Tapia, Mary Weismantel, Sergio G. Barrera, Matthew Leslie Santana, Kerry P. White, and Elizabeth F. S. Roberts for their assistance; and to the University of Michigan Institute for Research on Women and Gender; the College of Literature, Science, and the Arts; and the Office of Research. César Burgos Dávila would like to thank the *Consejo Nacional de Ciencia y Tecnología* (CONACyT), and the *Programa para el Desarrollo Profesional Docente* (PRODEP) for their support of his research. Cathy Ragland thanks Rogelio Nuñez (co-founder and director of the Narciso Martínez Cultural Arts Center), Reynaldo Avila (founder and director of the Conjunto Music Hall of Fame and Museum in San Benito), and art historian/photographer Carlos Roberto DeSouza. Jesús A. Ramos-Kittrell would like to thank Ágnes Vojtkó, Pálné Vojtkó, Pál Vojtkó, and Eszter Varjassy for providing the space necessary to finish drafting the introduction and editing the final manuscript of the book. Peter J. García is grateful to Mark Slobin, Su Zheng, and Eric Charry for organizing the 2011 summer institute "Ethnomusicology and Global Culture," sponsored by the National Endowment for the Humanities, the Society for Ethnomusicology, and Wesleyan University, which was the seed of the ideas developed in his chapter.

These are all of the people and entities that in one way or another influenced the production of this project, which now comes to completion.

Before the Sounding of Ideas, Before the Symbology of Sound
or
Radical Post-Border Studies: Music and the Decentered Nation-State

Foreword

Chela Sandoval

"[We must] consider processes of aural signification . . . in order to grasp the contradictions that lie at their core, and that outline political possibilities that have been lost in our purview, where the marginal subject is recognized only as the underdeveloped figure of history."

—Jesús A. Ramos-Kittrell

"Classifications of race and gender, now entangled with modern sexuality and class, remain fundamental to state authority and affiliated endeavors to concentrate power, property, and security in the hands of the few . . . However, a vibrant assortment of sounds, symbols, and practices performatively conjure [these classifications in relation to] mexicanidad and nationalist history, identity, and pride, even as the same elements serve, in this transnationally constituted space, to deconstruct, de-essentialize, and decenter mexicanidad, and to dilute nation and national identity."

—Nadine Hubbs

This book represents a major intervention in academic thought. Its chapters insist on and demonstrate how musicality, aurality, the sonic—and especially their myriad intersections with the bodily senses—are crucial to the ideological training that creates every person's sense of citizen-subjectivity.[1] The authors make it a point to show us how the aural participates in, positions, and narrativizes our social locations. But it is not enough to recognize how sound impacts the making and (un)making of citizen-subjectivity. *Decentering the Nation* also insists that we must identify and deploy the *methods* necessary to self-consciously decode and recode what is sonically perceived.[2]

This volume's contributions, however, extend beyond these methodological and theoretical interventions in the field of music studies, because its music authors have also brought their collective focus on globalization in relation to the U.S./Mexico borderlands. One result is that *Decentering the Nation* teaches us new ways to comprehend the aesthetic, cultural, and political tremors, the violence and mass murders that are taking place in contact zones everywhere. It is under these very conditions that authors have labored to bring eccentric routes towards emancipation, identified in part as unexpected and creative lines of resistance that, however, can also transform into accessories to domination. This phenomenon is part of what Ramos-Kittrell identifies as a complex "complicity with power." The "decentering of the nation," he continues, has turned cultures into "regionally situated" sites of "subversion and ferment," such that certain kinds of "collusions" with power should become recognized as "a necessary kind of political agency in globalization," and part and parcel of a postnational condition. (From the "Introduction.")

So begins a book that courageously tackles the effects of the sonic on the making and challenging of national ideologies, globalized cultures, and the forms of being encouraged (or not) to inhabit the worlds we have made. The volume challenges us to change the ways we comprehend the presence of bordered nation-states; redefines how we go about thinking and feeling our ways inside and through 'mexicanidad' and citizenship; and opens up new ways to perceive, and understand, what and how we are affected by, and trained to 'hear'.

These aims are achieved through analyses offered by leading thinkers in the fields of music, cultural anthropology, psychology, gender and sexuality, border and transnational ethnic studies. They ground their chapters in topics that include the sounds, musics, and meanings created among Indigenous communities; postnational expressions in conjunto musics; the sonic sides of identity politics; the queer and loving artistries of Chavela Vargas and Frida Kahlo; huapango arribeño music and its time-space re- and dis-locations; the magnetizing musics of a "Chicano Batman"; narco-musics and their political interventionism; the sonic assemblages captured in *cine de rumberas*; a form of queer mexicanidad wherein possibilities are opened for re-becoming gendered; and the ways in which the DJ's SWAPA[3] of a *sonidero* become a storytelling method for (re)historicizing sonic signifiers, and making them capable of crossing class, gender, epistemological, and geographical boundaries.[4]

The chapters are written from varying phenomenological sites and from wavering geo-national borders. Their combined outcomes set meanings in motion that demonstrate the liberatory and confining impacts of sound. What authors insist upon across all their engagements (whether with sound, nationality or borders, and regardless of their varying methodological approaches) is the possibility of a twenty-first-century form of being that is capable of crossing ontological enclosures and of reaching into broader contact zones. Today, negotiating boundaries has become a postnational necessity.

Decentering the Nation reevaluates the power tensions that take place in points of encounter, be it the borders of nation-states or even the borders of being. As I write this Foreword in August of 2019, U.S./Mexico, Hong Kong/ China, and Israel/Palestine contact zones are burning. Days ago, an assassination/mass murder by a U.S. white supremacist took the lives of twenty-seven "Mexican"/"Hispanic"/"Latinx"/"Indigenous" peoples in El Paso, Texas. Twenty minutes before the murders a manifesto was posted online that planned to stop a "Hispanic invasion": in order to ensure that "If we can get rid of enough people our way of life can be more sustainable. White people [will not be] replaced by foreigners."[5]

Decentering the Nation shows us how it is at such borders, understood as contact zones, where political/ideological sentiments are intensified; 'permissible' citizen-subjectivities are in constant formulation; and where processes of domination and subordination are set into place. At the same time, the book reveals how these boundaries can be understood as laboratories where new kinds of feeling, being, becoming, and making constantly converge. Each chapter offers readers an original diagnosis of sonic expressions understood as media that carry the symptoms and effects of current geo-political conditions. Sound, its authors insist, has been an important element in the constitution of patriotic nationalism. But so, too, they contend the sonic can work to challenge the structures of this ideational form. Ideas such as these allow the book's authors to identify and produce what can be considered a postnational scholarship, a contribution to what has also been engaged as "postcontinental," or as "third world decolonial" scholarship.[6] These are all approaches to knowledge formation that challenge the very bases of those imperial knowledge forms that rationalized the division of the planet into nation-states. The authors in this volume decode and release previous political, sonic, and aural significations, which in their hands are transformed into keys that open alternative modes of perception, doing, and being.

Third-world feminist thinkers including Gloria Anzaldúa, Paula Gunn Allen, Audre Lorde, and Janice Mirikitani also anticipated the intellectual and political possibilities of such analytic and political work.[7] In their political scholarship, hearing and active witnessing, understood in relation to the mobilities of the sensorium and perception, were advanced under the rubrics of "borderlands" or "third space" studies, "oppositional differential consciousness," or as radical "third world feminism." These are bio-semiotic approaches that expose and 'cross' the artificiality of governmentally imposed nation-state borders, and promote ways of comprehending how becoming a legitimized being is a *created* process. One goal of these thinker/activists was to bring attention to the lives of beings of the in-between—and of a racially (un) bordered beingness.[8] Their work leads us from Anzaldúa's final visions of a cross-border planetary "new tribalism" of "nepantleras", to Sylvia Wynters's denomination of the "human" as a western, patriarchal invention; and to Frantz Fanon's analysis of the "soul" as a "white man's construct." To investigate and dwell on these kinds of (de)borderings (i.e., to reside on Fanon's "threshold" of consciousness) is what also opened the possibility for cross-national solidarities. Their thinking prepared the grounds for transforming how and what we know, and for creating the new forms of political beingness referred to as intersectionality.

This is an alternative third-space politics that allowed them to develop a post-Descartian, post-Freudian theory of consciousness, conceived as a body/emotion/mind matrix (b/e/m matrix with the "mind" understood as one of the senses). Liberation philosophers Audre Lorde and Gloria Anzaldúa both identified this matrix as the location of the "soul," the place the soul is "made" (Anzaldúa's "making face, making soul"). This is a re-cognition that provides perceivers access to a "matrixing" identity that is always available to transformation. As Anzaldúa puts it, this matrixing is an effect and result of powers that also constantly and, in Lorde's words, "erotically" move into and through the senses differentially, in a manner that can potentially renew the perceiving being in an always-rising present time of body, emotions, and mind.

Decentering the Nation calls up these kinds of knowledges and practices through what some of its authors deploy as a "radical bio-semiology," the methodology of a practitioner who tracks the movement of meaning through its own body—its perceptual apparatus; that is, through its body/mind/emotion matrix. This tracking occurs through the ability of consciousness to "meta-witness" its own operation; the meta-witness is capable of wonder at the ways in which the body is 'conducted' in the atmosphere of social meanings to generate responses, emotions, images, thoughts, ideas, and narratives. Radical bio-semiology thus opens the lens of consciousness to "aesthesis." It is a method wherein practitioners self-consciously read the cultural production of their own senses. The sound worlds revealed in *Decentering the Nation* lead readers to a "meta-witnessing" consciousness, to what Fanon describes as the "open door" of every consciousness, or to what Anzaldúa describes as a "spiritual activism." In another place in this book, meta-witnessing is described as the place where a postnational "affective citizenship" begins to be possible—a feeling and state of being that can create country people of a shared psychic terrain, in the same way that 1980s third-world feminists also connected across their ethnic, class, genderized, and racialized differences inside a shared global site of belonging, what Anzaldúa hopefully described as a "new tribalism."

There is thus a kind of language shared by the authors of this volume through which they communicate new forms of meaning which I think of as a "soundlect" necessary to transinterpret aural impacts as they affect and effect our political beingness.[9] The transdisciplinary work in this book moves beyond normalized canons and categories in order to identify and analyze the poetic and political musicalities of Mexican, U.S., Indigenous, African, Asian, Xicanx, and hybrid sounds, auralities, gestures, speech, and their effects (self-aware or not) on b/m/e matrices. Each chapter demonstrates how different acts create or reveal national, pre- and/or post-national aesthetics, politics, identities, sites of loyalties, and memberships. They teach us to meta-witness the mobile and complex formations of political and personal realities. The collection opens up and points to how we can think through and enact methods capable of materializing *postnational* forms of thinking, decoding, understanding, doing, and being.

The designed forms of postnationality explored in this book challenge the borders of every condition, and move beyond the imposed violences through which bodies, minds, and the planet itself have been shaped and enclosed. A living poetic musicality of being, a differential, matrixing relation to the senses understood as a b/m/e matrix makes such postnational consciousness possible—and opens up new paths to follow. This book is one of these openings. Chapter titles can be read as an index of decolonial performantics. They reveal sonic significations as keys that allow us to enter terrains that cross the present enclosures of cartography, theory, and method making. This book teaches us to write, think, and become through what I recognize as the sonic physics of the social—which is similar in function to Audre Lorde's understanding of the social powers of emotion and sensation and their parts in generating the social physics of love. For in all social physics, the sonic is comprised of media that are carried through the frequencies and flows of power.

NOTES

1. See Ellie D. Hernández, *Postnationalism in Chicana/o Literature and Culture* (Austin, TX: University of Texas Press, 2009); Ellie D. Hernández and Eliza Rodriguez y Gibson, eds., *The Un/Making of Latina/o Citizenship: Culture, Politics, and Aesthetics* (New York: Palgrave Macmillan, 2014); and Dolores Inés Casillas, *Sounds of Belonging. U.S. Spanish-language Radio and Public Advocacy* (New York: New York University Press, 2014).

2. These are not necessarily new aims, they have been confronted by previous influential scholars of music, sound, performance and global studies. A few examples: Roland Barthes, *Image-Music-Text* (New York: Hill and Wang; 1977); Gloria Anzaldúa, *Borderlands La Frontera: The New Mestiza* (San Francisco: Aunt Lute Books, 1987); Rafael Pérez-Torres, *Mestizaje: Critical Uses of Race in Chicano Culture* (Minneapolis: University of Minnesota Press, 2006); Jacques Attali, *Noise: The Political Economy of Music* (Manchester: Manchester University Press, 1985); Diane Taylor, *The Archive and the Repertoire: Performing Cultural Memory in the Americas* (Durham: Duke University Press, 2003).

3. SWAPA is the acronym for "Storytelling-Witnessing/World-Art/Performance as Activism." See Eddy Francisco Alvarez Jr., "Jotería Pedagogy, SWAPA, and Sandovalian Approaches to Liberation," *Aztlán: A Journal of Chicano Studies* 39, 1 (Spring 2014): 215–227.

4. See the authors in this volume, Alegre González, Ragland, Madrid, Alonso-Minutti, Burgos Dávila and Simonett, Chávez, García, Gutiérrez, Hubbs, and Ramos-Kittrell.

5. Tim Arango, Nicholas Bogel-Burroughs, Katie Benner, "Minutes Before El Paso Killing, Hate-Filled Manifesto Appears Online," *The New York Times* (August 3, 2019): https://www.nytimes.com/2019/08/03/us/patrick-crusius-el-paso-shooter-manifesto.html.

6. See, for example, Nelson Maldonado-Torres, "Thinking through the Decolonial Turn: Post-continental Interventions in Theory, Philosophy, and Critique," *Transmodernity* (Fall 2011): and Chela Sandoval "U.S. Third World Feminism: The Theory and Method of Oppositional Consciousness in the Postmodern World," *Genders* 10 (Spring 1991): 1–24. Also, in her play *The Hungry Woman*, Cherríe Moraga critiques Aztlan, indeed, critiques all national borders. The location of the play is situated beyond the borders of Mexico, the U.S., and Xicanidad. This Xicana 'post-Aztlan' location puts identities in conversation from differing national and postnational locations. Some peoples argue that Chicanx reality cannot be contained by borders, and that borders completely fail to explain it, which is in part why Anzaldúa's work on an ever expanding 'borderlands' is so foundational to Chicana and Chicano studies.

7. Gloria Anzaldúa, *Borderlands La Frontera: The New Mestiza* (San Francisco: Aunt Lute Books, 1987); Paula Gunn Allen, *The Sacred Hoop: Recovering the Feminine in American Indian Traditions* (Boston: Beacon Press, 1992); Audre Lorde, *Sister Outsider: Essays and Speeches* (Trumansburg, NY: Crossing Press, 1984); Janice Mirikitani, *Time to Greeze!: Incantations from the Third World* (San Francisco: Third World Press,1975).

8. 1980s political activism and philosophies of third-wor(l)d feminism continue to reverberate today. This Foreword would be remiss should it not remind us of its continuing presence, and resistances to it, in the contemporary moment. On July 17, 2019, television anchorman George Stephanopulos reported on the ABC News program "Good Morning America": "Attacking four congresswomen, the president was met with raucus chants of support at his first campaign rally of 2012. The crowd ate him up." (This alternative sensorial eating ends with aural mayhem when the crowd begins chanting "Send her back.") This is how it happened:

President Trump at the podium, calling out: "Representative Ilhan Omar."

[The large audience roars its reaction to her name that coalesces into a unified chant filling the auditorium: "Send her back! Send her back! Send her back!"]

Reporter Terry Moran voice-over: "The crowd calling for U.S. State of Minnesota congresswoman Ilhan Omar to be sent back to the country she left as a child. Omar is a U.S. citizen. The president even proudly refused to call representative Alexandria Ocasio-Cortez by her full name." Trump, continuing: "I don't have time to go by three names. We'll call her 'Cortez'." Moran visual and audio: "For days Trump has hammered the four freshman lawmakers, all of them women of color, saying they should go back to where they originally came from…[Cut back to audio and visual of Trump.] Trump: "If they don't love it, tell them to leave it." [The crowd agrees in roaring unison.]

Moran, voice-over: "Three of the four lawmakers were born in America." Trump on-screen continuing his speech: "Do they want to be American or not? It's their choice . . ." [Cut back to Moran.] Moran: "The president's base doesn't see all this as race-based rhetoric, but as patriotism." Audience member, a middle-aged Anglo-American man in a baseball cap: "It has nothing to do with race—it has more to do with values: do they want to be American, or not?" [Cut back to Trump as he concludes his speech.]

Trump: "A vote for any democrat in 2020 is a vote for the rise of radical socialism and the destruction of our country, the destruction of the American dream; frankly, the destruction of our country.")

Stephanopoulos: "The president's crowd are ever more energetic, wild, revved up . . . a classic American nativist, populist playbook, out to define who gets to be an American. Not based on citizenship, but on loyalty as he, and they define it."

9. On "transinterpretation" see Alicia Gaspar de Alba's foundational work on the Codex Nepantla: www.codexnepantla.net.

Introduction

Post-Mexicanidad apropos of the Postnational

Jesús A. Ramos-Kittrell

The virulent attacks of presidential candidate Donald Trump against Mexican individuals in 2016 brought to mind Roger Bartra's analysis of Mexico's populist movement, which by the time of the presidential election in Mexico in 2012 had acquired significant strength. It was not that Trump's characterization of Mexicans as "criminals and rapists"—a mass of "bad hombres" (Ross 2016)—resonated with imaginings of Mexican populism. Rather, it was that in both cases the mediation of images of difference was a political strategy to tap into the emotions of people to appeal for the recovery of traditions linked to the idea of historical struggle. In the U.S., Trump's comments were meant to stir deep-seated sentiments among white, blue-collar Americans about being left out of a project of economic expansion. The corporate weight of agribusiness on rural communities, the effects of gentrification in urban public spaces, the lack of access to mechanisms and tools for social mobility (to which the increased corporatization of higher education should be added), the outsourcing of manufacture, and the uneven distribution of wealth and financial responsibilities towards the state (i.e., taxation) created an emotional reservoir of frustration that was exploited in the 2016 presidential campaign.

At this critical moment the answer to Roger Bartra's question from 1997 became clear: will the great changes in the world (i.e., the fall of the Berlin Wall, the end of the Cold War, and the demise of communism as the alterity that threatened all American cultural and political values and interests) have an effect on the political system of the United States (2013, 55–56)? In 2016, the harnessing of a collective emotional reservoir in support of a cultural project that looked back at historical greatness related to concerns over the loss of social and economic welfare in relation to a system that married the idea of progress to 'traditional American' values, upheld and defended against alien threat.[1] Historically present in this system, the stimulation of feelings about otherness found a new figure—that of the marginal, blue-collar immigrant Mexican worker, now criminalized—to channel feelings of resentment. Thus, the evocation of a sense of collective memory about a productive white society that had made the United States 'the greatest country in the world' became a rhetorical tool to address the socio-economic anxiety produced by the post-Cold War global realignment that had strained the American political system.

Trump's populism resonated with the disquiet caused by the encroachment of corporate, "rigged capitalism" on the structure of the state, a symptom of the intensifying effects of neo liberalism, which people feared could lead to the disenfranchisement of a large segment of the working class (Luce 2019). In Mexico, on the other hand, the crumbling down of a revolutionary political system (related to the fall of an authoritarian apparatus and its cultural project —what Mario Vargas Llosa once called "the perfect dictatorship"—and the rise of armed movements in Chiapas under the Ejército Zapatista de Liberación Nacional, EZLN in 1994) loosened the knot tied up by links that connected the political and cultural existence of individuals to the state, and that assured their identification with a social system organized by its institutions. The disintegration of this knot affected the credibility of political discourses advocating for development (from the right and the left); undermined identity canons; and brought about an acute sense of cultural disorientation.

1994 was a particularly significant year in the move toward this historical moment. This was the year when the political system of the *Partido Revolucionario Institucional* (PRI) showed clear signs of decline, which eventually brought an end to institutionally established forms of 'Mexican' socio-cultural and political validation. But even though the insurrection of Indigenous groups under the banner of the EZLN (for whom the North American Free Trade Agreement—NAFTA—meant opening the Mexican southeast to privatization and systematic exploitation), the murder of PRI presidential candidate Luis Donaldo Colosio Riojas (a left-oriented politician who sought to implement a system of social reform), and the consequent economic crisis in Mexico (which in the second quarter of 1994 registered an unemployment rate of 6.6%; a 3.4% increase in the first five months following the implementation of NAFTA. See González Madrid 1997, 213) were a trifecta that marked the beginning of the end, the symptoms had been, nonetheless, accumulating prior to this year.

The *Plan Nacional de Desarrollo 1989–1994* (NPD—National Plan for Development) designed by President Carlos Salinas de Gortari aimed to alleviate extreme poverty, create well-remunerated employment, and protect and raise the buying power and overall well-being of the working class (PND 1989, 36–37). Nevertheless, the socioeconomic analysis presented by the *Confederación de Trabajadores de México* (CTM Confederation of Workers of Mexico) in 1993 painted a bleaker picture: between 1989 and 1993 unemployment reached a cumulative rate of 15%, well above the cumulative rate of growth in population. Such a rise resulted from a process of privatization, increased dismissals due to the decorporatization of state industries, and a general deceleration of the national economy since 1992 (González Madrid 1997, 212). The state of the country's economic structure made it harder for constituencies to find niches of political representation in the public sphere, where the economically active sector of the population received the most attention. One of the state's choices was to open channels of representation through the market afforded by cultural industries; a very calibrated democratic turn to sooth feelings of disenfranchisement (Lomnitz 2016, 238). Thus, NAFTA brought Mexico *into* North America to form part of a platform of 'development' through the liberalization of trade and the pressures that it would pose on the productive sector.[2] More than immersion, NAFTA submerged Mexico in globalization, officially jeopardizing a system that organized sociopolitical and cultural (although not necessarily democratic) action.

In the United States, the increasing rates of migration following the events of 1994 started to show the failure of the Mexican state to look after the public-corporate body of civil society in its inability to keep civil order. The infamous War on Drugs put this in evidence when the government's tactics only accelerated the proliferation of kidnappings, massacres in plain daylight, and the hanging of dead bodies in public view, among other things. The War on Drugs also put in evidence the government's lack of control over law enforcement, as local police cooperated with the cartels to perpetrate these actions. This produced deep feelings of mistrust in state institutions and deteriorated the fiber of civil society with the rampant level of impunity experienced every day. It is thus that, for César Burgos Dávila and Helena Simonett, 'North-Americanization' implied a profound symbolic and institutional questioning of mexicanidad. In their chapter on the production and consumption of narco-music in California (see this volume) the authors consider how the transnational popularity of this music reflected a demise of state authority in Mexico. As Burgos Dávila and Simonett observe, censorship of this music and its artists by the Mexican government only brought attention to its incapacity to stop drug-related violence. Moreover, the recognition of this music by the American music industry reframed 'Mexican' images (e.g., that of the Mexican peasant dedicated to growing crops in the countryside) in a way that, in their relation to narcotrafficking, undermined the institutional and political legitimacy of the Mexican state.

The precarious functioning of the state apparatus and its failure to address the immediate needs of the society during a time of violent chaos fueled desires to establish new forms of social solidarity in order to find channels of representation. Guided by the idea that subaltern groups are repositories of recyclable traditions, populist activists saw in peripheral ethnic communities the possibility of social, political, and cultural renewal. According to Roger Bartra, such activists aimed at knitting an affective structure of ideas and emotions for the recovery of traditions produced in the struggle (Bartra 2013, 149). Populist activism gathered momentum under Andrés Manuel López Obrador, a national socialist who eventually won the Mexican presidency in 2018. The event marked the final hour of the revolutionary socio-political system that had shaped the idea of 'Mexico' for most of the twentieth century, setting the stage for the possible socio-political and cultural reconfiguration of the country.

Soon after López Obrador took office in 2019 ethnicity became a point of focus. That year, writer Paco Ignacio Taibo II (named chief editor of Fondo de Cultura Económica, the nation's non-profit publishing group, subsidized by the government) released the documentary *Patria* (based on his book trilogy of the same name, published by Editorial Planeta). The documentary recounts historical events that occurred between 1854 and 1867. This was a period of political and cultural intervention, when Mexico was prey to foreign interests, and when it was liberated by a president in exile, Benito Juárez, an Indigenous man from Oaxaca who fought his way back to the capital. At the end of the film, a genuflection by Taibo II in front of an imposing statue of Juárez begins the list of credits, forgoing any mention of Juárez's masonic activity or of his endorsement by the U.S. government—who supplied arms to fight a Habsburg emperor. Instead, the documentary ends with an exaltation of the president's Indigenous origins and of his activity during these years as the critical moment that forged the modern Mexican nation.

It would be far-fetched to say that Taibo II's reverential pose at the end of the film was a symbolic political maneuver to counter the class-laden, racist attacks towards López Obrador during both of his presidential campaigns, thereby identifying him with Juárez's stoic Indigenous figure. Nevertheless, given the strong pro-Indigenous stance of Mexico's president, Taibo II's gesture can hardly pass unnoticed. Not only has López Obrador's political career been supported by Indigenous groups for decades (Gallegos 2018), but he is also the first Mexican president to be given the *bastón de mando* (baton of command), a symbol of authority used by governing individuals in Indigenous societies. Throughout Latin America, Indigenous representatives have given this symbol to presidents who have shown a commitment to the interests and needs of groups neglected by previous governments (BBC News Mundo 2018). In López Obrador's case, the inauguration of the *Instituto Nacional de los Pueblos Indígenas* (Muñoz 2018), and the initiative to consult Indigenous and Afro-Mexican groups about constitutional and juridical reforms to civil rights policies are meant to highlight such commitment. Moreover, the president's demand to Spain for an apology to Mexico for the exploitation suffered during the colonial period was also symbolic of a disposition to enfranchise historically marginalized cultural groups. This moral gesture touched on a plethora of emotions that, for many people, arguably derive from an unhealed historical wound (Bartra 2013, 148). In this context, Taibo II's film presents an image of Juárez that comes across as a virtual transhistorical collage: that of a president representing the colonial Indigenous 'other,' converted into a mute symbol of 'tradition,' historically in struggle, and now making its voice heard.

The reckoning of Bartra's analysis was not so much because both cases—that of Mexico and the U.S.—are necessarily similar. It was because in both, the emotional appeal to historically loaded symbols of difference was a strategy to mobilize constituencies at a moment when the state had no credible mechanisms of representation. It was no longer possible for civil society to recognize itself in the structure of the nation. The need to create a representational space made it necessary to propose a historical 'place' where constituencies that have felt increasingly marginalized by the present neoliberal order could situate themselves. Yet, in each instance, 'Mexican' images (the American racialized figure of the blue-collar 'brown' immigrant, but also the Indigenous subject who under discourses of *indigenismo*, *mestizaje*, *campesinismo*, and *obrerismo* has informed the racialization of the working class and the agricultural sector) allude to difference as something that processes of collective arbitration need to grapple with to legitimize feelings of belonging that can situate people in these historical niches. In this respect that both projects contrast with each other: In Mexico, a project of social and political transformation accounts for the historical legacy of difference in order to enfranchise peripheral constituencies. In the U.S., the reframing of difference is a move to regain a sense of status quo, to make things 'great' again. As the U.S. looks back into the past, Mexico is trying to find a way of looking into the future.

* * *

These concerns for enfranchisement point to an anxiety for the validation of a sense of being, a subjectively experienced constitution of the world that produces a narrative of selfhood and that locates the subject 'somewhere.' As the political system that organizes the order of things breaks down—along with the symbols and narratives of heritage and history that inform its cultural project—the "who am I?" emerges as a temporal specter seeking to remap a space of being and belonging, along with its structuring mechanisms. "Where am I being?" (doing, making) produces an implicit "when" through the dynamics of collective bargaining that, in their interaction with institutions, constitute cultural memory in the imagination. The feeling of dislocation caused by the prevalent crisis of representation affecting the nation-state has led some scholars to inquire about a postnational condition.[3] In reaction to the effects that neoliberal capitalism has had on the capacity of the state to provide mechanisms for security, growth, and well-being to its citizens, postnational cultural studies gathered momentum in the early 2000s. Postnationalism became particularly pertinent in gaining insights into the globalizing and local elements that influence culture formation, and that challenge nationalist narratives of culture promoted by the state. Specifically, academic attention focused on issues of social justice in relation to cultural identity because scholars perceived culture as a potential resource of socio-political and economic improvement (Yúdice 2003, 9 and 82). Thus, postnational studies sharpened their scrutiny on the inability of the nation-state "to close the gap between the rich and the poor and its lack of capacity to provide tools for social mobility." A postnational condition, it was said, should aim not only for the adaptation of the nation-state to make it more responsive to human needs in global conditions (Dhanapala 2001), but also for the "recognition of the injustices, the omissions, the dismissals, and the repudiations that nationalist discourses have inflicted upon their citizens," thereby acknowledging "the ethnic, racial, sexual, and class diversity of the liminal citizens 'forgotten' by hegemonic nationalist discourses" in the cultural realm (Corona and Madrid 2008, 4–5).

While pointing to the shortcomings and pressures that dislodged a project of human development and the realization of potential from the state's apparatus, academic critique also denounced the state's suppression of diverse cultural subjectivities alien to its cultural project, and its incapacity to articulate an inclusive entelechy of human growth relevant to such diversity. Within the scope of this crisis, the nation became decentered because the global traffic of symbols, meanings, practices, people, and capital produced transnational sites of identification, which made nationalists' cultural narratives and symbols less important. The nation also became decentered because these sites realigned institutional structures, as the latter engaged with the local operational dynamics of the former. This last aspect prompts us to think of the decentered nation in terms of how its regulating structure has come to function regionally, and how people use it to articulate arenas of sustained political activity. Pundits on global economy have brought attention to this realignment, stressing that the state's regulatory capacity continues to mediate how corporations benefit from globally operating business strategies, such as aggregation (leveraging scalable assets across countries) and arbitrage (exploiting differences, such as labor costs, for example). The corporate economic "winners" in globalization, it has been said, will be those who can adjust to its international complexities instead of following global visions (Ghemawat and Altman 2019).

The rhetoric of interdependence among nations from the 2000s, therefore, has shifted to ideas about adaptability. This is of particular importance to cultural analyses given that the rhetoric of interdependence had previously considered culture a potential domain to foster strategies for social control. Culturally articulated and locally structured habits of exchange, it was said, could engage global forces in domains with less state control to be later assimilated. Close to two decades ago, this rhetoric was based on the idea that formed habits could eventually spill over into areas sensitive to institutional regulation and discipline. Thus, political and economic theorists thought that, once formed, chains of habits and behaviors could become collectively too strong to be broken (Dhanapala 2001). Yet, as the chapters in this volume show, local cultural fields remain important arenas of social action, where the articulation of habits, attitudes, and behaviors can be politically subversive against the globalizing effects of neoliberal policies (see Alegre González in this volume).

But what is the character of these cultural arenas and their political potential? What possibilities do they offer against disenfranchisement, one of the most alarming features characterizing the complex relationship between the state and the corporate economic system that seeks to regulate it? How do these cultural processes urge us to move beyond identitarian narratives of difference towards new strategies for representation and political inclusion? As far as a democratic intervention is concerned, these questions pose a formidable task in the domain of political action, for the social transactions transpiring in cultural fields are not necessarily alien to the effects of power. One cannot lose sight of the effects that asymmetrical power relations have had in the constitution of subjectivities, and of how these effects might shape the production of inclusive spaces of social participation. Foucault called for caution here, in terms of how any democratic and equitable advocacy in favor of peripheral constituencies derives from the very structures of power (and their regulating mechanisms) it attempts to critique.[4] In structuring the social and institutional landscape of agency (the doing and making of things), power relations also structure a temporal sense of being, which locates the subject historically. And yet, in their phenomenological dimensions (in the casting of behaviors, attitudes, and feelings), cultural arenas are highly contestatory given that affect can produce new links of social solidarity that resituate people and reorganize temporal imaginings of personhood. That is why for Claudio Lomnitz the importance of affect ought to make phenomenology a central component of cultural analyses, due to its implications in subjective temporal constitutions (2016, 305). Our task, then, ought to go against the impulse of embracing homogenized temporal nostalgias and focus on the processes of negotiation imbricated in the temporal rearrangements and relocations that emerge from cultural practices.[5] This type of analysis can hopefully lead to more audacious ideas that can intervene in the social and political challenges of the present.

These issues are not necessarily exclusive to questions of mexicanidad or of 'Mexican' culture. Nonetheless, these issues call, on the one hand, for an analytical lens to problematize the incumbent crisis of representation affecting the nation-state, and the rhetoric of difference that informs democratic inclusivist activism. On the other, they call for a cultural platform to contextualize this analysis. Mexicanidad is a topic most relevant to this volume: it is a construct historically steeped in difference, which nation-states (Mexico and the U.S.) have used to promote ideas of cultural legitimacy in relation to modern national political projects of social and economic development that are now under strain. The consideration of the emotions is central to this book, albeit not as sentimental textures prone to manipulation. Rather, we ought to consider them constitutive of the networks of agentive placement through which people negotiate the forces that mark them as different, and that allow them to reconfigure their sense of belonging. The present volume uses music as a phenomenological platform for this exploration in order to consider the performative elements that articulate cultural processes as arenas of politically subversive potential. Thus, the contributors to this volume seek neither to reframe mexicanidad as a cultural identity trope, nor to expound on what it is or ought to be. Rather, this book uses mexicanidad as a critical lens to shed light on the *trans*actional and *trans*gressive aspects of human imagination and behavior through which people negotiate difference in order to situate themselves, and that problematize mexicanidad as an identitarian construct. In doing so, these chapters do not hint at populism as a collective mechanism of political representation, nor do they suggest that such mechanism should focus its mediating efforts solely on the periphery. Instead, this volume focuses on the political character of cultural practices in light of the social alliances that emerge from phenomenological encounters, through which people stake claims on political enclosure.

The decentering of the nation in globalization, therefore, has made it necessary to think of the realignment of the state's structure in relation to the global flows that have upset nationalist symbologies and identitarian cultural narratives, and that urge us to rethink difference in order to find collective spaces of belonging in the public sphere. By addressing the otherizing tensions that, informed by issues of displacement, race, class, gender, and sexuality, have historically traversed mexicanidad in Mexico and the U.S., the chapters in this volume approach this premise as follows.

DE-TEMPORALIZING MEXICANIDAD

In Mexico, mexicanidad related to an identitarian sentiment—sometimes melancholic (see Chávez in this volume)—during the course of the twentieth century; a construct that the Mexican nation-state promoted as part of a revolutionary political and cultural project. Although an array of symbologies permeated mexicanidad through the different shapes that national identity acquired in different localities (Lomnitz 2016, 81), *indigenismo* vis-à-vis *mestizaje* articulated a large conceptual field through which state institutions and cultural industries deployed somewhat contradictory national images. It could be argued that, from the 1930s through the 1950s, indigenismo became a temporally imagined basis to forge mestizaje: a 'modern' notion of mexicanidad a by-product of the mixing of European and Indigenous cultures. The semi-western mestizo had a central symbolic place in the embodiment of mestizaje. Neither Indigenous (attempting to move beyond the socio-economic indicators of marginality that marked the *indio* as peripheral) nor white (dreaming of economic development and cosmopolitan inclusion as the undelivered promises of modernity), the mestizo was a desiring subject, liminal, engaged in the process of becoming modern. In contrast, *el indio* was a mute symbol, perennially on display in the waiting room of modernity, representing a point of departure and one of no return in the move towards 'progress' (see Alegre González in this volume). As such, mestizaje and indigenismo articulated racialized views of mexicanidad to the modern West: museum exhibits highlighted the monumental achievements of pre-Columbian cultures as the highest points of American (non-western) civilization. The promotion of local folk dances, handcrafts, and stories, and of excursions to emerging archeological sites further provided a focal point for indigenismo, and the historical girth that mestizaje needed as a cultural symbol of 'moving forward.' Government agencies channelled such constructs of mexicanidad through the tourism industry, advertising images of "sarape-clad, guitar strumming male figures in sombreros; young women in 'peasant' blouses and braids," and images of architectural sites dominated by pyramids (Saragoza 2001, 100–101). Mexico's film and radio industries were instrumental in forging a sonic representation of this imagery. Ranchera music and the mariachi ensemble became the most vivid aural symbols of mestizaje (for a discussion of this construct as a chrono-trope see Chávez in this volume), which the media propagated through films and a network of radio stations across America (Henriques 2006; see also Madrid 2013, 8–9). Thus, the western gaze towards Mexico focused on formalized exotic displays of class-based, gendered, contradictory otherness: mexicanidad as a symbol of the modern nation, yet assembled through its allusion to indigenismo and the ranchero, mestizo chrono-trope, both at the outskirts of modernity.

With this backdrop, the state promoted mexicanidad as a historical process of engagement with a political and cultural project for the formation of the modern 'Mexican' subject. In that project, the mestizo bore the racializing mark of coloniality: racialized as 'yet not western,' the mestizo also racialized otherness as regressive, alien to the environment where modernity happened. If *el rancho* (the ranch, the rural landscape) framed the image of the mestizo in ranchera music, the city became the space where this subject engaged in exoticizing, objectifying dynamics of racialization that formed part of the experience of modernity. Laura G. Gutiérrez shows us that it was in the city where the exotic objectification of the female body—through Afro-Caribbean rhythms and dance—became a strategy used by Mexican cultural industries to mediate anxieties around blackness. The production of films geared towards the urban population of the 1950s reproduced racialized desire as a way to experiment with 'otherization,' understood to be an aspect of the experience of modernity. The mestizo trope produced its own ethics of conduct in relation to patriarchal, gender-role-oriented forms of social and cultural behavior. As Gutiérrez explains, this middle-class, heteronormative form of desire was at the core of what the state saw as the ideal national subject who sought to become modern by consuming and discursively appropriating dominant narratives of race, gender, and sexuality.

The weakening of the state's political project after 1994 started to make visible cultural practices that contested these narratives. On the one hand, Indians, formerly silent signs used only to spill ink about 'Mexican identity roots,' became vocal subjects who could also spill blood in the Mexican southeast. As such, Indigenous subjects passed from being frozen symbols of atavistic tradition to being recognized as communities with histories of their own. In this regard, Lizette Alegre González's chapter on Nahua communities points out how the impact of globalization has made Indigenous groups re-approach the mechanisms that organize their social structures, in which music and dance rituals are pertinent to the affective configuration of their communities. Such re-approximation not only has disrupted the representational discourse that the Mexican state historically assigned to Indigenous societies, but also has reconfigured gender roles and the status of women in Nahua groups. As enunciative practices, music and dance have become affective strategies to reconstitute a sense of community, as well as to reframe ideas of race and gender.

At a deeper level, Alegre González emphasizes the political implications of phenomenological practices by stressing the subversive potential of affective labor, and its capacity to reconfigure subjectivity and sociability as processes that remap the production of community and that reposition subjects (Nahua women, in her chapter). Affective labor articulates territorial claims that localize culture through a system of uses and customs (*usos y costumbres*) prevalent in Indigenous communities. The subversive and political discursive potential of this system (as it pertains to the political visibility and agency of historical alterities and the organization of their affective practices) has not been immune to critique. Roger Bartra has mentioned that the notion of consensus—understood to be implicit in this Indigenous system—hides an oppressive mechanism of operation that does not allow for the possibility of dissent relative to the collective majority. In fact, Bartra argues that the affirmation of the Indigenous system of uses and customs involves the acceptance of an authoritarianism inherited from colonial forms of domination that have been naturalized by Indigenous groups. The system of uses and customs, therefore, has the repressive task of "blocking any 'non-traditional' minority. It is possible that mechanisms of government by unanimity are characteristic of some Indigenous communities. More than a pre-Hispanic flavor, however, what they release is an unequivocal PRIist stench" (2013, 39).

Bartra's commentary highlights an important concern for Indigenous forms of self-governmentality and cultural production that have been influenced by the political bureaucracy of previous governments. Likewise, his commentary shows skepticism about the rhetoric of political and cultural autonomy with which populist activists might try to manipulate the governing structures of Indigenous communities in order to stabilize the state's hegemony once again. Here, Alegre González cautions us about essentializing subjectivity either as Indigenous ancestral purity (understood as a system of uses and customs that reflects a 'true' Indigenous culture that has been suppressed and that should be acknowledged—a notion to which Bartra shrewdly objects) or as passive submission. Her chapter shows that Indigenous social structures indeed are not alien to the influence of power, and that negotiation is key to cultural sustainability and continuity. In this respect, her focus on affect shows the articulation of a biopolitics of resistance from below: affect produces sociability through the negotiation of state neoliberal policies in order to produce the community by an affective appeal to its members. Therefore, the constant re-adaptation of the system of uses and customs to an immediate political reality does not entail the operation of a suppressive unanimity or passive consensus. Rather, such transformation involves the negotiation of consensus, the consequent reconfiguration of community members, and of their status in the group, as well as of notions of personhood previously configured in and by that system.

On the other hand, affective claims on the body have also upset traditional views of gender and sexuality in relation to mexicanidad. In her chapter about

La Llorona, Ana R. Alonso-Minutti shows how the construction of a queer mexicanidad results from a homo-erotic gender encounter through this iconic figure of Mexican folklore. More specifically, Alonso-Minutti focuses on the relationship between Frida Kahlo and Chavela Vargas, and the lyrical character of La Llorona (in the song of the same name) to analyze views of womanhood that challenge narratives of femininity and gender binarism stemming from nationalist heteronormativity. Nadine Hubbs extends the scope of this critique by focusing on the Vaquero World as an affective arena where people from different Latin American nationalities engage in political acts of nation-branded affiliation and sentiment. These acts, Hubbs observes, splinter traditional images of mexicanidad in a transnationally participatory array of queer practices that evoke a 'Mexican' experience in order to bring people together socially and sexually. These performances cut against the grain of colonially constructed notions of gender, race, and sexuality that have informed cultural nationalist understandings of mexicanidad, and celebrate queer mexicanidad as a transnational and transgendered way of being in the world. The analyses of Alonso-Minutti and Hubbs raise important questions about phenomenology in relation to the body as a contestatory space. While Alonso-Minutti's chapter ponders decolonial notions of womanhood that upset traditionally conceived forms of femininity, Hubbs's chapter interrogates how binary readings of gender have subalternized queerness. Her analysis of transgendered performances problematizes the enactment of queerness in relation to mexicanidad as a multidimensional postgendered space through which gay Latin American migrants reclaim the liminality of their bodies. It is thus that the body functions as a phenomenological site to recast ideas of selfhood through queer experiences of gender and sexuality that have been historically marginalized.

In their focus on the body, these studies show a concern for the materiality of situated experience, which results from contesting institutionalized practices that have organized social and cultural behavior. More broadly, the examples of Alegre González, Alonso-Minutti, and Hubbs show how the negotiation of power relations situate the production of the subject, and that such negotiation has phenomenological implications. Other chapters expand this notion further, attending to memory as an element that situates the subject. The chapter dealing with Colombian music in Monterrey, Mexico (written by this author), addresses how middle-class DJs encrypted Colombian cumbia symbolically with images of urban marginality (the site where this music historically circulated in that city). DJs used that symbolism to cope with a concern for 'Mexican roots' in their globalized DJ practices. Thus, cultural representation involved the sounding of an imagined periphery by mixing cumbia (the sound of 'Mexican' urban marginality) with globalized sounds and DJ mixing practices (house, hip-hop). These efforts reflect an interest to re-situate the middle-class subject temporally by making class conflict (i.e., cumbia as a symbol of urban marginality articulating middle-class 'Mexican' nostalgia in the bourgeois space of electronic dance music) a condition for the reproduction of memory and subjecthood.

While this chapter reveals class-based claims to a discourse of territorial belonging, Alex E Chávez's chapter dealing with the performance of *son arribeño* by Mexican migrants in the U.S. addresses a different angle of this concern over memory and situatedness. His chapter delves into the phenomenological process through which musicians articulate a sense of memory and 'place' as part of an act of self-authorization. Self-authorization is a loaded term, as it alludes to both the musico-performative process through which people make sense out of their migratory experience, and to how this process legitimizes their sense of being territorially situated, despite their lack of legal recognition in the U.S. By making claims to "my land" (*mi tierra*) through the musical and lyrical performance of son arribeño, migrants articulate memory as a phenomenological construct that maps their surroundings affectively (referencing their Mexican origins through the performance of song in a new space), thereby legitimizing their territorial presence—even if momentarily—and challenging the power logics that, on the one hand, dislocated them from their place of origin to look for sustenance elsewhere; and on the other, attempt to make invisible the materiality of their presence in the U.S.

Cathy Ragland makes further insights into this process of territorialization and memory construction. Her chapter on conjunto music and cultural memory in San Benito, Texas comments on how power tensions between dominant U.S. culture and Mexicans and Mexican Americans in the Rio Grande Valley inform institutionalized ideas of border culture. While the presence of Mexican migrants has been constant in that region for decades, Mexican Americans with deeply entrenched family roots and a historical sense of lineage have ambivalent feelings about them. These attitudes notwithstanding, it is the liminal character of border life (neither fully 'American' nor fully 'Mexican') that moves both groups to stake territorial claims over ideas of heritage in San Benito. Conjunto music (identified with Mexican migrants through the figure of musician Narciso Martínez) and Tejano music (identified with Mexican Americans through the figure of musician Freddy Fender) are the affective sites to articulate these claims. Yet, the work of institutions such as music festivals, museums, and the municipal and state governments are instrumental in locating these claims territorially, and thus make San Benito a site to situate a sense of belonging through the institutionalization of cultural memory.

The chapters by Chávez, Ragland, and this author highlight how the articulation of memory points to a temporal process sensitive to power relations that configures the perception of reality in order to locate the subject. Peter J. García's chapter on Chicano music and culture in East Los Angeles makes a final commentary on the tensions that surround temporal claims on memory and belonging, while making a timely observation on the liminal character of difference. García argues that historically shifting notions of identity among Mexican Americans in California point to phenomenal changes in the experience of difference. While for a generation for whom *chicanismo* related to the experience of political struggle for enfranchisement, for a newer generation of "Chipsters" the racialization of the term "hipster" (mixing both words, Chicano and hipster) reflects an identitarian surveillance of their incursion into a mainstream culture of leisure. Yet, in contending whether the term Chiptser alludes to a derogatory sense of "selling out" to gentrification, García points out how differences in the political profiles of Chicanos (struggling against marginalization, and advocating for equal opportunities for development during the Chicano movement of the 1960s) and the newer generations of Mexican Americans (openly embracing mainstream consumerism) might be at the core of temporally seated identitarian feelings. In doing so, García voices the concerns of activists who see in these new patterns of conduct the potential loss of historical memory. At the same time, García leaves open an inquiry about whether going back to Chicano discourses based on the idea of resistance might imply recoiling into identity politics that make subalternity and racialization defining historical markers prone to reproduction. Thus, García leaves us pondering about the intricate character of difference, and about the liminality of its double-bind.

Alejandro L. Madrid addresses in detail the politics of this liminality in the final chapter of this volume. Taking as a point of departure Juan Gabriel's (one of Mexico's most popular singers and songwriters of the twentieth century) performance of diasporic self in the 1979 film *Del otro lado del puente* (in which a Mexican American raised in Mexico returns to the U.S. to witness the systematic discrimination experienced by people of Mexican descent), Madrid explores the possibility of seeing oneself from "the other side." By asking "what does it mean to look at oneself from the estranged perspective of the Other," Madrid considers how such gaze can reproduce the problematic fixed notions of national, ethnic, and gender identity that a transborder experience challenges. In doing so, Madrid opens a critique of intellectual projects in the humanities that celebrate the border as a metaphorical space of cultural contact in order to bring attention to the material reality of borders and the violence they perpetuate. By naturalizing such imaginary lines, Madrid argues, we reify structures that reproduce difference in order to celebrate it. This limits our ability to understand and engage with the 'cultural surpluses' (those cultural acts of difference not inscribed within the bounds of normative epistemological fields) that challenge the political ideologies that thrive on their asymmetrical reproduction. Instead of seeing marginal cultural surpluses through an Orientalizing estranged gaze, a productive estrangement could make us see them as indexes of shared histories of marginalization. Thus, estrangement without Orientalism can trigger a move away from difference and towards "critical sameness" in order to establish productive social spaces of communication where decolonial political action can occur.

Madrid's critique shows skepticism about democratically inclined intellectual efforts, and a concern for their potential blind spots. In this regard, his call for critical sameness does not entail the recognition of a tabula rasa articulating such communicative space. One should not lose sight of how the experience of difference can shape how cultural actors partake in this interrelational dynamic. As the chapters described above suggest, political structures, their cultural and intellectual projects, and the processes that generate and signify difference involve the experience of power relations, which leave embodied phenomenal traces that are negotiated, and which influence the production of memory and a sense of situatedness. The act of establishing critical sameness with seemingly estranged subjectivities (recognizing their temporal sense of being) should acknowledge this fact. The democratic bend of our intellectual efforts in this volume is guided by this awareness, paying heed to the regulatory effects that institutions have on these encounters.

Thinking in terms of social collusion might be a productive way to establish the type of connection advocated by critical sameness. Scholars like Madrid and Shunsuke Nozawa have shared insights into the dynamics transpiring in collusive spaces. Madrid has mentioned that the socially participatory character of cultural processes opens up the possibility to think of these practices as networks of loyalty produced by temporally different modes of participation. An important aspect of this process involves the development of circuits of membership through involvement in performative cultural acts, which acquire meaning the moment they are received (2012, 166). Such participatory involvement produces a narrative that is temporally dislodged, as the temporality permeating the performance of a cultural act (i.e., the notions of past, present, and future in the social field of its performers) informs the perception of such act in the reader's present both in terms of his/her interpretation of such act, and in relation to the place that such reading ultimately takes in his or her own cultural baggage. Any unidirectional conception of past, present, and future, therefore, disappears the moment a reader inserts him or herself in this process (Madrid 2012, 167). Shunsuke Nozawa has further theorized this participatory involvement in terms of the political agency afforded by temporal dislocation. Nozawa relates the disappearance of unidirectional temporality to a desirable sense of 'forgetting' that makes new forms of agency possible. For the performers, memory has the implicit expectation of being re-*collected* in the reader's temporal act of recognition (2012, 56–57). Thus, by enabling the participation of an external agent who can read the other, Nozawa argues, temporal forgetting involves an ethical disposition towards a performative cultural action in which both parties can have stakes.

The principle of social collusion might be conducive to creating spaces of political action. Collusion forges alliances, loyalties, and circuits of belonging that disrupt identitarian feelings through a communicative logic between apparently different constituencies. Chapters by Alegre González, Hubbs, Madrid, and this author highlight how mechanisms of collusion can reconfigure subjects temporally and position their desires for recognition in larger collective fields of participation. However, the chapters by Ragland, García, and Chávez suggest that vertical structures continue to affect and discipline such claims, and that the perpetuation of systems and ideologies that thrive on the reproduction of difference can lead to alienation and in some cases complete historical invisibility. It is not possible to argue for collusion as an equity-driven, democratic dynamic. For although the effects of global forces on vertical disciplining structures have transformed people and their practices, they have also produced political and cultural dilemmas without a clear solution. Thus, the present volume invites us to think of collusive spaces not in historically equalizing terms, but in terms of the new aporias that characterize the contact zones of complicity in globalization. It is in this way that we can think of collusion as a space for involvement, where shared histories of struggle make us want to be personally invested in the desire for visibility of others as it resonates with our own. This volume is looking for such a complicit reader who can posit ethical and moral stakes on the cases of those oppressed, marginalized, and brutally treated—denied of presence and memory—by the political mechanisms in which we participate. Such should be the spirit of democratic endeavors: my well-being, but also that of others.

By attending to the pressures of the global socioeconomic system that seeks to control the state and that has made the issue of representation an urgent political matter, the authors in this volume hope that our readers will approach mexicanidad not in the spirit of what it 'means' within the symbolic economy that feeds anodyne corporate interests of "Cultural Diversity and Inclusion."[6] Rather, we hope that by addressing the tensions that have made of mexicanidad a historical trope of otherized difference in that symbolic circuit, the reader can recognize a point of resonance in the asymmetrical experiences of displacement, race, class, gender, and sexuality contained in these chapters. In doing so, our goal is that the reader may find in difference the potential to forge alliances and collectively meaningful spaces for social action, through which to establish shared stakes over representation in the public sphere. It is thus that the decentering of the nation has made culture a regionally situated site of ferment and subversion, and collusion a necessary kind of political agency in globalization.

EDITORIAL REMARKS

Throughout the book, the use of double quotation marks has been applied only to direct quotations. Single quotation marks have been used to highlight the politicized character of certain terms or concepts within the logic of each chapter. The chapter by Lizette Alegre González was originally conceived in Spanish and it was the duty of this author to translate it into English. As Gayatri Chakravorty Spivak has said, to translate is to be suspended in another's text. In addressing the case of women who have learned how to speak (*saber hablar*) Alegre González was suspended in the effort of making the voices of these subaltern women audible. Since translation implies 'killing' the phonetic integrity of the original text, my task was, therefore, ethically very sensitive. I hope to have brought forth the spirit of the author's voice in this translation, although my real concern is that the reader can at least feel, intuitively, the presence of these women's speech. If such intuition is absent the translating failure is entirely mine and not the author's.

NOTES

1. Since then, localized examples of this concern for historical renewal have risen dramatically. The recent article in the *Financial Times*, "America's new redneck rebellion," is an example.
2. Not necessarily a matter of geography, the placement of Mexico in the north or center of the continent seems dependent on the way the country fares in relation to foreign interests. See Heredia Zubieta 2017.
3. Roger Bartra has commented on the "post-Mexican" condition that characterizes the current post-NAFTA scenario in Mexico. See Bartra 2013, 53.
4. In his debate over the concept of human nature with Noam Chomsky, Michel Foucault pointed to the danger of arguing for and defending a type of intrinsic human nature in individuals, which in actual society has not been given the rights and possibilities that would allow it to realize itself. In doing so, Foucault mentioned, we risk defining such nature in terms borrowed from such a society. Foucault set the Socialism of the end of the nineteenth and beginning of the twentieth century (with its

fierce critique of bourgeois capitalism) as an example. In this system, he observed, the concept of an alienated society was a society which gave pride of place for the benefit of all; to a bourgeois type of life in terms of the outlooks that defined a lifestyle conducive to self-realization. The example is not meant to state that all democratic advocacy aims to open access to dominant aesthetic forms as a preferred path towards self-development. It rather states that it is problematic to think about the constitution of marginalized subjectivities as independent from the structures of power that produce them and alienate them. See Chomsky and Foucault, 2006, 43–44).

5. In the U.S., the calls to 'Make America Great Again,' and 'Keep America Great' stem from an emotional appeal to go back to a temporal system of subject formation steeped in racial oppression. This appeal rests on the exaltation of nostalgic feelings and sentiments about 'greatness' vis-à-vis otherness, rather than on ideas and sound proposals to counter the actual problems affecting American society.

6. For an extended commentary on the problems with this corporate rhetoric and its effects on cultural competence in higher education see Jesús A. Ramos-Kittrell, "Teaching Music and Difference: Music, Culture, and Difference in Globalization," *Musicology Now* (July 10, 2018): http://www.musicologynow.org/2018/07/.

REFERENCES

Bartra, Roger. *La sangre y la tinta: Ensayos sobre la condición postmexicana*. México, D.F.: Océano, 1999.

Brescó de Luna, Ignacio. "The end into the beginning: Prolepsis and the reconstruction of the collective past." *Culture & Psychology* 23, no. 2 (2017): 280–294.

Chomsky, Noam and Michel Foucault. *The Chomsky-Foucault Debate on Human Nature*. New York: The New Press, 2006.

Corona, Ignacio and Alejandro L. Madrid, eds. *Postnational Musical Identities: Cultural Production, Distribution, and Consumption in a Globalized Scenario*. Lanham, MD: Lexington Books, 2008.

Dhanapala, Jayantha. "Globalization and the Nation-State. A Cartography of Governance: Exploring the Role of Environmental NGOs." *Global Policy Forum* (April 7, 2001): https://www.globalpolicy.org/component/content/article/172-general/29952.html.

Gallegos, Zorayda. "Viaje a los orígenes de López Obrador." *El País* (June 18, 2018): https://elpais.com/internacional/2018/06/16/mexico/1529167842_033751.html.

Ghemawat, Pankaj and Steven A. Altman. "The State of Globalization in 2019, and What It Means for Strategists." *Harvard Business Review* (February 6, 2019): https://hbr.org/2019/02/the-state-of-globalization-in-2019-and-what-it-means-for-strategists.

González Madrid, Miguel. "Pobreza y desempleo. Los saldos de la crisis de 1994–1995." *Polis—Política, Marco Electoral, Pensamiento Social y Economía* 96, vol. 1 (Junio 1997): 209–235.

Henriques, Donald. "Performing Nationalism: Mariachi, Media, and the Transformation of a Tradition." Ph.D. diss., The University of Texas at Austin, 2006.

Heredia Zubieta, Carlos. "México no es Norteamérica, como creía, pero tampoco se siente de los nuestros." *El Universal* (February 17, 2017): https://www.eluniversal.com.mx/entrada-de-opinion/articulo/carlos-heredia-zubieta/nacion/2017/02/17/mexico-no-es-norteamerica-com-0.

Lomnitz, Claudio. *La nación desdibujada: México en trece ensayos*. Barcelona: Malpaso ediciones, 2016.

Luce, Edward. "America's new redneck rebellion." *Financial Times* (June 27, 2019): https://amp.ft.com/content/327a9c4a-9799-11e9-9573-ee5cbb98ed36?__twitter_impression=true&fbclid=IwAR1bCady_6dBKQ3ZBTlcu3qHcdst4VwKqXcpqiUkdpMuG4gUiivqDDtaXPs.

Madrid, Alejandro L. *Music in Mexico: Experiencing Music, Expressing Culture*. New York: Oxford University Press, 2013.

———. "Retos multilineales y método prolépsico en el estudio posnacional del nacionalismo musical." In *Discursos y prácticas musicales nacionalistas (1900–1970): España, Argentina, Cuba, México*, edited by Pilar Ramos López, 161–172. Logroño: Universidad de La Rioja, 2012.

México, Poder Ejecutivo Federal. *Plan Nacional de Desarrollo 1989–1994*. Mexico: Diario Oficial, May 31, 1989.

Muñoz, Alma E. "AMLO presenta Programa Nacional de los Pueblos Indígenas." *La Jornada* (December 21, 2018): https://www.jornada.com.mx/ultimas/2018/12/21/amlo-presenta-programa-nacional-de-los-pueblos-indigenas-6308.html.

Nozawa, Shunsuke. "Discourses of the Coming: Ignorance, Forgetting, and Prolepsis in Japanese Life-Historiography." In *The Anthropology of Ignorance: An Ethnographic Approach*, edited by Casey High, Ann H. Kelly, and Jonathan Mair, 55–85. New York: Palgrave Macmillan, 2012.

Ramos-Kittrell, Jesús A. "Teaching Music and Difference: Music, Culture, and Difference in Globalization." *Musicology Now* (July 10, 2018): http://www.musicologynow.org/2018/07/.

Redacción. "Toma de protesta de AMLO: qué significado tiene el Bastón de Mando que los pueblos indígenas le entregaron al nuevo presidente de México." *BBC News Mundo* (December 3, 2018): https://www.bbc.com/mundo/noticias-america-latina-46427940.

Ross, Janell. "From Mexican rapists to bad hombres, the Trump campaign in two moments." *The Washington Post* (October 20, 2016): https://www.washingtonpost.com/news/the-fix/wp/2016/10/20/from-mexican-rapists-to-bad-hombres-the-trump-campaign-in-two-moments/?utm_term=.485dd08da421.

Sandoval, Chela. *Methodology of the Oppressed*. Minneapolis: University of Minnesota Press, 2000.

Saragoza, Alex. "The Selling of Mexico: Tourism and the State, 1929–1952." In *Fragments of a Golden Age: The Politics of Culture in Mexico since 1940*, edited by Gilbert M. Joseph, Anne Rubenstein, and Eric Zolov, 91–115. Durham, NC: Duke University Press, 2001.

Yúdice, George. *The Expediency of Culture: Uses of Culture in the Global Era*. Durham: Duke University Press, 2003.

Chapter 1

Afrodiasporic Visual and Sonic Assemblages

Racialized Anxieties and the Disruption of Mexicanidad in Cine de Rumberas

Laura G. Gutiérrez

Towards the end of the Mexican film *Coqueta* (1949), directed by Fernando A. Rivero and produced by Producciones Calderón, the Cuban-born dancer Ninón Sevilla, in her role as Marta del Valle, performs a dance number on a cabaret stage. While the cabaret's name has not been referenced before, we are to assume that we are in the Cabaret Mambo because we see the word "mambo" in the backdrop in huge bamboo stick graphics as the performers take to the stage. From stage left, we first see and hear the rumbero Kiko Mendive[1] leading the *bongoseros* (bongo players) to form a semicircle on the stage as they, along with the full orchestra that is already onstage, start to musicalize the guaracha "Qué cosas tiene la vida" ("What Things Life Has"), made famous by Daniel Santos and the Sonora Matancera. Sevilla, as Marta, the principal performer, follows them and takes her place at the center among the musicians and back-up dancers. In this scene, it is Ninón Sevilla who is vocalizing the song, and, at the same time, and with the assistance of Kiko Mendive and the bongoseros, we have the sense that certain elements and segments in the song are undergoing improvisation. A minute after, Marta starts singing—a performance that exceeds Daniel Santos's recorded version because of its even more boisterous laughter—she pauses her vocalizations, albeit she continues to sway her body across the stage. The sound we hear at this moment is being emitted by the bongoseros, the only musicians still playing; it is here that they modify the rhythm to a rumba, which leads Marta to adapt her corporeal movements: Marta's hips adjust to a fast-paced rhythm, moving mostly from side to side to set up a series of aggressive pelvic thrusts. This midway musical improvisation only lasts about thirty seconds. At that moment, Mendive announces yet another rhythmic shift, now to a mambo, or, as he yells out, "*mambo negro*" ("black mambo"). This musical portion lasts about a minute and does not include singing. The rest of the orchestra steps in and joins the bongoseros in a classic mambo composition accompanied, still, by Marta's solo dancing, although now one sees all of the musicians swaying to the music. Marta's dancing is almost always taking place at the center of that previously-mentioned semicircle, where she stands out not only because of her gender, but also because of her color (she is the lightest-skinned of all performers). The rest of the musicians, including the rumbero Kiko Mendive, are Afro-Cuban mulattos, while the dancer in this number, Ninón Sevilla, is a white Cuban performer (see Figure 1.1).

I describe this scene in full detail to highlight the ways in which Mexican cultural industries during the middle of the twentieth century arranged black diasporic sounds, images, and bodies for a national, and to a lesser extent, international mid-century audience. *Coqueta* is far from being unique in these arrangements; mid-twentieth century Mexican cinema trafficked extensively in this type of visual imagery and soundscapes. There were other urban melodramas during the height of Mexico's so-called cinematic golden age era, where the presence of blackness in the lives of central characters was cause for concern and even extreme panic among those in their immedi-

Figure 1.1. Lobby card of the film *Coqueta* (Azteca Films, Inc., 1949). *Source:* Benson Latin American Collection, LLILAS Benson Latin American Studies and Collections, The University of Texas at Austin (used with permission).

ate circles, specifically the blood relatives.² However, in this chapter I argue that the type of visual and sonic assemblages like the one mentioned above, occurred primarily in the subgenre of films that were clustered under the category *cine de rumberas* (woman rumba dancer cinema) and that, among other things, were instrumental in mediating Mexico's racialized anxieties around blackness or an African presence in Mexico. These films, which predominantly featured a cinematic cabaret space as a preferred social arena, depended heavily on Afrodiasporic sounds and corporeal movements to register two opposing and irreconcilable ideas regarding blackness: a desire to flirt and experiment with exoticism to approximate *a notion* of modernity and cosmopolitanism, while simultaneously condemning the ways in which blackness, particularly because of its perceived sensual excess, was a threat to the nation and its alleged sanctified traditions. While these sounds and movements were key elements in the rumbera films, it is important to mention that, more often than not, the only Afrodiasporic subjects were the music-makers, the back-up singers, and the dancers who performed in the cinematic numbers, some of which included Dámaso Pérez Prado, Beny Moré, Kiko Mendive, and Rita Montaner. The main rumbera, however, was always a white Hispanic performer (as is the case with Ninón Sevilla and other artists that participated in these films, some of which I will discuss in this chapter), and the cinematic mis-en-scène during these musical-dance numbers always centered on her white dancing body.³ I ultimately argue that these films, which were a phenomenon during the decade of the 1940s and the early 1950s, made blackness palatable for Mexicans as a consumable form of entertainment that was in conversation with a sense of modern cosmopolitanism for Mexican audiences. If, as Jayna Brown argues in *Babylon Girls* (2008), modern racialized subjects constituted themselves in part via a usable past, thus "the figure of the 'native' dancing girls was a central trope used in the discourses of primitivist modernism" (191). However, in contradistinction to certain spaces in the U.S. (New York, Chicago) and Europe (Paris, France), where the black dancing girl was the rage, in the context of an aspiring modern and cosmopolitan Mexico, with its rhetoric of *mestizaje* (which can be coded for a racial mixing that would ultimately produce white subjects), the black ancestral rhythms had to be carried out by non-black subjects. Because many of these films traveled throughout the hemisphere, their work in appeasing racialized anxieties extended beyond the national context of Mexico. Thus, the Hispanic, Cuban, gendered body of the rumbera became the site through which the threat of blackness could be minimized: her sensual moving figure recasts racial anxieties as desires for sexual exoticism in the safe haven of her white body.

The critical examination of the work of these women artists in these films necessitates an interdisciplinary approach that is attentive to race, gender, and sexuality, as played out on or manifested through the body. This approach, however, needs also to be mindful of the historically-specific processes happening in Mexico during the middle of the twentieth century, when the country experienced important socio-economic transformations. This methodological framework of analysis, where performance studies intermingles with film studies, and where global ethnic studies grapples with gender and sexuality studies, will urge us to think about the role of Mexican cultural industries in mediating the construction of blackness (as exotic otherness) vis-à-vis the construction of *mexicanidad*, and about the role of gender in this process. Most specifically, this approach will help us read and derive meaning from the whole conglomeration of signifying references and the tensions that they created—the dancing body/bodies, the sounds, the urban or not-so-urban landscapes, discourses of modernity, changing gender roles, to name a few—to grapple with the absence/presence of blackness in a Mexican context.

During the *sexenios* (six-year terms to serve as President of Mexico) of both Manuel Avila Camacho (1940–1946) and Miguel Alemán (1946–1952), the film industry churned out over two hundred films that were later categorized as cine de rumberas. The Afrodiasporic symbols featured in these films consisted not only of tropicalized cabaret spaces (with neon palm trees and stereotypical black Caribbean elements), but also bodies in movement meant to excite the multiple audiences viewing these films, thus creating what I call "tropicalized desire." While, on the one hand, this tropicalized desire via Afrodiasporic sounds and dancing bodies was able to disrupt a rigid Mexican gendered and sexual system of desire, on the other, it promoted racialized and gendered stereotypes of the Caribbean.[4] In addition to the (stereo)typical costuming that the different rumberas wore in their dance numbers (which featured the standard ruffled tops revealing the mid-section of the torso, skirts that opened at the front to reveal legs and allow for more movement, and a pair of platform shoes), the films specifically trafficked in the congealed symbology of blackness, which centered around two specific figures:[5] the black man as a non-threatening *negrito bailarín* (the dancing little black man), whose sole existence was to entertain non-black audiences; and the *mulata* (the mulatta), exotic and desirable, and a conduit for sinful pleasure. It is important to remember, as Edouard Glissant wrote, "[i]t is nothing new to declare that for us music, gesture, dance are forms of communication, just as important as the gift of speech (1999, 248–9). Albeit, such techniques are more than performative modes of communication; they are also about affective relational ties to Afrodiasporic subjects. What happens then, when those communication techniques are filtered through one of the most powerful cinematic industries in the spanish-speaking world in the middle of the twentieth century? How can we make sense of blackness being mediated through the white gendered body, in close proximity and in relation to blackness and black and mulatto performers, and urban desires for modern cosmopolitanism among film viewers? These are some of the questions that I will grapple with in this chapter.

FROM *SIBONEY* TO *MULATA*: A BRIEF HISTORY OF CINE DE RUMBERAS

Beginning in the 1930s, thanks in large part to the esoteric Spanish filmmaker, actor, and dancer Juan Orol, women from the Spanish-speaking Caribbean, particularly Cuba, began traveling to Mexico to work both in theater and in the emerging national film industry.[6] Women, such as Ninón Sevilla, mentioned above, along with her compatriots María Antonieta Pons, Amalia Aguilar, and, later, Rosa Carmina, would be the primary figures of the rumbera film canon. These rumberas centered their performance dance styles on Afrodiasporic rhythms, whether in theater or cinema. Although rumberas had appeared in films prior to 1938,[7] it was during this year, with Orol's film *Siboney* (featuring Pons), that the cine de rumberas subgenre emerged. In this film, Pons plays the title character, Siboney, a worker in a plantation in Cuba who becomes the love interest of the plantation owner. Through the performance of Afro-Cuban dance numbers and European-style operas, class and racial differences are bridged; love can overcome any obstacle. Pons and Orol, as well as others that soon followed suit, incorporated examples of Afrodiasporic expressive culture, and in some cases history and myths, in the onscreen theatrical and ritualistic performances. In addition to adopting melodrama as the blueprint of plots about the emotions and desires of the characters, the film *Siboney* is an example of how the Mexican film industry arranged Afrodiasporic elements, rhythms, and bodies for the cinematic gaze through this subgenre. Ernesto Caparrós's 1938 short fictional film (released in Cuba), *Tam Tam o el origen de la rumba*, merits comment in this regard. In her book *She is Cuba: A Genealogy of The Mulata Body* (2016), Melissa Blanco Borelli discusses the ways in which *Tam Tam* brings together the mulata body and rumba, and ponders if it may be possible that this short film would have informed the films that later came to be part of cine de rumberas, which was mostly a Mexican phenomenon, as the films were made or produced in that country, although not exclusively for national consumption. Blanco Borelli's conjecture is highly plausible, but this early cinematic rendering is not necessarily the singular source for the emergence of the cine de rumberas phenomenon; after all, *Aguila o sol*, which features an astounding dance number ("Un meneíto na' ma" by the Dominican-born Margarita Mora), and *Siboney* are also from that same year.[8]

In addition to Pons, Sevilla, Aguilar, and Carmina, all of whom performed in similar arrangements for the cinematic stage, there were other performers that are now part of the rumbera pantheon, including two U.S.-born ones, Meche Barba and Yolanda Montes Tongolele. The former moved to Mexico City at a very young age and is considered to be the best of national rumberas, and she is never thought to be anything but Mexican. Tongolele, on the other hand, may be considered more of an *exótica* than a rumbera because her performance attire was considered extremely risqué (even more so than the above-described typical rumbera dresses), and because on occasion she danced barefooted to South Pacific sounds. However, I do situate Tongolele on the rumbera spectrum because of the important dialogue she established with the bongoseros while performing Afrodiasporic rhythms in her dance numbers. It is important to reiterate, in the form of a question: What does it mean that these dancers, who also worked as actresses (some to greater success than others), were not born within Mexico's geopolitical borders? This not only raises questions about the migration of aesthetic images and cultural symbologies, but also forces us to think about the relationship between cultural industries, transnationalism, modernity, exoticism, sexuality, and, of course, race, within and beyond nationally specific contexts. Because of the mostly self-fashioned tropicalizations of rumberas for the stage and the screen, the cultural journalist and playwright Fernando Muñoz Castillo dubbed these women the "Queens of the Tropic" in his photo essay book *Las reinas del trópico* (1993). They all traveled to Mexico either in the 1930s or 1940s and began working on theatrical stages there, but soon after became part of a cinematic apparatus where melodramatic narratives and/or suspenseful film noir-type stories were interlaced with dance scenes, many quite elaborate. For almost two decades—coinciding with Mexico's golden age period of cinema—filmmakers such as the aforementioned Rivero and Orol, as well as Alberto Gout and Emilio "El Indio" Fernández, among others, exploited the appeal that these "reinas del trópico" had over their audiences. The seduction that these films produced was due to the fact that the intertwined dance numbers that were set in tropical or quasi-tropical settings—such as Cuba or a fictional island, or the Mexican state of Veracruz, or in Mexican urban centers, principally its capital city and mostly in the space of the cabaret—effected the tropicalized desire I mentioned above. The seeming redundancy of this statement is elided if we consider that Mexico's rhetoric of mestizaje stemmed from a state platform of cultural production propagated by corporate media (specifically radio, television, and film). This platform, I argue, not only included, but depended on the mediation/ mediatization of blackness via Mexico's corporate cultural industries. In this context, the rumbera body upset state-sponsored imaginings of the nation as resultant of mestizaje, a narrative that disavowed Mexico's participation in the transatlantic slave trade and its relationship and entanglement with Afrodiasporic history and culture.

One of the main aspects that I am interested in examining in this chapter is the theorization of movement in relation to the work of rumberas on the cinematic stage. More specifically, I would like to approach movement—both geopolitical and embodied onstage movement—as a way to explore the politics of embodied and scopic pleasure, which largely depend on the incorporation of Afrodiasporic elements and gestures; that is, if the scopic regimes necessitate the female figure, but excess sensuality is reserved for the non-Mexican body, particularly if she is able to embody exoticism and primitivism, yet is modern and cosmopolitan. The initial migratory movements of Afro-Cubans began, more or less, during Mexico's post-revolutionary period in the early 1920s. It was during this period of initial modernizing projects, urban growth, and the rise of the entertainment industries, that the stereotypical figures of the 'negrito' and the mulata began to acquire a Mexican presence, appeal, and therefore, marketability potential.

In her book, *Mulatas y negros en la escena mexicana (1920–1950),* Gabriela Pulido Llano examines this junction, paying particular attention to the geographical movements of musicians and dancers, and to the construction and dissemination of the 'negrito' and mulata stereotypes. Pulido's chapter devoted to the cine de rumberas phenomenon is a good background for the representation of these figures. However, I differ in Pulido's reading of the films given that the 'mulata' figure appears only and virtually in the dance and song numbers, because rumbera women were in fact white Hispanics, as a back-up character. Even the film that directly references the mulata figure, *Mulata* (Gilberto Martínez Solares 1954)—in which Ninón Sevilla performs in blackface, both as the mother figure who is black and, years later in the story, as the daughter figure who is a result of a sinful encounter between the mother and a white man—does not feature a mulata performer (see Figure 1.2). The figure of the mulata, at least as far as Mexican film production is concerned, is performative and relational: to be mulata is to dance as a mulata and/or to wear makeup to simulate a mulata in relation to a central character. A notable exception that is worthy of closer critical analysis is the work of the Afro-Cuban mulata Rita Montaner who appeared in a number of these rumbera films. While she never had a stellar role in them, her participation in *Al son del mambo* (Chano Urueta 1950) and *Victi-*

mas del pecado (Emilio "El Indio" Fernández 1951) is noteworthy as blackness and mulattaness are working in tandem and, one could argue, in closer relation to a white dancing rumbera body at the center of the story/stage. The Mexico-born mulata singer Toña La Negra, from the coastal state of Veracruz, is another figure that calls for critical analysis. Just as Montaner did, Toña La Negra participated in the production of several rumbera films, more often than not as a singer in the different cinematic cabarets and playing as herself. Some of these films included *Konga roja* (Alejandro Galindo 1943) and *Humo en los ojos* (Alberto Gout 1946). With the exception of a musical-dance number in *Konga roja,* where Toña La Negra is the central figure during the performance of the song "Babalú ayé," the mulattaness of these two figures, as well as other musicians and dancers visually arranged for the camera, serves to prop up the principal rumbera in these narratives and in the cabaret performances specifically.[9]

Figure 1.2. Lobby card of the film *Mulata* (Azteca Films, Inc., 1954). *Source*: Benson Latin American Collection, LLILAS Benson Latin American Studies and Collections, The University of Texas at Austin (used with permission).

RETHINKING MOVEMENTS, RETHINKING PAUSE(S)

As I have begun to suggest above, one of my underlying arguments in this chapter is that cine de rumberas does much to undo, however momentarily, socially and culturally conservative ideas regarding female sexuality in post-revolutionary Mexico. I posit that this undoing happens through the intra-textual corporeal movements, dancistic or otherwise, enacted by these foreign-born women that were featured in these films. It is the rise of these movements—*bailes telúricos* (earth-shaking dances) or the dances with the *meneíto* (gyrating hip dances) that Tongolele made famous—during the 1940s both on the theatrical stages of Mexico and, most importantly for our purposes here, on the cinematographical stages, that allow for the first public discussion regarding "what is prohibited and what is permitted in regard to corporeal movements" to take place in the Mexican cultural sphere.[10] The embodied performances of these rumberas in these films offer us a way to rethink mass-culturally constructed notions of mexicanidad beyond the traditional paradigms of indigeneity and discourses of mestizaje. The fact that these films incorporate elements associated with the embodiment of Afrodiasporic expressive culture—more explicitly, movements and rhythms that were encoded as *lo cubano* (that which is Cuban), *lo caribeño* (that which is Caribbean), and *lo exótico* (the exotic) in the film industry, works to expand otherwise rigid understandings of *lo mexicano*.

Additionally, these highly commercial B films also provide an avenue for scholars to think about the cross-border complicated relationship between Mexico and the Spanish-speaking Caribbean, thus disrupting north-south flows in academic discourse and cultural representations (as much of academic discourse that takes up questions of the transnational often puts the U.S. in relationship to a Latin American country). In other words, transnational studies in the United States often pivots around an understanding of this country as either the starting point or the desired destination. Thus, one of my aims here is to disrupt certain assumptions regarding the way we study culture and the way its producers move and think about transnational frames that intensify the understanding of south-to-south transactions. If we heed the cultural flows that were activated in part by the Mexican cultural industries of the middle of the twentieth century in their mediatized construction of blackness and sexuality, however constructed and stereotyped, we can decenter the predominance of scholarship that always thinks in relationship to the U.S., either as what it produces culturally and then exports or what it consumes that is imported. In other words, these films were very much in circulation as part of a transnational circuit, not just to the global north, but also within the global south. Thus, thinking about cultural flows and academic discourses as not nationally bounded can benefit from considering an Archipelagic mode of American Studies and Latin American Studies, which includes the continental U.S. and Mexico, the Antilles, but also the Pacific, as some of these films evoke such settings, too. In the spirit of thinking alongside other writers who have guided our thought processes regarding black culture as always being in flux and in motion I agree with Jayna Brown who, in *Babylon Girls*, as she leans on the writings by James Clifford, states: "I prefer [a suggestion from the cultural anthropologist] that these 'practices of displacement might emerge as constitutive of cultural meaning rather than as their simple transfer or extension'" (p. 13). In other words, it is not enough to consider the ways in which there is or there is not authenticity in how the rumberas in these films move to black music and song, or how closely they might reproduce a cultural context's reality. What is more interesting, perhaps, is to ponder the ways in which Mexican cine de rumberas is producing new, albeit problematic, meanings around notions of blackness for both national and transnational consuming audiences.

Having said this, I want to propose that the musical and dance number in these rumbera films, as the one described in the opening of this chapter, can also be read as a sort of pause. This pause, I posit, occurs within the narrative that is otherwise melodramatic and charged with suffering or suspensefulness, for both the characters and the film spectators. But these same dance scenes are paradoxically filled with frenetic movement as most rumba dancing is accompanied to the beats and rhythms stemming from the bongoseros and other musicians. One of the ways I am mobilizing the notion of pause is to think of it not as a break, yet we do feel a sort of respite—as I had said, from the suffering and suspense—when one of the rumberas walks onto the cinematic stage and moves to the rhythm of the drums. I propose that the cinematic pause enacted by these dance numbers, some highly orchestrated and beautifully choreographed, is functioning to expand racialized representations in the context of the height of Mexico's cultural nationalism, heavily determined by discourses of European and Indigenous mestizaje, where the Indigenous past has been repurposed for a nationalist ideology that has fully integrated it into the present. The rumbera films coexist within this ideological terrain in the Mexico of the 1930s, 1940s, and 1950s. And, in spite of the fact that they were mass-produced (or maybe because of it), I believe that they are worthy of study because of their capaciousness to make use of cross-cultural exchanges between the Antilles, the Pacific, and Mexico in ways that make the mestizaje nationalist rhetoric a racialized hierarchical construction of the modern Mexican subject. Again, as it is important to reiterate, this expansion is done via the embodied performances of these white rumberas. As Brown has so succinctly written:

The experiences of race and place in the modernizing world were sensorial phenomena, negotiated by bodies in motion. In the age of electricity and machines, the human body in its various motor capacities became the form through which the modern was designed. Dance was the lexicon reflecting the dialectic process of modern transformation: the modern body continually reinventing itself, in and against its environment, at the same time as the environment made its claims upon the body (15).

Mexico's project of nationalism necessitated the Indigenous and mestizo body to index modernity via these racialized bodies; however, it was more *provocatively* efficient to modernize notions of mexicanidad via the exotic and the tropical. Belonging to and in the modern world was as much about development as it was about the experiential through the sensorial, which was often transitory and ephemeral. That is, these films also register a desire for and enabled those experiences through the constructions of the exotic via the presence of the female body, in most cases scantily dressed women who dance to Afrodiasporic rhythms—incorporating pelvic thrusts, jerky inward and outward torso movements that move in opposition to the shoulders and elbows, and careful leg choreographies—who incite pleasure among the spectators, both within and outside the film's frames. In proposing this I am taking cues from David F. García who, in his book, *Listening for Africa: Freedom, Modernity, and the Logic of Black Music's African Origins*, writes: "an analysis of music and dance not as genre but as human actions of interactions that encapsulated no doubt people's planning and desires, and that were entangled in modernity's ways of knowing, yet were also immanently about people's experiences in the world" (7). This is the work that the rumberas and the films they starred in did during the middle of the twentieth century; they were not just images that traveled throughout the nation, in the different regions of the Caribbean, and the hemisphere as a whole, but offered possibilities to experience the modern world in ways that, musically, were deeply rooted and indebted to a historical alterity reckoned through ancestral movements and rhythms.

DESIRE AND SCREENED SEDUCTION

The rumberas featured in these films—as I said, most of whom were born outside of Mexico's borders—and their bodies in movement (whether they are dancing or just sashaying across the screen) served as repositories of desire at the same time as providing a way to calm the spectator's anxieties around blackness. In sum, I am interested in exploring "the relationship to blackness through sound" and movement[11] and the role that Mexican cultural industries played in this idea by showcasing embodied performances by black/mulato artists (the back-up dancers and musicians mostly sit in the background and are part of the décor) and non-black bodies.

Additionally, I also want to interrogate the transnational embodied performances of women who integrated Afrodiasporic expressive elements into their repertoire in order to think about racialized sexual formations in the context of the national. As the pace of Mexico's industrial development and urban growth accelerated during the 1940s and early 1950s, particularly during the Miguel Alemán *sexenio* (1946–1952), cabarets and dance halls also flourished. Rumberas traveled from the Spanish-speaking Caribbean to work in Mexico's capital, and had a significant role in the development of the entertainment industries at this moment. They were employed by the urban centers of nightlife culture and helped in their development. These urbanized forms of leisure activity were transferred onto the screen and functioned as contrasts to the other cinematographical representations at that time, specifically the ones that mythologized Mexico and helped construct mexicanidad as a chrono-trope: the rural landscape with the agave plants, the charros on horseback, and the shrouded Indigenous women (see Alex E. Chávez in this volume). Thus, the modernizing impulse was intertwined with an overt form of sexuality that was less about mestizaje or miscegenation, and more about the ways in which these rumberas danced on the screen, the pleasure they exuded, and the ways in which the spectators consumed these representations of pleasure.

The majority of rumberas I discuss were principally trained as dancers—in their home country of Cuba—and that was the highlight of their performances, but they also sang occasionally in staged cabaret or theatrical spectacles. When their onstage live performances were transferred to film roles, this gave them a wider audience and they became celebrities almost overnight because the films that they worked on were immensely popular. To say that these rumberas reached iconic status during the middle of the twentieth century would not be a far stretch. I would even argue that they continue to hold onto this status, as the rumbera figure has resurfaced in a number of contemporary performances, whether in theater or cinema.[12]

Such iconic status was principally achieved through the placement of the rumbera's body front and center of the cinematic screen: the camera's depiction of the rumbera as a seductress via her stance, gaze, attitude, and corporeal movements, monumentalized her at the time that the films were produced and beyond those years into the present. While there were other icons constructed for and by Mexican cinema, and that had an even more national and international appeal (I am specifically referring to Dolores del Río and María Félix, but there were others), the power of seduction that rumberas possessed was also a result of their highly sensual dancing, often coded as exotic because of its Afrodiasporic referents. One could say that these rumberas managed and dominated the performance space through their dancing, and that they were central to the ways the orchestra performed. The rumberas' dance steps did not follow, rather, they often led. This is particularly true of those performances where a more traditional rumba number took place, with only the sound of percussion. For example, at the beginning of this chapter I described a scene in *Coqueta* where Ninón Sevilla as Marta is dancing; when there is a break into a rumba with the bongoseros, the audience senses a more dominant Marta who is in control of the ways in which the drummers perform.[13]

Important to mention here is that the roles in which rumberas were cast often posited them as vamps or femme fatales, making them even more seductive, albeit dangerous. The rumbera had a hypnotic appeal on the screen—understood as the power to seduce via her corporeal movements—replicated by some of the major stars in the Mexican film industry, yet with a different slant. The ability to "hip-notically" captivate the attention of her onlookers via the movement of her (dancing) body, was also an ability to seduce, both within the film's narrative and the film's spectators.[14] I agree with dance studies scholar Melissa Blanco Borelli, who in her book *She is Cuba*, when discussing the short fiction film *Tam Tam o el origen de la rumba* (1938), states:

> According to the logic of the narrative, *rumba* (and other Afro-Cuban rhythms) leads bodies to frenetic and frenzied corporeal outbursts. These unregulated movements require dissolution and temperance through the *mulata* body in order to make them palatable and acceptable for *sensuality* (non-threatening when slightly removed from blackness) to successfully materialize (emphasis in original, 116).

In the context of post-revolutionary Mexico, and for the purposes of the films that are categorized as cine de rumberas, the distance from blackness is even more jarring as sensuality here operates through the white dancing body that moves to Afrodiasporic rhythms. This fact, however, calls for a tangential, but needed conversation.

In an interview for a program for Mexico's cultural channel, Canal 22, cultural critic Carlos Monsiváis once stated, almost in passing, that the production of rumbera films represents *la legalización del erotismo* ("the legalization of eroticism").[15] I use these words as a sort of theoretical provocation in order to highlight what I have already mentioned before: that these films momentarily disrupt Mexico's socially conservative understandings of gender and sexuality that were still very much in place after Mexico's revolution and during its accelerated modernization period. In another interview, Monsiváis discussed the cine de rumberas in general, but Ninón Sevilla specifically, particularly her role in *Aventurera* (Alberto Gout 1950): "The most subversive aspect, whether or not [the film] has a happy ending, is the way in which all the social conventions around morality don't stand a chance vis-à-vis . . . the way that Ninón Sevilla walks, the way she smokes, or the manner in which she dances" (my translation).[16] He goes on to say that in the late 1940s Mexican cinema was still plagued by *moralejas* (moralities), which were needed, hypocritically so, in order to avoid social and ecclesiastical censorship. However, once the viewer was in front of the screen watching Ninón Sevilla, or any of the other rumberas for that matter, these moralities were for naught. In Monsiváis's own words:

> But those moralities become undone by what you see. You may hear voices that condemn your sin, that may anathematize it, or make it completely condemnable. And you may be able to verbally multiply hell's flames. But it would be enough that one of the rumberas dances, or that one of the rumberas feels pleasure, or that one of the rumberas incites, seduces, and tempts the spectator in all the possible visual means for those moralities to crumble and become invisible. Ninón Sevilla, all by herself, eclipses Father Ripalda's catechism.[17]

Monsiváis's quote aids in a productive theorization of masochistic visual pleasure in rumbera cinema. More specifically, I draw attention precisely to those moments in which the rumbera dances frenetically, or simply moves defiantly onscreen, or looks boldly, yet seductively at the spectator, all of which are movements and gestures that distance her from the sort of characterizations that audiences had been accustomed to as film spectators in post-revolutionary Mexico. That is, while the figure of the *cabaretera*—a woman working at the cabaret, mostly as 'companion' to men—is customarily portrayed as a victim of her circumstances that must resolve to prostitution, she must be punished for it. However, the rumbera in the films produced during the Avila Camacho and Alemán sexenios is no longer a mere 'fallen woman.' The rumbera's embodied performance signifies power and sexuality; one may even argue that she becomes a quasi-heroine character. While it is important to reiterate that these rumberas are still constructed erotically for the cinematic gaze (the object of desire, particularly for the masculine characters within the film's narrative), I want to stress that this position is not static. The women in these films, the rumberas, are also exerting their power over different audiences that watch them move, on the dance floor or otherwise. It is within this location of sexualized power that they are able to counter the religious moralities that Monsiváis discusses in the interview I quoted from above. The Mexican cultural critic speculates that the visual pleasure that the spectator experiences helps to disrupt indoctrinations regarding sexuality in Mexican culture of the 1940s and 1950s. It is precisely this intersection of pleasure/punishment in these films that I want to theorize. It is not possible to think about these films in relation to the films that mostly transpired in the rural setting, such as *María Candelaria* (Emilio "El Indio" Fernández 1943). While remaining for the most part traditional in their overall message, films like those of Fernández's were produced according to a hetero-patriarchal cinematic narrative. In contrast, while still hetero-patriarchal, cine de rumberas shows fissures in this narrative in terms of how female characters are represented, which marks them as substantially different from female characters featured in Mexican chrono-tropic cinema. María Candelaria, for example, was stoned to death due to her ill-reputed image in the public sphere which she inherited from her mother.

Although the power of the rumberas' onscreen seduction could extend to other media, most specifically magazines, whether specialized in cinema or not, their power of seduction was delivered principally through their projection on the cinematic screen. Moreover, this seduction needs to be understood as extending beyond Mexico's geo-political borders, as the rumbera draws her power from movements related to Afrodiasporic musical elements. In order for this onscreen seduction to operate as a structuring mechanism in the Mexican cinematic context, Afrodiasporic elements have to be displaced and projected onto the white rumbera body.

THE ARCHIPELAGIC CONCATENATIONS: FURTHER DECENTERING THE NATION

Thus far two of my interconnected arguments have been to rethink the relationship between Mexico and its cultural industries (through production of blackness) and the Spanish-speaking Caribbean, particularly Cuba and the ways in which critical analysis of these products can decenter congealed understandings of Mexico specifically, how the production of blackness upsets rigid understandings of mexicanidad as a byproduct of a rigid nationalist cultural narrative centered on mestizaje. What happens when, as part of the imaginary in these rumbera films, the connections are extended further to the east through representations that reach to the rest of the Antilles and beyond? I propose that part of the project of decentering the nation through Mexican cultural industries' capaciousness for racial representations (even as they continue to be stereotypical assemblages of exotic elements, movements, and sounds for the cinematic stage), is to think about archipelagic concatenations. I propose the idea of an archipelago to help us rethink relations that are often assumed to be a north-south dynamic, again particularly when we think about the ways in which transnational studies have been developed in the context of U.S. academe, which centers on the United States. I argue, however, that it is important to think about these relations in regard to Mexico and the Caribbean to complicate the Caribbean's relationship to the ideas of 'mainland' that have been conceptualized in critical discourse about body and identity politics (to read further on this point, see Madrid in the volume). For better or for worse, Mexico is also a destination for Cuban and other Caribbean-born migrants from the Greater Antilles, some of whom are cultural workers, and the country, with its powerful mid-twentieth-century cultural industries, can be considered a sort of mainland with deep connections to the chain of islands in the region. Thus, it is also important to think about south-south connections in terms of the mainland(s) being in relation to island chains, that is an archipelago. From the vast corpus of films that fall under the category of cine de rumberas, the work of two particular dancers indexes a desire to configure a chain of signification through corporeal movements and gestures in more expansive terms. One is Rosa Carmina who, like the aforementioned Ninón Sevilla, is a Cuban-born rumbera who further pushed the notion of exoticism by incorporating elements from the West Indies and, in some instances, even from the South Pacific, into her own visual and aural repertoire, particularly in movies such as *Sandra, la mujer de fuego* (1954) and *La diosa de Tahití* (1953), both directed by her then husband Juan Orol.[18] The other is Yolanda Montes "Tongolele" who was born in Tacoma, Washington, but migrated to Mexico and made its capital city her home, where she still resides. Tongolele is the rumbera that is associated with the aforementioned "bailes telúricos" and the "meneíto." One may even argue that it was Tongolele who was considered the most seductive on screen of all her peers, as she was considered too sensual and therefore provocative, and was censored by conservative women's groups, such as the *Liga de la Decencia* (Decency League). Alternatively, one could also argue that the fact that these women's groups rallied priests and other conservative spokespersons to prohibit citizens (i.e., Mexican nationals) from watching Tongolele perform only enhanced her popularity and seductive allure. As discussed above, Tongolele's power was concentrated not only in her ability to move her mid-section in extraordinary ways, but in the ways in which she was able to conduct the bongoseros in their rhythm making.

Tongolele's most esoteric film, *Han matado a Tongolele* (Roberto Gavaldón 1948), can help us examine visual representations more expansively. In the film, several would-be exotic and highly stylized performances take place on a stage while drama ensues backstage. Tongolele, playing her namesake and the main star of that night's cabaret line-up, is supposedly killed. All of the drama and the onstage performances happen during one evening in a cabaret, the real Teatro Follies to be exact, both onstage and backstage. During Tongolele's three onstage performances, before she is allegedly killed, we are all ensconced within an operating concept of the 'exotic' with Polynesian and/or Afro-Cuban traces. Tongolele is only one of several acts that night, during which the famous star is to bid farewell to the stage as she is about to get married to a journalist (played by David Silva). More than any other of the films that featured her, *Han matado a Tongolele* flirts with factual references to Tongolele's performances and real life career trajectory. Outside of the intrigue surrounding her death and her marriage to a journalist, in real life Tongolele did appear in the Teatro Follies performing her 'exotic' dance numbers in front of adoring crowds for years.

A deeper analysis of Tongolele's film, as well as a few from Rosa Carmina's extensive film work, may serve as illustrations of the ways in which commercial and popular cultural representations at the height of Mexico's cultural renaissance decentered manufactured nationalist narratives of mexicanidad. That is, what I have been calling Afrodiasporic assemblages in cine de rumberas is augmented to include the Lesser Antilles and the Pacific Ocean islands. Thus, rather than thinking of nations, or even in terms of island-nations, as exceptions, we can think about a trans-islandic activity in some of these films, and about how this is also connected to mainlands (here Mexico, but also others). I'm envisioning further discussions (like those which some scholars have already begun) about such an archipelagic mode of doing Latin American studies, one that is comfortable inhabiting a transnational framework because cultural practices erase national specificities. Tongolele's choreographies for the cinematic stage are a way to begin to think in productive terms about these connections within the global south.

CONCLUDING REMARKS

In María Novaro's film *Danzón* (1991) well-known queer artist Tito Vasconcelos performs a cabaret number that echoes the rumberas' performances from the archive of the classic Mexican cinema that I have been discussing in this chapter. In my reading of this filmic cabaret performance, the drag cabaret artist Susy (Vasconcelos), friend to the main character in the film, Julia Solórzano (María Rojo), is most specifically referencing Ninón Sevilla's music and dance numbers, although Susy, in full rumbera drag, is doing a number that is a lip-synched performance of Ana María Fernández's version of "El coquero" ("The Man That Sells Coconuts") by the bolero composer Agustín Lara. During the same decade that *Danzón* was released, a political cabaret performance piece, *Víctimas del pecado neoliberal*, had a short run in from 1994–1995 in El Hábito, the infamous theater-bar space in

Mexico City, that was co-managed by romantic and business partners Jesusa Rodríguez and Liliana Felipe. *Víctimas del pecado neoliberal* is not only a direct reference to the film *Víctimas del pecado* (1951) by Emilio "El Indio" Fernández and starring Sevilla, but also featured two musical-dance numbers that (in)directly reference Sevilla and the rumbera phenomenon of the middle of the twentieth century. One of these numbers featured the song by Liliana Felipe "Que devuelvan" ("Give it back") toward the end of the close of the two-hour live production. The song is a critique of white-collar corporate and government corruption, as the full cast dances in full guarachera—rumbera garb (which includes the aforementioned Vasconcelos and Rodríguez, as well as Regina Orozco and Rosario Zúñiga).[19] These cinematographic and live performances from the 1990s, which could be considered either marginal or minor, perhaps even underground, as was the case with the performance at El Hábito, took up the figure of the rumbera and made these films popular among a small audience demographic (queer and feminist), mostly centered in Mexico City. However, on the other side of the spectrum, by the late 1990s and in the early 2000s, entrepreneurs in the entertainment industry tapped into the rumbera archive and produced several commercial musicals, specifically *Aventurera* (Carmen Salinas)—inspired by the film starring Sevilla—and *Perfume de gardenia* (Omar Suárez), both of which had year-long runs and were promoted heavily on all advertising platforms, from billboards to television gossip shows.

I close my chapter with brief descriptions of a few contemporary examples of what may be called the resurgence of the figure of the rumbera (although there are more) in order to bring up a question regarding the ways in which certain ideas about Mexico's history and cultural past are still mediated through embodied and gendered performances. My interest is also in the form of a question: What does it mean to use the rumbera figure, to queer her, to camp her up even more, and to monetize on her popularity through nostalgic reinterpretations, at a moment in which blackness in Mexico is finally entering into public discourse in ways that are not about entertainment or stereotypes, but about the country's legacy of African slavery and the socio-political status of people of African or Afro-mestizo heritage? The question is to serve as food for thought as we come to terms with the ways in which blackness has been invisibilized, marginalized, denigrated, or propped up for its 'entertainment value.' The issue becomes acutely important if we consider that, just as in the cine de rumberas of the 1940s and 1950s, more current revivals of the rumbera figure suggest the possibility that, through the mechanisms of the entertainment industry, the specter of blackness continues to mediate Mexican identity in racially palpable ways.

NOTES

1. According to the credits, the musicians that accompany Kiko Mendive are Esmeralda y Los Diablos del Ritmo. Kiko Mendive was a Cuban rumbero (male rumba dancer) who appeared as himself or as a character, but always as a singer and/or dancer, in about twenty rumbera films produced in Mexico in the middle of the twentieth century. After the rumbera phenomenon lapsed, he relocated to Venezuela where he continued to perform until shortly before his death in 2000.

2. I am referring to *Angelitos negros* (Joselito Rodríguez 1948), *Negro es mi color* (Tito Davidson 1951), *El derecho de nacer* (Zacarías Gómez Urquiza 1952), and *Píntame angelitos blancos* (Ismael Rodríguez 1954).

3. I use the term white Hispanic to distinguish from the Afrodiasporic subjects in the films analyzed here. In other words, my use of whiteness is not meant to register a notion that is exclusively associated with the Anglo-Saxon culture, but people of European extraction, which includes the Iberian Peninsula.

4. By Mexican gendered and sexual system of desire, particularly as presented by the cultural industries during the 1940s, namely song and film, I mean to say that desire was filtered through a heterosexual gendered dynamic where masculinity had the stronghold and femininity was the desired object. The dance numbers in the cine de rumberas, particularly those that feature solo dancing and center the feminine dancing body who is deriving pleasure from her own movements and for herself, despite the masculine gaze, helps to momentarily interrupt the system of desire that structure most melodramatic films.

5. In his book *Nationalizing Blackness: Afrocubanismo and Artistic Revolution in Havana: 1920–1940* Robin Moore discusses, with some extension, the origins of the rumbera dress (which is actually known as a guaracha costume), but which are mostly forgotten. Moore explains that during the rumba craze of the 1920s and early 1930s in Havana, the dress was standardized, as it seemed that all groups performing (in music or dance) at that time would either wear ruffled vests and sleeves (men) or long-ruffled tails—or open skirts—(women) (p. 54).

6. In the book project from which this chapter is culled, I argue that there is a renewed interest in rumbera films and the imaginaries that they unleashed. There are various examples of this, including the live musicals produced in the first two decades of the new millennium that were (in)directly influenced by cine de rumberas, such as *Aventurera* (produced by Carmen Salinas) and *Perfume de gardenia* (produced by Omar Suárez). In the cinematic world, the biopic *El fantástico mundo de Juan Orol* (Sebastián del Amo 2012), tells the story of Juan Orol's role in the film industry in Mexico during its so-called golden age period, showing that the bulk of his films can be categorized as cine de rumberas.

7. In *Aguila o sol* (Arcady Boytler 1938), the first feature film with Mario Moreno "Cantinflas," Margarita Mora performs a rumba number, "Un meneíto na' ma." While there is no identifiable rumba dance number like the one in *Aguila o sol* prior to this, in a previous Boytler film, *La mujer del puerto* (1933), and in the alleged first talkie of Mexican cinema, *Santa* (Antonio Moreno 1932), the cinematic space of the cabaret is a primary location from which to explore the nexus of modernity,

exoticism, dance, and desire. In these spaces, one could see early vestiges of dancing rumberas as the women in the cabarets were dancing to Afrodiasporic rhythms.

8. Whereas Blanco Borelli's critical analysis centers the figure of the mulata and argues that *Tam Tam* is the first film to join the mulata body and the rumba, and is therefore an influence on the cine de rumberas, it is important to mention that in the bulk of the rumbera films the white Cuban dancing body is the one that is centered, as I mentioned in the opening of this chapter. I will further elaborate on this in the next section of the chapter.

9. In my book project, from which this chapter is culled, I examine these films and the roles of these two mulatas, Cuban-born Rita Montaner, and Mexico-born Toña La Negra.

10. *Lo prohibido y lo permitido en materia de movimientos corporales*. This quote comes from Carlos Monsiváis, "Tongolele y el enriquecimiento de las buenas costumbres." In *No han matado a Tongolele*, by Arturo García Hernández, p. 12.

11. Idea borrowed from Licia Fiol-Matta's presentation "Vocal Pedagogy: Ruth Fernández and the Role of the 'Musical' in Colonial Puerto Rico," delivered at the "Sexing the Borderlands" symposium at The University of Texas at Austin, October 12–13, 2012.

12. The larger book project, *Rumberas in Motion (Pictures): Transnational Movements in the Archive of 'Classic' Mexican Cinema*, deals with this explicitly where I explore the multiple meanings that contemporary representations of the rumbera might have in the collective imaginary.

13. In an interview with Yolanda Montes "Tongolele," we discussed this particular aspect of her dancing style. As opposed to other rumberas, Tongolele's dancing was almost always to the sound of bongoseros. And, as she told me in the interview, she was the musical leader.

14. My use here of 'hip-notically' is riffing off the word 'hypnotic' and thinking about the ways in which the hips are conjoined with the eyes in their effort to seduce; it is hugely indebted to Melissa Blanco Borelli's essay "¿Y ahora qué vas a hacer, mulata?: Hip Choreographies in the Mexican Cabaretera Film *Mulata* (1954)," where she develops the concept of hip(g)nosis that conflates hips, hypnotism, and gnosis to help think through the mulata's identity as performed via the corporeal movements. Blanco Borelli further develops these ideas in her book *She is Cuba: A Genealogy of the Mulata Body*.

15. Canal 22 interview.

16. From the segment "Aventurera" for the television series *Los que hicieron nuestro cine* by Alejandro Pelayo. Direct transcription of the Carlos Monsiváis interview.

17. Ibid. Father Ripalda (Jerónimo Martínez de Ripalda) was a sixteenth-century Spanish priest who wrote the book of catechism that was used during the colonial period in Mexico. It continued to be edited in Mexico until the middle of the twentieth century.

18. Her character Sandra in *Sandra, la mujer de fuego* was the inspiration for the Mexican comic book character Rarotonga, a savage yet seductive woman who lives

in the jungle in an island of the same name and who enchants many men with her ritualistic dances.

19. In my book *Performing Mexicanidad: Vendidas y Cabareteras on the Transnational Stage*, I discuss the other performance, which features Vasconcelos with a full gender parody of Sevilla's character, Elena Tejero, in *Aventurera* (Alberto Gout 1950), arguably her most well-known film, at least in the contemporary moment.

REFERENCES

Blanco Borelli, Melissa. *She is Cuba: A Genealogy of the Mulata Body*. New York: Oxford University Press, 2016.

_____. "¿Y ahora qué vas a hacer, mulata?: Hip Choreographies in the Mexican Cabaretera film *Mulata* (1954)." *Women & Performance: A Journal of Feminist Theory* no. 18, vol. 3 (215–233): 2008.

Brown, Jayna. *Babylon Girls: Black Women Performers and the Shaping of the Modern*. Durham: Duke University Press, 2008.

Galvadón, Roberto. *Han matado a Tongolele*. Producciones Juno, S.A. 1948.

García, David F. *Listening for Africa: Freedom, Modernity, and the Logic of Black Music's African Origins*. Durham: Duke University Press, 2017.

Glissant, Edouard, *Caribbean Discourse: Selected Essays*, translated and with an introduction by J. Michael Dash. Charlottesville: University of Virginia Press, 1999.

Madrid, Alejandro L. and Robin D. Moore. *Danzón*: Circum-Caribbean Dialogues in Music and Dance. New York: Oxford University Press, 2013.

Martínez Solares, Gilberto. *Mulata*. Productora Mier y Brooks, S.A. 1954.

Monsiváis, Carlos. "Tongolele y el enriquecimiento de las buenas costumbres." In *No han matado a Tongolele*, edited by Arturo García Hernández, 11–19. Mexico: La Jornada Ediciones, 1998.

Montes, Yolanda "Tongolele." Dancer and Star of Cine de Rumberas Films. Personal Communication. Mexico City, Mexico. August 5, 2011.

Moore, Robin. *Nationalizing Blackness: Afrocubanismo and Artistic Revolution in Havana, 1920–1940*. Pittsburgh: University of Pittsburgh Press, 1997.

Pulido Llano, Gabriela. *Mulatas y negros en la escena mexicana (1920–1950)*. Mexico: INAH, 2010.

Rivero, Fernando A. *Coqueta*. Producciones Calderón. 1949.

Vásquez, Alexandra T. *Listening in Detail: Performances of Cuban Music*. Durham: Duke University Press, 2013.

Chapter 2

The *Danza de Inditas* in the Mexican Huasteca Region
Decolonizing Nationalist Discourse
Lizette Alegre González

The celebration of transnational identities in current scholarly discourse has pointed to the demise of the nation-state as a category of cultural analysis in globalization, and to its inability to account for and mediate political and socio-cultural conflicts that emerge in diverse social sectors of its national territory. Stemming out of this narrative, the rhetoric of cultural diversity—intensified by the corporate advocacy for international human rights (Briones 2005)—has inspired studies that show how Indigenous groups have become visible throughout the geopolitical boundaries of nation-states in order to reclaim rights over their own identity. These analyses, however, rarely register the ethnic experience of groups that, although traversed by the effects of globalization and neoliberal governmentality, constitute historical alterities within the horizon of the nation-state, where they have reproduced dynamics of social exchange from time gone by. Historical alterities pertain to groups that were formed and sustained under control from the state and that were articulated through a structure of inequity during the course of national history (Segato 2002). These groups are internal *others*, the result of forms of subjectification that can be traced back to European colonial times, an important historical backdrop often overlooked by current socioeconomic and cultural critiques of globalization, along with the conflicts that characterized this period.

While the nation does not have an ontological existence, the way in which it mobilizes practices as part of its pedagogic and performative exhibition (Bhabha 2002) certainly produces effects. And thus, cultural difference continues until today to inform the state's ordering and administration of populations. Although 'nation' and 'state' should not be confused, the conjunction of both terms—nation-state—is a referent to a specific place of enunciation: a place for the apparatus that speaks for the nation and that adjudicates its representation according to how it produces a legitimate national subject (Rufer 2012). Moreover, the notions of 'time' that constitute the basis for the discursive operations of history are political notions. Such notions buttress the modern (and western) uses of empty time—linear, homogeneous, and progressive—that articulate a narrative of progress as destiny, in which the nation-state becomes the synthesis of political realization (Rufer 2010). Based on these notions of time, Latin American modernity produced the idea of a homogenous nation, a construct that could absorb the multiple temporalities that emerged from divergent modes of living. This process did not entail the elimination of these other temporal orders as much as the undermining of their contemporaneity. Thus, they were given a place in the past within the temporality of the nation, thereby making a distinction between societies of culture and societies of history, a differentiation that still persists today. Such distinction eradicated Indigenous groups from the national, history-destiny field of enunciation and placed them in the category of 'atavistic tradition,' an anachronistic representation of 'primal origins.'

Modern notions of national time operate as part of a type of signification that homogenizes the subject in order to position him/her in the (supposedly) universalizing space of citizenship, realized at the moment when the subject attains corporate visibility in relation to the state's progressivist rhetoric (see Ramos-Kittrell in this volume). In reality, Indigenous societies are denied this political condition in light of the atavistic backwardness that keeps them in the 'waiting room' of progress. The state perpetuates and exploits this positioning in the ways it indexes Indigenous atavistic temporalities as relics of the present, their subjects being in here today as living proof of a memorable past (Rufer 2016). Even in our times of national multiculturalism, the notion of empty time remains current. For, although the nation recognizes its cultural diversity, its place of enunciation does not change. Through the consistent displacement of Indigenous societies into the terrain of otherness the state continues the production of identities without implying a politics of intervention on the notion of 'time', or on the perpetuation of historical inequities (Rufer 2010). In this way, the state disavows the violence implicit in the production of national identity by a plundering and racializing mechanism of asymmetrical biopolitical engineering that articulates its historical narrative.

These processes comprise mechanisms of social classification through the naturalization of territorial, racial, and epistemological hierarchies, which define the colonialist framework that has historically constituted America until today (Quijano 2000a, 2000b). Thus, the Mexican nation emerged as a phenomenological construct steeped in the logics of coloniality.[1] In this chapter I argue that the *danza de Inditas* practiced by Nahua women from the Huasteca region disrupts the Mexican state's representational discourse of Indigenous societies—particularly their designated place as harbingers of atavistic tradition—likewise problematizing the state's auto-designated place of enunciation. Among Nahua communities of the Huasteca region in the states of Hidalgo, Veracruz, and San Luis Potosí (in the Mexican northeast), the main purpose of the *danza* is to praise the Virgin of Guadalupe. Traditionally, only young girls (children and non-married adolescents) could participate in the dance, as virginity was regarded an indispensable attribute of dancers involved in this bodily expressive form of praise. More than a decade ago, however, groups of married women—whom the community regards as *señoras*, and who do not possess the culturally prescribed attribute of *pureza* (purity)—began to take part in the ritual. The community describes these señoras (as they describe themselves too) as women that "know how to speak" (*saben hablar*). More specifically, *saber hablar* or knowing how to speak refers to a discursive and political iterative strategy: it is an instance of enunciation that Nahua women articulate through their work and activity in the community, and that upsets the logic of individual rights characteristic of liberal notions of citizenship. My research in the community of Atotomoc (in the municipality of Atlapexco) shows how the elements that conform *saber hablar* among señoras stem, on the one hand, from processes that reconfigure their status in the community, and on the other, from the way in which such processes redefine the communal notion of 'we,' an autonomous and socio-political form of organization, as well as a collective physical space. Thus, the 'speaking' of señoras takes form by defying cultural expectations in the production of their social personhood through the production of the collective within the framework of the dance-musical system of this region. The chapter also emphasizes how these processes are part of a series of transformations experienced by Huastecan Indigenous societies as a result of neoliberal state policies enforced in past decades.

INDIGENOUS COMMUNITIES AND THEIR SOCIO-POLITICAL REPRODUCTION

Contemporary Indigenous communities are the result of a historical process of struggle to preserve a territory through which to reproduce themselves socially and epistemically. Since the time of Spanish colonization, the development of Indigenous societies in the Huasteca region has been permeated by constant changes in their territorial and political organization: the *encomienda* system (Pérez 2010, 2001; Aguilar 1997; Gibson 1990); the policy of congregations and the instauration of the republic of Indians (*República de Indios*—Ariel de Vidas 2009, Cabrera 2002, Ávila, Barthas, y Cervantes

1995); the *hacienda* (Florescano 1990, Chevalier 1999, Escobar Ohmstede 1999); the creation of town councils (*ayuntamientos*—Escobar 1996); policies and initiatives to dismantle corporate assets, and silence Indigenous responses to these effects—such as the invasion of land and the creation of territorial enclosures by Indigenous communities (Escobar 1993, 1999; Gutiérrez, 2001); the agrarian redistribution of land under Mexican President Lázaro Cárdenas—which in the Huasteca region happened under the control of *caciques* (Shryer 1986, Escobar y Sandre 2007, Ávila, Barthas, y Cervantes 1995); and the agrarian movement (*movimiento campesino*) for the recovery of land of the 1970s and early 1980s (Ávila 1990, Suárez 2004, Briseño 1994, Ariel de Vidas 1993). More historically current challenges faced by Indigenous communities include the state's implementation of the *Programa de Certificación de Derechos Ejidales* (PROCEDE—Program for the Certification of Ejido[2] Rights), as well as fracking, intensified by the *Reforma Energética* (reform on energy) passed in 2013. The creation of town councils (*ayuntamientos*) substituted Indigenous governance with non-Indigenous governments in the nineteenth century. Town councils moved Indigenous political and collective life out from larger social and territorial spaces and pushed it into the confines of their local community. As a result, the community became the main site for the articulation of Indigenous social identity (Bartolomé 1997). Nevertheless, such a push enabled communities to autonomously organize their internal socio-political structure. The System of Duties (*sistema de cargos*) and the Domestic Group (*grupo doméstico*) are two of the structuring mechanisms that emerged from this internal form of organization. The System of Duties is a hierarchical echelon of charges or duties relevant to the public, civil, and even religious administration of the community. Only male members of the community are eligible to carry one of these duties, for which they are elected by vote, and on a rotating basis. This organizational dynamic establishes a reciprocity between governance and those governed by structuring and reproducing, on the one hand, labor duties aimed for the communal good (these are called *faenas*), and on the other, norms that stipulate the requirements, functions, and election process for someone to be assigned this form of labor. Far from being a static structure, the System of Duties shows a constant re-engineering of institutions in response to challenges against communal autonomy, land, and its resources (Ávila 2013, Iciek 2013).

Domestic groups, however, are the base of the social organization of the community. According to Sandstrom (2005), these are groups defined by their internal relationships of kin and aspects of their common life: they live together, prepare and consume their own food, share a household budget, and work together to reproduce these dynamics. Ultimately, the development of these groups creates localized patrilineal collectivities, especially because postmarital residence (i.e., for a woman leaving her family after getting married) is still patrilocal—that is, the new couple goes to live with the family of the husband until they can gather the necessary resources to build and form their own home (Sandstrom 2005, Robichaux 2005). The exchange of women—along with the product of their work—and the return of their parental descent as they enter a new domestic group after marriage are essential to the continuity of patrilineal collectivities. Nahua people define the arrangements of domestic groups as *se kosa tekitli* (working for something in common), given that they fulfill communal obligations such as carrying out duties (as part of the System of Duties), participating in *faenas*, and contributing to community works and festivities, among others. In exchange, the socio-political structure of the community grants two important rights to contributing groups, which are necessary to carry out agricultural labor or activities that require collective participation: access to land and the exchange of labor. Thus, the System of Duties and domestic groups are both catalysts of a project to produce society, which contrasts and opposes the power logics behind *mestizo* social initiatives;[3] it is through the rights that emerge directly from the collective work of all members of the community that such a project is possible.

SABER HABLAR: DISLOCATING THE NOTION OF LIBERAL CITIZENSHIP

The notion of *saber hablar* makes it necessary to account for what makes *señoras* 'speaking subjects' in light of the subalternity that national history has assigned to Indigenous people in general, and to women in particular. Expressions such as *saber hablar* and *poder hablar* (being able to speak)—but also their opposites: not knowing how to speak, or being afraid or ashamed to speak—emerge constantly in conversation with and among Nahua people of the Huasteca region. Today, señoras from Atotomoc recognize that the devaluation of women and their work, their imperatively expected obedience to men, and their domestic confinement form the basis of the 'not being able to speak'—of being afraid or ashamed to speak—that affected their mothers and grandmothers. 'Not being able to speak' alluded to the impossibility of women to complain, to defend themselves, to express their wishes or needs, or to have an opinion—let alone decide—over the dynamics of their domestic groups. *Saber hablar*, however, points today to discursive situations enabled by changes in the region over the last three decades, which reconfigure the status of women within their domestic groups and the community.

Since the 1980s, the burden of neoliberal economic policies over the agrarian sector (started by President Carlos Salinas de Gortari, see Harvey 2015, Rubio 2001, Ávila 1996) has transformed radically the relationship of Nahua communities with the national public sphere. On the one hand, the progressive decay of the agricultural economy increased the rate of migration (Mora 2012, Duquesnoy 2010, Pérez 2007, Camacho 2006, Alonso 2003), and the number of people entering the tertiary sector of the economy (either as domestic servants or in other services, see Arellanos 2012). Given the effects that neoliberal initiatives have had on the means of sustenance and reproduction of Nahua domestic groups (for which agricultural production and auto-consumption are no longer sufficient), their members have had to diversify their labor. Women in the tertiary sector have had to leave the local limits of their patrilineal communities in order to generate income are such an example. On the other hand, the expansion of the public school network (particularly at the elementary and middle levels) has also had an impact in the region since the 1980s (Valle 2004, 24–25). Such growth accelerated the spread of literacy and the castilianization of the Nahua community, especially among people (of both genders) that are thirty-five years old, or younger. Moreover, social welfare initiatives like OPORTUNIDADES (*Opportunities*)—a federal program officially launched in 2002 but preceded by similar programs—with their focus on health and nutrition strengthened the position of women in the family and in their community (González 2006). On general terms, the program allocates money every two months to women and children, making the mothers the central family liaison and the one responsible for managing these funds.

Either by laboring outside of the community or through federal assistance programs like OPORTUNIDADES, señoras have gained a degree of autonomy, as access to streams of income—and the legitimacy that they receive from state institutions, which recognizes women as central decision makers within domestic groups—enables them to be dynamic participants in the administration of their household, and therefore, productive members of their communities (Arellanos 2008). Moreover, their acquisition of Castilian literacy skills—through their involvement in the expansion of the public school system—has enabled them to engage the mestizo social sphere, and thus, act as mediators between their communities and state entities in matters pertaining to the distribution of different types of resources, thereby upsetting the historically gendered structure of their communities in which women depended on the labor of men. These changes have allowed Nahua women (especially señoras) to participate in the federal rhetoric of "rights for women" and "citizenship rights," which has created an interlegal bond between consuetudinary law (or customary law) and positivistic enacted policies which women have learned to negotiate (Sierra 2009). Thus, by exiting their domestic and cultural space, women have become dynamic social actors in the public sphere—the space in which social groups discuss, decide, and define themselves politically—thereby becoming key players in the legal and socioeconomic sustenance and representation of their communities.[4] Such transformations, especially as they pertain to the subjectivity of Nahua women, form part of the semantic field that they articulate by saying that they have lost fear or shame of speaking.[5]

The pillaging colonial effects of neoliberal capitalism in the Huasteca region notwithstanding—in which disenfranchisement from the public sphere has been the historical sign of economic marginalization[6]—Nahua señoras are acutely aware of a change in their status, which for them reflects a subjective process of self-reconfiguration and valuation in the phrase "having lost the fear of speaking." Their enunciations urge us to problematize the effects of coloniality and to question the extent in which it can truly affect the micro-social. In this respect, it is pertinent to consider Castro Gómez's heterarchical reading of power (2007) as a way of thinking about the relative independence of the local within the system—a type of independence that goes unnoticed in hierarchical representations of power—especially pertaining to the micro-physical terrain. Such heterarchical reading contests the notion that structures act independently and disengaged from the agency of subjects, and highlights the need to account for practices of subjectification. Yet, it should be emphasized that patrilineal communities continue working together, and that the income earned by women, far from being a means of fracture, constitutes a new basis for the reproduction of their communities and domestic groups without subverting the principle of postmarital patrilocal life. Moreover, women's engagement with and appropriation of the institutional rhetoric of "rights" has not been translated into a modern and liberal notion of emancipation. The new awareness that Nahua women have about gender equality tends to be informed by ideas of mutual complementarity, and particularly, of complementarity related to joint labor (*trabajo en común*). Such realization has enabled women to engage with their community and its internal inconsistencies and contradictions, thereby changing from the inside aspects of consuetudinary law that did not benefit them. The reconfiguration of women's status, therefore, suggests that Indigenous domestic groups act as autonomous estates in order to protect territory (Tzul 2014). In other words, while the state attempts to produce and administer individual subjects, Nahua women respond by safeguarding the collective.

THE BODY TAKES THE WORD: THE *DANZA DE INDITAS SEÑORAS* AS RECONFIGURATION OF THE COLLECTIVE

The *danza de Inditas* was introduced in the Huasteca region in the early 1960s. In addition to its celebration as part of the festivities for the Virgin of Guadalupe on December 12—the patron saint of this dance—the *Inditas* also take part in festivities for the Christmas season, as well as feasts for saints and Marian advocations. The music accompanying the dance is usually played by a *trio huasteco*, which typically features a violin, a jarana, and a *guitarra huapanguera* (huapango guitar, see Alex E. Chávez in this volume), although it is not unusual to find duets consisting of just violin and jarana. While the music (at least until today) is usually performed by men, dancing *Inditas* also play maracas and sing Nahuatl or Spanish songs telling the story of the apparition of the Virgin to Juan Diego in the hill of Tepeyac in the sixteenth century. It is in this performative context that the 'speaking' of señoras (i.e., who know how to speak, that is, *saben hablar*) takes form as they challenge the cultural expectations that construct their sense of social personhood while they reproduce and sustain the collective.

The Dance-Musical System and the Regulating Production of Identity

The *danza de Inditas* is just one of a group of local cultural expressions that conform the dance-musical system of the Huasteca region (see Figure 2.1). Comprehensibly, such system is:

> [...] a series of musical and dance acts within a structure that contains codified information derived from a play between what is similar and what is different. The contrast between the features that characterize such acts allows for differences to emerge and to become charged with meaning. Thus, the sounds, musical structures, genres, instrumentations, choreographies, and performative occasions are established according to grammatical codes that organize sound phenomena, and that are linked to other social dimensions, thereby articulating a grand system of communication (Camacho 2007, 169).

Following this conceptualization, I propose that the differences[7] that enable the regulative production of identity (i.e., the norms that produce the sense of *social personhood* within the community) emerge among the differences codified by this dance-musical system. By social personhood I am referring to the image that society subjectively constructs about what one of its subjects ought to be, an image that is necessarily internalized by its members in response to existing expectations (Bartolomé 1997, 150). This is to say that parental and

The Danza de Inditas *in the Mexican Huasteca Region* 31

Figure 2.1. Dance during the watch for the *Virgen de Guadalupe*. Atotomoc, municipality of Atlapexco, Hidalgo. Photo by Lizette Alegre González, 2011.

political systems of classification, age groups, ceremonial hierarchies, and even collective conceptions about the soul bestow meaning on the social person.

Social expectations regarding what women ought to be are informed and signified by age, as it relates to their physiological capacity for reproduction. In this way, the community establishes differences between girl-children (*niñas*), adolescents (*muchachas*), *señoras*, and grandmothers (*abuelas*), each understood as a type of social person. Women are eligible for marriage only after menstruation, which prompts a passage from their original domestic group to that of their husband (i.e., after marriage); it is at this point that women enter the social category of *señoras*. The loss of their physiological capacity for reproduction usually coincides with the moment in which their domestic group is expanded, that is, when their sons grow up and get married, at which point post-reproductive women become head of their households and articulating agents of their domestic units. At this point, women enter the category of *abuelas*, and they assume certain ritualistic obligations.

In the Huastecan dance-musical system, musical and choreographic genres are performatively deployed as part of acts related to two large spheres: that pertaining to the divine, and that pertaining to the human.[8] The divine sphere is associated with public festivities (i.e., those that pull the entire community together), while the human sphere is regarded in connection with private, familial, and domestic celebrations. Prior to the introduction of the *danza de Inditas* in the region, ceremonies related to the divine/public fostered the participation of children, youths, adults, and even elder musicians and/or dancers of both genders, excluding *señoras* altogether.

It is noteworthy that the preparation and realization of ceremonies of the divine/public type are structured through the System of Duties, which means that such ceremonies are instances of the political organization of the community. The political character of these ceremonies—in addition to their formalized and ritualized aspect—makes them texts that operate as meta-descriptions of culture (Lotman 1996) and of the communal 'we,' conceptions that point to how the community has changed historically. Not so long ago, this meta-description excluded señoras, whose sense of social personhood was formed in the domestic space of the household. The articulation of the dominant concept of 'we' entailed the negation of the categorical term embodied by married women (señoras) in the very same way that the private and the domestic domains of experience were hierarchically subordinate in the public sphere. The absent voice of married, reproductive women in the public arena of the dance-musical system (i.e., the presence of their dancing, performative bodies), thus, was a catalyst to reproduce the impossibility to position their voice (their speaking) both inside the domestic group and in the public sphere. In this respect, the notion that the *danza de Inditas* had to be performed by children or unmarried adolescent girls—while dancing outside of these conditions was sinful—reveals a cultural prescription (an expectation) that imposed limits on the bodies of señoras, and that created a differentiated subject by exclusion (see Figure 2.2).

A performative understanding of identity (Butler 2016)[9] urges us to think of culturally intelligible subjects—social persons—as the result of a discourse that, as defined by established norms, emerges from quotidian and generalizable acts of signification marked by difference in everyday experience. Such discourse is the citational, iterative structure where performative identity occurs, which allows signs to be dislodged and recontextualized, thereby opening terrain for the emergence of new identitarian constructions. This means that a chain of iterative acts can be delinked in order to signify bodies and ways of life thus far excluded by a dominant symbolic logic: what is excluded has the possibility of being produced as a rearticulation of the symbolic horizon and of the expectations it establishes in order to define categories of social personhood in relation to the body. It is right here that señoras—through the performative space of the *danza de Inditas*—effect processes that transform their reality. The irruptive positioning of their

Figure 2.2. *Inditas* of the "Virgen Morena" group. Atotomoc, municipality of Atlapexco, Hidalgo. Photo by Lizette Alegre González, 2011.

bodies in the dance-musical system reveals a profoundly transgressive process of signification that defies the descriptive force of established social categories, which formerly assigned married women a particular role.

In conversations with señoras—as well as with other people from Atotomoc and other communities—regarding how they understand what their dance practice means and has meant, general comments allude to chains of signifiers that have denaturalized and reconfigured perceptions of their social personhood. Prior to the incursion of señoras in the *danza de Inditas*, the dance produced the dance-child-Virgin-purity chain of signifiers. This symbolic linkage produced expectations about what child and adolescent girls ought to be in relation to the dance, while excluding señoras from any possibility of dancing altogether. Comments by members of the Atotomoc community about the incursion of señoras in the *danza* corroborate the rupture of this chain: their surprise (when señoras danced for the first time) and acceptance meant the recognition of married women's desire to dance, which they had not been able to enunciate before. However, there is a distance between the formulation of desire and its consummation, which can only be bridged by overcoming shame. It is important to highlight this feeling, as the shame related to their subversion against established norms around the dance-musical system is parallel to the feelings of insecurity and incapacity that they felt while confined to domestic spaces and subordinated to masculine rule. This challenge to the supposed inviolability of the norm that precluded señoras from dancing due to their loss of purity (i.e., their non-virgin bodies) has also prompted a reformulation of meanings in relation to the Virgin of Guadalupe. Recurring to divinity was the only way to legitimize their right to dance: "If you dance people say it is a sin, but I say that it is not because it is for the Virgin."

For señoras, being viewed dancing in public is also an enunciative mark tied to the notion of participation. This is because the *principle of participation* is a basic requisite to establish membership with the community, which makes individuals connect to the community's social network through a complex system of reciprocal exchange. This is why, according to Bartolomé, festivities are instances that exponentially institute communal relationships, because it is at that moment when such relationships become overtly visible (Bartolomé 1997, 137). Therefore, the way in which señoras emphasize their participation in the festivities for the Virgin—of making what was excluded a part of 'we'—reveals a gesture that upsets the defining stability of the notion of 'we' to enable a reconstruction of the collective.

Parody is also a feature that characterizes the agency of these women dancers. The presence of norms not only determines an undeniable place for the enactment of power. They also provide a space for parody and subversion against the naturalized premises active in the construction of social personhood (Butler 2007). Some dancing women mention that whenever they go dance for other communities, people do not believe that they are señoras because their agility and high-pitched voices give the impression that they are youths. This seeming ambiguity upsets the distinction between signs and their corresponding bodies, thus displacing the significations usually assigned to the different categories of social person. Señoras imitate adolescent girls in their performance, but in so doing they implicitly stipulate that the social personhood of the latter—and that of child-girls, as their social personhood was also originally encoded in the chain of signifiers related to the dance for the Virgin—has become an imitative, citational category, and therefore contingent, which makes the social person of the *señora* contingent as well. Ultimately, this imitative act alters the regulating function and descriptive force of identitarian effects.

One of the most radical aspects of dance practices in the Huasteca region is how the curing of illness is perceived as deriving from the destabilization of social categories. All of the señoras that take part in the *danza de Inditas* claim to have suffered from an illness that disappeared at the moment when they started dancing, a miracle they attribute to the Virgin. Referring to the types of ailments that affected señoras at different points of their lives (and that they overcame by dancing), they mention things such as sadness, bitterness, and fear. This transaction between language and body points to how the overcoming of pain and suffering has a direct correlation with the social reconstitution of señoras and their world. They associate the chain of terms no-dance / still-body / death / sadness / sickness / domestic-space as a juxtaposition of dance / body-in-movement / life / happiness / cure / public-space. These linkages reflect how the body is constituted through a type of mediation that objectifies the suffering from illness by breaking away from complacency with their private and domestic world—especially with the place assigned to the private and the domestic space in relation to the sentiments associated with them—thereby resisting their complete assimilation. The linkages also reflect a connection between social structures and the phenomenological experience of illness, implying that the personal and private world—traversed by sentiments such as sadness, bitterness, and fear—has a history tied to the social and political organization of the community.

"The Virgin gave me strength, it's a miracle" (*La Virgen me dio fuerza, milagro*), dancers usually say. An impulse towards the affirmation of life and existence is part of the miracle that has cured them and saved them. It is not out of coincidence that people say that the Inditas señoras "came to dance to make it known that they still exist" (*vinieron a bailar para que se sepa que todavía existen*). Thus, dancers irrupt to establish a speaking (*un habla*) that takes the shape of the body in movement to enunciate their presence in this world by advocating it in the other. Señoras are constituted as collective body-subjects by a resulting sorority out of their shared experience of illness and cure. This constitution emerges in the structured relationships that produce the symbolic, from which they become interlocuters and advocates to the other side (the afterlife) affirming "we are alive" (*estamos vivas*). Ultimately, the emergence of this collective body-subject, made possible only through the displacement of a group of practices and instituted signifiers, is what gives the *danza* its political character, what makes it a political performative instance (Arditi 2014). This is because señoras actually experience and produce the very things that they strive for in the very act of striving for them: the capacity for agency of señoras lies not in who they are, but in the projects that they build and realize. It is through this process that they are transformed into what they are, by transforming their social and cultural universe (Ortner 1995).

The Community: Living Subject of a History and Project of the Future

Currently, the continuity of their community is among one of the challenges faced by Nahua people in the Huasteca region. This is because such sustenance requires solidary rearticulations among community members in order to reconfigure a legitimate collective sense of the *we*.[10] Social ascriptions related to the community are expressed in very particular ways during festivities. Festivities engage community structures, which range from the social net woven by parentage to diverse organizational instances that conform the System of Duties. Participating in festivities implies the acknowledgment of responsibility towards the physical space that supports and sustains Nahua life (Briseño 1995). The notion of participation is readily apparent in the social irruption of señoras in relation to their desire to dance. Notwithstanding initial resistance by some people, the *danza de Inditas señoras* has been now accepted in the entire region. In the case of Atotomoc, the entire community (including its representative authorities) has accepted the *danza* as it is conformed today. For this, the community called for a solemn assembly in order to pass a referendum that stipulated the common accord of the community to not criticize and respect señoras. It is out of this act that the *danza de Inditas* señoras is now considered *of* the community, which implies the visible insertion of señoras within the collective logic of mutual rights and responsibilities.

The idea that a festivity without dance is a sad festivity emerges frequently in conversations with señoras and other people from Atotomoc. People associate this sadness with the fact that without expressive practices such as the *danza* people would not get together. Likewise, it is said that people should share in the experience of the festivity with each other happily, because anger alienates people, which makes collective, cooperative work impossible. These comments suggest that festivities and dances constitute mechanisms of collective cohesion, as they contribute to the maintenance of the solidarity and commitment required for the exchange of labor. However, the successful execution of labor requires *organization*. This concept is central to the operational dynamics of dancers: señoras use this term systematically to refer, on the one hand, to the load of efforts and tasks that have been necessary to undertake in order to "put the dance up" (*levantar la danza*)—that is, to form a dance group, manage it, and direct it successfully—and on the other, to their valuation—related to their performative enactment of chants and choreographies. Similarly, the term *organization* also refers to the internal structure of the group, which is constituted as a committee in close connection with entities in the System of Duties, particularly with the delegate and *mayordomo* (an officer in charge of the logistics involved in the organization and production of religious festivities). This organizational activity takes place without remuneration, even if it takes time and energy to realize it. The labor of dancers is thus configured as a *faena* (a duty aimed at the communal good), which transforms both the dance-musical system and the System of Duties. This is how the *danza* not only gathers, but in fact produces the community. Given that the labor of the faena is done "from the heart" (*de corazón*, as señoras mention), the end result is highly affectual, expressed through happiness;

such feeling, in itself, represents the very constitution of the community insofar as it creates collective subjectivities and affectual dynamics of sociability (Hardt 1999). While the exploitation of affect and sociability for the sake of material production is not a new phenomenon, the degree to which affect is a productive resource, and how its use-value has become generalized in different sectors of the economy, is indeed a novelty. Nevertheless, such fact does not mean that affect, as immaterial labor, is not useful in anticapitalist projects. Affectual labor has an extraordinary subversive potential, which can be geared towards autonomous collective constitution. In fact, scholars like Hardt recognize in affectual labor biopolitical potential.[11] By attending to the labor involved in biopolitical production one can see the operation of biopower from below in terms of the capacity that affectual labor has to sustain life through the production and reproduction of subjectivities and sociability: "A focus on affect and on the networks that produce affect highlights such processes of social constitution. What is created through networks of affectual labor is a way-of-life" (Hardt 1999, 98).

Ultimately, this perspective reveals that, historically, the labor of biopolitical production has been strongly constituted as gendered labor. Feminist studies have shed light on this issue, showing the place that the labor involved in caretaking has in the production of social networks, community, and life. The recognition of this type of labor breaks away from traditionally distinctive notions between production and reproduction, and between the public and the domestic sphere. For Graeber (2006), one of the most outstanding features of the capitalist system is that its way of production is the only one that systematically divides households and workplaces. Graeber believes that it is possible to reimagine the notion of *modes of production* from a perspective that considers the complicit creation of human beings, and not just the making and struggling for a form of material value. From this perspective, Graeber argues that the labor involved in caretaking, maintenance, and education (among others), which sustains the functioning of societies and that has been performed overwhelmingly by women, ought to be considered as productive labor given that it *produces people*.

Thus, the labor of señoras through the *danza de Inditas* articulates a biopolitics from below: dancing produces affect, while affect produces sociability, community, and life. In light of the challenges that the neoliberal policies of the Mexican state pose to Indigenous communities (and their implications regarding territoriality, political structure, and consuetudinary law), a biopolitics from below is an important mechanism of resistance, as it produces the community by affectual appeal to its members. What makes this fact even more important is that, while the affectual and immaterial labor of señoras is not exclusive of the *danza de Inditas* (i.e., other dance and musical rituals can produce it too), it is their appearance in the public sphere through a dance-musical system that previously denied them a place that ultimately makes visible and valuable the product of activities that they had historically performed: immaterial, affectual labor. By appearing in the social sphere through this dance-musical system, by joining the community's political structure through the operation of the dance group as a committee, by accessing the logic of responsibilities and rights of the System of Duties, and—I insist—by doing all of this through the performance of what I have described as immaterial, affectual labor, the women of the *danza de Inditas* repair, unify, and communicate the public and the domestic fields, thereby making inroads towards the de-patriarchalization of the territory of the community. There, where their own culture did not allow them to participate, women built alliances with their community and reestablished mutual relationships in order to position their speaking bodies, and decolonize and depatriarchalize speech and body. Their practice is a political-cultural performance proper to self-reflexive subjects who learn to transform themselves while they resist the logics of coloniality. The communal collective subject takes form, and the body takes the word to speak, to speak by doing.

FINAL CONSIDERATIONS

The *we*, being a category of representativity, is also a political category. As such, it is impossible for this category to personify the particular demands and desires of all of those who seek to be represented by it. Nevertheless, such absence of in-full content (*contenido pleno*) is what makes possible the rearticulations produced by practices that at a given moment can be anomalous—even transgressive—such as the participation of señoras dancing in festivities. Far from static, the in-fullness of the *we* is an actual succession of contingent contents that emerge from socially, politically, and historically situated claims. This is what constitutes the foundation of radical historicism. Thus, I echo Rita Segato's proposition that relativism must make space for historical arguments through what she calls *historical pluralism*, a non-culturalist variation of relativism, though without the latter's fundamentalist tendencies. The author writes:

> "More than a fixed horizon of culture, each social group knits its history through the path of debate and internal deliberation, rearranging the inconsistencies of its own cultural discourse, enduring its contradictions, and choosing alternatives [. . .] which are activated by circulating ideas that come from the surrounding world" (Segato 2011, 26).

Therefore, when señoras affirm that they dance so that "the custom endures" (*para que la costumbre se mantenga*), such enunciation cannot be understood as an essentialist interpretation of culture, let alone associate it with the rhetoric of atavistic tradition (custom, actually, prohibited women to dance in the first place). What sustains custom is not a stable cultural patrimony but rather the common perception—although not free from dissent and conflict—of sharing a history, as well as the will to construct one's own historical project.

The recognition of señoras of the *danza de Inditas* as women that 'know how to speak' (*saben hablar*) implies that they have reached an enunciating status. What emerges behind such status, however, is the community as a collective subject, political actor, and interlocutor. This phenomenon points to a consideration, on the one hand, of the speaking of the subaltern (Spivak 2003), and on the other, of the enunciative place of the nation-state (Rufer 2012). As it is well known, in denying that the subaltern can speak Spivak was not referring to an incapacity to express desires, of forging alliances, or of producing political or cultural effects. Rather, she referred to the fact that the subaltern's representativity is not legible within the dominant framework of conceptualized representation. In this regard, the speech that claims rights while maintaining its particularity, without the sponsorship of institutional power (which establishes what is recognizable as a claim), lies usually ignored. Nevertheless, the present chapter sheds light on processes of agency that aim to sustain alternative constructions to the ways in which the nation-state conceals inequity through the administration of cultural difference. The lack of convergence between both discourses highlights the epistemic foundational violence that structures relationships between the institutions of the modern colonial nation-state and Indigenous social groups, questioning ultimately the legitimacy of the first.

Speech, realized as dancing body, restitutes the enunciative status of corporeal acts by making them prone to be listened to. Such acts problematize and expand the notions of speaking and listening. These acts also contest the idea that the music and dance of Indigenous groups are expressions inscribed in pre-political forms of action, linked to the ill-termed *uses and customs*, a contestation that reinforces the political and epistemic value of Indigenous ideas and practices. This is not only because the *danza de Inditas* constitutes an act of contestation that denaturalizes the social category that once constructed señoras, and that reconfigured the communal *we* right at the heart of the dance-musical system; in other words, not only because dancers re-stage and displace the epistemic scheme of their culture, but because this actually gives place to a critique of the concept of *tradition*—construed as negativity, as something that implies the idea of 'not-yet-modern'—so dear to the teleological construct of the Mexican nation-state. In this way, señoras contort that "powerful imaginary of narratives that privilege modern institutions, such as those of 'citizenship,' 'nation,' or the 'modern liberal subject' above other forms of social solidarity or experiences of subjectivity" (Restrepo 2007, 295).

The *danza de Inditas señoras* dismembers the uses of the past through which the Mexican nation-state has represented the Indigenous, either as heraldry or as relic. Thus, the *danza* hybridizes the apparently purified, empty, and homogenous time of the nation as it reclaims the legitimacy of that which the nation-state has historically seized from Indigenous social groups: the capacity to speak.

NOTES

1. Given the structuring effects of coloniality in the present (Escobar 2003), feminist critiques of modernity have pointed not only to the modernity-coloniality dimension lying at the core of notions of nation, law, democracy, and citizenship in modern states, but also to its patriarchal character (see Mendoza 2014, 2006; Rivera 2014; Ochoa 2014).

2. The ejido is a common land in a small town, typically used for cultivation, for gathering cattle, or for other activities, depending on the region. As such, the ejido is characterized by being an indivisible, collective land, which can be neither sold nor inherited.

3. In Mexico, the term *mestizo* refers to a social and cultural category historically articulated by racializing relationships of power. The construction of a national state implied the necessary construction of a national subject as a strategy to rationalize the category of 'Mexican citizen,' through which *mestizaje* acquired the character of 'national race.' See Laura Gutiérrez in this volume for further discussion about the politics that have permeated this construct.

4. Rita Segato observes that the marginalization of the domestic space in Indigenous communities derives from the historical coloniality of gender (2011). The contact of the Indigenous village with modernity's discourse of equity—or the "crossroad of patriarchies," as Paredes calls them (2010)—has had two consequences. On the one hand, the 'otherization' and marginalization of the domestic space eroded the political character that its internal activity could have. On the other, such erosion robbed Indigenous communities of their political presence within the republican public sphere.

5. The relationship between changes in the household economy and the restructuring of womanhood within domestic spaces has been addressed in decolonial feminist scholarship. See Hernández (2014) and Pavia (2014).

6. The incapacity by state agents to distinguish between citizenship—a mass of individuals entitled to rights—and the organization of collective life has usually had a disruptive effect on the dynamics of collective bargaining and on the system of authority of communities. In this way, the state emphasized individual rights while eroding the rights of collective subjects.

7. Here I am referring to the principle of differentiality that constitutes a unified grammar as a system of signs that generates meaning from its internal differences.

8. Conceptualizations of the divine and the human relate to Indigenous native categories that emphasize the directionality of musical and dance actions: in one instance they are directed toward divinities, and in another, toward human beings (Camacho 2007, 169).

9. As the reader might be aware, the citational—iterative—structure of the sign proposed by Derrida in his critique of Austin's performativity (1990, 1994) led Judith Butler to propose that the stylized reiteration of performative acts constructs gender—as well as social persons and identities (2007).

10. A construct not politicized in quotation marks, which points to its gendered exclusionary politics, but an integrated concept that recognizes and values the subjectivity of its women members.

11. Here, Hardt considers biopower as a term that adopts and also inverts the faculties that characterize it according to its Foucaultian meaning. Foucault perceives biopower as something that emerges from above: it is the power that controls lives; the forces stemming out of governmentality that create and control populations.

REFERENCES

Aguilar Robledo, Miguel. "Indios, ganado, tenencia de tierra e impacto en la Huasteca Potosina, siglos XVI y XVII." *Huaxteca. El hombre y su pasado* 2, no. 3 (1997): 15–25.

Alonso Meneses, Guillermo. "Indígenas, campesinos, ejidatarios y emigrantes. Migración y transformación de las comunidades nahuas de la Huasteca hidalguense." Paper presented at Primer Coloquio Internacional Migración y Desarrollo: Transnacionalismo y Nuevas Perspectivas de Integración, Zacatecas, México, 2003.

Arditi, Benjamín. "Insurgencies Don't Have a Plan—They Are the Plan." In *The Promise and Perils of Populism: Global Perspectives*, edited by Carlos de la Torre, 113–39. Lexington: University Press of Kentucky, 2014.

Arellanos Mares, María Liliana. "En busca de la vida. Grupos domésticos y estrategias de sobrevivencia en Tzicatlán, Veracruz." Master's thesis, Universidad Nacional Autónoma de México, 2012.

———. "La participación de las mujeres nahuas en Oportunidades." In *Memoria de papel. Actas del primer coloquio sobre otomíes de la sierra madre oriental y grupos vecinos*, 237–246. México: Instituto Nacional de Antropología e Historia, 2008.

Ariel de Vidas, Anath. *Huastecos a pesar de todo: Breve historia del origen de las comunidades teenek (Huastecas) de Tantoyuca, Norte de Veracruz*. México: Centro de Estudios Mexicanos y Centroamericanos, 2009.

———. "Una piedrita en los zapatos de los caciques. Ecos y repercusiones de las políticas de desarrollo rural en la Huasteca veracruzana." *Estudios Sociológicos* IX, no. 33 (1993): 741–746.

Austin, John L. *Cómo hacer cosas con palabras*. Barcelona: Paidós, 2014.

Ávila, Agustín. "Aproximaciones al gobierno indígena y la justicia comunitaria en San Luis Potosí." In *La Huaxteca. Concierto de saberes en homenaje a Lorenzo Ochoa*, edited by Ana Bella Pérez Castro, 227–267. México: Instituto de Investigaciones Antropológicas, Universidad Nacional Autónoma de México: El Colegio de San Luis, 2013.

———. "Etnia y movimiento campesino en la Huasteca hidalguense." In *Las organizaciones de productores rurales en México*, edited by Fernando Rello, 65–96. México: Universidad Nacional Autónoma de México, 1990.

———. "¿A dónde va la Huasteca?" *Estudios Agrarios* 2, no. 5 (1996): 9–30.

Ávila, Agustín, Brigitte Barthas, and Alma Cervantes. "Los huastecos de San Luis Potosí." In *Etnografía contemporánea de los pueblos indígenas de México. Región Oriental*, III. México: Instituto Nacional Indigenista, 1995.

Bartolomé, Miguel. *Gente de Costumbre y Gente de Razón. Las identidades étnicas en México*. México: Siglo XXI Editores, 1997.

Bhabha, Homi K. *El lugar de la cultura*. Buenos Aires: Manantial, 2002.

Briones, Claudia. *(Meta) cultura del estado-nación y estado de la (meta) cultura*. Popayán, Colombia: Editorial Universidad del Cauca, 2005.

Briseño Guerrero, Juan. "Los desvaríos del poder ante la autoridad: El sistema político del pueblo nahua de la Huasteca." In *Pueblos indígenas ante el derecho*, edited by Victoria Cheanut and María Teresa Sierra, 171–190. México: CIESAS, 1995.

———. *Aquí nomás . . . aquí somos. Reproducción de la organización comunal de Ocuiltzapoyo, S.L.P.* México: CIESAS, 1994.

Butler, Judith. *El género en disputa: el feminismo y la subversión de la identidad*. Madrid: Paidós, 2007.

Cabrera, Antonio J. *La Huasteca potosina: Ligeros apuntes sobre este país*. Colección Huasteca. México, D.F. and San Luis Potosi: Centro de Investigaciones y de Estudios Superiores en Antropología Social and El Colegio de San Luis, 2002.

Camacho Díaz, Gonzalo. "La cumbia de los ancestros. Música ritual y mass media en la Huasteca." In *Equilibrio, intercambio y reciprocidad: Principios de vida y sentidos de muerte en la Huasteca*, edited by Ana Bella Pérez Castro, 166–180. Veracruz: Consejo Veracruzano de Arte Popular, 2007.

———. "El vuelo de la golondrina, música y migración en la Huasteca." In *Música sin fronteras. Ensayos de música, migración e identidad*, compiled by Fernando Híjar, 251–288. México: Conaculta, 2006.

Castro-Gómez, Santiago. "Michel Foucault y la colonialidad del poder." *Tabula Rasa*, no. 6 (2007): 153–172.

Chevalier, François. *La formación de los latifundios en México: Haciendas y sociedad en los siglos XVI, XVII y XVIII*. 3. ed. (corr. y aum.). México: Fondo de Cultura Económica, 1999.

Derrida, Jacques. *Márgenes de la filosofía*. Madrid: Cátedra, 1994.

Duquesnoy, Michel. "La Huasteca hidalguense, migración y retos locales en una región de fuerte concentración indígena." *Revista LIDER* year 12, no. 15 (2010): 85–103.

"¿Es la familia el núcleo de la sociedad? Entrevista a Gladys Tzul." YouTube video, 15:19. Posted by "desde abajo," September 25, 2014. https://www.youtube.com/watch?v=zgr-LdsP8ZQ.

Escobar Ohmstede, Antonio. "Los pueblos indios de las Huastecas a través de cien años de historia." In *Los Pueblos indios y el parteaguas de la independencia de México*, compiled by Manuel Ferrer, 105–165. México: Instituto de Investigaciones Jurídicas, Universidad Nacional Autónoma de México, 1999.

———. "Del gobierno indígena al Ayuntamiento en las Huastecas hidalguense y veracruzana, 1730-1853." *Mexican Studies/Estudios Mexicanos* 12, no. 1 (1996): 1–26.

———. "Los condueñazgos indígenas en las Huastecas hidalguense y veracruzana: ¿Defensa del espacio comunal?" In *Indio, nación y comunidad en el México del siglo XIX*, edited by Antonio Escobar Ohmstede, 171–88. México: Centro de Estudios Mexicanos y Centroamericanos: Centro de Investigaciones y Estudios Superiores en Antropología Social, 1993.

Escobar Ohmstede, Antonio, and Israel Sandre Osorio. "Repartos agrarios 'en seco'. Agua y tierra en el cardenismo." *Boletín del Archivo Histórico del Agua*, no. 36 (2007): 70–87.

Escobar, Arturo. "Mundos y conocimientos de otro modo. El programa de investigación de modernidad/colonialidad latinoamericano." *Tabula Rasa*, no. 1 (2003): 51–86.

Florescano, Enrique. "Formación y estructura económica de la hacienda en Nueva España." In *Historia de América Latina. Tomo III. América Latina colonial: economía*, edited by Leslie Bethell, 92–121. Barcelona: Crítica, 1990.

Gibson, Charles. "Las sociedades indias bajo el dominio español." In *Historia de América Latina. Tomo IV América Latina colonial: población, sociedad y cultura*, edited by Leslie Bethell, 157–88. Barcelona: Crítica, 1990.

González de la Rocha, Mercedes, ed. *Procesos domésticos y vulnerabilidad: Perspectivas antropológicas de los hogares con Oportunidades*. México: Centro de Investigaciones y Estudios Superiores en Antropología Social, 2006.

Graeber, David. "Turning Modes of Production Inside Out: Or, Why Capitalism is a Transformation of Slavery." *Critique of Anthropology*, no. 26 (2006): 61–85.

Gutiérrez Rivas, Ana María. "El proceso agrario en las huastecas hidalguense y veracruzana, 1825–1874." *Sotavento*, no. 11 (2001): 9–38.

Hardt, Michael. "Affective Labor." *Boundary 2* 26, no. 2 (1999): 89–100.

Harvey, David. *Breve historia del neoliberalismo*. Madrid: Akal, 2015.

Hernández Castillo, Rosalva Aída. "Entre el etnocentrismo feminista y el esencialismo étnico. Las mujeres indígenas y sus demandas de género." In *Tejiendo de otro modo: Feminismo, epistemología y apuestas descoloniales en Abya Yala*, edited by Yuderkys Espinosa Miñoso, Diana Marcela Gómez Correal, and Karina Ochoa Muñoz, 279–293. Popayán, Colombia: Editorial Universidad del Cauca, 2014.

Iciek, Alexandra A. "'Servir, organizar y vigilar, sufrir e ir por delante'. El concepto de autoridad en una comunidad nahua en el contexto de la globalización y la interlegalidad." In *La terca realidad: La Huasteca como espejo cultural*, edited by

Jesús Ruvalcaba Mercado, 125–180. México: Centro de Investigaciones y Estudios Superiores en Antropoligía Social, 2013.

Lotman, Iuri. *La semiosfera I. Semiótica de la cultura y el texto*. Madrid: Cátedra, 1996.

Mendoza, Breny. "La epistemología del sur, la colonialidad del género y el feminismo latinoamericano." In *Tejiendo de otro modo: Feminismo, epistemología y apuestas decoloniales en Abya Yala*, edited by Yuderkys Espinosa Miñoso, Diana Marcela Gómez Correal, and Karina Ochoa Muñoz, 91–103. Popayán, Colombia: Editorial Universidad del Cauca, 2014.

Mora, Libertad. "Migración transnacional, TIC's y nuevos procesos identitarios en el sur de la Huasteca." In *Diásporas, migraciones, tecnologías de la comunicación e identidades transnacionales*, edited by Denise Cogo, Mohammed ElHajji, and Amparo Huertas, 399–432. Bellaterra: Institut de la Comunicació, Universitat Autònoma de Barcelona, 2012.

Ochoa Muñoz, Karina. "El debate sobre las y los amerindios: El discurso de la bestialización, la feminización y la racialización." In *Tejiendo de otro modo: Feminismo, epistemología y apuestas descoloniales en Abya Yala*, edited by Yuderkys Espinosa Miñoso, Diana Marcela Gómez Correal, and Karina Ochoa Muñoz, 105–118. Popayán, Colombia: Editorial Universidad del Cauca, 2014.

Ortner, Sherry. "Resistance and the Problem of Ethnographic Refusal." *Comparative Studies in Society and History* 37, no. 1 (1995): 173–193.

Paiva, Rosalía. "Feminismo paritario indígena andino." In *Tejiendo de otro modo: Feminismo, epistemología y apuestas descoloniales en Abya Yala*, edited by Yuderkys Espinosa Miñoso, Diana Marcela Gómez Correal, and Karina Ochoa Muñoz, 295–308. Popayán, Colombia: Editorial Universidad del Cauca, 2014.

Paredes, Julieta. *Hilando fino desde el feminismo comunitario*. La Paz, Bolivia: CEDEC, 2010.

Pérez Castro, Ana Bella. "Activando el mundo simbólico para enfrentar la emigración." *Chungara. Revista de Antropología Chilena* 39, no. 1 (2007): 51–68.

Pérez Zevallos, Juan Manuel. "Las visitas como fuente de estudio del tributo y población de la Huasteca (siglo XVI)." *Itinerarios*, no. 12 (2010): 41–64.

———. *La visita de Gómez Nieto a Huasteca, 1532–1533*. Colección Huasteca. México, D.F. and San Luis Potosí: Centro de Investigaciones y Estudios Superiores en Antropología Social, Centro de Estudios Mexicanos y Centroamericanos, Archivo General de la Nación, El Colegio de San Luis, 2001.

Quijano, Aníbal. "Colonialidad del poder, eurocentrismo y América Latina." In *La colonialidad del saber: Eurocentrismo y ciencias sociales. Perspectivas latinoamericanas*, edited by Edgardo Lander, 201–245. Caracas: CLACCSO, 2000a.

———. "Colonialidad del Poder y Clasificación Social." *Journal of World-Systems Research* VI, no. 2 (2000b): 342–386.

Restrepo, Eduardo. "Antropología y colonialidad." En *El giro decolonial. Reflexiones para una diversidad epistémica más allá del capitalismo global*, edited by Santiago Castro-Gómez and Ramón Grosfoguel, 287–305. Bogotá: Siglo del Hombre Editores; Universidad Central; Instituto de Estudios Sociales Contemporáneos, Pontificia Universidad Javeriana, Instituto de Estudios Sociales y Culturales; Pensar, 2007.

Rivera Cusicanqui, Silvia. "La noción de 'derecho' o las paradojas de la modernidad postcolonial: indígenas y mujeres en Bolivia." In *Tejiendo de otro modo: Feminismo, epistemología y apuestas descoloniales en Abya Yala*, edited by Yuderkys Espinosa Miñoso, Diana Marcela Gómez Correal, and Karina Ochoa Muñoz, 121–134. Popayán, Colombia: Editorial Universidad del Cauca, 2014.

Robichaux, David. "Principios patrilineales en un sistema bilateral de parentesco: residencia, herencia y el sistema familiar mesoamericano." In *Familia y parentesco en México y Mesoamérica*, edited by David Robichaux, 167–272. México: Universidad Iberoamericana, 2005.

Rubio, Blanca. *Explotados y excluidos. Los campesinos latinoamericanos en la fase agroexportadora neoliberal*. México: Plaza y Valdés, 2001.

Rufer, Mario. "La tradición como reliquia: Nación e identidad desde los estudios culturales." In *Nación y estudios culturales: Debates desde la poscolonialidad*, compilado por María Carmen de la Peza y Mario Rufer, 61–89. México: Itaca, 2016.

———. "Introducción: Nación, diferencia, poscolonialismo". In *Nación y diferencia. Procesos de identificación y formaciones de otredad en contextos poscoloniales*, compiled by Mario Rufer, 9–43. México: Editorial Itaca, 2012.

———. "La temporalidad como política: Nación, formas de pasado y perspectivas poscoloniales." *Memoria y Sociedad* 14, no. 28 (2010): 11–31.

Sandstrom, Alan. "Grupos toponímicos y organización de casas entre los nahuas del norte de Veracruz." In *Familia y parentesco en México y Mesoamérica: Unas miradas antropológicas*, edited by David Robichaux, 139–166. México: Universidad Iberoamericana, 2005.

Segato, Rita. "Género y colonialidad: En busca de claves de lectura y de un vocabulario estratégico descolonial." In *Feminismos y poscolonialidad: Descolonizando el feminismo desde y en América Latina*, edited by Karina Bidaseca and Vanesa Vázquez Laba, 17–48. Buenos Aires: Ediciones Godot, 2011.

———. "El color de la cárcel en América Latina. Apuntes sobre la colonialidad de la justicia en un continente en deconstrucción." *Nueva Sociedad*, no. 208 (2007): 142–161.

———. "Identidades políticas y alteridades históricas. Una crítica a las certezas del pluralismo global." *Nueva Sociedad*, no. 178 (2002): 104–125.

Shryer, Frans J. "Peasants and the Law: A History of Land Tenure and Conflict in the Huasteca." *Journal of Latin American Studies* 18, no. 2 (1986): 283–311.

Sierra, María Teresa. "La renovación de la justicia indígena en tiempos de derechos: Etnicidad, género y diversidad." In *Estado, violencia y ciudadanía en América Latina*, compiled by Ruth Stanley, 221–249. Madrid: Entinema, 2009.

Spivak, Gayatri Chakravorty. "¿Puede hablar el subalterno?" *Revista colombiana de antropología*, no. 39 (2003): 297–364.

Suárez Soto, María de la Luz. *Eusebio García Ávalos (Chebo) y el Campamento Tierra y Libertad en la Huasteca potosina (1973–1976)*. México: Universidad Autónoma de Chapingo, 2004.

Valle Esquivel, Julieta. *Nahuas de la Huasteca*. México: Comisión Nacional para el Desarrollo de los Pueblos Indígenas: Programa de las Naciones Unidas para el Desarrollo, 2004.

Chapter 3

Chavela's Frida

Decolonial Performativity of the Queer Llorona[*]

Ana R. Alonso-Minutti

The title of this chapter includes the names of two iconic figures in the *mexicana* imaginary, Chavela Vargas (1919–2012) and Frida Kahlo (1907–1954), in association with a female Mexican prototype: La Llorona. While the construction of *mexicanidad* by both figures is something that has been widely covered in academic and non-academic sources, rarely do we find these discussions addressing Chavela and Frida in connection with each other. Frida, arguably the best-known Mexican female artist, has received overwhelming attention, especially during the last three decades. On the other hand, while regarded as one of the leading proponents of Mexican music of the twentieth century, Chavela has received marginal popularity, primarily within music scholarship.

This chapter is not about Frida or Chavela in any biographical sense, but about the performative construction of Frida as La Llorona in the eyes and voice of Chavela Vargas. This construction illuminates intricate nuances of a queer mexicanidad, one in which gender binarism crumbles and femininity prototypes crack.[1] Moreover, the performative construction of Frida in the voice of Chavela reflects a decolonial mexicanidad, one in which spirituality and desire are fused in a non-linear experience of time. By examining Chavela's Frida we are able to discern the multiple entangled views of Mexican womanhood that challenge normative heterosexual constructions of *mexicanidad y nación*, which are notions grounded in the coloniality of power.[2]

As Norma Alarcón, Caren Kaplan, and Minoo Moallem have shown women have been 'ex-centric subjects' in the construction of the modern nation-state and of national subjectivity, meaning, outside of male-centered pillars of citizenship.[3] The defining lines of national subjecthood have involved a heterosexualization of women and an adherence to gender binarism. Moreover, as María Lugones has noted, heterosexuality has not only been normative within the colonial modern gender system, but has been violently exercised in order to construct a worldwide system of power.[4] While maintaining male supremacy, this system also perpetuates a racial/ethnic hierarchy that privileges whites. In her positionality as a brown, lesbian performer, Chavela subverts the colonial paradigm of gendered subjecthood by drawing on pre-Columbian epistemologies and by projecting nonbinary gender and sexual practices. Her openly gay performances in general, and the performativity of her romantic relationship with Frida in particular, expose the practical and ideological racism and sexism of the colonial precepts and suggest a more nuanced connection between the cultural products of womanhood and nation-ness. Although regarded as archetypes of mexicanidad, Chavela and Frida, as cultural products, are rich sites to explore the levels in which nonbinary individuals forcefully resist the imposed defining lines of national identification for women.

The ideological and practical sexism at the core of notions of mexicanidad could explain, on one hand, the popularity of Frida Kahlo—especially during the rise of 'Fridamania' in the 1980s and 1990s—and on the other, the marginal position of Chavela Vargas in popular culture. Although Frida gathered excessive attention at the global level on such diverse platforms as fashion, education, activism, and even cuisine, her heterosexual relationship with Diego Rivera dominated discourses around her sexuality, while downplaying her nonbinary positionality and active bisexuality. On the other hand, Chavela's openness in regard to her lesbianism in performance placed her at the margins of popular and commercial arenas.

My research on this topic began in 2017, about six months after the 2016 U.S. presidential election. I was invited to give a lecture at the University of New Mexico Art Museum as part of programming for an exhibition of Frida's personal photographs, and as part of the Southwest Gay and Lesbian Film Festival, which was to offer a screening of Catherine Gund and Daresha Kyi's newly released documentary film, *Chavela*.[5] My presentation took place in the central museum gallery, surrounded by Frida's photographs, and in front of about a hundred enthusiastic spectators. The audience in general, to my surprise, was not only utterly receptive, but overtly emotional—especially during the instances where I played excerpts of Chavela's songs. It was hard not to read the audience's overly emotional reaction as reflective of a desperate need to come together in solidarity amidst a hostile environment to people of color, to women, to migrants (Mexicans in particular), and to the LGBTQIA community, an environment heightened after the forty-fifth president took office. That night at the UNM Art Museum, from my vantage point, I observed how the audience was deeply moved—many to the point of tears—while listening to one of Chavela's last renditions of the song, "La

Llorona." (And, as will be explored here, Chavela's discursive articulations of Frida as her greatest love were best evidenced by her singing that particular song.) Given Albuquerque's politically liberal community and its proximity to the border, Chavela's raspy and cry-felt singing was, at the local level, loudly resonant with the audience's sentiments and political dissent.

Chavela's voice and artistic persona have also symbolized political dissent at global levels. The British newspaper *The Guardian*, reporting on Gund and Kyi's documentary screened at the 2017 Berlin film festival, introduced Chavela as "Donald Trump's ultimate nightmare—a Mexican lesbian diva who can wring your very soul."[6] To repressive political systems Chavela represents a nightmare and a threat; a type of individual that is to be kept out of national borders. Cuban leader Fidel Castro is credited as having said, "Don't let this *vieja* come to Cuba, because she stirs up a hornet's nest."[7] At a time of loud political rhetoric about wall building—now declared a "national emergency"—accompanied by racial and racist ideologies at the core of the notion of illegality—Chavela's voice materializes a decolonial opposition.[8] Her story embodies the condition of many Latinxs, and migrants in general, and carries with it histories of dispossession, displacement, and abuse, while granting an example of endurance, resilience, and hope.

BECOMING CHAVELA, *LA CANTANTE MEXICANA*

María Isabel Anita Carmen de Jesús Vargas Lizano, known best as Chavela Vargas, was born in Costa Rica in 1919 to a very modest and conservative family. Her childhood was not a happy one; she had been in fragile health since she was a baby and had poliomyelitis at three years old. She suffered rejection from both parents; one time her mother begged the Virgin to take Chavela's life, and her father used to call her *rara*.[9] Chavela's experienced *rareza* was accompanied by a fierce rejection and marginalization by all around her. She was growing up in a conservative society that was cruel to women, and even more so, to homosexuals who refused to hide. Feeling rara became part of Chavela's core and only through her creative outlook did that rareza become her utmost strength. Given this unsustainable hostile atmosphere, Chavela decided to leave her homeland at age fourteen in search of freedom, and travelled with her cousin to Mexico.

"¿Para qué vine a México?"—Chavela rhetorically asks as she narrates her migration in her autobiography. "Yo quería cantar, como los mexicanos"—she responds.[10] Her young aspiration was to sing. However, she did not want to become *any* kind of singer; she wanted to sing as Mexicans do. Sharing an idyllic memory, Chavela recounts that, when walking the fields of Costa Rica as a young girl, all she wanted was to sing like a Mexican.[11] This declaration reveals that the singer grew up with a desire of becoming the Other; to embrace an identity that would allow her to be *who she really was*. Chavela achieved her dream not only of "singing like Mexicans do," but *becoming* Mexican. She has been regarded as an *ícono de la cultura mexicana* in Mexico and abroad.[12] As she used to say, "I happened to be born in Costa Rica, but my life, my true life, I was to find in Mexico."[13] To this day, it is puzzling for many to discover that she was not born in Mexico. While Chavela's biographic details might not be widely known, one thing is certain: she is regarded as *una cantante mexicana*. One of Chavela's most famous sayings, broadly reproduced, with small variations, reads: "¡Los mexicanos nacemos donde se nos da la rechingada gana!"[14] Chavela's embodied mexicanidad challenges discourses of nationalism tied to national borders. Moreover, as we will shortly see, her performative construction of her mexicana identity is tied to a decolonial queerness connected to nature, to indigeneity, and to lesbian desire.

Throughout the 1940s Chavela held various types of jobs, and by the late 1950s she had gained a significant presence in Mexico City's thriving bohemian club scene. Her first recording, however, was not released until the early 1960s, when she reached a peak of popularity with her first hit, "Macorina," that was to become "the Lesbian hymn." The text comes from a poem by Spanish poet Alfonso Camín (1890–1982), and the music is Chavela's. Narrated in first person, Camín wrote these lines to María Calvo Nodarse (1892–1977), a beautiful Cuban woman—of scandalous reputation—who would be the first woman to be granted permission to drive an automobile in Havana. The insistent refrain of the song says: "Ponme la mano aquí, Macorina / ponme la mano aquí" (Put your hand right here, Macorina / put your hand right here). When singing these lines in performance, Chavela would place her hand between her legs while engaging the gaze of a woman in the audience.[15] Chavela would alter her singing style, from declamatory to sweet. She wouldn't *sing* the words *mano aquí*, but instead, with her mouth closed, she would emulate the sexual pleasure of feeling the lover's hand touching the desired part of the body. "Macorina" became, to Chavela, her guide and banner.[16]

Chavela used her voice in a powerful manner to play with codes of sensuality and her performances of this song have always been openly suggestive of lesbian desire.[17] While the *canción ranchera,* as a musical genre, had been predominantly reflective of the male experience—a man expressing dramatic feelings of love, pain, and longing for a woman (see Alex E. Chávez in this volume)—Chavela queered these conventions with her 'masculine,' raspy voice and her unchanged gender pronouns, assuming herself as male.[18] The genre of *música ranchera*, as Olga Nájera-Ramírez, Laura G. Guitiérrez, and others have demonstrated, is a particularly useful site for exploring issues of mexicanidad, especially when performed by women.[19] By participating as ranchera performers, Nájera-Ramírez states, "women, by virtue of singing in their 'female' voice, recontextualize a text even when they do not change a single word. . . . Hence each performance presents women with the opportunity to take control of the text to convey their own, subversive message."[20] When performed on stage, canciones rancheras are typically accompanied by large instrumental forces—mariachi ensembles, most often. Chavela, in contrast, usually accompanied herself with two guitars. This thin instrumental texture allowed her voice to be the main carrier of dramatic content.[21]

Not only were her vocal gestures transgressive, her appearance was too. Instead of wearing the traditional outfit of ranchera singers, such as female versions of the *charro* suit, long or short skirts, or Adelita dresses, Chavela's choices did not carry any feminine associations. She, on the contrary, preferred the 'masculine' combination of trousers and *jorongo*, wearing no makeup, with her hair up, oftentimes appearing on stage without shoes, and smoking and drinking tequila.[22] These choices corresponded, in part, to a larger attitude of cultural nationalism shared by singers and performers throughout Latin America associated with the *Nueva Canción*. A validation of Indigenous and folk signifiers was also accompanied by protesting imperialism and promoting national autonomy.[23] Although Chavela's songs were not overtly political, Lorena Alvarado has pointed out that Chavela's incorporation of *campesino* cultural indicators coincides with the revolutionary fervor of the time.[24] Moreover, Alvarado observes that the masculine campesino look that Chavela projected and her avoidance of singing with a full mariachi ensemble set her apart from typical performers of the genre, thus preventing her from mainstream commercial popularity. In this sense, Chavela's performances, "decentered the hyper-nationalist imaginary, as well as the heteronormative fantasy it engendered."[25] Moreover, the fusion of Chavela's butch image and her public view as a "hallmark of Mexico," according to Yvonne Yarbro-Bejarano, provided a space for lesbian subjectivity within the notion of what could be regarded as "authentically Mexican."[26]

With her performances of songs like "Macorina" and "Cruz de olvido," Chavela was becoming an international icon. She gained significant success throughout the 1960s and early 1970s, and toured in Mexico and abroad. However, in the late 1970s Chavela withdrew from the public, given her struggle with alcoholism, which lasted for fifteen years. Many had thought she was dead. To the surprise of many, in the early 1990s she returned to the stage and after her lengthy hiatus appeared in public for the first time at Mexico City's queer-friendly, Teatro-Bar El Hábito, after receiving an invitation by the venue's cofounder Jesusa Rodríguez.[27] Chavela's career progressively recovered international prominence throughout Latin America, the U.S., and—significantly—in Spain, largely due to her friendship with Spanish film director, Pedro Almodóvar, who cast her in various films.[28] This return, which was labeled *El chavelazo,* was accompanied by an unprecedented popularity.[29] Chavela's voice, resurrected from the dead, was fiercer than ever. The last two decades of her life were the most prolific. At age eighty-three she debuted at Carnegie Hall and a few months before her death, at ninety-three, she gave a concert in Mexico City's Palace of Fine Arts—the most prominent and prestigious performance venue of the country.

FRIDA AS LLORONA: THE OTHERWORLDLY, SUFFERING, INSATIABLE, AND MOTHERLY LOVER

Before Chavela reached popularity with "Macorina", or had obtained the international recognition of her later years, she met Frida Kahlo and Diego Rivera, sometime in the early 1940s.[30] Chavela must have been in her early twenties and Frida in her late thirties. Chavela was invited to a party at the famous Casa Azul, Frida's house located in Mexico City's Coyoacán neighborhood, now a museum dedicated to her work. The night of the party, according to Chavela, Frida invited her to stay overnight, for Chavela lived far away. Eventually, Chavela would stay many nights at La Casa Azul, spending countless hours in Frida's company, singing for her while Frida painted.[31] While their romance has been a matter of much speculation, the love and devotion Chavela had for that "beautiful woman"—fifteen years her senior—whom she called a friend, a mentor, and her "greatest love," was undeniable.[32]

Throughout her life Chavela retold the story of her first encounter with Frida multiple times and wrote about it with detail in her autobiography. However, Chavela's most compelling narration of her encounter with Frida, where she makes the strongest declaration of their romance, is found in a recorded interview with film composer Elliot Goldenthal, which is included in the special features of Julie Taymor's film *Frida* (2002). When this interview took place Chavela must have been around eighty-three years old, and it was in that setting where Chavela offered one of the most moving accounts of her relationship with Frida, one that I'm taking the liberty to transcribe here:

> It was love at first sight. It was dazzling but not of this world. It was a light from another dimension, from another planet. To look at her face and her eyes I thought that she wasn't a being from this world. Without yet having the maturity of a woman in myself. I was too young. And nevertheless, I guessed by the way of talking, by the way of looking. Her joined eyebrows were a swallow

in full flight. If she was in the bed, she flew when she opened her eyes by the eyebrows, two wings of a swallow. And I sensed that I could love this being with the purest love in the world. With the most devoted love in the world. With the most painful love in the world, the happiest in the world, the saddest in the world. The freest love in the world. The most inhibited in the world. And one day my words possibly hurt her very much one time when I told her that I was going. And that I would go from her side forever some day. And she told me, "I know. I know that you are going. And I am not going to cry. Nor will you. Some evening when you want to, in whatever country in the world, and you have time, remember me. Just remember me and think that one time in life there was a being who loved you, who loves you. Because I gave birth to you and I give you freedom. I can't tie you up to my crutches and to my bed. Go." And one day I opened the door and I didn't return.[33]

In this interview, Chavela strongly outlines a constructed version of her lover, Frida. Firstly, Chavela's Frida was an otherworldly lover, "a light from another dimension, from another planet." Secondly, Chavela's Frida was a suffering lover. Chavela reveals to Goldenthal that she and Frida shared a love tainted with passion and suffering. And thirdly, Chavela's Frida was a motherly lover, as she recounts how Frida's love granted her both life and freedom.[34]

These aspects of Chavela's Frida are most present in Chavela's singing voice. Chavela recounted singing endless songs for Frida, and one of Frida's favorites, "La Llorona," became forever linked to the painter's mass media image through Taymor's film. In a climactic scene of the movie, Chavela appears singing "La Llorona" to Frida, played by actress Salma Hayek. At this point in the plot Frida is at a bar drowning her sorrows in liquor for she had just found out that her husband Diego was having an affair with Cristina, Frida's sister. Introduced as "La Pelona" (Death), Chavela begins to sing, and her singing draws Frida to her table. Her voice and gaze are intensely directed to Frida, who returns the intensity back. While Sofía Ruiz-Alfaro points out that the encounter between these two characters is purposefully "void of any homoerotic charge," I sustain that the diagetic singing of "La Llorona" encapsulates the most intimate moment Frida had with any other character throughout the movie. The camera work, especially through close-ups, and the use of dim light emphasize the closeness between the two.[35] Beyond the realms of Taymor's film, I sustain that Chavela's recurrent performances of "La Llorona" throughout her career were a public testimony to her adoration of the visual artist and performative utterances in which Chavela articulated her own versions of Frida. In what follows, I explore the performative construction of Frida *as* La Llorona. A comparison of multiple renditions of the song renders visible the parallels Chavela also insists in redrawing between herself and her lover. Defiance, suffering, spirituality, and homoerotic desire inhabit the mythology of Chavela's Frida and permeate Chavela's emancipatory songs of love and pain.[36]

In her 1993 album, *La Llorona*, Chavela introduces a rendition of the song that she will follow more or less faithfully in later performances (up to 2007), in terms of instrumentation, tempo, key signature, and lyrics. The traditional song "La Llorona" is a nineteenth-century *son istmeño*, originally from the region of the Isthmus of Tehuantepec, Mexico. Traditionally, sones istmeños are performed in social gatherings and religious festivities by a small group of musicians playing guitar, *requinto*, and *bajo quinto*,[37] and singing in both Spanish and Zapotec, the local Indigenous language. Since the nineteenth century this *son* has been orally transmitted throughout the Americas and has had a significant presence in Mexico and across the U.S. Southwest. There is not an 'authoritative' version of this song; there are as many different versions of "La Llorona" as there are performances. Singers are free to choose among hundreds of documented verses, or to create or improvise their own lines on the spot, which is significant for my analysis, since the verses Chavela sings articulate a personal version of Frida.

This son istmeño is based on the legend of La Llorona, which dates back to pre-Columbian times and has persisted until the present. Some of the earliest accounts of the legend link La Llorona with the Aztec goddesses Cihuacóatl or *mujer serpiente* (woman serpent), a figure that would appear at night crying out for dead children.[38] While the cultural history behind the legend is fascinating, here I will limit myself to highlighting a few aspects of the narrative that are directly connected to Chavela's construction of Frida as La Llorona. La Llorona is one of the three dominant female figures of the Mexicana/Chicana imaginary—the other two being La Malinche and La Virgen de Guadalupe. The legend of La Llorona exists in many variants—some of them contradictory—but all share the existence of a female figure, La Llorona, or the weeping woman. Why does she weep? Firstly, because she has been betrayed by her (assumed male) lover. Some variants state that this betrayal involved a difference in social class: the male lover belonging to a higher social class than La Llorona. Other variants point out an ethnic difference: he is a Spaniard, she is an Indigenous Mexican. Most versions of the legend affirm that, angered after her lover's infidelity, La Llorona drowned her children in the river and was condemned to spend eternity weeping in search of them. In the version that I was told as a kid, while living in Puebla, La Llorona can be heard at night, meandering on the streets while wailing, "¡Ay, mis hijos, mis hijos!"

As many folklorists have pointed out, this legend remains largely in the hands of women and has mostly been transmitted by women.[39] Chicana feminists have claimed that the figure of La Llorona symbolizes a voice of resistance against male domination and heteronormative expectations of the role of women inside the family unit. In patriarchal societies women are expected to be submissive wives, to quietly endure betrayals by their male partners, and to bear *his* children. Motherhood is viewed as the fulfillment of the major task a woman is expected to fulfill. La Llorona, by contrast, reacts against these expectations and carries out an act of utmost defiance. Killing *his* children becomes an act of resistance and liberation. She becomes a solitary defiant figure whose cries and yells are to resound for eternity.

Given that "La Llorona" is a *son* that originated on the Isthmus of Tehuantepec, it should be noted that, throughout that region, Zapotec women have occupied authoritarian roles since pre-Columbian times. In Juchitán, for example, women control the market and manage the household. Scholars have recorded that women in the Isthmus have a significant degree of independence and an unusual sexual/erotic openness. Alfredo Mirandé notes a balanced equality between the sexes in the region—a prominent contrast to the gender inequality of the country at large (see also Lizette Alegre González in this volume).[40] In his study, Mirandé explores the area's gender hybridity and, in particular, Juchitán's reputation as a site of significant acceptance of gay and transgender people—a "gay paradise." There is an unusual nonbinary assignation of genders and an acceptance of a third gender, which may have had pre-Columbian origins. This acceptance, in Mirandé's words, "is consistent with the history of resistance in the Isthmus in general, and Juchitán in particular, to both colonial rule and national control."[41] The region's embrace of gender hybridity provides an appropriate lens in which to read Chavela's renditions of the song "La Llorona." Frida as La Llorona is based on a strong femme, unafraid of voicing erotic desires and carrying out unexpected degrees of independence. "[Frida] taught me not to be afraid of anything," Chavela once stated, "she taught me how to break molds." Frida's assertive personality, and her resistance to normative expectations of gender and sexuality, represented to Chavela "un modelo como mujer."[42]

There are many parallelisms that can be drawn between Chavela and Frida. As little girls, both suffered from serious health problems, including poliomyelitis. Also, both had distant, rejecting mothers. As women living in conservative societies, both had to break through in order to find their own artistic voices in male-dominated scenes. In addition to sharing similar circumstances, there are important parallelisms that Chavela drew with Frida throughout her life, one being a *naturaleza rara*—a weird nature. They are not normal beings; they belong to an abnormal world (*un mundo raro*). Chavela expressed: "We used to share the same thoughts at the same time. We thought about the same things and we wanted the world to be as we dreamed."[43] To Chavela, the *mundo raro* was a space where she could freely articulate her sexuality, and it was through a song—specifically a canción ranchera—that Chavela most beautifully articulated her need (and desire) to inhabit it:

> Y si quieren saber de mi pasado,
> es preciso decir otra mentira:
> les diré que llegué de un mundo raro,
> que no sé del dolor,
> que triunfé en el amor,
> y que nunca he llorado.
>
> And if they want to know about my past,
> I will have to say another lie:
> I'll tell them I arrived from a strange world,
> that I don't know about pain,
> that I triumphed in love,
> and that I have never cried.

This song, "Un mundo raro," written by talented and prolific songwriter José Alfredo Jiménez (1926–1973), became so ingrained in Chavela's construction of her self-identity that she titled her 2002 autobiography, *Y si quieres saber de mi pasado*. While much scholarship, especially among Chicana feminists, has elaborated on Chavela's *rareza* as a site where she constructs her lesbian self, little has been written about the connection between Chavela's rareza and her self-identification as a *chamana*—with the notable exception of Ruiz-Alfaro's work. *Chamanes* possess extraordinary perceptive abilities that allow them to act as intermediaries between the spiritual and the physical realms.[44] According to Ruiz-Alfaro, in Chavela's construction of her own identity as a rara, her strangeness includes a subjectivity that is intimately connected to nature, to the native, and to the shamanic. This subjectivity is also one that reaffirms a consciousness of a sexuality felt as *out of the norm*—the norm here understood as the heterosexuality and heteronormativity of the society in which Chavela lived.[45]

Chavela reaffirmed this rareza through singing. In Chavela's songs "there is a heterosexual subversion in the passionate declaration of love from a female singer to another woman."[46] This is evident in the first two stanzas of Chavela's renditions of "La Llorona." As my analysis of ten post-1993 renditions of "La Llorona" shows, with the exception of her last concert in Mexico, Chavela invariably opened the song with these verses:

> Todos me dicen el Negro, Llorona,
> Negro pero cariñoso.
> Yo soy como el chile verde, Llorona,
> picante, pero sabroso.

> Everybody calls me the Black man, Llorona,
> Black, but very affectionate.
> I am like the green chile, Llorona,
> spicy hot, but tasty.

In the first line, Chavela identifies herself as both male and dark-skinned. In the third line, she establishes her sexuality in connection with nature; as a *chile verde*, Chavela's queerness is as natural as it is poignant, and her sexual offering is as hot as it is flavorful.[47] As Yarbro-Bejarano has noted, Chavela's most transgressive interventions "are those in which the voice of the song is either unmarked or identified as male, and the object of desire is marked as female in the text." In the case of songs like "La Llorona," which assume a male narrator, Chavela, "dons a kind of musical drag, writing/speaking/singing lesbian desire through the butch appropriation of the active heterosexual male subject position."[48] In choosing these lines to open almost every rendition of "La Llorona," I argue that Chavela asserted her erotic desire for Frida. Frida was Chavela's *gran amor*, and according to Chavela, Frida reciprocated the sentiment fully.

A photograph and a letter, both of unconfirmed authenticity, have been extensively used as proof of the romantic relationship between Chavela and

Figure 3.1. Frida Kahlo and, allegedly, Chavela Vargas. Unknown photographer, ca. 1945, gelatin silver print, 3.25 × 5.8 inch. Courtesy of Throckmorton Gallery.

Frida. The photograph, wrongly credited to Nickolas Muray, depicts Frida with her head reclining on the chest of a young woman lying in the grass with a guitar next to her (see Figure 3.1).[49] This exquisite image is one of the few that captures Frida's smile, which she partially covers with her hand. Multiple sources identify the young woman as Chavela. In a 2015 exhibition devoted to photographs of Frida, New York City's Throckmorton Gallery credited this image to Muray and labeled it as "Frida Kahlo and Chavela Vargas."[50] While the identity of the woman accompanying Frida has not been confirmed, the photograph now forms part of the constructed imaginary of the romantic relationship between Frida and Chavela, as it also played a central role as supporting visual material used by directors Catherine Gund and Daresha Kyi's documentary *Chavela* when depicting Chavela's encounter with Frida.

Moreover, the existence of a letter that Frida allegedly wrote to Mexican poet, Carlos Pellicer (1897–1977) describing her passionate and erotic feelings after meeting Chavela, has brought plenty to speculate about. While Hilda Trujillo Soto, director of the Frida Kahlo Museum, publicly denied its legitimacy in 2012,[51] this letter continues to have a strong presence in various online sites, especially among the LGBTQIA fans of both artists. Chavela herself granted credit to the letter in public interviews and included a copy of it in the 2009 co-authored autobiographical book, *Las verdades de Chavela*.[52] The lack of hard evidence regarding Frida's feelings for Chavela prompted Chavela to react strongly, claiming that whoever is in search of proof, should open her chest to find her memories.[53] Moreover, Chavela attested to having burned a letter by Frida where Frida declared her love and stated, "I live for Diego and for you. No more."[54]

Chavela dedicates an entire chapter of her autobiography to Frida; the only chapter devoted to a single person.[55] The central message of the chapter is an enunciation of Chavela's love for Frida. Aware of the overwhelming international attention Frida was gathering in the late 1990s and early 2000s, Chavela went to great lengths to clarify that, although she admired the painter, she loved the woman.[56] When writing about Frida's biography Chavela mostly focuses on one aspect: Frida's suffering. Chavela includes a detailed and quite moving narration of the tragic bus accident the painter had when she was eighteen. In that event, Frida suffered terrible injuries that almost killed her, leaving her with life-long severe pain. After the accident, she was hospitalized numerous times and underwent more than thirty surgeries. To Chavela, pain and suffering were at the core of Frida's existence. She writes: "Pain. Frida, *la niña* Frida believed to have been born to love, to love and to enjoy life. But no: her life was torment, grief; permanent, continuous bitterness."[57] To accompany the narration of Frida's suffering, Chavela includes a brief description of Frida's painting, *La columna rota*. She begins her description as follows:

"In 1944 Frida painted herself again. She is naked, with loose hair, and it is not me who looks at the painting: *it is she* who is looking at me."[58] This line is revealing: to Chavela, Frida's gaze is on her; Frida's expression of pain, her suffering, and her tears, are *directed* to Chavela.

Among the multiple self-portraits Frida painted, Chavela chose one where Frida is portraying herself alone, in front of a cracked and barren landscape.[59] Frida is crying, and her chest is opened to reveal her inner brokenness. In selecting the painting, *The Broken Column* to describe Frida's painful life, I claim that Chavela is affirming Frida *as* La Llorona: a weeping woman, unapologetically sexual, meandering in solitude, enduring exorbitant pain, yet resolute and determined to remain standing.

Critics have noted that the white sheet wrapping Frida's lower body in *La columna rota* mirrors the Christian iconography of the Crucifixion, as do the piercing nails. In a similar vein, Chavela also associated Frida with Christian symbolism. To her, Frida was like the Virgin. In her own words: "I admired her, I saw her as the virgin of an altarpiece, a virgin that would detach herself from an altarpiece . . . with her eyebrows, almost to fly away."[60] Not surprisingly, Chavela would incorporate these verses in her renditions of "La Llorona":

> Salías del templo un día, Llorona,
> cuando al pasar yo te vi.
> Hermoso huipil llevabas, Llorona,
> que la Virgen te creí.

> You were coming out of the temple one day, Llorona,
> when in passing, I saw you.
> You were wearing such a beautiful huipil, Llorona,
> that I thought you were the Virgin.

Given that the figure La Llorona is originally from the Isthmus of Tehuantepec, it is not hard to imagine her wearing a Tehuana dress which consists of two basic pieces, a *huipil*—a traditional embroidered blouse—and a skirt. On one hand, Frida painted herself numerous times wearing a Tehuana dress and also appeared in public wearing Tehuana costumes. While her dressing choice represented a "fashionable nativist primitivism,"[61] it also manifested her desire to construct her mexicana identity by adopting the image of the strong Indigenous woman, "the undefeated counterpart to the despised 'Chingada,' who, conversely is the female embodiment of Mexico's hybrid post-conquest culture."[62] By fashioning herself as Tehuana, Frida adopted an anti-colonial position and a feminist resistance.[63] On the other hand, Chavela associated

Frida with the Tehuana dresses and notes in her autobiography how much Frida liked to wear them.[64]

To love Frida and to be loved by her demanded everything Chavela had or was. In a documented interview with María Cortina, Chavela states: "What I felt for [Frida] was never repeated . . . what I gave of myself to her was everything I had. My energy and all the energy of the world, the warmth, the sensibility, all the strength of the love I have ever felt in me, I gave it to her."[65] This type of demanding love is best expressed in the verses Chavela chose to end "La Llorona" in almost every performance after 1993:

> Si porque te quiero, quieres, Llorona,
> quieres que te quiera más.
> Si ya te he dado la vida, Llorona,
> ¿qué más quieres?
> ¡Quieres más!
>
> If because I love you, you want, Llorona,
> you want me to love you more.
> If I have given you my life, Llorona,
> what else do you want?
> You want more!

As previously noted, there is no fixed version of the song "La Llorona"; singers choose and rearrange existent stanzas, and compose or improvise verses as they see fit. Traditionally, singers keep the strophic musical form throughout. In these ending verses Chavela didn't. She disrupted the form by altering the versification, and more so, by yelling the last two lines, instead of singing them. In every utterance of these lines, Chavela's voice is angry, frustrated, desperate, and resolute. Moreover, these lines mark an abrupt end of the song. Chavela becomes a *gritona,* resembling La Llorona, who according to Anna Marie Sandoval, "is a *gritona,* demanding to be recognized as a strong, resistant figure who commands her own life."[66] La Llorona, Chavela's Frida, is an insatiable goddess, and Chavela's performances of "La Llorona" become shamanic rituals where she invokes her goddess to heal her soul.

A *chamán* is dedicated to healing; to heal the body, the soul, and the spirit. In her self-identification as a *chamana*, when she sings, Chavela heals first and foremost her own wounds, especially the ones she carried since childhood: the estrangement, rejection, and abandonment she felt from her family. As Chavela expressed: "it's true that I grew up with a huge lack of affection, that I wasn't loved, that [my] family was a knot of solitudes, and that as a small girl, I was forced to learn how to defend myself."[67] Hence, I assert here that every rendition of "La Llorona" allows Chavela to embrace her shamanic identity to heal herself by identifying in the figure of La Llorona-as-Frida the familial embrace that she lacked.

Chavela's performative construction of Frida as a motherly lover is also accompanied by a visualization of Frida as a central role model and mentor, roles that Chavela's biological mother did not fulfill. Chavela describes that Frida taught her how to overcome the suffering caused by family abandonment. From Frida, Chavela not only learned how to 'break molds,' but also how to fully embrace her own life. In her own words, "Because of her, if I am born again, I would be named the same."[68] As a motherly figure, Frida represented an ideal for womanhood in general, and Mexican womanhood in particular: "She was who she was. We were two women that . . . well, we were *muy mujeres*, as Mexicans say, and we had to love each other because we were women."[69] According to Ruiz-Alfaro, the assertion of being *muy mujeres* is intrinsically connected to a shared notion of female masculinity; a queerness that was, "breaking traditional gender and sexuality norms, embodying female masculinity and desire, and, ultimately, being who they wanted to be."[70] Understanding *being born* of Frida, Chavela takes refuge in La Llorona's guidance, *llévame al río*—the river here understood as the site of rebirth, of restoration. By asking La Llorona to cover her, *tápame con tu reboso, Llorona, porque me muero de frío,* Chavela recognizes her need for warmth, the type of warmth that only a mother's arms can provide while covering her child with a blanket:

> ¡Ay de mí! Llorona,
> Llorona, llévame al río.
> Tápame con tu reboso, Llorona,
> porque me muero de frío.
>
> Oh woe is me! Llorona,
> Llorona, take me to the river.
> Cover me with your shawl, Llorona,
> because I'm dying of cold.

These verses obtained yet deeper meaning when Chavela sang them at the end of her life, in the concert she gave at El Palacio de Bellas Artes on April 2012, a few months before she died.[71] Being fully aware of her short time left on earth, the ninety-three-year-old Chavela ended that legendary performance singing "La Llorona."[72] Her rendition of the song stands apart from all her other previous renditions in important ways. Here, Chavela felt free to improvise verses, reflecting on her own life and giving a personalized farewell to her audience. Moreover, she completely departed from the tune's melody, rhythm, and pacing, making her autobiographical declaration even more poignant:

Sonaban doce campanadas, Llorona,
en lo alto de la montaña.
Era Dios que bajaba, Llorona,
buscándote donde estabas.

Solo yo sabía, Llorona,
que estabas ahí, parada,
oyendo la voz de Cristo.
Tú y yo nada más, Llorona, casi sentada.

Y así termina mi historia,
que comenzó de la nada.
Dame la mano, Llorona,
que vengo muy lastimada.
Señora, dame la mano,
que vengo mucho, muy cansada.

¡Ay de mí! Llorona,
Llorona, llévame al río.
Tápame con tu reboso, Llorona,
porque me muero de frío.

Twelve strikes of the bells sounded, Llorona,
at the top of the mountain.
It was God coming down, Llorona,
searching for you.

I only knew, Llorona,
that you were there, standing,
hearing the voice of Christ.
Only you and I, Llorona,
[you] almost sitting down.

And this is how my story ends,
which started from nothing.
Give me your hand, Llorona,
for I come very hurt.
Madam, give me your hand,
for I come very, very tired.

Oh, woe is me! Llorona,
Llorona, take me to the river.
Cover me with your shawl, Llorona,
because I'm dying of cold.

This time Frida, as La Llorona, is the Virgin who "hears the voice of Christ." For the first—and only—time, in this rendition La Llorona has another name; Chavela calls her *Señora* and asks her to take her by the hand, to sustain her. Here it is pertinent to recall that Chavela felt she was *born* of Frida, that she felt Frida's blood running in her own blood,[73] and more so, that Frida taught her how to live.[74] At the end of her life, Chavela reached out to Frida for the sustenance necessary to transition from life to death. She asked her lover to take her to the river of rebirth, where they could be together again. Chavela was ready to meet her Frida, and she had made peace with it. Appropriately, Chavela chose to end the song *not* with the usual abrupt demanding yelling of previous renditions, but with a plea to Frida to take her to the river and to cover her with her shawl because she is, this time literally, dying.

TOWARDS A MARGINAL, QUEER AND DECOLONIAL MEXICANIDAD

Is there hard evidence that Chavela and Frida had a romantic relationship? Do we know for sure that they actually met?[75] These questions have instigated heated debates and controversy. If they had a romantic relationship, nobody knows with certainty how long it lasted, or why it ended. Although I have been asked those questions multiple times, I respond by saying that what fuels my interest in this research topic is not to achieve clarity on these issues. What I pursue is an exploration into Chavela's performative constructions of her love for Frida as entangled in her own performative constructions of a queer, decolonial mexicanidad.

In this chapter I have proposed that in every iteration of "La Llorona" Chavela invoked, first and foremost, *su gran amor*, Frida: an otherworldly lover, a suffering lover, an insatiable lover, and a motherly lover. However, what has been proposed here is not intended to portray a complete picture of Frida as La Llorona. A further image needs desperate attention, however brief, and that is of Chavela herself *as* La Llorona. She conceived herself as someone not from this world, but from *un mundo raro*. She also saw her life as marked by suffering, by *una cruz de olvido*. She was insatiable; she wanted it all and had it all. In her own words, "I have already drunk it all, I have traveled until exhaustion, I have enjoyed friendships, and took pleasure (and suffering) from my lovers."[76] Chavela's excesses and her exaggerated dramatism together with her embraced opposition reflect the performative codes of those whom Deborah R. Vargas calls *dissonant divas*. Through reclaiming the term *diva* from its derogatory reference to "women of color who are said to be too much, too dramatic, too demanding," Vargas illustrates the ways in which their embodiments of excess were connected to critical examinations and negotiations with systems of power.[77]

By performing a lesbian masculinity, Chavela destabilized the heteronormativity imposed on Mexican womanhood. In this sense, we can read Chavela's performativity as representative of what José Esteban Muñoz calls *disidentifications*, "survival strategies the minority subject practices in order to negotiate a phobic majoritarian public sphere that continuously elides or punishes the existence of subjects who do not conform to the phantasm of normative citizenship."[78] Artists who adopt disidentification as a performative strategy while dealing with dominant ideology, Muñoz says, neither assimilate nor oppose it, but try to "transform a cultural logic from within, always laboring to enact permanent structural change while at the same time valuing the importance of local or everyday struggles of resistance."[79]

Chavela's disidentificatory performances allowed for the creation of new social relations within minoritarian counterpublic spheres.[80] While affirming herself as a non-conformist unapologetic singer unafraid of transgressing long-held musical and social conventions, Chavela was providing a strong alternative figure of the female ranchera performer. Given her unusual voice timbre—powerful and defiant, forceful and uncompromising—her rural campesino image, and her open queerness, Chavela challenged the socially constructed binaries assigned to gender and sexuality in conservative mid-twentieth-century Mexico. Moreover, by offering critical counter-discourses while entertaining the audience, Chavela became an artist that, in the words of Laura G. Gutiérrez, "make evident societal hypocrisies in relationship to sexuality, particularly female and queer."[81]

Margins, as bell hooks reminds us, have been both sites of repression and resistance.[82] A site of creativity and power, the margin is an "inclusive space where we recover ourselves, where we move in solidarity to erase the category colonized/colonizer."[83] The voice of Chavela articulating her love for Frida as La Llorona opens such an inclusive space and embodies liberation. It is in the potential of the margins that we find a more nuanced, yet no less complex, notion of mexicanidad. The queer mexicanidad performed by Chavela from the margins confronts the normative discourses of Mexicanness and at the same time, articulates new dimensions of such Mexicanness.

Chavela's wails, yells, and cries have come to be taken not as personal expression, but as the voice of Latin America: "somebody said that she was the eternal lament of the South American plateau."[84] As Alvarado reminds us, Chavela "evokes indignation of the abandoned and neglected, one that resonates with historical and contemporary struggles of migrants, particularly Central American migrants."[85] This indignation is best felt in Chavela's piercing voice. Often described as *desgarradora* (heartwrenching), Chavela's voice has been perceived as a symbol of her 'authentic' feelings. What is imperative to note is that the power granted to Chavela's piercing voice is coming out of an aging body. In this sense, Chavela's aging voice and her aging body were physical manifestations of her queered decolonial mexicanidad, one that empowers the elderly and that disrupts the colonial adherence to a progressive, linear time.

The aging voice of Chavela, as opposed to her younger voice, is the one known throughout the world. It is in her old age when Chavela continued to articulate her sexuality, and it is in the aesthetics of her aging voice that critics found, "La voz de América Latina." Her broken, piercing, crying, demanding voice is best felt in every iteration of the son istmeño "La Llorona." As previously mentioned, Chavela's post-1993 renditions of the *son* were characterized by a thin instrumental texture (two guitars), a repeated instrumental *ritornello* (see example 3.1), and a predilection for certain opening and closing strophes. These particular musical choices that Chavela adopted to sing "La Llorona" have been emulated by a myriad of younger Mexican female singers, such as Eugenia León, Lila Downs, Ximena Sariñana, and many others. Most recently, the version performed by Angela Aguilar, Aida Cuevas, and Natalia Lafourcade during the sixty-first GRAMMY Awards Premiere Ceremony (2019) is clearly indebted to Chavela's rendition.

Example 3.1.

One can say that there was a *before and after* Chavela's "La Llorona," for her particular style of performing the song was followed by most popular singers after her, a phenomenon that could be compared to the construction of a "performance practice" of that son istmeño. For Chavela, and for many other artists and listeners across the world, La Llorona is a mirror in which one understands oneself to be. The story of La Llorona is a story of resistance, of female sexuality, of resilience, of rivers and borders crossed. It is one that speaks to all of us, for all of us face our own struggles. Our tears, weeping, and wails, are necessary for survival, and our solitary meandering takes us, again and again, back to the river of rebirth.

NOTES

* A preliminary version of this chapter was presented at the XIII Conference of the International Association for the Study of Popular Music Latin American Branch in San Juan, and at the 2018 national meeting of the Latin American Studies Association in Barcelona. I'm utterly thankful for the feedback I received during those occasions, particularly from Susan Campos Fonseca, Silvia Martínez, Pepa Anastasio, and Carlota Aguilar while in Puerto Rico, and from Laura G. Gutiérrez, Marysol Quevedo, Amanda Petersen, Kency Cornejo, Hettie Malcomson, and Henry Stobart in Spain. I'm equally grateful for the commentaries I received from Sergio de la Mora, Alex E. Chávez, and Jesús A. Ramos-Kittrell. Thanks to my graduate assistants Lisa White, Tim Mallette, and Aubrie Powell for their help during the elaboration of this chapter.

1. The concept of "queer *mexicanidad*" was used by Marie Sarita Gaytán and Sergio de la Mora to describe the ways in which *ranchera* singer Lucha Reyes, "visually and vocally queered the ranchera genre and challenged the heteronormative contours of traditional mexicanidad." See Marie Sarita Gaytán and Sergio de la Mora, "Queening/Queering *Mexicanidad*: Lucha Reyes and the *Canción Ranchera*," *Feminist Formations* 28, no. 3 (Winter 2017): 197. See also, Ramón H. Rivera-Servera, *Performing Queer Latinidad: Dance, Sexuality, Politics* (Ann Arbor: The University of Michigan Press, 2012). Nadine Hubbs's chapter in this volume provides yet a further elaboration of the concept of a "queer mexicanidad."

2. Coloniality of power, a phrase coined by Peruvian sociologist Aníbal Quijano, identifies social discrimination throughout Latin America as a legacy of colonialism. The concept has been expanded upon by Walter Mignolo, Ramón Grosfoguel, Nelson Maldonado Torres, and María Lugones, among others. See Aníbal Quijano, "Coloniality of Power, Eurocentrism, and Latin America," *Nepantla: Views from South* 1, no. 3 (2000): 533–80; María Lugones, "Heterosexualism and the Colonial/Modern Gender System," *Hypatia* 22, no. 1 (Winter 2007): 186–209; Walter Mignolo and Catherine E. Walsh, *On Decoloniality: Concepts, Analytics, Praxis* (Durham and London: Duke University Press, 2018).

3. Norma Alarcón, Caren Kaplan, and Minoo Moallem, "Introduction: Between Woman and Nation," in *Between Woman and Nation: Nationalism, Transnational Feminisms, and the State,* edited by Caren Kaplan, Norma Alarcón, and Minoo Moallem (Durham and London: Duke University Press, 1999), 1. For more on notions of citizenship in Mexico, see Lizette Alegre González, and Jesús A. Ramos Kittrell in this volume.

4. María Lugones, "Heterosexualism and the Colonial/Modern Gender System," *Hypatia* 22, no. 1 (Winter 2007): 186–209.

5. I want to thank my colleague and friend, art historian Ray Hernández-Durán, for inviting me to participate in the UNM Art Museum's exhibit and the 2017 iteration of the Southwest Gay and Lesbian Film Festival, for suggesting this topic, and for his generous and timely feedback.

6. Jonathan Romney, "Berlin Film Festival 2017 Roundup: An SOS for a World Without Walls," *The Guardian*, February 19, 2017, https://www.theguardian.com/film/2017/feb/19/berlin-film-festival-2017-roundup-the-party-viceroys-house-a-fantastic-woman. Catherine Gund and Daresha Kyi's documentary *Chavela* won second place in the festival.

7. Fidel Castro's credited phrase says, "No dejen entrar a esta vieja a Cuba, porque me alborota el gallinero." See Celia Dosio, *Las transgresoras: Anaïs Nin, Simone de Beavoir, Alfonsina Storni, Chavela Vargas* (México, D.F.: Lectorum, 2007), 182.

8. Alex E. Chávez's contribution to this volume provides illuminating remarks about political and symbolic economies of national borders.

9. The word *rara* is translated to English as strange, odd, weird. Chavela's father used to tell her, "Eres mi hija, pero eres rara" (you are my daughter but you are weird). Sandra Barneda, *Hablarán de nosotras: diecisiete mujeres poderosas que pecaron para ser libres* (Madrid: Aguilar, 2016), 277.

10. Chavela Vargas, *Y si quieres saber de mi pasado* (Madrid: Aguilar, 2002), 103.

11. It is interesting to note that Chavela shares this particular memory in relation to her first encounter with Frida.

12. Redacción Digital Enciclopedia, "Chavela Vargas, ícono de la cultura mexicana," Radio Enciclopedia, June 8, 2012, http://www.radioenciclopedia.cu/noticias/chavela-vargas-icono-cultura-mexicana-20120806/. This online publication is hosted in Havana, Cuba.

13. María Cortina, Enrique Helguera de la Villa, Chavela Vargas, *Dos vidas necesito. Las verdades de Chavela* (Barcelona: Montesinos, 2012), 39. All translations are mine, unless otherwise indicated.

14. "We, Mexicans, are born where we fucking want to." This phrase has become a popular idiom among people of Mexican origin. It is found in multiple variants throughout the web. See Pedro Carrillo Baltazar, *Yo soy México* (Copenhagen, Denmark: SAXO, 2018).

15. Yvonne Yarbro-Bejarano, "Crossing the Border with Chabela Vargas: A Chicana Femme's Tribute," in *Sex and Sexuality in Latin America*, ed. Daniel Balderston and Donna J. Guy (New York: New York University Press, 1997), 39.

16. "Macorina" was included in Chavela's first album, *Noche Bohemia*, released in 1961 on Orfeón.

17. Lorena Alvarado, "Never Late: Unwelcome Desires and Diasporas in Chavela Vargas' Last Works," *Women & Performance: A Journal of Feminist Theory* 26, no. 1 (2016): 27. Although Chavela carried out an openly homosexual life, she did not come out publicly as a lesbian until she was in her eighties. The first public record of this announcement was published a day after she was awarded La Gran Cruz de Isabel la

Católica by the Spanish government in 2000, in the Spanish newspaper *El País*. See Rosa María Pereda, "Una cruz distinta para Chavela: El Consejo de Ministros condecora a la cantante mexicana, de 81 años," *El País* (October 14, 2000), https://elpais.com/diario/2000/10/14/ultima/971474401_850215.html. As Sofía Ruiz-Alfaro points out, "Chavela's announcement occurred amid an intense political debate in Spain about civil unions and same-sex marriages.... [It] only reaffirmed the question of giving visibility to the invisible." See Sofía Ruiz-Alfaro, "Out in the Jungle: The Queer World of Chavela Vargas," in *Queer Exoticism: Examining the Queer Exotic Within*, ed. David A. Powell and Tamara Powell (Cambridge: Cambridge Scholars Publishing, 2010), 15.

18. Chavela was not the first singer whose ranchera voice was perceived as 'masculine'. Earlier in the twentieth century, Lucha Reyes popularized a defiant assertive attitude. See Yolanda Moreno Rivas, *Historia de la música popular mexicana* (México, D.F.: CONACULTA/Alianza Editorial Mexicana/Editorial Patria, 1989); Olga Nájera-Ramírez, "Unruly Passions: Poetics, Performance, and Gender in the Ranchera Song," in *Chicana Feminisms: A Critical Reader*, ed. Patricia Zavella et al. (Durham and London: Duke University Press, 2003), 184–210; and Marie Sarita Gaytán and Sergio de la Mora, "Queening/Queering *Mexicanidad*: Lucha Reyes and the *Canción Ranchera*," *Feminist Formations* 28, no. 3 (2016): 196–221.

19. Olga Nájera-Ramírez, "Unruly Passions: Poetics, Performance, and Gender in the Ranchera Song," in *Chicana Feminisms: A Critical Reader*, ed. Patricia Zavella, Gabriela F. Arredondo, et al. (Durham and London: Duke University Press, 2003), 184–210; Laura G. Gutiérrez, *Performing Mexicanidad: Vendidas y Cabareteras on the Transnational Stage* (Austin: University of Texas Press, 2010).

20. Nájera-Ramírez, "Unruly Passions," 196.

21. Chavela's decision of accompanying herself with only two guitars was regarded by Miguel Peña—one of her guitar players—as a sign of Chavela's uniqueness, and as a mark for a new route in the female ranchera tradition. To Chavela's musicians, Miguel Peña and Juan Carlos Allende, "Los Macorinos," this thin texture was a lesson about *sencillez* (simplicity/humbleness). See "Miguel Peña y Juan Carlos Allende: Los Macorinos de Chavela Vargas," YouTube video, 10:35, posted by "Discos Corasón," November 5, 2012, https://www.youtube.com/watch?v=ZPMVm18bMY8.

22. Celia Dosio, *Las transgresoras: Anaïs Nin, Simone de Beavoir, Alfonsina Storni, Chavela Vargas* (México, D.F.: Lectorum, 2007), 167. As Deborah R. Vargas has noted, singers Rita Vidaurri and Lucha Reyes, "were among the first *mexicanas* to wear charro pants while performing rancheras, thereby bucking the gendered norms of Mexican female performance and disrupting gendered national iconography." See Deborah R. Vargas, *Dissonant Divas in Chicana Music. The Limits of La Onda* (Minneapolis: University of Minnesota Press, 2012), vii. Also see Gaytán and de la Mora, "Queening/Queering Mexicanidad."

23. According to Lorena Alvarado, Chavela's choice to dress as *gente de campo* (country people), "reflected the cultural nationalism that emerged at the time she debuted professionally." See Lorena Alvarado, "Never Late: Unwelcome Desires and Diasporas in Chavela Vargas' Last Works," *Women & Performance: A Journal of Feminist Theory* 26, no. 1 (2016), 33.

24. Ibid., 32–33.
25. Ibid., 21.
26. Yvonne Yarbro-Bejarano, "Crossing the Border with Chabela Vargas," in *Sex and Sexuality in Latin America*, ed. Daniel Balderston and Donna J. Guy (New York: New York University Press, 1997), 33–43.
27. Chavela's return to the stage at El Hábito happened in November 1991. She began her performance singing "Macorina." An uncut video of that performance is found here: http://hidvl.nyu.edu/video/001097505.html.
28. Chavela was the first Latin American female singer to perform at Paris's Olympia. Some of Pedro Almodóvar's films where you can hear the voice of Chavela Vargas are: *Kika* (1993), *La flor de mi secreto* (1995), *Carne trémula* (1997), and *Julieta* (2016). Apart from Almodóvar, Chavela was befriended by other Spanish celebrities, such as Joaquín Sabina and Miguel Bosé. Chavela achieved significant recognition in Spain and performed throughout renowned theaters in the country. She was granted prestigious honors, such as the Spanish Government's Gran Cruz de la Orden de Isabel la Católica, the *Premio de Honor* granted by the Sociedad General de Autores y Editores (SGAE), and the title Señora Excelentísima e Ilustrísima by the Universidad de Alcalá and the Universidad Complutense de Madrid.
29. Yarbro-Bejarano, "Crossing the Border with Chabela Vargas," 35.
30. The exact date when Chavela Vargas met Frida Kahlo is uncertain. In her autobiography, Chavela states that she hadn't turned twenty-five when she met Frida. See Vargas, *Y si quieres saber de mi pasado*, 103. Pino Cacucci signals 1939 as the year of their encounter—an earlier date. See Pino Cacucci, "Chavela, l'essenza della *mexicanidad*," preface to *Un mondo raro. Vita e incanto di Chavela Vargas*, by Antonio Di Martino and Fabrizio Cammarata (Milan: La nave di Teseo, 2017), 10.
31. Chavela recounts Frida telling her, "Cántame, mientras yo pinto" (sing to me while I paint). See Vargas and Cortina, *Las verdades de Chavela*, 53. It was commonly said that Chavela lived in La Casa Azul for a year. And, although the singer denied that belief in her 2002 autobiography, later in life she confirmed the rumor in a televised interview. See Vargas, *Y si quieres saber de mi pasado*, 119; "Frida Kahlo y Chavela Vargas," YouTube video, 8:14, posted by "República Musicana," June 22, 2011, https://www.youtube.com/watch?v=F72QF_t6b7c.
32. "Siempre será mi gran amor" ([Frida] will always be my greatest love)—Chavela told María Cortina. Surprised by this declaration, Cortina explains that, up to that point, Chavela had not confessed that Frida was her greatest love. See Vargas and Cortina, *Las verdades de Chavela*, 58. While Chavela repeatedly professed that there was a reciprocal love between herself and Frida in her autobiography and in multiple interviews, it should be understood that in this chapter I am not interested in establishing the veracity of that claim. My primary concern is Chavela's performative construction of her romantic relationship with Frida.
33. Special Features: Chavela Vargas, in interview with Elliot Goldenthal, *Frida*, directed by Julie Taymor (Los Angeles: Miramax Films, 2002). "Fue amor a primera vista. Fue un deslumbramiento pero no del mundo, fue una luz de otra dimensión, de otro planeta. Al verle la cara, los ojos, pensé que no era un ser de este mundo. Sin tener todavía la madurez de la mujer en mí, era muy niña, y sin embargo, adiviné por

la manera de hablar, por la manera de mirar, sus cejas juntas eran una golondrina en pleno vuelo. Si estaba en la cama, volaba cuando abría los ojos, por las cejas, dos alas de golondrina. Presentí que podía amar a ese ser con el amor más puro del mundo, con el amor más de entrega del mundo, con el amor más doliente del mundo, más alegre del mundo, más triste del mundo, el amor más libre del mundo, el amor más atado del mundo. Y un día mis palabras posiblemente la hirieron mucho cuando le dije que me iba alguna vez. Que iba a levantar el vuelo, que me iría de su lado para siempre, algún día. Y ella me dijo: 'Lo sé. Lo sé que te vas. Y no voy a llorar, ni tú tampoco. Cuando quieras en un atardecer, en cualquier país del mundo y tengas tiempo, recuérdame. Sólo recuérdame. Piensa que hubo una vez en la vida un ser que te amó, que te ama, porque yo te nací, y te doy la libertad. No te puedo atar a mis muletas ni a mi cama, vete'. Y un día, abrí la puerta, y no volví". Translation taken from English subtitles provided in the DVD.

34. In another source, Chavela recounts Frida telling her: "Yo te nací. Agarra las cosas buenas de mí, hasta nútrete de mi propio dolor" (Take the good things from me, nurture yourself from my own suffering). See Rubén García Badillo, *Frida se confiesa* (Bloomington, IN: Trafford Publishing, 2012), 138.

35. Sofía Ruiz-Alfaro, "From Chavela to Frida: Loving from the Margins," *Journal of Homosexuality* 59, no. 8 (2012), 1137.

36. For this chapter I compared ten versions of Chavela's renditions of "La Llorona" from 1993 up to 2012. This comparison was useful to determine that Chavela maintained the same instrumental accompaniment in all performances of the song and, although she varied some strophes, she mostly kept the same verses to begin and end the song.

37. The *requinto* guitar is smaller than a standard guitar, and tuned a fourth higher. The *bajo quinto* is larger than a standard guitar and has five courses of doubled steel strings.

38. The testimonies about Cihuacóatl were recorded in Fray Bernardino de Sahagún's *Historia de las cosas de la Nueva España* (1569). Luis Leal points out that, apparently, the myth of the goddess Cihuacóatl transformed into La Llorona as the frightener of little children soon after the Conquest of Tenochtitlán. See Luis Leal, "The Malinche-Llorona Dichotomy: The Evolution of a Myth," in *Feminism, Nation and Myth: La Malinche*, ed. Rolando Romero and Amanda Nolacea Harris (Houston: Arte Público Press, 2005), 136.

39. José Limón, "La Llorona, The Third Legend of Greater Mexico: Cultural Symbols, Women, and the Political Unconscious," in *Between Borders: Essays on Mexicana/Chicana History*, ed. Adelaida R. Del Castillo (Mountain View, CA: Floricanto Press, 2005), 399–432.

40. Alfredo Mirandé, *Behind the Mask: Gender Hybridity in a Zapotec Community* (Tucson: The University of Arizona Press, 2017), 8.

41. Ibid., 15.

42. Vargas, *Y si quieres saber de mi pasado*, 114. Frida was a role model to Chavela.

43. Ibid.

44. Sofía Ruiz-Alfaro, "Nos/otras las Chamanas. Metáfora y Curación en Gloria Anzaldúa y Chavela Vargas," *Aztlán: A Journal of Chicano Studies* 41, no. 2 (2016), 66.

45. Ibid., 70.

46. Deborah Shaw, "Remaking Frida Kahlo through Song in *Frida*," in *Screening Songs in Hispanic and Lusophone Cinema*, ed. L. Shaw and R. Stone (Manchester: Manchester University Press, 2012), 230.

47. The word *chile* is also used in Mexico as a slang word for penis.

48. Yarbro-Bejarano, 38.

49. Upon inquiry, Nickolas Muray's daughter, Mimi Levitt, confirmed that this photograph was not taken by her father. She expressed that, in trying to assess the identity of the photographer, someone also had claimed that the woman accompanying Frida was Teresa Proenza. Mimi Levitt, email message to author, June 5, 2019.

50. See Helena Calmfors, "Mirror, Mirror. . . . Frida Kahlo Photographs at Throckmorton Fine Art," Musée Vanguard of Photography Culture, May 27, 2015, http://museemagazine.com/culture/culture/art-out/mirror-mirrorfrida-kahlo-photographs-at-throckmorton-fine-art.

51. DPA, "Cartas de Frida Kahlo a Chavela Vargas no corresponden a la caligrafía de la pintora," *La Jornada*, August 29, 2012, http://www.jornada.unam.mx/2012/08/29/cultura/a06n2cul.

52. The image of this letter is reproduced in *Las verdades de Chavela* with this caption: "Carta de Frida Kahlo dirigida al poeta Carlos Pellicer. (Colección Fernández-Noyola, donada a la señora Chavela Vargas)." There is no further commentary about it in the body of the text. The letter reads: "Hoy conocí a Chavela Vargas. Extraordinaria, Lesbiana, es más se me antojó Eróticamente. No sé si ella sintió lo que yo. Pero creo que es una mujer lo bastante liberal que si me lo pide, no dudaría un segundo en desnudarme ante ella. Ella, repito, es erótica. Acaso es un regalo que el cielo me envía. Frida." See Vargas and Cortina, *Las verdades de Chavela*, 59.

53. Vargas, *Y si quieres saber de mi pasado*, 112.

54. Ibid.

55. The centrality of Frida in Chavela's own recounting of her life, as evident by this autobiography, is noteworthy.

56. Vargas, *Y si quieres saber de mi pasado*, 112.

57. Ibid., 99.

58. Ibid., 102. Emphasis is mine.

59. A reproduction of Frida's *La columa rota* is available here: https://www.wikiart.org/en/frida-kahlo/the-broken-column-1944.

60. Vargas, *Y si quieres saber de mi pasado,* 115.

61. Wendy B. Faris, "Primitivist Construction of Identity in the Work of Frida Kahlo," in *Primitivism and Identity in Latin America: Essays on Art, Literature and Culture*, ed. Erik Camayd-Freixas and José Eduardo González (Tucson: The University of Arizona Press, 2000), 228.

62. Oriana Baddeley, "'Her Dress Hangs Here': De-Frocking the Kahlo Cult," *Oxford Art Journal* 14, no. 1 (1991), 13.

63. Baddeley, 13. See Margaret A. Lindauer, *Devouring Frida: The Art History and Popular Celebrity of Frida Kahlo* (Middletown, CT: Wesleyan University Press, 1999).

64. Vargas, *Y si quieres saber de mi pasado*, 101.

65. Vargas and Cortina, *Las verdades de Chavela*, 58.

66. Anna Marie Sandoval, *Toward a Latina Feminism of the Americas: Repression and Resistance in Chicana and Mexicana Literature* (Austin: University of Texas Press, 2008), 43.

67. Vargas, *Y si quieres saber de mi pasado*, 23.

68. Ibid., 114.

69. Ibid., 116.

70. Ruiz-Alfaro, "From Chavela to Frida: Loving from the Margins," 1137.

71. See, "Chavela Vargas en Bellas Artes 2012 (Concierto COMPLETO)," YouTube video, 1:15:25, posted by "Enrique Vázquez Maravilla," September 2, 2012, https://www.youtube.com/watch?v=uYuRTG02qdk. This was not the first time Chavela performed at El Palacio de Bellas Artes. In 1995, at seventy-five, she offered two concerts in that venue, which were introduced by filmmaker Pedro Almodóvar. Singing in Bellas Artes was, to Chavela, a dream come true. Considered the most prestigious performance venue in the country, El Palacio de Bellas Artes had also functioned as a gatekeeper of "high art music." The first popular music singer to perform in that venue was Juan Gabriel, in 1990. As Alejandro L. Madrid has pointed out, this event, which marked a historical moment in Juan Gabriel's career, was also demonstrative of "the type of discursive excess and cultural surplus that such an act of cultural reterritorialization presupposes" (p. 86). Moreover, the queerness of Juan Gabriel's camp vocality, or *jotería*, as Madrid puts it, revealed the "open secret of homosexuality in a traditionally homophobic society, thus voicing the history of erasures, silences, and discrimination behind the 'don't-ask-don't-tell' kind of attitude that many Mexicans use to deal with homosexuality" (p. 97). The success of Juan Gabriel's performance in Bellas Artes created a precedent for Chavela's. Both artists queered mexicanidad by transgressing the conventions of a venue that is still considered a symbol of Mexican nationalism. See Alejandro L. Madrid, "*Secreto a Voces*: Excess, Performance, and *Jotería* in Juan Gabriel's Vocality," *GLQ: A Journal of Lesbian and Gay Studies* 24, no. 1 (2018), 85–111.

72. This was not the last time Chavela performed "La Llorona." She sung a version of the song less than a month before her death in Madrid's Residencia de Estudiantes, on July 10, 2012. See, "La última vez que Chavela Vargas cantó La Llorona," YouTube video, 1:36, posted by "Carlos Muñoz," August 14, 2012, https://www.youtube.com/watch?v=ZMcpQDuMoTc.

73. "Chavela Vargas & Frida Kahlo," YouTube video, 4:30, posted by "Frankie Olaya," April 6, 2009, https://www.youtube.com/watch?v=O1W7rsBY7y8.

74. Vargas, *Y si quieres saber de mi pasado*, 114.

75. After learning about my research on this topic, in an email conversation film director Daresha Kyi posed the following question: "Were you able to find proof that they actually even met?" She continued to explain that, even in spite of the controversy surrounding Muray's photograph, she decided to incorporate the image in the

documentary *Chavela*, which she co-directed with Catherine Gund. Daresha Kyi, email message to author, February 8, 2018.

76. DPA, "Chavela Vargas escribe su biografía para dejar como legado," *Emol.com*, July 5, 2001, http://www.emol.com/noticias/magazine/2001/07/05/59451/chavela-vargas-escribe-su-biografia-para-dejar-como-legado.html.

77. Vargas, *Dissonant Divas in Chicana Music*, xv.

78. José Esteban Muñoz, *Disidentifications: Queers of Color and the Performance of Politics* (Minneapolis: University of Minnesota Press, 1999), 4.

79. Ibid., 11–12.

80. Ibid., 5.

81. Gutiérrez, *Performing Mexicanidad*, 7.

82. bell hooks, "Choosing the Margin as a Space of Radical Openness," *Framework: The Journal of Cinema and Media* 36 (1989), 21.

83. Ibid., 36

84. See "Chavela Vargas en Concierto | Sala Caracol (Madrid)—01.05.1993," YouTube video, 1:11:20, posted by "TerritorioFlamenko," April 20, 2014, https://www.youtube.com/watch?v=-CoaZSggeSI.

85. Lorena Alvarado, "Never Late: Unwelcome Desires and Diasporas in Chavela Vargas' Last Works," *Women & Performance: A Journal of Feminist Theory* 26, no. 1 (2016), 22.

REFERENCES

Alarcón, Norma, Caren Kaplan, and Minoo Moallem. "Introduction: Between Woman and Nation." In *Between Woman and Nation: Nationalism, Transnational Feminisms, and the State*, edited by Caren Kaplan, Norma Alarcón, and Minoo Moallem, 1–18. Durham and London: Duke University Press, 1999.

Alvarado, Lorena. "Never Late: Unwelcome Desires and Diasporas in Chavela Vargas' Last Works." *Women & Performance: A Journal of Feminist Theory* 26, no. 1 (2016): 17–35.

Baddeley, Oriana. "'Her Dress Hangs Here': De-Frocking the Kahlo Cult." *Oxford Art Journal* 14, no. 1 (1991): 10–17.

Badillo, Rubén García. *Frida se confiesa*. Bloomington, IN: Trafford Publishing, 2012.

Baltazar, Pedro Carrillo. *Yo soy México*. Copenhagen, Denmark: SAXO.com Hispanic Ap5, 2018.

Barneda, Sandra. *Hablarán de nosotras: diecisiete mujeres poderosas que pecaron para ser libres*. Barcelona: Aguilar, 2016.

Cacucci, Pino. "Chavela, l'essenza della *mexicanidad*." Preface to *Un mondo raro. Vita e incanto di Chavela Vargas*, edited by Antonio Di Martino and Fabrizio Cammarata, 7–18. Milan: La nave di Teseo, 2017.

"Chavela Vargas & Frida Kahlo." YouTube video, 4:30. Posted by "Frankie Olaya," April 6, 2009. https://www.youtube.com/watch?v=O1W7rsBY7y8.

"Chavela Vargas en Bellas Artes 2012 (Concierto COMPLETO)." YouTube video, 1:15:25. Posted by "Enrique Vázquez Maravilla," September 2, 2012, https://www.youtube.com/watch?v=uYuRTG02qdk.

"Chavela Vargas en Concierto | Sala Caracol (Madrid) - 01.05.1993." YouTube video, 1:11:20. Posted by "Territorio Flamenko," April 20, 2014. https://www.youtube.com/watch?v=-CoaZSggeSI.

Cortina, María, Enrique Helguera de la Villa, and Chavela Vargas. *Dos vidas necesito. Las verdades de Chavela.* Barcelona: Montesinos, 2012.

Cortina, María, and Chavela Vargas. *Las verdades de Chavela.* México D.F.: Editorial Océano, 2009.

Dosio, Celia. *Las transgresoras: Anaïs Nin, Simone de Beavoir, Alfonsina Storni, Chavela Vargas.* México D.F.: Lectorum, 2007.

Faris, Wendy B. "Primitivist Construction of Identity in the Work of Frida Kahlo." In *Primitivism and Identity in Latin America: Essays on Art, Literature and Culture*, edited by Erik Camayd-Freixas and José Eduardo González, 221–240. Tucson: The University of Arizona Press, 2000.

"Frida Kahlo y Chavela Vargas." YouTube video, 8:14. Posted by "República Musicana," June 22, 2011. https://www.youtube.com/watch?v=F72QF_t6b7c.

Gaytán, Marie Sarita, and Sergio de la Mora. "Queening/Queering *Mexicanidad*: Lucha Reyes and the *Canción Ranchera*." *Feminist Formations* 28, no. 3 (2016): 196–221.

Gutiérrez, Laura G. *Performing Mexicanidad: Vendidas y Cabareteras on the Transnational Stage.* Austin: University of Texas Press, 2010.

hooks, bell. "Choosing the Margin as a Space of Radical Openness." *Framework: The Journal of Cinema and Media* 36 (1989): 15–23.

"La última vez que Chavela Vargas cantó La Llorona." YouTube video, 1:36. Posted by "Carlos Muñoz," August 14, 2012. https://www.youtube.com/watch?v=ZMcpQDuMoTc.

Leal, Luis. "The Malinche-Llorona Dichotomy: The Evolution of a Myth." *Feminism, Nation and Myth: La Malinche*, edited by Rolando Romero and Amanda Nolacea Harris, 134–138. Houston: Arte Público Press, 2005.

Limón, José. "La Llorona, The Third Legend of Greater Mexico: Cultural Symbols, Women, and the Political Unconscious." In *Between Borders: Essays on Mexicana/Chicana History*, edited by Adelaida R. Del Castillo, 399–432. Mountain View, California: Floricanto Press, 2005.

Lindauer, Margaret A. *Devouring Frida: The Art History and Popular Celebrity of Frida Kahlo.* Middletown, CT: Wesleyan University Press, 1999.

Lugones, María. "Heterosexualism and the Colonial/Modern Gender System." *Hypatia* 22, no. 1 (Winter 2007): 186–209.

Madrid, Alejandro L. "*Secreto a Voces*: Excess, Performance, and *Jotería* in Juan Gabriel's Vocality." *GLQ: A Journal of Lesbian and Gay Studies* 24, no. 1 (2018): 85–111.

Mignolo, Walter, and Catherine E. Walsh. *On Decoloniality: Concepts, Analytics, Praxis.* Durham and London: Duke University Press, 2018.

"Miguel Peña y Juan Carlos Allende: Los Macorinos de Chavela Vargas." YouTube video, 10:35. Posted by "Discos Corasón," November 5, 2012. https://www.youtube.com/watch?v=ZPMVm18bMY8.

Mirandé, Alfredo. *Behind the Mask: Gender Hybridity in a Zapotec Community.* Tucson: University of Arizona Press, 2017.

Nájera-Ramírez, Olga. "Unruly Passions: Poetics, Performance, and Gender in the Ranchera Song." In *Chicana Feminisms: A Critical Reader,* edited by Patricia Zavella, Gabriela F. Arredondo, Aída Hurtdao, et al., 184–210. Durham and London: Duke University Press, 2003.

Quijano, Aníbal. "Coloniality of Power, Eurocentrism, and Latin America." *Nepantla: Views from South* 1, no. 3 (2000): 533–580.

Rivas, Yolanda Moreno. *Historia de la música popular mexicana.* México, D.F.: CONACULTA/Alianza Editorial Mexicana/Editorial Patria, 1989.

Rivera-Servera, Ramón H. *Performing Queer Latinidad: Dance, Sexuality, Politics.* Ann Arbor: The University of Michigan Press, 2012.

Ruiz-Alfaro, Sofía. "Nos/otras las Chamanas. Metáfora y Curación en Gloria Anzaldúa y Chavela Vargas." *Aztlán: A Journal of Chicano Studies* 41, no. 2 (Fall 2016): 65–85.

———. "From Chavela to Frida: Loving from the Margins." *Journal of Homosexuality* 59, no. 8 (2012): 1131–1144.

———. "Out in the Jungle: The Queer World of Chavela Vargas." In *Queer Exoticism: Examining the Queer Exotic Within,* edited by David A. Powell and Tamara Powell, 15–25. Cambridge: Cambridge Scholars Publishing, 2010.

Sandoval, Anna Marie. *Toward a Latina Feminism of the Americas: Repression and Resistance in Chicana and Mexicana Literature.* Austin: University of Texas Press, 2008.

Shaw, Deborah. "Remaking Frida Kahlo through Song in *Frida.*" In *Screening Songs in Hispanic and Lusophone Cinema,* edited by Lisa Shaw, Rob Stone, and Ian Biddle, 220–234. Manchester: Manchester University Press, 2012.

Taymor, Julie. *Frida.* DVD. Miramax Films. 2002.

Vargas, Chavela. *Y si quieres saber de mi pasado.* México D.F.: Aguilar, Altea, Taurus, Alfaguara, 2002.

Vargas, Deborah R. *Dissonant Divas in Chicana Music: The Limits of La Onda.* Minneapolis: University of Minnesota Press, 2012.

Yarbro-Bejarano, Yvonne. "Crossing the Border with Chabela Vargas: A Chicana Femme's Tribute." In *Sex and Sexuality in Latin America,* edited by Daniel Balderston and Donna J. Guy, 33–43. New York: New York University Press, 1997.

Chapter 4

Vaquero World

Queer Mexicanidad, Trans Performance, and the Undoing of Nation[1*]

Nadine Hubbs

Over the past decade, at some distance from mainstream view, a network of gatherings has emerged and given rise to new queer Latinx world-space. Fostering queer sociality, sexuality, and performance, the world thus created stages nonessentialist, *trans* representations of gender and nation bearing decolonial implications. In the United States, Spanish-speaking queer Latinx men, most of Mexican descent, don hats and boots and travel to meet at weekend *reuniones vaqueras* (cowboy gatherings), converging on six cities that currently host annual *vaquero* conventions at different times of the year: Dallas, Denver, Las Vegas, Los Angeles, and Phoenix in the Southwest, and Chicago in the Midwest.[2] Details of the events vary, but every *reunión* features regional Mexican music and social dancing, Mexican food and drink, and live performance in many forms.[3] Each one also includes a competitive pageant for the local vaquero title, called Rey Vaquero (King Cowboy), Mr. Vaquero, Mr. Encuentro Vaquero (Mr. Cowboy Encounter, following the name of Chicago's reunión), or something similar. "Mr." commonly appears in these titles (as in the long-running Mr. Leather competitions in gay kink communities), and I will use "Mr. Vaquero" here to refer generically to the pageant portions of U.S. reuniones vaqueras.

Held in Mexican-American LGBTQ nightclubs and in Spanish, the pageants draw out-of-town male vaquero attendees and contestants, and locals including straight attendees and numerous queer women who participate as attendees, organizers, and performers.[4] The competition entails multiple categories of performance. For example, 2018 contestants at Las Vegas's BackDoor Lounge competed in a *presentación* (presentation), *talento* (talent), *traje de gala* (gala wear), and finally, *pregunta* (question) segment, responding on mic to a social or humanitarian question. Categories were nearly the same at the 2018 Chicago contest, except that *la pregunta* was replaced by *toro mecánico* (mechanical bull riding). Equally vital to the festivities, on both sites, were the intervals before, between, and after the competition segments: in these, past vaquero champions, *transformistas* (drag queens), and others performed to recorded music, or attendees took the floor to dance. The music—mostly *norteño, duranguense,* and, especially, *banda*—fell under the heading of regional Mexican music, a "catchall category" of music "with roots in rural Mexico" that rose in the 1990s to become the most popular U.S. category of Latinx music (Martínez 2011).

In this chapter, I draw on fieldwork at vaquero events in Las Vegas and Chicago to examine a little-known transnational space of working-class Latinx sociality and entertainment where music and multidimensional performance meet reverberative forms of sexuality and gender, nationalism, and *mexicanidad*. I use mexicanidad here to name a shifting array of practices and objects, material, sensorial, and ideational, that serve to evoke Mexican experience and identification and bring people together socially, sexually, and musically in online and physical realms of (what I am calling) Vaquero World. I use the term *nationalism* in a delimited sense to refer not to any perceptibly political acts or utterances, but to declarative performances of nation-branded affiliation and sentiment in the late-capitalist and markedly transnational space of Vaquero World.

For example, Mr. Vaquero contestants in both Las Vegas and Chicago—a significant number of whom were non-Mexican Latinos—donned MÉXICO-emblazoned ponchos in performance; and I discuss below a choreographed performance featuring Mexican flag waving to song lyrics celebrating the Mexican land and people—sung by a Sonora-born Angeleno star of banda, a "fully transnational" music (Simonett 2001, 21). I recognize queer vaqueros and allies' displays of nationalism and mexicanidad as collaborative productions of globalized transnational performative labor, and I analyze these in relation to trans forms of gender expression (as defined below) and transnational queer sexuality in Vaquero World.[5] In the process, I diverge from recent discourses on vaquero gatherings that view them as enactments of essentialized macho gender (Delgado 2015, Rosen 2017, Snyder 2018). Finally, considering the constitutive roles of gender and race in the colonial establishment of the modern nation-state (Silverblatt 2004), I ask what decolonial effects might link to Vaquero World's trans-performances of both nationalism and nonessentialist gender, including their undoing of nation.

GENDER, RACE, AND THE ORIGINS OF NATION

In *Imagined Communities: Reflections on the Origin and Spread of Nationalism*, Benedict Anderson noted that "in the modern world everyone can, should, will 'have' a nationality, as he or she 'has' a gender" (Anderson [1983] 2006). Indeed, the properties are constitutively linked, according to the historian and anthropologist Irene Silverblatt (2004). Her work shows that the modern nation stands on classifications of both gender and race, and it was these classifications that brought the nation, brutally and violently, into being. Drawing on archives of the Spanish Inquisition in Peru, Silverblatt has argued that sixteenth- and seventeenth-century Spanish imperialism in Latin America ushered in the modern nation-state, through its bureaucratic and bloody institution of racial and gender classification. In order to be legible beneath the lens of the colonial bureaucracy, individuals were compelled to occupy stable categories as men, women, whites, Indians. On these bases, subjects were sorted according to who would perform labor and what kind, who would couple with whom, who could possess power and property in various forms, and who could access citizenship.

Against this historical backdrop I will consider the contemporary world created by queer vaqueros. In broad perspective, performance on the vaquero sites encompasses the self-presentations of all in attendance, not only designated performers but also every patron, and includes bodily stylings, with clothing, accessories, and more; behaviors and interactions; movement on the dance floor and beyond; and vocal utterances and expressions. Performance at vaquero events thus adds up to an abundant mix of gender, sexuality, class, race, ethnicity, nationality, and other significations (Butler [1991] 1993).

Vaquero scenes have received little public attention up to now, but when they have received U.S. coverage, they have often been viewed as gay enactments of a machismo that is essentialized as male and, at times, Latin. The most substantive article I have seen in this regard is the journalist Michael Snyder's essay "Vaqueros" in the literary quarterly *VQR* (Snyder 2018). A gay-identified U.S. travel writer currently based in Mexico City, Snyder paints a vivid and absorbing picture of his experience taking part in a gay vaquero gathering in Real de Catorce, Mexico. The scene is an emphatically male "fantasia of nostalgic masculinity" marked by urban weekend "cowboys' studied, frozen pouts." I do not question Snyder's characterization of the vaquero weekend in Real de Catorce. Indeed, I cannot, having never attended that event or any of the gay vaquero events that have been established in Mexico since about 2008.

I can attest, however, that Snyder's account of gender among Real de Catorce vaqueros does not describe what I experienced at U.S. vaquero events. To be sure, I observed machismo, in both onstage and civilian performances—but not as an essentialized gender form upholding traditional social and civic structures. While some male-bodied participants displayed machismo, others presented as more feminine vaqueros or as drag queens.

And notably, machismo was also accessed by female-bodied vaqueros. In other words, the context for gender performance collectively enacted on these sites was not essentializing. It was trans.

The transgender historian Susan Stryker has illustrated the recent historical shift from essentialized gender (pinning femininity to biological femaleness and masculinity to biological maleness) to transgender representations through a comparison to analog and digital representation:

> The current fascination with transgender . . . probably has something to do with new ideas about how representation works in the age of digital media. Back in the analog era, a representation (word, image, idea) was commonly assumed to point to some real thing, the same way a photograph was an image produced by light bouncing off a physical object and causing a chemical change on a piece of paper, or the way a sound recording was a groove cut in a piece of vinyl by sound waves produced by a musical instrument or a person's voice. A person's social and psychological gender was commonly assumed to point to that person's biological sex in exactly the same way: Gender was considered a representation of a physical sex. But a digital image or sound is something else entirely. It's unclear exactly how it's related to the world of physical objects. It doesn't point to some 'real' thing in quite the same way, and it might in fact be a complete fabrication built up pixel by pixel or bit by bit—but a fabrication that nevertheless exists as an image or a sound as real as any other. Transgender gender representation works the same way (Stryker 2017, 26 and 28).

At this point, recalling Silverblatt, we might ask: If the construction of bodily difference through racial and gender classification launched the modern nation under Spanish colonialism and still sustains it, what does it mean, for the nation and nationalism, to perform gender in the "digital" mode described by Stryker and demonstrated in Vaquero World—a mode that leaves gender itself, feminine and masculine, largely intact but deletes the indexing of gender to material embodiment, thus de-essentializing it? I will return to this question later, but I must first draw a distinction here. Stryker's account of a move from analog to digital representations of gender serves to illuminate recent and ongoing shifts in the United States, Canada, Australia, and Europe, among other places, but we cannot assume it applies equally everywhere. In fact, Mexico, and Latin America generally, has not been part of the same shift. This is not to say that Latin Americans are stuck in an analog gender mode, but rather that they were never very analog. Race in Latin America has long been nonessentialist and digital, and so, arguably, has gender, relative to the nations just listed; I will elaborate these points below. Finally, I would note that nation does not only surface indirectly through gender performance in Vaquero World but also receives lavish representation in its own right, insofar as queer vaquero events brim with Mexican nationalism performed through musical sounds and styles, song lyrics, clothing and costumes, and vibrant aromas and flavors evocative, for participants, of mexicanidad.

THE BACKSTORY: COUNTRY MEXICANS

The queer vaquero scene I discuss here is subcultural and not widely known. I had no knowledge of its existence until I received a tip while working on another research front, conducting focus groups with Mexican-American country music lovers in Texas and California. Following a focus-group conversation in the Texas borderlands, one participant, a twenty-something queer-identified Mexican-American country fan named Roxy, spoke to me of having recently helped her gay friend compete in Texas's Rey Vaquero contest. Roxy had served as her friend's interlocutor in a video interview that helped carry him to the finals at a Dallas gay bar. She thought that I might like to know about this scene. And so began the story of how a non-Mexican female-bodied queer musicologist wound up traveling to, writing about, and staying up late at queer vaquero events.

The focus groups were part of my research for a forthcoming book, *Country Mexicans: Sounding Mexican American Life, Love, and Belonging in Country Music*. This project arose from issues and questions I had been ruminating on for years, concerning certain tendencies in cultural representation and music scholarship, and individuals and communities I had known since childhood. It struck me, for example, that while people of Mexican descent in the United States listened to a variety of musical styles—including, in my 1970s Midwestern youth, country, mariachi, ranchera, and rock—representations of Mexican Americans' listening and other musical engagements, in both the media and academe, often focused exclusively on music of Mexico.[6] And while Mexican American music lovers may construct their social identities in relation to Mexican music, they construct social selves in relation to other, non-Mexican music, too—today including Puerto Rican reggaetón and mainland-U.S. ska, rap, pop, punk, R&B, and country, among other styles.[7] Depicting Mexican-Americans' authentic musical tastes, lives, and selves only in relation to music labeled *Mexican* can serve to exoticize, inscribe difference, and essentialize, and to reify boundaries that have been racially, culturally, and geographically constructed. An empirical reckoning of listening practices on the ground readily reveals such a view as inadequate to the transnationalism of actual musical engagements and desires of people of Mexican descent, in both Mexico and the United States.

In country music studies over the past decade, a growing body of academics and journalists from a range of disciplines have significantly expanded the field with new perspectives on gender, race, sexuality, and class. We know vastly more today, for example, about African-American influence and involvements in country music than we did just a few years ago, thanks to work like Diane Pecknold's *Hidden in the Mix* (2013), Charles Hughes's *Country Soul* (2015), and Karl Hagstrom Miller's *Segregating Sound* (2010). But country music scholarship up to now has included scarce mention of Mexican-American engagements.[8] I knew Mexican-American country lovers as a kid in the seventies, the decade of Johnny Rodriguez, Linda Ronstadt, and Freddy Fender's star turns in country music. And today, country has even more Mexican-American constituents: in 2016, the Country Music Association identified Latinxs as one of the fastest-growing U.S. fan groups. But Mexican-American engagements and contributions have yet to be studied in this music that for many has symbolized whiteness, working-classness, and quintessential Americanness (Hubbs 2014).

Attention to Mexican and Mexican-American country influences and involvements can help to recover the Mexican origins of U.S. culture, extend histories of transcultural musical exchange, counter false images of a uniformly white U.S. working class, and de-essentialize country as (putatively) white Anglo-American music. The cultural scholar Curtis Márez (1996), for example, focuses on the *tejano* country music of Freddy Fender in his analysis of brown style. And Mexican-American fans have attested in my focus groups that country is Mexican—in its themes and values, its *corrido*-like storytelling, and (according to one of my interlocutors) its fiddle parts resembling banda clarinet lines. Country music is Mexican, too, in its visual and sartorial style. It owes its boots and hats, belt buckles and western shirts to a distinctly Mexican figure, which it shares with Vaquero World.[9]

EL VAQUERO

The central figure of queer vaquero weekends, at once timeless icon and living, breathing everyman, is the cowboy: in Spanish, *el vaquero;* from *vaca:* cow. Americans know him, via Hollywood, as a solitary romantic nomad galloping over untamed, wide-open spaces, driving cattle under the big sky with only his horse for companionship and the sometime society of his fellow cowboys. Many know him, in the United States and around the world, as a masculine symbol of Americana, a paragon of American freedom, independence, and restlessness; hard work and can-do spirit; toughness and courage. And overwhelmingly he is Anglo and white. The image of the nineteenth-century Anglo-American cowboy has been cemented in U.S. and global consciousness by western films since the silent picture era and by mediatized music since the 1930s, through singing cowboys on the silver screen and western swing and country music on the airwaves and in the dancehall. Today, U.S. country artists still wear cowboy hats, boots, and other western clothing, and cowboy themes continue to feature in their music—for example, in the most-played country track of the 1990s, Toby Keith's "Should've Been a Cowboy."

But the American cowboy romance is flawed to the extent that it stands on the image of the cowboy as a U.S. original. In fact, as the border studies pioneer Américo Paredes elucidated (Paredes [1958] 1971, 1993; Saldívar 2012), the cowboy originated in Mexico, and the Anglo-American version arose later out of a "complicated history of cross-cultural borrowings" (Márez 1996, 111). Spanish conquistadores brought horses to the New World in 1519, when Cortés landed in what is now Mexico, and they introduced cattle and bullfights soon after. The colonizers imposed a law restricting rights of land ownership and horseback riding exclusively to Spaniards but later granted Mexican Indigenous and mestizo land workers the coveted right to ride so that they could perform the labor on colonial *haciendas* (estates). Mexican *charros* (horsemen) developed a highly skilled style of horsemanship adapted from that of the Spanish, who had learned from the Moors. They practiced their *jinetea* (breaking a horse in), *colear* (fancy lassoing and roping), *rodeo* (round-up), and *jaripeo* (bull-riding) skills, among others, on the open range and in the contest and show arena. *Charrería* refers collectively to these practices and is the official national sport of Mexico. *Charro* dress became the national costume, too, following charros' contributions to the fight for Mexican independence in 1821 (LeCompte 1985).

In the United States, the jinetea methods of the charros were adopted in the nineteenth century by working cowboys and by the Texas Rangers. The cowboy emerged as a popular U.S. figure only in the mid-1880s, the result of Buffalo Bill's Wild West show and its many imitators touring the United States and Europe in 1883–1916 (which introduced charros' trick and fancy roping techniques to the United States for the first time). The American heritage of the Wild West frontier as represented by "Buffalo" Bill Cody in his roping, riding, and shooting shows and contests was actually a collection of Mexican charro traditions (in early performances, Buffalo Bill himself appeared in a charro suit). All-day *fiestas* (parties) of charrería in rural Mexico, with music, food, and dancing through the night, were the apparent precursors of American rodeo. A description of one such fiesta in 1846 at the Hacienda Santa Fe was erroneously cited in many sources as the first U.S. rodeo, but in fact, the hacienda was located near Veracruz, Mexico, and rodeo appeared in the United States only in the latter half of the nineteenth century (LeCompte 1985).

In the twenty-first century, Mexican nationalist expressions continue to invoke the vaquero. The vaquero is a defining figure, for example, in contemporary regional Mexican music styles including ranchera, tejano, norteño, *onda grupera,* duranguense, and banda. A popular style with roots in the military band and polka music of mid-nineteenth-century European-Mexican immigrants, banda in its contemporary form is transnational music created and consumed in both Mexico and the United States (Simonett 2001).[10] Singers, band members, dancers, and audiences dress in vaquero style. The early 1990s saw the rise of contemporary banda music on both sides of the border, and young fans' adoption of *moda vaquera* (cowboy wear) represented a significant expression of Chicanx identity in Los Angeles and elsewhere (Simonett 2001, 61–64).

VAQUERO WORLD: CHICAGO AND LAS VEGAS

Chicago's Sexto Encuentro Vaquero Medio Oeste (Sixth Midwest Cowboy Encounter) was a convention for queer men presented under the auspices of Vaqueros Chicago, Inc., and part of what publicity materials refer to as *el movimiento vaquero* (the vaquero movement). Taking place each year in mid-August, Encuentro Vaquero comprises a full weekend packed with well-organized and -attended vaquero-themed events. The 2018 festivities began Friday night with Mr. Encuentro Vaquero 2018 y Noche de Bienvenida (Mr. Vaquero Encounter 2018 and Welcome Night) at a Mexican-American gay club in the city. Featuring five contestants, the 2018 pageant started at 9:30 p.m. and culminated just after midnight with the crowning of the winner, Plebito S., a handsome young Mexican-immigrant factory worker from Alabama who showed impressive poise and dance moves. Then, without pause, the party shifted into Welcome Night, with the DJ spinning crowd favorites. Yet to appear was the headline musical act, Adolfo Urías y Su Lobo Norteño, a well-known norteño singer and accordionist from Ojinaga, Chihuahua, and his four-man band. The revelry continued into the wee hours of Saturday morning.

Day two's events began with a Tardeada Vaquera (Cowboy Afternoon) from 1:30 to 7:30 p.m., featuring a local banda group in the later afternoon. Attendees could catch a chartered shuttle from the convention hotel to the *tardeada* site just outside Chicago, north of O'Hare airport (see Figure 4.1). The Saturday night event, titled After Party, took place at a second Chicago Latinx gay club. Running from 9:00 p.m. to 3:00 a.m., it hosted a sixteen-piece Chicago banda group, and a seven-piece group playing música duranguense. True to its name, the twenty-first-century regional style focuses on rural Durango, but it originated in the Chicago Mexican-American community in the mid-2000s (Giraud 2006). Sunday night's closing event, Cierre con Broche de Oro (Putting the Cherry on Top), was scheduled from 10 p.m.

Figure 4.1. Tardeada Vaquera outside Chicago, August 2018. Photo by Nadine Hubbs, 2018.

to 4 a.m. at another gay Latinx night club. The bill again included a DJ, plus two well-known Chicagoland acts: a six-piece norteño band and a pair of singing, guitar-playing sisters, Dueto K-Poneras de Chicago. Out of forty-two musicians booked throughout this weekend (plus several DJs), they were the only women. Such numbers are not peculiar to the gay male-centered vaquero context. It is common to hear and see only male performers in spectacularly instrumental, male-dominated regional Mexican music styles where women figure mostly as singers, when they figure at all.

Mr. Vaquero competitions in both Chicago and Las Vegas centered on performance modes familiar to U.S. queer clubgoers. A DJ played music for patrons' social dancing between staged performances by the vaquero contestants and others including past vaquero winners, local amateurs, and house drag queens. Operating solo or paired with gay cis-male co-emcees, the drag queens performed musical numbers between the competition segments and just generally ran the show, keeping things lively with witty commentary and sexual innuendo. What constituted performance for all the participants was lip-syncing to, and sometimes acting out, well-known songs and dancing, alone or in an ensemble.[11] In modes familiar to patrons of queer Latinx clubs, the music in both Chicago and Las Vegas included various regional Mexican styles—banda, norteño, duranguense, ranchera, onda grupera—and all commentary and dialogue on mic was in Latin American Spanish.[12]

Snyder's account from Central Mexico (2018) and a few others focused on U.S. vaquero events piqued my curiosity about gender performance on the scene (Delgado 2015, Rosen 2017). I approached the Las Vegas and Chicago events eager to observe gender performance and audiences' sex and gender makeup. On my first night in Vaquero World, I found myself the lone patron in Las Vegas's BackDoor Lounge. I had made the rookie error of showing up at 10:00 p.m., just as the club manager advised me to do. Saúl, a young gay bartender, made friendly conversation while slicing lime wedges in preparation for a night of countless *Coronas con limónes* (bottled Corona beers with lime). I asked about starting time, and he replied that the show would start at 2:00 a.m. (5:00 a.m. Eastern, my body reminded me), and the bar would close whenever everyone was gone—maybe 6:00 a.m. "Is the crowd mostly gay men?" I asked, images of a hypermale vaquero scene still lingering from my readings. "No." Saúl explained that vaquero nights bring out gay men, lesbians, and straight people—"everybody." That was indeed what I witnessed on both Friday and Saturday at the BackDoor Lounge, and later at México Moderno, a spacious gay bar in Chicago.

Contrary to male-focused representations, the Mr. Vaquero crowds I experienced were significantly *non*-homosocial, and both the gender flavor and the hook-up vibe in the spaces were inflected by this: the room felt more dance focused than sex focused.¹³ Moreover, a good number of the male-bodied vaquero participants and attendees presented some degree of femininity, including the plentiful drag queens (I saw at least a dozen in Chicago, where the peak crowd numbered about 240). Masculinity and machismo were surely present, but these were not the exclusive property of men. Rather, they were spread around among cowboys both male- and female-bodied. Dashing butches turned out in their *moda vaquera* of hats, boots, and cowboy shirts and were an integral part of the scene on both sites. The Latin American, Spanish-speaking crowd was mixed in age, from twenty-somethings to fifty- or sixty-somethings, and in gender and sexuality. There were queer men, drag queens, and queer women (including both butches and femmes, not always in mixed pairings: two-femme couples were common) together with straight couples, all dancing, socializing, and cheering on the contestants. Patrons arrived and stayed in groups or pairs; if any social type was conspicuously absent, it was the loner (though Las Vegas had one: me).

GENDER AND QUEER MEXICANIDAD

Is the U.S. reunión vaquera about machismo? I asked this question of Sergio C. on a sunny August Saturday at the Tardeada Vaquera outside Chicago. We were at a leafy municipal park. The local vaquero organizers had provided a comfortable setup in and around a shelter festooned with colorful fiesta banners. Long picnic tables inside the shelter were surrounded by a sound system and DJs playing banda and other dance music, grills that filled the air with aromas of meat and seasonings, and a mechanical bull with its inflatable landing pad. Walking paths led into the woods, and occasionally I saw a vaquero heading in or out, maybe to pee, I imagined, or to make out with another guy. Any more serious *encuentro vaquero* seemed risky here.

So, this scene that brings together well-groomed Latinx men in tejanos ("Texans": straw or felt cowboy hats), boots, and vaquero wear, this *movimiento vaquero*, is it about machismo? Sergio, a Toluca-bred Tennessean and ten-year vaquero attendee, shook his head. "No. There are always some gay men who are masculine and some who are feminine," he pointed out matter-of-factly, invoking nonessentialist common knowledge. "If it's not about machismo, is it about mexicanidad?" I asked. He nodded and shrugged, and offered an illustration. "I grew up in Mexico, and I've worn cowboy boots all my life. I wear them for everything: I even play basketball in cowboy boots! And I wear a [tejano] hat all the time."¹⁴ Sergio thus suggested that his *moda vaquera* is not a statement of macho gender but a functional choice and a sign of his Mexican origins, a marker of mexicanidad as he understands it. He was disappointed that this year's tardeada was set in a park. For five years it was held at a working ranch, and he liked it that way. In this instant it dawned on me how a change of venue could transform vaquero clothing from practical, comfortable gear to the sort of conspicuously gendered peacockery evoked by Michael Snyder (2018).[15] Sergio, meanwhile, said he wouldn't come back to Chicago if the organizers repeated this setup.

The reason grew clearer when he abruptly returned to the question of what vaqueros is about. I was not expecting his answer: "It's about the animals." I learned that Sergio has a *ranchito* (small farm) in rural Tennessee. He flashed me a portrait: Sergio and his dappled grey horse, heads side by side on his phone screen. Chatting with my friends, he spoke of his chickens, too. Sergio dislikes U.S. gay bars. And *gringos* cannot stay on the mechanical bull—he cringed—not past six seconds. But he values vaquero events, which allow him to meet and stay connected with queer Latinx friends from around the country. Sergio travels to three vaquero weekends each year and would attend all six if he could. He stressed, however, "I don't really like the competition," referring to the Mr. Vaquero contest. "That's not what vaqueros is about."

TRANS PERFORMANCES: -GENDER AND -NATIONALISM

The U.S. gay vaquero events I attended were celebrations of queer mexicanidad enacted by attendees and contestants of Mexican and, sometimes, other Latin American descent. In Chicago, out of four aspirants to the title of Mr. Encuentro Vaquero 2018, one had migrated from Honduras and one from Ecuador. The evening, however, and the entire vaquero weekend was structured and permeated by performative expressions of Mexican nationalism. Many, if not most, vaquero attendees had crossed national borders in their lifetimes and had descended from people and lands that had been crossed by shifting borders. A vibrant assortment of sounds, symbols, and practices performatively conjured mexicanidad and nationalist history, identity, and pride, even as the same elements served, in this transnationally constituted space, to deconstruct, de-essentialize, and decenter mexicanidad and to dilute nation and national identity—as the following five examples illustrate.

The Las Vegas vaquero weekend opened on Friday night with a performance by a local performer dressed as a mariachi, including a magnificent *sombrero charro.* He danced and lip-synched to a crowd favorite, El Dasa's "Alegre y enamorado" ("Happy and In Love" 2014). From start to finish, by dint of its lyrics, music video, and (for cognoscenti) its musical sounds, this banda track is a nationalist paean to the Mexican land and people. The Las Vegas performance featured a pair of sidekick vaqueros, one male and one *macha,* or butch. Dancing on either side of the mariachi, the two vaqueros waved giant Mexican flags in rhythm throughout El Dasa's second verse, which dedicates the song to "his" Mexican land and people, with shout-outs to over twenty cities and regions from Aguas Calientes to Zacatecas.

In this track, El Dasa delivers a brief declamatory break after verse 1, exuberantly calling for a round of applause for his dancing horse. He then leaps, no less exuberant, into verse 2: "I sing to Michoacan and to the Bajas Californias, to my beautiful Mexico City, to Durango and Sinaloa."[16] Beyond these five cities, states, and towns, El Dasa lists fourteen more—Aguas Calientes, Chiapas, Coahuila, Colima, Guanajuato, Guerrero, Hidalgo, Jalisco, Nayarit, Nuevo León, Oaxaca, Puebla, Tamaulipas, and Zacatecas—and concludes the verse by adding another city and state, "his" country, and "his people": "Veracruz y Chihuahua y a toda mi raza de todo mi México dedico este son". (Veracruz and Chihuahua and to all my people of all my Mexico I dedicate this song.)

The music is impossibly energetic, from El Dasa's gleaming vocals to the big, ebullient sound of his crack thirteen-piece ensemble, like a village wind band on steroids. Clarinets, trumpets, and *charchetas* (alto horns) present the banda treble layer, pushing out a florid arrangement with such precision that even their wide vibrato is in perfect unison. Beneath it churn the trombones, a driving drumbeat, percussion fills, and surging waves of bass line from a blasting sousaphone. In "Alegre y enamorado," all of this goes to create a nationalist spectacle led by a Mexican expat. Like many banda musicians before him, El Dasa traded Mexico for Southern California. The Sonora-born singer has made his home in Los Angeles since age eighteen (ca. 2007).

Another banda star whose life and work moved in transnational directions was the late Jenni Rivera. One of the drag queens in Las Vegas specialized in performing her songs and persona. Known as *La Diva de la Banda*, Rivera was a beloved 'Mexican' musician and actor, and a U.S. national. Born and raised in Long Beach, California, she died in a tragic 2012 plane crash outside Monterrey, Nuevo León. Her continual crossing of multiple borders—in her case, national, cultural, artistic, music-stylistic, and linguistic—is mirrored, often extending into realms of gender and sexuality, in the life stories of the vaquero contestants and attendees I saw and spoke with.

Further blurring of national boundaries arose in my 2017 focus-group discussions with young adult Mexican-American country music lovers in the borderlands of South Texas. When I asked these first-generation-immigrant fans how they felt about patriotic Red, White, and Blue country songs, they replied that the songs inspired in them feelings of pride and gratitude. Their response contradicted the reception of distaste and distancing predicted by some of my non-Mexican, non-country-loving colleagues, who expected that these songs would strike Mexican-American listeners as corny, offensive, or both. Moreover, it became apparent that patriotic country songs inspired such feelings in shades of Red, White, and Blue and, concurrently, Green, White, and Red. The feelings and identifications the songs roused for these millennial borderlands country fans were not U.S. *or* Mexican but U.S. *and* Mexican, engendering an excess of nationalism that strains against conventional definitions of the term.

Further markers of transnationalism and mexicanidad appeared in specifically queer forms that were expressed performatively through gender and sexual styles on the vaquero sites. One instance involved a sexualized style of female masculine self-presentation I will call "butch cleavage." I saw it on a handsome young female-bodied masculine in Las Vegas's BackDoor Lounge. This macha sported close-clipped hair and vaquero dress, from black felt tejano hat to jeans, flashy silver-mirror belt, and pointy boots. Her well-fitting vaquero shirt lay directly against the skin with nothing underneath, and was open from the neck to below the sternum, exposing the inner surfaces of her breasts and accentuating the outside contours pressed against the shirt fabric—which, judging by its appearance and by the fact that the delicate arrangement held, seemed to have been attached by wardrobe tape. I was struck by this look, which ran counter to cross-cultural practices of generations of masculine female queers who have devised various means, including ACE bandages, medical compression binders, and in recent years, surgery, to de-emphasize curves and create a smooth, flat chest.

Talking with friends and family about the Las Vegas macha, I learned that my partner had repeatedly encountered butch cleavage among machas in a Mexico City queer disco in 2014–2015. Thus, it seems likely that this style, too, appeared to cognoscenti in Las Vegas as an element of queer mexicanidad. In any case, its social and civic implications are radical: butch cleavage visibly thwarts essentialist gender binaries, replacing monogendrous consistency with polygendrous abundance. It constructs macha sex appeal by combining multiple markers of masculinity with bodily curves that have long been feminized, and thus performatively gives rise to distinctive forms of gender and sexiness. Butch cleavage does not "leave gender intact" (to recall my earlier phrase). It jams the circuitry of binary gender, whether this is understood in analog or digital terms (to borrow Stryker's language), and of binary object choice, too: Can sexual or gender identities predict the appeal of a good-looking butch whose masculine swagger is replete with swells of boldly arrayed breasts?

A final instance involves gay Mexican immigrant men's sexuality as described in research by Héctor Carrillo and Jorge Fontdevila. The sociologists reveal prior scholarly characterizations of (what I will call) gay sexual mexicanidad as narrow and out of sync with migrant Mexican gay men's actual sex and gender lives and personas in the U.S., and sometimes in Mexico, too. Jesús A. Ramos-Kittrell's phrase "cosmopolitan desires" (in this volume) seems apt to the processes of transnational migration and exchange whereby gay Mexican immigrant men at times exceed the putatively "premodern" and "working-class" passive/active gendered model that researchers have long attributed to them and instead adopt homo/hetero *sexuality* models, in which either partner may top or bottom and sexual positions are not linked to gender roles (Carrillo and Fontdevila 2014, Carrillo 2017). I would emphasize that neither model of queerness is in fact more progressive or retrograde than the other, but the gendered model, associated in the United States and elsewhere with sex-gender life of the folk and of the street, has been viewed from above as subaltern by contrast to the modern sexuality model that was announced by elite European medical and sexological experts circa 1870 (Chauncey 1994, Boyd 2005, Hubbs 2014).

At a basic level, this example shows that gay sexual practices and identities have themselves been classified in relation to essentializing, othering perceptions of mexicanidad. Notably, it also illustrates a long-standing devaluation of 'primitive' trans enactments of gender by contrast to authoritative 'scientific' gender essentialism. In reality, the sexualities of men like those who participated in the Las Vegas and Chicago vaquero gatherings have been shaped by transnational encounters, 'cosmopolitan desires,' and dynamic migrations of ideas, bodies, and practices. These men's sexualities and practices often exceed the binaries imposed on them in bureaucratic imaginings—of sexuality models/gender models, modern/premodern, white/brown, middle class/working class—and thus, they challenge essentialist notions of mexicanidad.

CONCLUSION: QUEER MEXICANIDAD AND DECOLONIALISM

Mexicanidad is central to the multidimensional performance space of the vaqueros, a subculture that brings together people of varied sexualities and genders, and so, is not narrowly gay but broadly queer.[17] Clearly, mexicanidad here is not the exclusive property of those in whom it is supposedly inborn. Rather, like transgender, it, too, is performed 'digitally'—by Angelenos as well as mexicano/a/xs, and by Hondurans and Ecuadorians, among others. The same goes for machismo, accessed here by scene figures of whatever biological sex and of various binary and nonbinary gender expressions. Historically, machismo and the vaquero have been essentialized through repeated performance by male bodies, and mexicanidad in turn has been essentialized through the vaquero figure that has long been a core element in its construction. But in Vaquero World, trans performances of nationalism and gender, mutually mirroring and reinforcing one another, serve to de-essentialize machismo, the vaquero, and mexicanidad.

Spanish colonialism in Latin America ushered in the modern nation-state through the violent bureaucratic establishment of racial and gender classification. But as Silverblatt (2004) has shown, these social classifications, and particularly racial classifications, did not become essentialized in Latin America in the same ways they did in such settler-colonized lands as Canada, Australia, and the United States. To be sure, Latin American subjects both colonial and contemporary have lived categories of race and class as real—but also as malleable by means of education, language, profession, and region (Stepan 1992, de la Cadena 2000, Weismantel 2001, Roberts 2012). And as butch cleavage might suggest, there is evidence that gender, too (contrary to U.S.-based assumptions), is less essentialized in this realm (see, e.g., Lancaster 1997, de la Cadena 2000, Weismantel 2001). For these reasons, Latin Americans may be well poised to decolonize the future, and queer vaquero participants could lead the way. To the extent that their performative engagements with the colonial classificatory apparatus of gender, race, and nation sever or omit the indexical link between particular bodies and the categories to which they 'belong', these must be seen as decolonizing.

Of course, much more has been done to build up the modern nation-state since the colonial establishment of racial and gender classification, difference, and hierarchization. At this late date, we cannot assume that undoing these would suffice to undo colonialism and its ubiquitous, enduring effects. But neither can we underestimate the impact of such undoing when the classifications of race and of gender, now entangled with those of modern sexuality and class, remain fundamental to state authority and affiliated endeavors to concentrate power, property, and security in the hands of the few.

CODA: COUNTRY VAQUEROS

Chicago's Mr. Encuentro Vaquero contest featured one country track, Trace Adkins's "Honky Tonk Badonkadonk." The 2006 No. 2 country hit is a straight-white-bro' paean to female bootyliciousness, voiced in a growling bass-baritone. Unusually, the emcee offered a pre-performance explanation: he announced that the talento competition stipulates use of "regional, cowboy, or country" music, thus validating the Adkins selection. But if Chicago organizers anticipated objections to the English-language country track, there were none. In the transnational space of Vaquero World, audience members clapped along in rhythm to the lip-synching dance performance by Diego T., a Chicagoan of Ecuadorian origins. Country music also surfaced in Las Vegas, albeit tacitly, as the source of "No rompas más mi pobre corazón" by the onda grupera band Caballo Dorado. The 1995 Mexican megahit is a Spanish-language cover of Billy Ray Cyrus's 1992 U.S. country megahit "Achy Breaky Heart."

But even if the music played is rarely country, the queer vaquero scene is nevertheless relevant to my chapter on Mexican-American country music involvements. The two overlap in participants and in aspects of style, perhaps most obviously in visual and clothing style. I will investigate these connections in my pursuit of past and present links between Mexico and Mexican Americans and country music. My research has already suggested that country music is not just a means of belonging for Mexican-American fans but, in very real ways, belongs to them. This is a crucial distinction in the present moment, when President Donald Trump frequently slurs people of Mexican origins, ignoring their contributions, denying their legitimacy, and showing no knowledge of the histories of Mexican-American cultural and territorial belonging in the United States.

It is an important distinction, too, when progressive Mexican-American intellectuals impute assimilation to working-class Mexican-American country fans and, citing the pernicious political context of Trump and his racist and anti-immigrant stances, raise questions of collaboration around these fans' engagements with country music (read as white here, whether or not among Mexican-American fans) versus rap and reggaetón (read here as black).[18] Like the Spanish colonizers, the U.S. music industry at its founding imposed racialized classifications, confecting racially separate R&B ('race') and country ('old-time') categories out of shared working-class music in the Jim Crow South—and these essentialist categories, now naturalized, continue to shape modes of hearing and interpreting popular music nearly a century later (Tosches [1977] 1996, Lewis 2001, Miller 2010, Hubbs 2014).

In *Country Mexicans* I will further explore the valences of music branded in the U.S. racial imaginary as white or black and Mexican Americans' musical and socio-political situation under this binary regime. I will also complicate the racial analysis of Mexican-American musical engagements with intersectional gender analysis—crucially, given that suspicions of racial assimilation and collaboration emerged at some point in my fieldwork when young female Mexican-American country fans drew musical (country, rap, and reggaetón) comparisons in relation to their feelings of embodied vulnerability, which is gendered and all too real in the public space of the dance club and elsewhere throughout U.S. society. Pivotally for all these questions, I will engage Mexican-American fan accounts of country music as neither Anglo-American nor white, but Mexican and brown.

NOTES

1. * I am grateful to Jesús Ramos-Kittrell for his editorial and organizing work and for conceiving and inviting me in on this project, and to all my fellow participants in the September 2018 colloquium Decentering the Nation for their valuable suggestions and dialogue. Thanks to Laura G. Gutiérrez, Cáel Keegan, Curtis Marez, Lorena Munoz, Nancy de los Santos, Barry Shank, Ruby Tapia, and Mary Weismantel for sharing perspectives, sources, and leads. Sergio G. Barrera provided essential assistance in recruiting and conducting 2017 focus groups in South Texas. Matthew Leslie Santana and Kerry P. White provided generous, timely, and pivotal assistance in Chicago and essential research before the event, and this project has been helped enormously by their expert contributions. I am grateful to the University of Michigan Institute for Research on Women and Gender; College of Literature, Science, and the Arts; and Office of Research for funding my research, and to Elizabeth F. S. Roberts for crucial sources and critical insight, food, and love.

2. The first such U.S. event was apparently the 2009 vaquero weekend in Las Vegas. According to my Chicago vaquero interlocutor Sergio C., Zacatecas, Mexico, was the site of the first reunión vaquero ca. 2008, and Las Vegas followed the next year with the establishment of a reunión at Piranha Nightclub. The Las Vegas gathering is held annually over Memorial Day weekend, like Chicago's Mr. Leather contest ever since its 1979 founding (the July vaquero competition I attended at BackDoor Lounge began more recently). Sergio also provided the list of U.S. host cities that I cite. Still earlier precedent for the vaquero weekend can be found in the regular Vaquero Night, running from 1991 to the present, at Club Tempo, a Latinx queer bar in East Los Angeles (Rosen 2017).

3. My use of the term *regional Mexican music* echoes its use in Chicago's Mr. Encuentro Vaquero contest, in comments preceding one contestant's performance to a U.S. country song (see above).

4. I will retain the Spanish word *vaquero* throughout. For purposes of discussing the gay vaquero events I attended, 'cowboy' would be counterproductive. It evokes Anglo-American images and histories (discussed above) distinct from the images and performances I witnessed among gay vaquero contestants, organizers, and attendees.

5. See Kulick (1999) for another study that considers transgender in relation to transnationalism, and also in a musical setting, a discussion of Israeli trans pop singer Dana International.

6. To ascribe narrow, fixed, or localized tastes to a group also carries negative class and status implications. In the sociology of the arts, Richard A. Peterson and his collaborators built an influential theory on the figure they dubbed the *cultural omnivore,* a high-status social agent with expansive tastes and cosmopolitan connoisseurship, by contrast to the *cultural univore,* a low-status cultural consumer of supposedly narrow, parochial tastes (Peterson 1992). See Ollivier (2005) for a cogent critique of anti-working-class bias in the univore concept.

7. I made similar points in an interview with Ludwig Hurtado (2019).

8. Important exceptions include Lewis (1991) and, outside country music studies, Márez (1996).

9. In future work I will consider the ways in which the legendary clothing designer Manuel (Cuevas) has infused postwar country music style and fashion with Mexican styles and symbols, drawing on my December 2018 interview with the costumer for Johnny Cash, Dolly Parton, Porter Wagoner, Dwight Yoakam, and countless other artists.

10. See Helena Simonett (2001) for discussion of regionalism and nationalism in *banda*. Her book's pivotal emphasis on the role of transnationalism in banda is reflected in the subtitle "Mexican Musical Life across Borders." As Roberto, a music student I met in a U.S. Gulf Coast university, attested, banda is deemed a *naco* (tacky proletarian) taste in the middle-class Mexico City world in which he was raised. In Northern Mexico, however, banda crosses class lines, much as country music does in Texas and elsewhere in the U.S. Southwest. On banda's low-class image, see Simonett (2001: 130–31).

11. The staging of a live norteño band Friday night in Las Vegas and multiple live music performances in Chicago departed from standard performance practice in most U.S. LGBTQ clubs, which typically offer recorded music spun by DJs.

12. Onda grupera (group wave) bands use electric guitar, synthesizers, and vocals to make transnational pop music "characterized by a common-denominator style or 'bubblegum sound' rather than a distinctive Mexican regional style or flavor" (Simonett 2011). Caballo Dorado's music featured in one Las Vegas vaquero performance (discussed above). The superstar band has been categorized under grupera but also "Mexican country music." Their 2001 album *Contra el Viento* is often described as a collection of Spanish-translated U.S. country songs, although half the songs are pop or rock, including the title track, Bob Seger's 1980 Heartland rock classic "Against the Wind."

13. One possibility that could account for the differences in our perceptions would be that the other writers were describing vaquero events other than the Mr. Vaquero contest. As I discuss above, I found the contest crowd mixed, but I found non-night club vaquero events like Chicago's Tardeada Vaquera to be predominantly homosocial (see photo above).

14. It seems possible and even probable that the significance of the U.S. events for attendees may be more about mexicanidad than is the case at the events in Mexico. Simonett noted a comparable pattern in certain overt expressions of regionalism and nationalism among 1990s U.S. banda dancers that Mexican aficionados did not exhibit (2001: 63–64).

15. I would also note that rodeo fashion is not unequivocally masculine—not by U.S. standards, at least. Rather, in both U.S. and Mexican stylings, it is an arena of flamboyance in which "Men and women are equally positioned to be peacocks . . . colorful and striking," in the words of Patty Limerick, director of the Center for the American West at University of Colorado, Boulder (Turkewitz 2019).

16. *Yo le canto a Michoacán y a las Bajas Californias, a mi bella Ciudad de México, a Durango y Sinaloa.*

17. I invoke here a long-standing colloquial usage of *queer* as LGBTQ catch-all designation. This differs from the more specific political definition attached to it by

queer theorists in the 1990s, which rendered *queer* a sexual identity positioned in opposition to social norms (e.g., see Halperin 1995: 66).

18. I take seriously these questions, which Mexican-American academics have sometimes raised when I have presented my research publicly. In a fall 2018 conversation, the ethnomusicologist Peter J. García recalled to me his feelings, as a Mexican-American teenager in 1980s New Mexico, of having to choose between 'black' and 'white' music along lines comparable to those described above.

REFERENCES

Anderson, Benedict. *Imagined Communities: Reflections on the Origin and Spread of Nationalism.* revised ed. New York, NY: Verso, [1983] 2006.

Boyd, Nan Alamilla. *Wide-Open Town: A History of Queer San Francisco to 1965.* Berkeley: University of California Press, 2005.

Butler, Judith. "Imitation and Gender Insubordination." In *The Lesbian and Gay Studies Reader*, edited by Henry Abelove, Michèle Aina Barale, and David M. Halperin, 307–320. New York: Routledge, [1991] 1993.

Carrillo, Héctor. *Pathways of Desire: The Sexual Migration of Mexican Gay Men.* Chicago: The University of Chicago Press, 2017.

Carrillo, Héctor, and Jorge Fontdevila. "Border Crossings and Shifting Sexualities among Mexican Gay Immigrant Men: Beyond Monolithic Conceptions." *Sexualities* 17, no. 8 (2014): 919–938.

Chauncey, George. *Gay New York: Gender, Urban Culture, and the Makings of the Gay Male World, 1890–1940.* New York: Basic Books, 1994.

de la Cadena, Marisol. *Indigenous Mestizos: The Politics of Race and Culture in Cuzco, Peru, 1910–1991.* Durham, NC: Duke University Press, 2000.

Delgado, Eduardo. 2015. "Machos, vaqueros y gays." *Telemundo 39* (August 14, 2014). https://www.telemundo51.com/noticias/Machos-vaqueros-y-gays-noche-vaquero-club-musica-banda--video-271280251.html.

Giraud, Melissa. 2006. "Duranguense: Mexico Meets the Midwest." *Weekend Edition Saturday*—National Public Radio (January 14, 2006). https://www.npr.org/templates/story/story.php?storyId=5156569.

Halperin, David M. *Saint Foucault: Towards a Gay Hagiography.* New York: Oxford University Press, 1995.

Hubbs, Nadine. *Rednecks, Queers, and Country Music.* Berkeley: University of California Press, 2014.

Hughes, Charles L. *Country Soul: Making Music and Making Race in the American South.* Chapel Hill: University of North Carolina Press, 2015.

Hurtado, Ludwig. "Country Music Is Also Mexican Music." *The Nation*, January 3, 2019.

Kulick, Don. "Transgender and Language: A Review of the Literature and Suggestions for the Future." *GLQ: A Journal of Lesbian and Gay Studies* 5, no. 4 (1999): 605–622.

Lancaster, Roger N. "Guto's Performance: Notes on the Transvestism of Everyday Life." In *Sex and Sexuality in Latin America: An Interdisciplinary Reader*, edited by Daniel Balderston and Donna Guy, 9–32. New York: New York University Press, 1997.

LeCompte, Mary Lou. "The Hispanic Influence on the History of Rodeo, 1823–1922." *Journal of Sport History* 12, no. 1 (1985): 21–38.

Lewis, George H. "Ghosts, Ragged but Beautiful: Influences of Mexican Music on American Country-Western and Rock 'n' Roll." *Popular Music and Society* 15, no. 4 (1991): 85–103.

Lewis, George H. "The Color of Country: Black Influence and Experience in American Country Music." *Popular Music and Society* 25, no. 3 (2001): 3–4, 107–19.

Márez, Curtis. "Brown: The Politics of Working-Class Chicano Style." *Social Text* 14, no. 3 (1996): 109–132.

Martínez, Katynka Z. "Regional Mexican Music." In *Grove Music Online*. New York, NY: Oxford University Press, 2011.

Miller, Karl Hagstrom. *Segregating Sound: Inventing Folk and Pop Music in the Age of Jim Crow*. Durham, NC: Duke University Press, 2010.

Ollivier, Michèle. "Modes of Openness to Cultural Diversity: Humanist, Populist, Practical, and Indifferent." *Poetics* 36, nos. 2–3 (2008): 120–147.

Paredes, Américo. *"With His Pistol in His Hand": A Border Ballad and Its Hero*. Austin: University of Texas Press, [1958] 1971.

Paredes, Américo. "The Problem of Identity in a Changing Culture: Popular Expressions of Culture Conflict along the Lower Rio Grande Border." In *Folklore and Culture on the Texas-Mexican Border*, edited by Richard Bauman, 19–48. Austin: University of Texas, Center for Mexican American Studies, 1993.

Pecknold, Diane, ed. *Hidden in the Mix: The African American Presence in Country Music*. Durham, NC: Duke University Press, 2013.

Peterson, Richard A. "Understanding Audience Segmentation: From Elite and Mass to Omnivore and Univore." *Poetics* 21, no. 4 (1992): 243–258.

Roberts, Elizabeth F. S. *God's Laboratory: Assisted Reproduction in the Andes*. Berkeley: University of California Press, 2012.

Rosen, Miss. "A Night on the Town with LA's Queer Vaqueros." *Huck* (November 1, 2017). https://www.huckmag.com/art-and-culture/photography-2/lgbt-latinx-cowboy/.

Saldívar, José David. *Trans-Americanity: Subaltern Modernities, Global Coloniality, and the Cultures of Greater Mexico*. Durham, NC: Duke University Press, 2012.

Silverblatt, Irene. *Modern Inquisitions: Peru and the Colonial Origins of the Civilized World*. Durham, NC: Duke University Press, 2004.

Simonett, Helena. *Banda: Mexican Musical Life Across Borders*. Middletown, CT: Wesleyan University Press. History, 2001.

Simonett, Helena. "Onda Grupera [Música Grupera]." In *Grove Music Online*. New York, NY: Oxford University Press, 2011.

Snyder, Michael. "Vaqueros." *VQR: A National Journal of Literature & Discussion* 94, no. 1 (2018).

Stepan, Nancy Leys. *"The Hour of Eugenics": Race, Gender, and Nation in Latin America*. Ithaca, NY: Cornell University Press, 1992.

Stryker, Susan. *Transgender History: The Roots of Today's Revolution*. 2nd ed. New York: Seal Press, 2017.

Tosches, Nick. *Country: The Twisted Roots of Rock 'N' Roll*. New York: Da Capo, [1977] 1996.

Turkewitz, Julie. "Where the Wild West Wears Its Heritage." *The New York Times*, February 5, 2019.

Weismantel, Mary. *Cholas and Pishtacos: Stories of Race and Sex in the Andes*. Chicago: University of Chicago Press, 2001.

Chapter 5

Soy gallo de Sinaloa jugado en varios palenques

Production and Consumption of Narco-music in a Transnational World

César Burgos Dávila and Helena Simonett[1]

Shouting in excitement, the audience moved toward the bandstand to take pictures and videos of Ariel Camacho and Los Plebes del Rancho entering the stage.[2] Beams of light and heavy smoke blurred the band's appearance which was accompanied by fragments of its popular narcocorridos and ballads—"El karma" (Karma), "La fuga del dorian" (Dorian's Escape), "Toro encartado" (Imprisoned Bull), "Los talibanes del prieto" (Prieto's Talibans), "Entre pláticas y dudas" (Between Talks and Doubts), "El señor de los cielos" (The Lord of the Skies), "Te metiste" (You Got In), "Hablemos" (Let's Talk), "Rey de corazones" (King of Hearts)—introducing Ariel Camacho and Los Plebes del Rancho as follows:

> It's music from the Sierra. And this genre that was, is, and will always be of and for the people has a new leader . . . with his youth, talent and guts he has accomplished by this day to become the new lord and master of the corrido . . . His skill and musical power are as high as the pines . . . Country [*peasant*] music has a new leader . . . Mexico and the United States stand at attention for the 'King of Hearts' [reference to one of his songs]: Ariel Camacho. And he does not come alone, he comes well escorted by Los Plebes del Rancho [The Fellows from the Ranch] . . . Take good note, the instruction is very simple: Let's everyone dance, drink and sing with full Sinaloan force. Here he is: Ariel Camacho. . .[3]

Then Ariel Camacho addressed the audience: "Good evening. We'll play some songs for you . . . Everybody, let's drink and dance . . . Go Culiacán, Sinaloa, and Sunnyvale Palladium!"—the latter a nightclub in the San Francisco Bay Area where the band was performing that night. Cheerfully and energetically they opened their gig with "El sinaloense" (The Sinaloan), a song that celebrates the boisterous and upbeat Sinaloan character.[4] The dance floor began to fill up with young couples, and the festive mood continued throughout the night as the young people were drinking, shouting emotionally, and singing along to the songs and narcocorridos the band performed.

Reflecting the development of drug trafficking and drug-related violent crime, the content of the narcocorridos is ever changing (Burgos 2013, 158–60). The transnational musical connection between California and Sinaloa, based on drug trafficking, specifically, has been a long-standing one, and has allowed for the articulation of both social realities and cultural resignifications in relation to changes in narcocorridos. This chapter, thus, examines how transnational music production, circulation, and listening practices among *mexicanos* in California have changed since Chalino Sánchez, the now legendary Sinaloan narco-singer, was brutally murdered in 1992 for singing the 'wrong' corridos (Simonett 1998). We are particularly interested in how narco-music is influenced by the different settings in which it is created, distributed, evaluated, and consumed.

During Simonett's ethnographic fieldwork in the 1990s, "Nuevo Los Ángeles" or "Nuevo L.A.," as the predominantly Mexican and Latino area that in earlier decades comprised the industrial heartland had been dubbed, was the hub of the production of this emerging musical genre (Acuña 1996, 3; Simonett 2001a, 226–54). A number of small, independent record labels began to record narcocorridos that were commissioned and performed at local nightclubs frequented by Mexican immigrants. Cassettes and compact discs with this music were distributed locally by small stores or at carwashes and swap meets. Carried by the *technobanda* craze in California, narco-music eventually seeped into Spanish-language radio broadcasting and reached a wider audience. Although music related to drug trafficking and traffickers was stigmatized as a subcultural expression, relevant to a minor population only, compositions about drug trafficking quickly kindled an interest among young second- and third-generation Mexicans who felt empowered by this 'very Mexican' music they could call their own. The new genre became a symbol of pride in one's Mexican roots and served for the formation of cultural self-imaginings during a time when the American political environment that had grown increasingly hostile towards anyone of Mexican descent (Simonett 2001b).

At the dawn of the new millennium, the so-called "Regional Mexican" music had become the most popular Latin music genre in the United States in terms of radio promotions and sales (Cobo 2001, 2005). This was partly due to the popularity of the *duranguense* bands that originated in Chicago in the early 2000s (Simonett 2012), and partly to a 'rejuvenated' style of narco-music produced and promoted by the Sinaloan immigrant siblings Omar and Adolfo Valenzuela—better known as Los Cuates Valenzuela (the Valenzuela twins)—owners of Los Angeles-based Twiins Enterprise. Their target audience not only included recently arrived Mexicans, but young first- and second-generation Mexican Americans as well—a market largely ignored by mainstream media producers (Kun 2006). It was, therefore, more lucrative to produce narco-music in California than in Mexico: Twiins speculated that once popular in the United States, the music would "cross back into the market in Mexico" (Adolfo Valenzuela quoted in Kun 2006). Given that record labels dedicated to narco-music are located in Los Angeles, there is a constant musical exchange between California and Sinaloa, the reason why they are considered today the main sites of production, diffusion, and consumption of the genre.

Unlike in the early 1990s, today's bands are no longer confined to small, local audiences that attend their live performances; their music is being consumed by many millions of virtual listeners. Ariel Camacho y Los Plebes del Rancho shall serve as an example to illustrate this phenomenon: by October 2016 the official video of "Hablemos" (posted on YouTube in March 2014) generated 220 million views, and two years later the number doubled. There are other YouTube postings of the same video that score in the millions as well. Another of Camacho's songs, "Te metiste" (posted by a fan with audio only) has received over one hundred million clicks in one year, and three years later the number increased to 250 million. Other narco-songs by this particular band, though less popular, still score in the millions. For example, "El karma" (posted by the original video producer in March 2014) was re-produced by DEL Records in East Los Angeles as the band's U.S. debut album. Since then, the song has generated over 77 million views.[5] Moreover, the music video of "El señor de los cielos" (The Lord of the Skies, as Sinaloan drug lord Amado Carrillo Fuentes was known), posted by DEL Records in January 2015, had generated 141 million views by the time this chapter was written. Furthermore, "El negociante" (The Dealer), received 380 million clicks in less than a year. In addition to these YouTube streamings, the songs have been digitally downloaded and given significant airplay, thus multiplying their consumption. Over the last years, YouTube and similar social media networks have established new practices of use and cultural consumption, as well as new modes of music reception, production, circulation, and socialization.[6]

While we cannot know who the millions of virtual consumers of this music are, why they listen to this music or what it means to them, we believe that the massive consumption of narco-music sheds light on the kind of mobile identities that emerge under the influence of transnational marketing and consumption practices. As such, narco-music is a postmodern expression *par excellence*, an aesthetic production that has become integrated into commodity production outside the nation-state's control. This latest stage of capitalism, according to Fredric Jameson (1991), is characterized, among other things, by the international division of labor, the explosion of financial markets and communication media across national borders.

Ultimately, the existence of a thriving transnational narco-music culture—and the way it has redressed notions of 'Mexican music'—points to the culturally decentered position of the nation-state in globalization. The phenomenon, however, also interrogates the complicity between state representatives, the media, and cultural brokers, as well as the ambiguity of their positions in the articulation of narco-music culture. The narco-music genre allows us to critically examine this process from three angles. Number one is narco-music's role in the production of meaning and in the shaping of communities and socio-musical practices. Number two refers to the joint effect of media and migration on the work of imagination as a constitutive feature of modern subjectivity. And number three points to the messy articulation of transnationally-produced values, ideologies, and aesthetics.

SOY GALLO DE SINALOA JUGADO EN VARIOS PALENQUES

Born in 1960, Chalino Sánchez grew up in a large family in Sanalona, a village thirty kilometers east of Culiacán. At the age of eighteen, he migrated to California like many other poor Mexicans hoping to find a better future in the North. Chalino's dream of becoming a professional singer eventually came true in Los Angeles, his second home.[7] Chalino began to compose corridos on commission and later, from 1989 on, recorded them on cassettes for his clients with local *norteño* groups and *bandas*. He produced some of his best songs with Los Amables del Norte and Banda Flor del Campo, both bands based in the Los Angeles area. Chalino's success was partly due to his ability to fabricate his own 'tough guy' image, drawing from Sinaloan folklore, the bandit-hero myth, and the corrido tradition. Immortalized with and through his songs, Chalino's persona embodied the character of a Mexican drug-trafficking subculture transpiring in Mexico and the United States (see Figure 5.1).

After his violent death, Chalino Sanchéz became a key figure in the musical landscape of Mexican Los Angeles. Although his corridos did not receive any airplay on radio at the time, he prompted a cultural movement known as *el chalinazo*: dozens of youngsters in the Los Angeles area emerged imitating his voice, his singing style, and his particular way of dressing in *ranchero* (cowboy) style—a style that journalist Sam Quinones (1998) coined as 'narcotraficante chic.'[8]

Figure 5.1. Screen shot of Chalino Sánchez from the music video "A ti mi grandota."

"El gallo de Sinaloa" (The Rooster from Sinaloa) was one of Chalino's most popular corridos. In the first line of the song, the singer refers to himself as a "rooster that has played many cockfighting rings." The rooster is a metaphor for the aggressive fighter with a strongly pronounced sexual potency, commonly used by rural people to boast about one's proficiency and power (in this song, enforced with potent weapons) and to intimidate potential enemies such as traitors and U.S. drug enforcement agents. Chalino's posthumous rise in fame brought along a 'Sinaloaization' of Mexican cultural expressions in California.[9] As Quinones suggested:

> If tourists thought mariachi synonymous with Mexico, in L.A. the Mexican working class were really listening to the music of Sinaloa: the norteño *conjunto* and the banda, a tuba-anchored marching band playing dance music. And if being Sinaloan—with its drug undertones—was suddenly cool, even more so was to be from the Sinaloan rancho (2001, 24).[10]

During the two decades since Quinones's observation, the Sinaloaization of Mexican cultural practices has grown stronger. It is customary to "go cowboy style" (*ir vaquero*) and "have a look as if from the ranch" (*parecer de rancho*) when attending concerts or dances.[11] It seems that the dress codes of the *quebradita* and the *pasito duranguense* eras (popular dance crazes in the United States in the 1990s and 2000s, respectively) had been appropriated by yet another generation of music-and-dance practitioners who reclaim and renovate their own traditions away from their, or their parents', places of origin (Simonett 2008). El Komander's 2014 hit song boosts the vaquero pride: "Yes sir, I'm from the ranch; I'm on boots and on a horse."[12] After signing with Twiins Music Group, Los Angeles, the Sinaloan-born *corridista* Alfredo Ríos (aka El Komander) quickly became the main representative of the controversial "altered movement" (*movimiento alterado*), narcocorridos of extremely aggressive, violent content (Miserachi 2016).[13] Accompanied by a (combined) norteño-banda group that plays in an accelerated tempo, typical for this new genre, the singer alludes to the disreputable Sinaloa known from the news while celebrating its rural life style.[14]

In Regional Mexican music productions, the idea of a bucolic (*campirano*) Mexico, a country where men make and live by their own laws, is prevalent both aurally and visually. Similarly, the corrido genre itself insists on a rootedness in the Mexican northern borderlands of an anarchistic time: deeply embedded in rural society, it evolved as a mestizo cultural form in the context of border conflicts with the United States and later became associated with the rise of Mexico's national consciousness during the early decades of the twentieth century (see Chávez in this volume).[15] In their introduction to *Music, National Identity and the Politics of Location*, Ian Biddle and Vanessa Knights remind us to not be surprised "to find that new forms of nationalism continue to emerge and the force of the nation as a cultural trope continues to adapt to new political and material conditions." Globalization has not erased nationalist tropes; rather, "new forms of nationhood and the continued operative force of 'older' imaginations of nation" are both dynamic agencies in contemporary musical identity (Biddle and Knights 2007, 11).

While Mexican nationalist tropes still influence contemporary music production, the identification with the northern part of the country, and in particular the Sinaloan rancho, seems to be the way to commercial success.[16] According to corrido scholar Juan Carlos Ramírez-Pimienta (2011, 188), the periphery has become the new center: in the world of the corrido, to be or appear to be from the *sierra*, specifically the Sinaloan Sierra, carries much symbolic capital.[17] Allusions to the sierra—the refuge of the persecuted, the revolutionary fighters, *guerrilleros*, and the *narcos* alike—are omnipresent in band names, song lyrics, video images, logos, and clothing.

The generation of singers following in Chalino's footsteps took a pass on his handmade *huarache* sandals, typical footwear in Mexican countryside farming communities. Instead they transformed themselves into Wrangler- and boots-wearing "badasses" (*perrones*), dedicated to a tougher style of narco-music, the so-called *música perrona* (badass music).[18] In the early 2000s, Lupillo Rivera broke with the cowboy image and, as an elegantly and expensively dressed cigar-smoking *pelón* (bald-headed man), set a new fashion that sparked a new generation of bilingual, bicultural Los Angeles-Mexican artists. Today's artists of the altered movement feel equally comfortable in a T-shirt and wearing a baseball cap or in a stylish suit with a tejano cowboy hat.

In 2011, inspired by the popular corrido, "El muchacho de la barba" (The Bearded Youngster) by Código FN and Enigma Norteño, a young man by the name of Edgar Ramírez created a logo off a selfie, showing the silhouette of a man's face with full beard.[19] He then sold baseball hats and T-shirts with the imprinted logo via social media and equipped musicians who helped to promote the new Barba Norteña label. On the company website, the young entrepreneur advertised Barba Norteña as a 'life style' expressed in this unpretentious logo.[20] "The idea was to start a brand that focused on stuff I could relate to. I've always loved certain brands here and there, but I never found anything I could really relate to," Ramírez recalled (quoted in Lara 2015). The label, with its affirmation of *lo norteño* (anything northern), became an instant success. Although not exceedingly expensive, the Barba Norteña brand is intended for urbanites that cultivate their relationship with Mexico's rural north through music. Its everyday products, such as hats, shirts and other accessories, feature imprinted images from the world of norteño music. For example, the motif of a rooster printed on a T-shirt with the caption "played in many cockfighting rings" (*jugado en varios palenques*), refers to Chalino's corrido, "El gallo de Sinaloa." The silhouette of a pistol with the caption "so, you said you wouldn't fire" (*no que no tronabas*) alludes to the popular phrase that the norteño comedian-actor Lalo González "El Piporro" popularized: "so, you said you wouldn't fire, little pistol?" (*¿No que no tronabas, pistolita?*)[21]

"As design and fashion become quasi-independent forces closely connected to the movements of capital and the rapid growth of specialized technologies for manufacture, the world of commodities undergoes a galactic expansion," Appadurai contends (2013, 256). The global production and distribution of consumer goods, however, obscures the fact that even commercial geographies are historically produced. "It is historical agents, institutions, actors and powers that make the geography" (66). The circulation and consumption of Barba Norteña commodities point to a specific kind of identity politics, one in which consumption habits, situated in social forms of everyday life of mexicanos in California, produce a transnationally articulated locality. Rather than valuing Mexico as simply "a repository of cultural nostalgia," it becomes a dynamic part of "the geopolitical present" (Spivak 1999, 402).

MEXICO AND 'EL OTRO MÉXICO'

Since the War on Drugs was unleashed in 2006, tens of thousands of people have become victims of the bloody turf wars between drug cartels and between the cartels and the army. Homicide rates in the embattled border city of Ciudad Juárez reached unprecedented heights between 2008 and 2012. Banda and norteño music became the soundtrack to this horrendous violence: a local official of Ciudad Juárez said that gunmen would announce executions on police radio frequencies via narcocorridos (Schwarz 2011). In 2013, photojournalist Shaul Schwarz (2013) documented this gruesome reality in his film *Narco Cultura* with footage from the front lines.[22] The condition of violence—massacres, beheadings, kidnappings, and extortions—that many Mexicans experience in everyday life has become material for entertainment. Schwarz shows how the growing music industry based in Los Angeles plays with these coexisting realities. "If there wasn't so much violence in Mexico, we wouldn't have such badass corridos," Twiins Enterprises cofounder Adolfo Valenzuela reasons (featured in Schwarz 2013). Oscar López, director of a low-budget Mexican action movie business specializing in the narco genre, believes that people who have "never been affected by this drug war are on the side of the narcos—or they want to be. That's why narco culture has grown so much; because these guys see narcos as modern-day Robin Hoods. They go against the government, against the system" (featured in Schwarz 2013).

This connection with the shady underworld of drug traffickers increased the visibility and consumption of narco-music produced by small-scale record labels in metropolitan Los Angeles. Spanish-language radio stations across the United States now broadcast narco-music, and movies inspired by narcocorridos, previously sold in Mexican neighborhood grocery stores, are now found in major chain stores such as Walmart and Target. Whilst in Mexico, narco-music has been banned from the public for decades, and new governmental regulations continue to do so today, as we will address in more detail below.

Territorialism remains an important force in today's politics as rising nationalism, border protectionism, and isolationism worldwide show (Martell 2007, 173). Although the global flow of people and goods may deceive us into thinking that territorial boundaries no longer serve as markers of identity in today's world, identities that are created and performed in the context of transnational economies do not negate borders, rather they emphasize their fluidity. Mexican migrants residing in "the other Mexico" (*el otro México*, as band Los Tigres del Norte named the territory north of the border in a song by this very title in 1986), reshape and rearticulate their Mexicanness based on perceived Mexican identities and cultural practices. Referring to the current popularity of narco-music, a member of a local Californian norteño group problematizes what he sees as a cultural misconstruction as follows:

> There is a lot of liberty of expression here in the U.S. But the problem is that many youths lack life experience, maturity; they don't know how to listen to a corrido in a healthy way. They hear something and want to do it as well . . . they too want to wear things they can't afford, to live a lifestyle that's not theirs: and yet, through the corridos they can live it, they can do it.[23]

Other musicians agree: they have been commissioned to compose narcocorridos for everyday men who want to experience the fame of the corrido heroes, "the guys that are making the money and are flashing around the neighborhood; because there is no other way to get out of the neighborhood."[24] It is a vanity game, commented documentary filmmaker Schwarz. "I can totally understand why teenagers valorize narcos, and it's actually simple. At the end of the day, our policy has let the bad guys win for such a long time and it's never been worse . . . at the end of the day these kids see our failed policies as evidence of what success looks like" (quoted in Viscarrondo 2013).

The current popularity of the corrido relates to how the music industry has produced a music that appeals to an audience sensitive to the fluidity of social, regional, national, and gender boundaries that they experience. Hector Amaya believes that:

> The claims of Mexicanity and the way [narco-]performers . . . have embodied the narco-brand are thus not only commercial tactics. They are also the means by which Mexican-American urban youths, who are the typical consumers of narcocorridos, reconfigure their marginalization through the tactical deployment of counterhegemonic fantasies that narcocorridos activate (2014, 226).

The widespread popularity of narcocorridos in the U.S. has no single cause, as the abovementioned opinions suggest. Yet, economic deprivation, social exclusion, and the ongoing pervasive othering of people of Mexican heritage may indeed affect individuals' life stance. An analysis of commissioned corridos of the 1990s suggests that social acceptance was of prime importance to drug traffickers and wannabes alike. According to Quinones, by the end of the 1990s, the corrido had "adapted to the new reality of Mexicans having to live and work away from Mexico" (2001, 27). A commissioned corrido was considered tangible proof of economic success—one that placed the owner close to Mexico's drug traffickers who, by that time, had acquired significant social status and an important cultural position in the Mexican social imagination: they had become the new patrons of this regional music style (Simonett 2001a, 201–25).

In a recent article on "The Ballad of Narcomexico," folklorist and corrido scholar John McDowell somewhat disdainfully states: "Examining the corridos on YouTube, one might imagine that the corrido tradition has become captive of drug cartels or the production studios, that the corrido is now and will forever be the narcocorrido" (2012, 268). Yet, ethnographic evidence draws a more nuanced picture of narco-musical production and consumption than that provided by internet consultation and secondhand journalistic sources alone. Having witnessed local music productions and talked to musicians, composers, fans and music producers alike, we believe that there are no clear-cut answers to the messy articulation of transnationally produced values, ideologies, and aesthetics related to the narcocorrido, let alone the corrido genre as a whole.

Openly celebrated commemorative practices that unite and fuse folklore with delinquency and violence such as the ones of the Sinaloan Robin Hood-like outlaw Malverde, have coerced the idea of the *valiente*, the brave man who raised his arms against the established social order and the representatives of the ruling class (Córdova 1993, 39). Narcos are often compared to the bandit-hero Robin Hood, but no one we have met who has experienced narco-terror upholds such a glamorized view. Rather, social bandits "are heroes not in spite of the fear and horror their actions inspire, but in some ways because of them," Eric Hobsbawm stated in his classic book on bandits in pre-capitalist societies. "They are not so much men who right wrongs, but avengers, and exerters of power; their appeal is not that of the agents of justice, but of men who prove that even the poor and weak can be terrible" (1969, 50).

The drug trafficker of today is, as Marc Edberg pointed out, "a commodified persona that sells—a fact not lost on the media industry that markets CDs, ringtones, and movies; or among narcotraffickers themselves, who commission narcocorridos as advertisements to enshrine their reputation in the public memory" (2011, 68). Outlaws have long been mystified in popular culture: their sensational stories have undeniable commercial appeal. Al Capone's deeds are exploited in numerous action movies and Colombian kingpin Pablo Escobar's life has become an American crime web television series (*Narcos*) so popular that Netflix recently announced a fourth season, to premier in November 2018.

Appadurai described cultural commodities disseminated by the media as "image-centered and narrative-based accounts of strips of reality" (1990, 9). According to prolific corrido songsmiths, such as Enrique Franco and

Teodoro Bello, "all the stories are entirely truthful" (Guardado 1996), they are "based on what the press, the radio, and the television say" (Cruz 2000). El Komander follows in their footsteps claiming to be 'a reporter of reality.' Corridos indeed once were the 'history books' of the illiterate, providing an intriguing folk counterpoint to Mexico's 'official' history. But rather than functioning as a kind of folk newspaper—as commonly believed—corridos depended on a prior transmission of news: their goal was to interpret, celebrate, and ultimately dignify events already thoroughly familiar to the corrido audience or community (McDowell 1981, 47). Similarly, narcocorridos—if not simply fictitious—usually retell what has already been disseminated by the news media. Amanda Morrison finds *corridistas*'s claims to truthfulness interesting, "considering the fact that the 'objective' journalism offered by the mainstream news media . . . walks a similarly fine line between spectacle and reality" (Morrison 2008, 393).

Los Angeles-born Edgar Quintero, lead singer of the narco-band BuKnas de Culiacán featured in Schwarz's documentary (2013), sings about people and events he knows and learns about mainly from the internet. For him and his fans, the appeal of narco-music is based on a simulacrum that has little to do with the violent reality of the drug war as it is experienced daily by thousands of people south of the border. The twenty-two-year-old lead singer of the San Jose-based group Nueva Mentalidad wishes for nothing more than to be commissioned by a famous narco. He told Burgos that he has always dreamed of playing for the head of the Sinaloa cartel, "El Chapo" Guzmán: "Like Enigma Norteño and the others in Culiacán who know and live with these guys."[25] Similarly, Quintero yearns to cross the border and see the 'real Mexico.' For Quintero, the real Mexico is the state of Sinaloa, home to the world's "deadliest drug cartel" (quoted in McAllester 2013). "If you're born here [in the U.S.], you don't have the same vocabulary as someone from Mexico" (Quintero featured in Schwarz 2013). Aspiring narco-musicians, especially those born and raised in *el otro* México, ache for street credibility such as personal contact to someone influential in the drug business.

On the other hand, many musicians lament their dependency on clients that make their money illegally. Not only has their work environment become exceedingly violent—El Komander says that there are fights in eight out of ten shows he does—but the quality of the music has suffered as well. "Sinaloa has produced many great artists, several wonderful bandas, with excellent, excellent musical skills," a member of Nueva Mentalidad says, "but if they play 'beautiful music' they go out of business."[26] Musicians are forced to play the "ugly and brave" (*feo y bravo*) repertory that is in vogue in order to survive economically. He hopes that the current violent corridos are just a passing fad like the ones that came before:

> When Los Razos and Los Originales [de San Juan] came out, everyone was from Michoacán. Later, when [*pasito*] *duranguense* became fashionable, everyone was from Durango. *Tribal* came out and everyone was *tribalero*. Everyone follows the fashion. When the *corrido alterado* came out, everyone became a bloodthirsty bully and *buchón*, a Sinaloan drug cartel hit-man wannabe.[27]

Narcocorrido's decline, though, had long been prognosticated. But its recent popularity on the internet has revitalized the genre tremendously, and this has caused some critics to say that "the narcocorrido style—in song, dress, and lifestyle—forms an expressive cluster within which the interests of the cartels and the efforts of the promoters coincide in producing a climate favorable to the distinct YouTube narcocorrido videos" (McDowell 2012, 259).

One should keep in mind, however, that the altered movement was launched during the bloodiest time in Mexico's history since the revolution a century ago. In 2006, President Felipe Calderón declared war on drugs just a few days after entering office with the goal to recover the spaces occupied by the drug cartels and to restore security (Astorga 2015). Yet, the military intervention had devastating consequences for the Mexican people: drug-trafficking violence grew to unprecedented levels as a result of gruesome fights between drug cartels caused by the elimination of a number of key cartel leaders (Chabat 2010). Calderón's militarization of Mexico left the country with an estimated death toll of 120,000 and tens of thousands of people disappeared.[28]

Mexico's grisly reality was reflected in the narcocorridos of the young composers and performers. Stories about the victories and defeats of the capos, the alliances and retaliations of the drug cartels, the deals with politicians, corruption, crimes, extortions, massacres, beheadings, and disappearances were also the material of norteño and banda music (Burgos 2013, 175). Explicit and violent song lyrics generate huge economic profits, which led BMI (Broadcast Music, Inc.) to recognize the Valenzuela twins as leading producers of Mexican regional music.[29] Moreover, El Komander, one of Twiins's strongest-going altered movement acts, won a Billboard Latin Music Awards in 2016 in the category of "Regional Mexican Song Artist of the Year, Solo" (McIntyre 2016).[30] Furthermore, narco-singer Gerardo Ortiz received an award for the best "Regional Mexican Album of the Year," despite protests against a controversial music video for which he was arrested by the Federal Police in Mexico a few months later, and charged with "criminal exaltation" (Cobo 2016b). By that time the song had hit the Top 10 of Billboard's Hot Latin Songs chart. Thus, the glorification of violence in music videos eventually turned out to be positive for Ortiz's career. Leila Cobo, Billboard's Executive Director of Content and Programming for Latin Music, summarized the intricacy of the Ortiz case: "What started as a genuinely productive look at hard-core music videos that indeed exalt criminal activities has backfired, with many in the media, including serious columnists, accusing the Mexican government of overzealousness (2016a)."

By celebrating artists' (and by extension their own) economic success, the music industries have consistently downplayed their moral complicity in producing and disseminating artistic representations of various forms of violence—a violence that south of the border has caused thousands of deaths and that continues to take an enormous toll on society.

CENSORSHIP AND THE STATE'S COMPLICITY

In the late 1980s, the San Jose, CA-based norteño band Los Tigres del Norte became a leading voice for the plight of Mexican immigrants with socially conscious songs such as "La jaula de oro" (1986), a story about life in "the gilded cage," a metaphor for the experience of undocumented immigrants living in the United States. Before that, the band launched its breathtaking career with the hit songs "Contrabando y traición" (Contraband and Betrayal, 1971), a tale starring drug trafficking couple Emilio Varela and Camelia La Tejana; and "La banda del carro rojo" (The Gang of the Red Car, 1973), a story about the fate of a gang of cocaine smugglers. Although norteño groups experienced governmental suppression of their musical activities as early as the 1970s, censorship of corridos telling stories about drug smuggling was not a hot topic until bands began to record corridos that pointed to the involvement of high officials in the illegal business. In 1989 Los Tigres del Norte released an entire album with songs about drug trafficking with the title *Corridos prohibidos* (Forbidden Corridos), ridiculing the Mexican government's attempts to repress its music.

This marketing strategy helped push norteño music to the top of Mexican regional music and shaped a new generation of corrido performers (Simonett 2001b, 320). Los Tigres del Norte, admired by millions of Mexicans and Mexican Americans as "the idols of the people" (*los ídolos del pueblo*), is the most influential norteño group and, after more than three decades of activity, still one of the top-selling groups in the U.S. Latino market. The band's success and popularity has enabled its members to exercise harsh criticism against the Mexican government and official authorities, accusing both of corruption and blaming them for the failure to win the War on Drugs.[31]

In 1995 Los Tigres del Norte launched a song that portrayed (former) President Carlos Salinas de Gortari and his brother Raúl as heads of the Sinaloa drug cartel. Simonett, then doing fieldwork in Sinaloa, noticed that soon everyone in the streets could sing along the catchy melody and knew the words by heart: "Carlos and Raúl were the owners of a circus; Carlos was the tamer, the younger brother, Raúl the coordinator, hungry to get rich."[32] In the second verse, the word 'circus' alluded to 'cartel,' and suggested that the Salinas brothers were deeply entangled in Mexico's drug business. "El circo" (The Circus, written by Jesse Armenta) dominated Sinaloa's airwaves much to the dismay of the PRI (Institutional Revolutionary Party), the political party that had held power in Mexico since its inception in 1929, but had lost many of its voters after the country's economy spiraled downward. Much was at stake and such a direct accusation against prominent members of the PRI elite was politically damaging.

Carlos Salinas began office in 1988 after controversial elections. An economist and alumni of Harvard University, Salinas continued the PRI's neoliberal policy: both the banking system and the national phone company were privatized. He also negotiated the North American Free Trade Agreement (NAFTA) between Mexico, the United States, and Canada in 1994. Nonetheless, scandalous accusations offset his political accomplishments. By the end of his six-year term in office, Mexico slipped into a deep economic crisis (see the introduction to this volume). The assassination of the two most visible and powerful official heads of the PRI in the election year of 1994—the presidential candidate Luis Donaldo Colosio and the secretary-general José Francisco Ruíz Massieu, once married to Adriana Salinas, sister of Carlos and Raúl—tinted the president's political reputation. The following year, Raúl Salinas was arrested (and eventually convicted) for his involvement in Ruíz Massieu's assassination, and the former president went into self-imposed exile twelve days after his brother's arrest (Bruce 2005).[33] Carlos Salinas de Gortari also became the target of a drug-money laundering investigation involving authorities in at least ten countries. (In Switzerland, for example, the attorney general seized US$114 million deposited by Salinas in numbered Swiss bank accounts under false names, see Ward and Moore 1999.)

Until 1994, high-level corruption was rarely linked to drug trafficking and minor drug-fighting activities dismissed potential critiques of the government (Patenostro 1995, 46). While President Salinas joined U.S. President George H. W. Bush in his militarized war on drugs, the arrest of Mexico's most powerful kingpin, Miguel Ángel Félix Gallardo, was read as a success of the Salinas administration against organized crime. Sinaloan sociologist Luis Astorga, however, called it an "act of symbolic power" (1995, 76–77). It was no secret that Félix Gallardo's drug trafficking network had been protected by many high-level government officials within the PRI, and that he was a house guest of Sinaloa's then governor Antonio Toledo Corro (Grayson 2013, 27).

In their music, Los Tigres del Norte criticized the Salinas administration for all of this havoc. Their song "El circo" suggests that Carlos Salinas 'tamed' the cartels to empower himself, thus offering a counter discourse to the discourse of power. The song closes with the rather pessimistic assertion that similar 'circuses' will follow ("until a new circus arrives / and then the same trick again).[34] Indeed, the allusion to the *avionazo*—the arrest of Sinaloan kingpin Héctor Luis Palma Salazar in 1995 after a crash landing of his jet—indicates that despite such political power acts, the cartels remain a Mexican reality.

Fast forward: In May 2011, Los Tigres del Norte dined at the home of Sinaloa's governor Mario López Valdez (elected for the period of 2011–2016).[35] The governor had just passed a new decree that prohibited the dissemination of narcocorridos in public spaces as part of a new strategy to combat violence, and he was in dire need of public support for his controversial law (Cabrera and Morales 2011; Notimex 2011). López Valdez, a populist politician with the demeanor of a television actor, grandly staged himself with the widely popular Los Tigres del Norte, pledging to help him improve Sinaloa's reputation—the very same band that is, at least partially, responsible for the wide acceptance of narcocorridos.

Despite their commercial exploitation of the narco theme, such as the Grammy-nominated corrido "Jefe de jefes" (Boss of Bosses, 1997—an allusion to the almighty Sinaloan cartel boss Félix Gallardo), Los Tigres see themselves as true-to-life storytellers[36] rather than *narcocorridistas* (narco-balladeers). But so does El Komander, the best-known representative of the kind of violent corridos the Sinaloan governor tried to ban. "Does being a corrido singer or making this kind of music cause violence? Of course not!" El Komander opinionates (featured in Schwarz 2013). Two of the major "badass music" (*música perrona*) advocates, Long Beach natives Jenni and Lupillo Rivera, were similarly unconcerned about possible negative effects of their 'bad stuff' on young audiences. On the contrary, Jenni believed that "it gives [the listeners] an adrenaline rush, they get hyped up and it makes them happy. It makes them feel tough and it makes them feel, like, really, really Mexican. And I think we all like to feel like that" (Jenni Rivera quoted in Wald 2002, 144).

While the music's sonic and verbal messages may provide young listeners with some sense of empowerment, narcocorrido opponents on both sides of the border are concerned about this sort of nationalist display: they feel that the narco attitude further contributes to an already widespread stereotypical image of the Mexican as a criminal. Indeed, narcocorridos' wide acceptance among a public not directly involved in drug trafficking had alerted the Mexican authorities in the 1980s already. Sinaloa was one of the first states to put partial censorship policies for the protection of children and adolescents in place. In light of an ever-growing production and accessibility of music and music videos with exacerbated violent content, several states have issued new decrees to curb the problems of the drug war on a cultural level (Burgos 2012, 32–33).

Governor López Valdez's recent strike against narco-music, however, has taken the debate to another level: he claims that banning the music from public life prevents crimes, increases public security, and encourages positive attitudes among youths. He understands his cultural policies as a national strategy to combat drug trafficking. Therefore, cultural policy has become an instrument to censor cultural manifestations associated with drug trafficking activities, which could potentially tarnish the state's image (Burgos 2016, 3-4). Such policies have stigmatized, persecuted, and labeled regional musicians as promoters of drug culture. Thus, while the country's powerful drug trafficking organizations are spreading violence and fear and have infiltrated federal and local institutions economically and politically, narcocorridos are portrayed as the real "enemy of the state" (Valenzuela et al. 2017, 72–73).

On the other hand, narcocorridos are not simply people's chronicles that transgress, desecrate, or question the official view, as José Manuel Valenzuela (2002) suggests in his book on the genre. Rather, they are intrinsically linked to complex ideas about nationhood based on different life experiences (Simonett 2006). Censorship of narco-music vividly demonstrates that "claims against popular music are not just about music. They are also expressions of political, cultural, and social disagreements over images, meaning, and behavior. They are contests for control over public images and expressions" (Gray 1989, 143).

CONCLUDING THOUGHTS

As Biddle and Knights (2007, 14) state, "popular musics can productively open out the national not simply as the space in which nationalist ideology located itself, but also as a 'territory' that has symbolic force beyond its parochial-political needs. This territory is fluid, open-ended and productively unstable in its encounter with 'real' nation-states, as well as with 'real' national and nationalist aspirations." Since the signing of NAFTA in 1994 Mexico has fully embraced neoliberal practices and ideologies that shape its economic development. The rise of new forms of communication and cultural circulation made possible by digital media among Mexicans on both sides of the border has challenged ideas of fixed musical identities and styles bound to specific social groups or cultural areas. Community is constructed, lived, and expressed at a local level. But as the narcocorrido phenomenon so demonstrates, "the new power of the imagination in the fabrication of social lives is inescapably tied up with images, ideas, and opportunities that come from elsewhere, often moved around by the vehicles of mass media" (Appadurai 1991, 199).

Mexican regional music has come to interrogate the very 'Mexicanness' of Mexican music, as a Californian musician concludes:

> It is championed by *pochos*, people born here [in the U.S.] and not there [in Mexico] . . . they grew up here, and just because their family is from there, and because it's fashionable right now, they [claim to be] from there. I think these are their fantasies, illusions they try to live out [in this music].[37]

Adolfo Valenzuela of Twiins Enterprises, on the other hand, thinks that "it's cool to see regular people go to a club to feel narco for that night" (featured in Schwarz 2013). El Komander, hailed by the Las Vegas International Press Association as "Supreme Hispanic Pride" (*Máximo Orgullo Hispano*, Univision 2016) for his outstanding artistic career, recently released the song "El méxicoamericano" (The Mexican American, 2017) in an attempt to capture these Mexican-American fantasies. The music video presents clips of a festive atmosphere, supposedly somewhere in Sinaloa, where "good-quality cocaine" (*un pericón de lavado*), "icecold beer and marijuana" (*forjadito de hierba*) abound. The singer's T-shirt and baseball cap featuring Culiacán's league team, Los Tomateros, make visual his Sinaloan Mexican stance while, courted by scantly-dressed ladies, he sings to a bouncy banda-norteño tune. In the idealized festive ambiance of the song he "is awaiting his cousin" and a "gorgeous light-skinned girl" to arrive by a propeller plane on a dirt road, images that prompt an association with clandestine drug trafficking. Indeed, the cousin brings "a Colombian detail" (cocaine), a gift from Bogotá. The singer's conclusion: "It's more relaxed here [in Mexico] than there with the *güeros* [slang for white-Americans]. Cousin, let's step aside to pull the AK-47!" Within a couple of months El Komander's music video had been watched by close to three million people on different internet channels.

Since its emergence in the 1980s, the music video had been one of the most significant developments in the field of popular music. In the following decades, global computer networks and modern technology have expanded the circulation and accessibility of this medium. The internet has enabled artists to bypass the vetting of music and media industries while appealing to wide audiences. These new forms of music production, circulation, and consumption have made the altered movement a success among a young generation of Mexicans and Mexican Americans. Ángel Del Villar, founder of DEL Records, recalled:

young people with a musical concept different from the Regional Mexican genre post their music directly on the internet . . . Many young people play their guitars at home and upload their videos to YouTube . . . Their way of composing, singing and performing instruments was a drastic change in the genre (interviewed by Garza 2016).

Spanish-language radio stations had broadcasted narcocorridos for many years, but the ones circulating on the internet were different in style. Twiins co-owner Adolfo Valenzuela remembers that it was "a style, a movement that had no name, nothing. It was simply there. It was viable, it was happening. Artists were starting to come out of it" (interviewed by El Llanito 2010). This was the moment when savvy music entrepreneurs began to invest in the movement.

At the presentation of the fourth album in the *Movimiento Alterado* series in 2010 Twiins credited the young people for 'spreading the virus': "The different social networks helped young people to create and develop a new way of life never seen before," Valenzuela said (quoted in Burgos 2016, 14). "This is more than just producing music for us. This is a big political movement. We have *a voice* now as *a people*, and we hope that our music can help make the voice be heard" (Omar Valenzuela quoted in Kun 2006). While this may sound empowering for a politically marginalized and disenfranchised population in the United States, the relationship between music and politics, as we have shown in this chapter, is much more complex than that.

Narcocorridos, specifically YouTube narcocorrido videos, are aesthetic productions generated from 'the margins.' As symbolic responses to experienced realities, the content of this genre is constantly adapting to changing historical, political, economic and cultural conditions. Although the genre has recently been absorbed into the transnational circuit of popular music production, young people across the border continue to be the active, critical, and creative actors in its production, diffusion, and consumption. Narcocorridos reflect their experiences, expectations, practices, and ways of positioning themselves in transnational contexts ravaged by violence and drug trafficking, thus articulating what 'being Mexican' means to them.

NOTES

1. This collaborative chapter is based on ethnographic fieldwork in Sinaloa and in California. Simonett began her ethnomusicological research on narco-music as a transnational phenomenon in 1994 while studying ethnomusicology at the University of Los Angeles, California. Burgos Dávila began his fieldwork in Sinaloa in 2008 when he was a Ph.D. candidate in social psychology at the Universitat Autònoma de

Barcelona, Spain, and continued his research as a postdoctoral fellow in the Department of Ethnic Studies at the University of California, Berkeley, from 2014 to 2015.

2. Ariel Camacho (1992–2015) was a Mexican singer-songwriter known for his soft, nasal Sinaloan 'country' voice—similar to that of the legendary Chalino Sánchez—and his particular style of playing the *bajo sexto*, a type of Mexican guitar with six double courses of strings. He is also recognized for popularizing the Sinaloan 'sierreño' (Sierra) style in the United States. Accompanied by César Sánchez on guitar, the two guitarists nicely harmonized their voices, accentuated by a fast tuba bass line played by Omar Burgos. With only three members, the band is the smallest unit to which one can reduce a *banda sinaloense* and a *norteño* ensemble and still sound typically 'sinaloense' (see Simonett 2001b, 139–140). Norteño features a core instrumentation of button accordion and bajo sexto. Banda sinaloense is a full-fledged brass band consisting of eleven to sixteen musicians.

3. Original text: *Es música de la sierra. Y este género que ha sido, es y será del pueblo y para el pueblo tiene un nuevo patrón . . . que con su juventud, talento y agallas hoy por hoy ha logrado convertirse en el nuevo amo y señor del corrido . . . Su destreza y poder musical son tan altos como los pinos . . . La música campirana tiene un nuevo patrón . . . México y Estados Unidos se le cuadran como el Rey de Corazones: Ariel Camacho. Y no viene solo, viene bien escoltado por Los Plebes del Rancho . . . Tome bien la nota, la instrucción es muy sencilla, a bailar, a tomar y a cantar todo mundo, con todo el poder sinaloense. Aquí está, Ariel Camacho . . . Ariel, Ariel Camacho y Los Plebes del Rancho . . . Ariel, Ariel Camacho y Los Plebes del Rancho* (Burgos, field notes, Palladium Night Club, Sunnyvale, California, January 15, 2015).

4. Severiano Briseño registered "El sinaloense" in 1945 in his name. According to various Sinaloan musicians, however, this piece was composed by Enrique Sánchez Alonso "El negrumo" (from Culiacán) who later sold the composition to Briseño. This was not an unusual praxis among composers at that time (Simonett 2004, 158).

5. Although Camacho's untimely death at the age of twenty-two may have had some impact on the surge in streaming, sales, and radio airplay of "El karma," it is nevertheless astonishing that the song is one of only a few of the regional Mexican genre that have reached the top of Hot Latin Songs (Mendizabal 2015).

6. We have shown in detail in a recent article on *música tribal* how these new channels of communication change music production and consumption (see Simonett and Burgos 2015, 14–16).

7. Marisela Vallejo (Chalino's widow), interview by Simonett, Los Angeles, 1996.

8. For a summary of Chalino's life and work, see Meza (2014).

9. See "El mito del Pela Vacas, Chalino Sánchez" in Ramírez-Pimienta (2011, 159–90); "The Ballad of Chalino Sánchez" in Quinones (2001, 11–29).

10. Mariachi scholar Jesús Jáuregui (2007, 309–10) argued similarly that mariachi has become overshadowed by genres from the U.S.-Mexico borderlands that are "más coherentes con la lógica de la globalización, y en las que se manifiestan las nuevas

identidades que se producen bajo su influencia: identidades más flexibles, híbridas, más móviles."

11. Burgos, field notes, November 23, 2014.

12. *Sí señor, yo soy de rancho; soy de botas y a caballo*. Half a year after "Soy de rancho" (2014) was launched by Twiins Culiacán TV, it peaked at #8 on Billboard's Hot Latin Songs (https://www.billboard.com/music/el-komander/chart-history/latin-songs/song/812058); the song has since received 97 million hits.

13. *Alterado* in colloquial language means upset, deranged or infuriated. It can also mean to be under the influence of drugs. The music productions of the alterado movement are called *pura enfermedad* (pure disease).

14. A representative example of this style is the music video "Leyenda M1" by El Komander, a corrido about the legendary Manuel Torres Félix, aka M1 (1958–2012), a high-ranking leading member of the Sinaloa cartel.

15. For a concise definition of the corrido genre, see Simonett (2014, 548–51). For an in-depth analysis of a contemporary corrido tradition in Mexico, see McDowell (2000). Early recordings can be heard on the double-album *Corridos y Tragedias de la Frontera*, which includes a 167-page commentary in English, with discography, photographs, and song lyrics in Spanish with English translation, by Chris Strachwitz and Philip Sonnichsen.

16. DEL Records celebrated the appearance of the new Los Plebes del Rancho, highlighting their bucolic Sinaloan roots: *Los miembros de la banda vienen de un México de sol, de desierto, de la sierra. Llegan con la música de su tierra en su máxima y más auténtica expresión – una gran agrupación cargada con todo el misterio campirano y el talento desenfrenado de su Sinaloa* ("Del negociante" [Of The Dealer]; half a year later the site showed 106 million views; in September 2018, the number of views had grown to 380 million).

17. Ramírez-Pimienta elaborated on this phenomenon in the chapter on "El mito del Pela Vacas, Chalino Sánchez" (2011, 159–190): *Con sangre cien por ciento mexicana* means "of one hundred percent Mexican blood." Burgos, a native of Sinaloa's capital Culiacán, felt that during his fieldwork in northern California, interviewees often paid him respect for being an insider with 'natural' knowledge.

18. *Perrón*, which literally means 'big dog,' became a slang word among young *Mexicanos* (Mexican Americans) in the 1990s, describing anything superlative. According to Gabriel Francisco Kleriga, founder and owner of the music fanzine *Perrona* (literally 'big bitch'), the slang originated in Guadalajara and was soon appropriated by Los Angeles's Mexican youths as an attribute to the narco-subculture (interview by Simonett, Mazatlán, 2004).

19. Vidal and Damián (Los Plebes Eztilo Violento), interview by Burgos, Oakland, California, 2015.

20. *Lo que empezó en el 2011 como una marca dedicada al uso de la barba y el estilo regional hoy ha evolucionado a algo mucho más allá gracias a sus seguidores que adoptaron la marca como parte de su personalidad*, https://www.barbanortena.com (accessed January 15, 2017).

21. The saying is applicable to a thing or person that resists but ends up yielding.

22. The film was honored with an IDA (International Documentary Association) Creative Recognition Award for Best Music.

23. Johny (Nueva Mentalidad), interview by Burgos, San Jose, California, 2015.

24. According to narco-music promoter Joel Vázquez (Twiins Enterprises), featured in Schwarz (2013).

25. Enigma Norteño's corrido "El Chapo Guzmán" (2015) had generated ten million views within one year after it was posted on YouTube.

26. Interview by Burgos, San Jose, California 2015.

27. *Buchón* is a regionalism used in Mexico to refer in a derogatory way to the peasants of Sinaloa who are involved in drug trafficking. The word derives from a brand of whiskey (Buchanan). It is now commonly used to describe the kind of extravagant material culture that drug trafficking has generated. For *tribal* music see Simonett and Burgos (2015).

28. Mexicans' hope in their new president, Enrique Peña Nieto, to combat drug trafficking and organized crime and ensure citizen security quickly dwindled as the country's institutional failures keep staggering (Redacción Proceso 2013). Beleaguered by charges of corruption, the federal government has been unable to enforce the rule of law. By 2014, a third of the country's population considered the lack of security as the most important problem facing the nation: over 40% knew of sales of illegal drugs in their neighborhood and 23% were aware of a murder that occurred in their neighborhood (Cohen et al. 2017).

29. "Sanguinarios del M1" is a praise song to a leading member of the Sinaloa cartel, Manuel Torres Félix, also known as M1 (a firearm). Half a year after the song came out 100,000 copies had been sold. The official music video, "Movimiento Alterado—Sanguinarios del M1," was uploaded on YouTube by Twiins Culiacán TV in 2011 and has since been seen forty million times. For comments on the alterado movement see Redacción Animal Político (2012), Redacción SinEmbargo (2013), and Denselow (2012).

30. Also on the list of winners were Ariel Camacho y Los Plebes del Rancho ("Artist of the Year, New" and "Regional Mexican Song of the Year").

31. For example, in "El General" (The General) by Teodoro Bello on Los Tigres's Grammy-nominated 1997 album *Jefe de jefes* (The Boss of Bosses).

32. *Entre Carlos y Raúl eran los dueños de un circo: Carlos era el domador, el hermano más chico, Raúl el coordinador, con hambre de hacerse rico.* In an interview with Elijah Wald, Los Tigres's leader, Jorge Hernández, explained how the song came into being: "one day I told [Jesse Armenta]: you are falling behind, you have to work. I am going to give you an idea. I want you to do me a favor. Get on it, get sources. Right now there is an alarming problem in Mexico [with] the politicians. Buy all of the newspapers, learn about the Salinas issue, the president. Get good source material and write me a story about the politicians, because I will go into the recording studio next month and now is the time to record these stories. Because right now the president just signed a treaty, supposedly to give us more freedom of expression, and we can sing what we are allowed by the Secretariat of Foreign Relations. We are a bit more open, let's see what happens. (*Un día le dije [a Jesse Armenta]: Te estas quedando atrás tú, tienes que trabajar, te voy a dar una idea, quiero que me hagas*

un favor, ponte, documéntate ahorita hay un problema muy grave en México, los políticos; cómprate todos los periódicos, agárrate como está la cuestión de Salinas, el Presidente, documéntate bien y hazme una historia de los políticos, porque yo voy a grabar el mes que entra y ahorita es el momento de que grabemos esas historias, porque ahorita acaba de firmar el Presidente de la República un tratado donde dice que nos da un poquito más de libre expresión y podemos cantar lo que la Secretaría de Relaciones Exteriores nos da permiso de cantar, estamos un poquito más abiertos, vamos a ver qué pasa, a ver cómo nos sale) Http://www.elijahwald.com/jhernan.html (accessed September 1, 2018).

33. After having served ten years of his twenty-seven-year sentence in prison, the conviction was overturned in 2005 and Raúl Salinas was released.

34. *Hasta que llegue otro circo / y otra vez la misma transa.*

35. Espinosa (2011). The governor has long been plagued by accusations of corruption and links to organized crime (Gómez 2013). For a detailed analysis of the impact of narco-music on Sinaloan youths, see Burgos (2011).

36. According to the band's own website, "About Los Tigres del Norte," http://www.lostigresdelnorte.com/english/about.html (accessed September 5, 2018).

37. Interview by Burgos, Oakland, California, 2015.

REFERENCES

Acuña, Rodolfo. *Anything But Mexican: Chicanos in Contemporary Los Angeles.* London: Verso, 1996.

"Adolfo Valenzuela (Twiins)–Entrevista con El Llanito Pt.I 2010." YouTube video, 7:06. Posted by "Daniel Brancato," December 27, 2010. https://www.youtube.com/watch?v=klggH_qHhs8.

Amaya, Hector. "The Dark Side of Transnational Latinidad: Narcocorridos and the Branding of Authenticity." In *Contemporary Latina/o Media: Production, Circulation, Politics*, edited by Arlene Dávila and Yeidy M. Rivero, 223–242. New York: New York University Press, 2014.

"Ángel Del Villar revela el secreto de su éxito." YouTube video, 29:30. Posted by "Pepe Garza," January 25, 2016. https://www.youtube.com/watch?v=8OZaPBeQYlw&t=4s.

Appadurai, Arjun. *The Future as Cultural Fact: Essays on the Global Condition.* London and New York: Verso, 2013.

———. "Global Ethnoscapes: Notes and Queries for a Transnational Anthropology." In *Recapturing Anthropology: Working in the Present*, edited by Richard G. Fox, 191–210. Santa Fe: School of American Research Press, 1991.

———. "Disjuncture and Difference in the Global Cultural Economy." *Public Culture* 2, no. 2 (1990): 1–24.

"Ariel Camacho – El karma (Video Oficial)." YouTube video, 3:15. Posted by "EstiloSucioTV," March 12, 2014. https://www.youtube.com/watch?v=v56532ojZ-s.

"Ariel Camacho—Hablemos." YouTube video, 3:09. Posted by "Ariel Camacho," March 12, 2014. https://www.youtube.com/watch?v=bN3G5gXKPkY.

"Ariel Camacho—Te Metiste." YouTube video, 3:31. Posted by "Marilin CRV," October 6, 2014. https://www.youtube.com/watch?v=AXpAsfF_b_o.

Astorga, Luis. *"¿Qué querían que hiciera?" Inseguridad y delincuencia organizada en el gobierno de Felipe Calderón*. Mexico, D.F.: Grijalbo, 2015.

———. *Mitología del "narcotraficante" en México*. Mexico, D.F.: Universidad Nacional Autónoma de México, 1995.

Biddle, Ian and Vanessa Knights. "Introduction: National Popular Music: Betwixt and Beyond the Local and Global." In *Music, National Identity and the Politics of Location: Between the Local and the Global*, edited by Ian Biddle and Vanessa Knights, 1–15. Aldershot: Ashgate, 2007.

Bruce, Ian. "Mexico Frees Ex-Leader's Brother." *BBC News* (June 10, 2005). http://news.bbc.co.uk/2/hi/americas/4079372.stm.

Burgos, César. "'¡Que truene la tambora y que suene el acordeón': Composición, difusión y consumo juvenil de narcocorridos en Sinaloa." *Trans. Revista Transcultural de Música* 20 (2016): 1–24.

———. "Narcocorridos: Antecedentes de la tradición corridística y del narcotráfico en México." *Studies in Latin American Popular Culture* 31 (2013): 157–183.

———. "Mediación musical: Aproximación etnográfica al narcocorrido." Ph.D. dissertation, Universitat Autònoma de Barcelona, Spain, 2012.

———. "Expresiones musicales del narcotráfico en México: Los narcocorridos en la cotidianidad de los jóvenes sinaloenses." Lecture at Vanderbilt University, Nashville, TN. December 5, 2011.

Cabrera, Javier and Alberto Morales. "Malova impulsará veto de narcocorridos en todo el país." *El Universal* (May 21, 2011). http://archivo.eluniversal.com.mx/sociedad/7036.html.

Chabat, Jorge. "La respuesta del gobierno de Calderón al desafío del narcotráfico: Entre lo malo y lo peor." *Centro de Investigación y Docencia Económicas* 196 (2010): 1–18.

"Chalino Sánchez—A Ti Mi Grandota (Video Oficial) (Original)." YouTube video, 2:35. Posted by "Musica de Arranque," August 22, 2013. https://www.youtube.com/watch?v=3yXcEMnyIXw.

Chalino Sánchez. *Chalino Sánchez con Los Amables del Norte*. Cintas Acuario. CAN-094.

Cobo, Leila. "Gerardo Ortiz Apologizes for Graphic 'Fuiste Mia' Video But Should He Be Prosecuted?" *Billboard* (July 22, 2016a). http://www.billboard.com/articles/columns/latin/7446673/gerardo-ortiz-apologizes-fuiste-mia-video-arrest.

———. "Mexican Star Gerardo Ortiz Arrested on Charges Stemming from Violent Video." *Billboard* (July 17, 2016b). http://www.billboard.com/articles/columns/latin/7439092/gerardo-ortiz-arrested-charges-fuiste-mia-video.

———. "Regional Mexican Acts Hit the Road." *Billboard* 117, no. 26 (2005): 29.

———. "Regional Mexican Music Moves North of the Border." *Billboard* 113, no. 29 (2001): 1, 92.

Cohen, Mollie et al. *The Political Culture of Democracy in the Americas*. Nashville: Vanderbilt University, USAID, LAPOP, 2017.

Córdova, Nery. "Las mediaciones culturales y la comunicación." In *Sinaloa: Historia, cultura y violencia*, edited by Difocur Sinaloa, 37–47. Culiacán: Dirección de Investigación y Fomento Cultural Regional del Gobierno del Estado de Sinaloa, 1993.

Corridos y Tragedias de la Frontera. First Recordings of Historic Mexican-American Ballads (1928–1937). Arhoolie Folklyric. 7019/7020.

Cruz, Mary Carmen. "Teodoro Bello cobra . . . ¡20 mil dólares por canción!" *Furia Musical* (USA Edition), no. 7 (2000): 13.

Damián. Band member of Los Plebes Eztilo Violento. Personal Communication. Oakland, California. March 16, 2015.

"Del Negociante—Los Plebes del Rancho de Ariel Camacho (Video Oficial)—DEL Records." YouTube video, 4:07. Posted by "DEL Records," February 14, 2016. https://www.youtube.com/watch?v=sAw8aiU5Ris.

Denselow, Robin. "Narcocorrido, the Sound of Los Angeles." *The Guardian* (March 28, 2012). https://www.theguardian.com/music/2012/mar/28/narcocorrido-sound-los-angeles?INTCMP=SRCH.

Edberg, Marc C. "Narcocorridos: Narratives of a Cultural Persona and Power on the Border." In *Transnational Encounters: Music and Performance at the U.S.-Mexico Border*, edited by Alejandro L. Madrid, 67–82. New York: Oxford University Press, 2011.

"El Mexicoamericano (Video Oficial 2017)—El Komander." YouTube video, 3:58. Posted by "El Komander," January 31, 2017. https://www.youtube.com/watch?v=zlZdiLwRrnw.

"El Muchacho De La Barba—Enigma Norteño ft Codigo FN 2012." YouTube video, 2:29. Posted by "joseMG020," August 26, 2012. https://www.youtube.com/watch?v=uI52eGk0GrQ.

"El Señor De Los Cielos – Ariel Camacho (Video Underground)—DEL Records 2015." YouTube video, 3:33. Posted by "DEL Records," January 6, 2015. https://www.youtube.com/watch?v=Y4r3LrlpW7c.

"Enigma Norteño—El Chapo Guzmán ft. Hijos De Barrón." YouTube video, 4:21. Posted by "Enigma Norteno TV," September 28, 2015. https://www.youtube.com/watch?v=tgpJGu0VhTQ.

Espinosa, Alberto. "Se reúne Malova con Los Tigres del Norte: La agrupación musical trabajará para mejorar la imagen de Sinaloa." *Sexenio* (May 11, 2011). http://www.sexenio.com.mx/articulo.php?id=4511.

Gómez, Felicia. "Governor López of Sinaloa Accused of Having Ties with Sinaloa Cartel." *Justice in Mexico* (July 10, 2013). https://justiceinmexico.org/governor-lopez-of-sinaloa-accused-of-having-ties-with-sinaloa-cartel.

Gray, Herman. "Popular Music as a Social Problem: A Social History of Claims against Popular Music." In *Images of Issues: Typifying Contemporary Social Problems*, edited by Joel Best, 143–158. New York: Aldine de Gruyter, 1989.

Grayson, George W. *The Cartels: The Story of Mexico's Most Dangerous Criminal Organizations and Their Impact on U.S. Security.* Santa Barbara, CA: Praeger, 2013.

Guardado, Héctor. "Los Tigres del Norte." *Noroeste* (November 9, 1996).

Hobsbawm, Eric. *Bandits*. New York: Delacorte Press, 1969.
Jameson, Fredric. *Postmodernism, or, The Cultural Logic of Late Capitalism*. Durham, N.C.: Duke University Press, 1991.
Jáuregui, Jesús. *El Mariachi. Símbolo musical de México*. Mexico, D.F.: CONACULTA, Taurus, 2007.
Johny. Band member of Nueva Mentalidad. Personal Communication. San Jose, California. February 21, 2015.
Kleriga, Gabriel Francisco. Founder and owner of the music fanzine *Perrona*. Personal Communication. Mazatlán, Mexico. 2004.
Kun, Josh. "The Twiins: Mexican Music, Made in America." *The New York Times* (May 14, 2006). http://www.nytimes.com/2006/05/14/arts/music/14kun.html?pagewanted=all.
Lara, Julio. "Ramirez's Barba Nortena Trending Upward." *Latino Entrepreneur Series* (November 2015). http://lam-network.com/ramirez-barba-nortena.
Los Tigres del Norte, *Contrabando y traición*. Diana. LPD-265.
———. *La Banda del Carro Rojo*. Fama. 536.
———. *La jaula de oro*. Profono International, Inc. PRL 90408.
———. *El otro México*. Golondrina. LPLPG-3151.
———. *Corridos prohibidos*. Musivisa. MUTV/6000.
———. *Unidos para siempre*. Fonovisa. SDC-6049.
———. *Jefe de jefes*. Fonovisa. SDC-6049.
Martell, Luke. "The Third Wave in Globalizing Theory." *International Studies Review* 9 (2007): 173–196.
McAllester, Matt. "Mexico's Narco Cultura: Glorifying Drug War Death and Destruction." *Time* (November 18, 2013). http://time.com/3804417/mexicos-narco-cultura-glorifing-drug-war-death-and-destruction.
McDowell, John. "The Ballad of Narcomexico." *Journal of Folklore Research* 49, no. 3 (2012): 249–274.
———. *Poetry and Violence: The Ballad Tradition of Mexico's Costa Chica*. Urbana and Chicago: University of Illinois Press, 2000.
———. "The *Corrido* of Greater Mexico as Discourse, Music, and Event." In *"And Other Neighborly Names": Social Process and Cultural Image in Texas Folklore*, edited by Richard Bauman and Roger D. Abrahams, 44–75. Austin, TX: University of Texas Press, 1981.
McIntyre, Hugh. "These Are the Winners of the 2016 Billboard Latin Music Awards." *Forbes* (April 29, 2016). https://www.forbes.com/sites/hughmcintyre/2016/04/29/these-are-the-winners-of-the-2016-billboard-latin-music-awards/#339ff7522543.
Mendizabal, Amaya. "Ariel Camacho's Death Leads to Hot Latin Songs No. 1." *Billboard* (March 5, 2015). https://www.billboard.com/articles/columns/chart-beat/6494386/ariel-camacho-death-hot-latin-songs.
Meza, Silber. "La recia vida de 'Chalino' Sánchez." *El Universal Domingo* (January 1, 2014). http://www.domingoeluniversal.mx/Historias/detalle/La+recia+vida+de+'Chalino'+S%C3%A1nchez-2086.
Misarachi, Raquel. "La historia de los narcocorridos, el Twiins Music Group y el movimiento alterado." *Univisión Noticias* (August 1, 2016). https://www

.univision.com/musica/uforia-music-showcase/la-historia-de-los-narcocorridos-el-twiins-music-group-y-el-movimiento-alterado.

Morrison, Amanda M. "Musical Trafficking: Urban Youth and the Narcocorrido-Hardcore Rap Nexus." *Western Folkore* 67, no. 4 (2008): 379–396.

"Movimiento Alterado—Sanguinarios del M1." YouTube video, 2:35. Posted by "TwiinsCuliacanTv," October 26, 2011. https://www.youtube.com/watch?v=rzod0gFjHIw.

Nico. Band member of Nueva Mentalidad. Personal Communication. San Jose, California. February 21, 2015.

Notimex. "Los narcocorridos calientan la sangre, afirma el gobernador Malova." *Excelsior* (May 31, 2011). http://www.excelsior.com.mx/2011/05/30/nacional/741074.

Patenostro, Silvana. "Mexico as a Narco-Democracy." *World Policy Journal* 12, no. 1 (1995): 41–47.

Quinones, Sam. *True Tales from Another Mexico: The Lynch Mob, the Popsicle Kings, Chalino and the Bronx.* Albuquerque: New Mexico Press, 2001.

———. "Narco Pop's Bloody Polkas: On Both Sides of the Border, Drug Lord Ballads Shoot to the Top." *The Washington Post* (March 1, 1998): G1, G8.

Ramírez-Pimienta, Juan. *Voces y versos del narcocorrido.* Mexico, D.F.: Planeta, 2011.

Redacción Animal Político. "Los corridos sobre el narco, en auge en Los Ángeles." *Animal Político* (March 30, 2012). http://www.animalpolitico.com/2012/03/los-corridos-sobre-el-narco-en-auge-en-los-angeles.

Redacción Proceso. "Más de 121 mil muertos, el saldo de la narcoguerra de Calderón: Inegi (Instituto Nacional de Estadística y Geografía)." *Proceso* (July 30, 2013). http://www.proceso.com.mx/348816/mas-de-121-mil-muertos-el-saldo-de-la-narcoguerra-de-calderon-inegi.

Redacción SinEmbargo. "Movimiento Alterado: las polémicas 'Canciones Enfermas' y la violencia como negocio." *SinEmbargo* (January 8, 2013). http://www.sinembargo.mx/08-01-2013/483513.

Schwarz, Shaul. "Singing Songs of Drug Violence." *Time Video* (2011). http://content.time.com/time/video/player/0,32068,651073925001_2027104,00.html.

———. *Narco Cultura.* Ocean Size Pictures, Parts and Labor. 2013.

Simonett, Helena and César Burgos. "Mexican Pointy Boots and the Tribal Scene: Global Appropriations of Local Cultural Practices in the Virtual Age." *Transatlantica. Revue d'études américaines* 1 (2015): 1–24.

Simonett, Helena. "Corrido." In *Bloomsbury Encyclopedia of Popular Music of the World,* vol. 9, Genres: Caribbean and Latin America, edited by John Shepherd and David Horn, 548–551. New York: Bloomsbury, 2014.

———. "Duranguense." In *Continuum Encyclopedia of Popular Music of the World,* vol. 8, Genres: North America, edited by John Shepherd and David Horn, 191–192. New York: Continuum, 2012.

———. "Quest for the Local: Building Musical Ties between Mexico and the United States." In *Postnational Musical Identities: Cultural Production, Distribution and*

Consumption in a Globalized Scenario, edited by Ignacio Corona and Alejandro L. Madrid, 119–35. Lanham, MD: Rowman & Littlefield Publishers, 2008.

———. "*Los gallos valientes*: Examining Violence in Popular Mexican Music." *Revista Transcultural de Música/Transcultural Music Review* 10 (2006): 1–14.

———. *En Sinaloa nací: Historia de la música de banda.* Mazatlán, México: Asociación de Gestores del Patrimonio Histórico y Cultural de Mazatlán, 2004.

———. "Narcocorridos: An Emerging Micromusic of Nuevo L.A." *Ethnomusicology* 44, no. 2 (2001a): 315–337.

———. *Banda: Mexican Musical Life across Borders.* Middletown, Conn.: Wesleyan University Press, 2001b.

———. "He Lived Singing the Corrido, the Corrido Was His Death: Chalino Sánchez's Lasting Legacy." Paper presented at the 3rd International Conference on the Corrido, Los Angeles, California, June 1998.

"Soy de Rancho (Video Oficial)—El Komander." YouTube video, 2:56. Posted by "TwiinsCuliacanTv," February 7, 2014. https://www.youtube.com/watch?v=dDp3lfE_In8.

Spivak, Gayatri C. *A Critique of Postcolonial Reason: Toward a History of the Vanishing Present.* Cambridge: Harvard University Press, 1999.

Univision. "Alfredo Ríos 'El Komander' recibe reconocimiento como Máximo Orgullo Hispano." *Univision* (March 7, 2016). http://www.univision.com/dallas/klno/musica/alfredo-rios-el-komander-recibe-reconocimiento-como-maximo-orgullo-hispano.

Valenzuela, José M. *Jefe de jefes: Corridos y narcocultura en México.* Mexico, D.F.: Plaza y Janés, 2002.

Valenzuela, Jorge et al. "Culturas juveniles y narcotráfico en Sinaloa. Vida cotidiana y transgresión desde la lírica del narcocorrido." *Revista Conjeturas Sociológicas* 14, no. 5 (2017): 69–92.

Vallejo, Marisela. Chalino's widow. Personal Communication. Los Angeles, California. 1996.

Vidal. Band member of Los Plebes Eztilo Violento. Personal Communication. Oakland, California. March 19, 2015.

Vizcarrondo, Sara. "Songs from the Drug War: 'Narco Cultura' Infiltrated both Sides of the Struggle." 2013. http://www.documentary.org/feature/songs-drug-war-narco-cultura-infiltrates-both-sides-struggle.

Wald, Elijah. *Narcocorrido: A Journey into the Music of Drugs, Guns, and Guerrillas.* New York: Harper Collins, 2002.

Ward, John and Molly Moore. "Mexican Politician Convicted of Murder." *Washington Post Foreign Service* (January 22, 1999): A01. http://www.washingtonpost.com/wp-srv/inatl/longterm/mexico/stories/990122.htm.

Chapter 6

Yo lo digo sin tristezas (I say it without lament)

Transnational Migration, Postnational Voicings, and the Aural Politics of Nation

Alex E. Chávez

"Our songs, proverbs, fiestas and popular beliefs show very clearly that the reason death cannot frighten us is that life has cured us of fear. It is natural, even desirable, to die and the sooner the better" (Paz 1985, 58). If the task, here, is to question the moral authority of national culture—or better still, to foreground the tensions between contemporary experiences of globalization and the political and symbolic economies of national borders—then it seems appropriate to begin with the words of one the most influential figures of the Mexican literati in the twentieth century and what is perhaps his most infamous treatise on fatalism as a distinctive feature of the Mexican character. In the face of intensified transnational economic integration between Mexico and the United States in the last quarter of the twentieth century and into the twenty-first, brazen appeals to death as cultural desire—given the human toll of undocumented border crossings—seem misplaced, yet they continue to circulate. And while the aim here, too, is to foreground how ambiguity is a dimension of the postnational condition—for the nation-state, arguably, is no longer the primary identitarian unit in the present-tense global moment—it must be stated explicitly, however, that there is nothing ambiguous about death as a social consequence of official border policy. With this complexity in mind, in what follows I highlight how migrant practitioners of *huapango arribeño*—a musical style from north-central Mexico—stake nuanced and defiant claims of belonging amid fraught politics and transnational human flows in ways that disturb nationalist models for understanding cultural attachments to place.

In recent years, cultural geographers have taken up Deleuze and Guattari to retheorize geographic concepts, including borders. This application, however, has neither spread widely into Border Studies, nor has the U.S.-Mexico border been taken up as studied example in cultural geography to any great extent. In an edited volume of speculation around the border called *B/Ordering Space* (2005), Woodward and Jones offer three ways the border has heretofore been approached. First, there are immaterial and discursive social categories (a reference to the *borderlands* analytic as a metaphorical gloss for liminality); second, there are the material effects of physical boundaries (the Border Studies' focus on the border as concrete physical space) both of which have been criticized as lacking the other. With respect to the latter, I agree that in some cases the border has been oversimplified when reduced to geographic boundary—a critique made long ago by Américo Paredes (1958) and continued in contemporary works (Madrid 2011). And with respect to the former, while borderlands aids in understanding the symbolic divides among various social groups, the geopolitical perspective of border studies is inherently undergirded by a broader consideration of the boundary work implicit in social and cultural ideologies of difference making, for one cannot fully understand the physical presence of the U.S.-Mexico border as a result of U.S. imperialism without accounting for the racial ideologies that drove westward expansion in the nineteenth century and which remain pervasive today. From a strictly anthropological perspective, the critical and ethnographically grounded integration of geographic/physical and cultural/conceptual perspectives is what Robert R. Alvarez Jr. (1995) termed an "anthropology of borderlands." And so, this third approach should provide both material and immaterial insights, for reliance on geographic and geometric notions of places and distances requires that any argument dwell upon a "localizable relation going from one thing to the other and back again"—the affects of coming and going and, for our purposes, the juridical legalities surrounding such movements (Deleuze and Guattari 1987, 25). This opens up a "transversal movement that sweeps one and the other away, a stream without beginning or end that undermines its banks [and borders] and picks up speed in the middle" (Deleuze and Guattari 1987, 25). Such nuance offers a way of rejecting the verticality of structuralist thought, while retaining a useful emphasis on the material and real productive consequences of flows and interruptions. Thus, I build upon this approach and open up the possibility for thinking of the border *poetically*, this is to say, bridging into its affective nature in which the border operates as both an ordered zone of difference making while simultaneously existing as an assemblage of affective and poetic metamorphoses.[1]

Any why might this *matter*? The present-tense juridical-political boundaries of the state are intensely undermined by global capitalism, yet because they are perceived to be under assault, those whose identities are deeply entrenched in ethno-nationalist ideologies of belonging, in particular, have resurrected an aggrieved politics of xenophobia that calls for isolation from world markets and an intensified need for borders and their protection, all of which is braced by discursive forms of racial animus. While in the United States some aspects of this are indeed novel, this is by and large non-exceptional (Rosa and Bonilla 2017), and it is thus revelatory of a persistent and generalizable colonial situation, or a continuation of structuring logics of cultural, economic, political, and sexual oppression wielded over and against subordinated racialized groups (Grosfoguel 2011). Given this context, the contemporary politics that surround Mexican migrants' musical expression within the cultural space of the U.S. nation-state have taken on heightened significance as expressive forms that participate in broader social projects of belonging that grate against the officialized technologies of citizenship. Apprehending this postnational voicing, as it were, requires we trace the aural constructions of Mexican culture as a nationalist project in Mexico and a racializing discourse in the United States, and of course the dialectical relationship between the two. For the "American audio-racial imagination" (Kun 2005, 26) is not only about how America hears itself domestically, but equally about what it hears itself against, particularly sounds from beyond its national borders. The policing of American national culture is a segregationist project that necessarily extends its aural gaze beyond the physical space of the nation wherein sonic cultural flows across borders are resignified and appropriated to effect social silences in the service of a broader nationalism. More specifically, Mexican music operates as an audible signifier of an otherness against which the United States has defined its own racial project and thus hears itself in opposition to. Among other things, Mexican music in the American mainstream sounds out as a racialized index that connotes both primal revelry and pastoral backwardness—ideas metonymically linked to ethnic Mexicans as a whole and presently wielded politically to brace the efficacy of the migrant-detention-industrial-complex, for undocumented ethnic Mexicans are perceived to be an unruly source of criminality. This aural construction owes, however, much to the project of Mexican musical nationalism and its concomitant chrono-tropic lexicon (concerning authentic Mexican culture, or *Mexicanidad*—explained in greater detail in the following section). Mexican music making is thus burdened by 'the national' in dual senses: (1) it participates in a U.S. racial markedness structure as a sonic index for a derided Mexican otherness, and (2) it is also the soundtrack to a powerful antimodernist Mexican national sentiment. Again, a transnational perspective is necessary in apprehending the aural politics of Mexican migrant musical expression.

To clarify, I deploy 'trans' in the sense of active crossing, as signaled above, and as such attend to the correlative social decentering of the space of the nation-state. This paradigmatic shift bypasses nationalist and essentialist models that cling to an "originary Mexican space" (De Genova 2005,

99–100). Still, transnationalism is not a paradigmatic solution that neatly frames the experiences of migrants, but rather, a problem to be engaged with, as they do in daily life. Therefore, in what follows, 'belonging' is not a catch-all appeal to juridical citizenship, rather I intend it as a phenomenological address to account for embodied affects that coalesce around the complex relationality between immaterial and material registers of experience—in this case sound and place—which in turn generate bonds of sociability that expose cultural-social-legal-physical borders experienced in everyday life. To belong, within this transnational perspective, is an ongoing enterprise that attends the various semiotic arrangements, expressive practices, and artistic repertoires—or voicings—enacted at the vernacular level that engender intimate, symbolic, and oppositional senses of existing. Moreover, to claim that migrant voicings *matter*—that is, resonate both materially and immaterially—is to account for embodied musico-poetic performance as a form of communication attuned to interaffective states of attachment, of living, of solidarity within a field of U.S.-Mexico transnational social and economic relations. This is indeed how voicing *takes place*, this is to say, how its material enactment maps the ways social actors move through the world (across borders), or desire to do so (a process I have elsewhere referred to as *self-authorization*) (Chávez 2015; 2017). And so I argue the sounds of Mexican music are heard through culturally and historically situated forms of listening, through aural modes of attention that circulate within transnational social fields of meaning and experience. This phenomenological consideration challenges the calcified essentialism of Mexicanidad; in other words, taken on their own terms, the huapango arribeño communities in question, while objectively considered Mexican, exercise agency by subjectively configuring who they are in relation to struggles in daily life and intimacies amid the pressures and borders—both discursive and material—of transnational migration. Neither the Mexican nation-state nor its jingoistic excess that condemn ethnic Mexicans to the "savage slot"—to invoke Michel-Rolph Trouillot (2003)—have a monopoly on who these communities are, for they actively engage in configuring their own Mexicanness, for lack of a better word, through the ways they go about living.

THE NATIONAL

Cultural discourses of *the nation* are concerned with upholding the political legitimacy of an imagined community (Anderson 1983) and the concomitant sense of national sentiment necessary to this project is often derived through a constellation of symbols, mythology, and expressive practices—this includes music and ideas about music (Turino 2003). In the Mexican case, there is a long-established project of musical nationalism that has relied on the relationship between music and a specific geographic landscape—*el rancho*, or the idealized countryside. Indeed, ranching and agriculture, as important modes of organizing regional economies existed for most of colonial New Spain and Mexico's history up through the twentieth century, at which point Mexico experienced accelerated processes of industrialization and urbanization that transformed its geopolitical landscape. Rural migration to Mexico's urban centers also has a long and complicated history, but occurred on a particularly massive scale in the wake of the Mexican Revolution's devastation, itself a populist uprising in opposition to the displacement associated with President Porfirio Diaz's modernization of Mexico's subsistence economies in the late nineteenth century. This political-economic transformation, it is suggested, subsequently found expression in the Mexican *canción típica* (traditional song), soon labeled *canción ranchera* (country song), the themes of which became increasingly pastoral in scope, symbolically indexing the failed promises of the Revolution (Nájera-Ramírez 1997). The *rancho* symbol-complex that emerged at the tensive crossroads of early twentieth century Mexico, and articulated through its musical canon, speaks of a nation struggling to both define itself and reimagine its past in the wake of centuries of institutional racism (certainly during the *Porfiriato*) that devalued or altogether criminalized homegrown musical expressions. As communities, musicians, and music making reconstituted themselves in new urban environments like Mexico City, a blurring of stylistic regional distinctions occurred, giving rise to a more-or-less uniform ranchera song by the mid-twentieth century, a form which became standardized through its increasing circulation through new media technologies (Gradante 1982; Peña 1985). Whether the emblems that became ranchero fixtures reflect: (1) a nostalgia for something lost (recently arrived migrants from the countryside longing for home in an alien urban environment (Nájera-Ramírez 1997)) or (2) a conservative response to the progressive social policies of President Lázaro Cárdenas[2], they assisted in an essentializing of Mexican culture as nearly equivalent to the space and time of el rancho. This placial imagining is what I term the *ranchero chrono-trope*. Drawing on Mikhail Bakhtin's ([1935] 1981) concept of the chronotope as an optic with which to explore the time-space relational dimensions that contour narrative representations of cultural systems, I propose the ranchero chrono-trope as a way of understanding how essentialist representations of Mexican cultural identity are placed in the rancho and are thus inseparable from the stereotypes—or tropes—engendered in that time-space construct.[3] This utopian rural backdrop inscribes Mexico as unmodern, perhaps stubbornly so, and inadvertently braces derisive claims of Mexicans as backward (at best).

Certain difficulties arise when studying specific forms of regional music in the context of this overriding sense of Mexican musical nationalism. Specifically, the role of the rancho removes expressive forms—deemed authentic— from their temporal, social, and placial contexts. It resignifies them, binding them to a romanticized time-space located somewhere out there at the (supposed) periphery of modernity, or the mythical realm of *allá* (out on the big ranch, perhaps).[4] *Allá* (out there), however, is quite materially the hacienda, the heart of the colonial project, and when examined critically, folklorized musical overtures woven into this dreamlike landscape play a role in silencing the history of empire building in the guise of a simpler "social structure where everyone knew their place, where certain privileged men ruled"(Nájera-Ramírez 1997, 25). This picturesque folklore disembodies vernacular forms of expressive culture so appropriated, obliterating their meanings and histories— women are marginalized (Nájera-Ramírez), blackness is erased (González 2010), regional specificity is flattened (Turino 2003)—and it is perhaps why cultural theorists like Roger Bartra ultimately ask, does it mean anything to be Mexican? In *The Cage of Melancholy* (1992), Bartra describes how the invention of the nation of Mexico has been an othering process in which the Mexican peasant from the countryside is inextricable from the folklore of the nation along with a whole range of characterizations. This othering is racial, classist, and ahistorical, despite claims to critical historicity, and the final result is the invention of a form of institutional culture that obfuscates the actual workings of power. Bartra explores the knotting of backwardness and melancholy, as if a lack of industrial desire connotes lack of any desire or vitality. This set of associations also connotes isolation, particularly from progress, which through dualistic thinking flips to "primordial savagery" (1992, 32). It is never a purely psychological condition, this idea of melancholy. The body is always involved in othering. Black bile, one of the Hippocratic humors that manifests as bodily illness, is also tied to melancholy. Here, pathology, disease, blight, melanchology, bodies, race, and class intertwine. Even further, madness and death intertwine. Thus, indifference to death (and therefore life as well) is a type of myth originating in a combination of religious fatalism and *danses macabres*, an invention of modernity which trails also into a miserable kind of heroic fatalism—as apparent in the ranchero chrono-trope—that gets picked up by Octavio Paz and others (1992, 61). As such, romanticized characteristics like melancholy, mourning, and fatalism should therefore be available for disarticulation rather than common use, given their continued circulation as part of nationalist cultural projects and politics across borders.

In his survey of folklore—as scholarly enterprise and expressive form—in American intellectual and cultural history, Simon J. Bronner (2002) discusses its importance in shaping the American social vision. Fast-forward to a more recent moment's witness to the rise of "multi-culturalism"—to quote Bronner's language—he writes, "folklore can be understood as ground zero in the culture wars" (53). Indeed, folklore's role in fashioning, maintaining, and reinforcing social boundaries—on the basis of traditional, ethnic, or otherwise identitarian traits—has long been the focus of scholarly inquiry. Thus, it is worth considering how American folklore—particularly romanticized myths about rugged individualism bound up with westward expansion—is but one backdrop to the contemporary rise of white supremacist ideology in mainstream American society. Indeed, a national literature is comprised of distinctive narrative genres, among them legend and myth, which in the U.S.-Mexico context has involved the (en)gendering of myths about Mexicans operative in sustaining an anatomy of racial othering. A historically constituted terrain of derided Mexican otherness is a cornerstone of American ethno-nationalist discourse that dates back to the nineteenth century. One contemporary point of analytical departure, to be sure, is the current regime's attitudes toward ethnic Mexicans, all of which is braced by gendered and racializing discourses concerning "drop-and-leave culprit mothers" and "rapists" as threats to be contained. This language is part of a much larger rhetorical project—a well-worn discursive genre in U.S.-American racial talk, evincing a deep-seated myth-making enterprise that has produced 'the Mexican' in the American racial imagination. Pathological notions of gender identities in excess, in particular, have operated as a metonym for Mexico—a mythic and primitive site against which constructions of North American white masculinity and white womanhood have been historically and symbolically constructed. This binary interpretive structure (Flores 2002)—premised on notions of progress—is not only the guiding cultural logic that operates as an (invented) allegorical social divide in the U.S.-American imagination inseparable from the U.S.-Mexico border as a concrete physical site, but is also the central polemic of folklore's disciplinary legacy as an anti-modernist cultural project. In sum, anti-Mexicanism constitutes a myth—touted as a commonsensical form of truth—which operates as a powerful fetish that disguises (and therefore silences) the racism and misogyny at the center of the American white racial project, from westward expansion to contemporary immigration politics. (The aural politics of "build the wall!" chants start to become clearer in this regard.) And herein looms a spectacle braced by racial ideologies that produce the commonsensical notion of illegality, at the center of which rests an exploitable Mexican other whose identity is tethered to a certain primitivism (in which the ranchero chrono-trope participates).

POSTNATIONAL SUBJECTIVITY

Recent music scholarship has tasked itself with tracing how flows of music take shape within this exceedingly xenophobic context. Drawing on Arjun Appadurai's (1996) theorizing in the wake of what he suggests is a crisis of modernity and a collapsing of hegemonic national identities, scholars contend that music shared across the boundaries of nation-states reveals not only how identities are forged and performed in a context of transnational economies (or the complicated relationship between the local and the global), but also how borders themselves are ultimately "fluid, give-and-take areas where complexity, negotiation, and hybridity are everyday constants" (Madrid 2008, 3–4).

In *Audiotopia: Music, Race, and America* (2005), Josh Kun argues "popular music is one of our most valuable tools for understanding the impact of nationalism and citizenship on the formation of our individual identities," and to this point deems it a postnational formation. While the argument partially refers to the way in which music traffics across borders, it also pushes us to consider solidarities beyond the national form. I extend his argument to consider modes of belonging beyond current models of citizenship (again, belonging being a phenomenological address that attends bonds of sociability that disturb cultural-social-legal-physical borderings in daily life). Imagining postnational subjectivities within the broader U.S.-Mexico perspective is, therefore, to acknowledge modes of belonging fashioned beyond the exclusionary juridical practices of the nation-state in order to recognize subjectivities that gesture toward its reimagining to be more inclusive of undocumented migrants. Embedded in this point is a critique of what is perhaps a common meaning postnationalism has taken on in certain music scholarship, operating as a gloss for transnationalism. To account for the ways in which musics are increasingly geographically diffuse in the current global moment, however, isn't necessarily the same as providing an understanding of how these practices go beyond the politics of the nation-state. For instance, the spatial movement of Mexican folk-derived popular musics across national boundaries certainly speaks to the transnational growth of their respective markets for production and consumption, given labor migration occurring between the United States and Mexico. But it must be asked how such musics speak to the racialized politics of illegality and to people's needs to fashion expressive practices of self-valorization within this context. Accounting for how music in everyday life becomes politicized in relation to border logics is necessary in deepening our understanding of how migrants disarticulate—in homegrown expressive ways—the material reality of the brutal juridical-economic logics administered by nation-states and corporate interests in their ruthless management of human and capital flows.

Though attentive to intensified U.S.-Mexico transnationalization in the post-NAFTA era, I move beyond the interpretation of "dissemination as 'immigritude'" (Grossberg 1996, 103) as postnational and instead turn my attention to how embodied performance is leveraged in meeting everyday needs for intimacy, place, and belonging beyond the logics of the nation-state. Thus, I explore how subjectivities are fashioned and necessary, aquí (here), not allá. Nicholas De Genova's interpretation of counterpublic slogans like *"¡Aquí estamos, y no nos vamos!"* (Here we are, and we're not leaving!) is useful in conceptualizing this very point, for such slogans represent an incorrigible, irreversible presence of migrants in the space of the U.S. nation-state whose politics "both identifies and is committed to the impossibility of inclusivity" (2010, 105). The performance of these and other expressions embodies a rejection of the state's dehumanizing categories and the ruthless subjugation of migrant life (Rosas 2012), for "the human activity from which [performance] is produced is founded on a process that accentuates the social relations that constitute it" (Flores 1994, 278). In other words, expressive enactments are fundamentally social acts that stake claims of belonging through a vitality and conviviality otherwise severed or denied amid the material reality of a hypermilitarized U.S.-Mexico border and its ubiquitous logics.[5]

TRANSNATIONAL MOVEMENTS

In December 2005, the Border Protection, Anti-terrorism, and Illegal Immigration Control Act (h.r. 4437), otherwise known as the Sensenbrenner Bill, was proposed in the U.S. Congress—another legislative act in a long line of policy initiatives aimed at expanding restrictions on migrants. Its provisions sought to make unauthorized migration a felony, punish those who aided undocumented migrants, provide $2.2 billion for the construction of seven hundred miles of fencing along the U.S.-Mexico border, and require the federal government take custody of undocumented migrants detained by local authorities. The more extreme version of the Sensenbrenner Bill was ratified by the House of Representatives but failed in the Senate, which in the end passed a more moderate bill that left out the felony provision. In response, millions of migrants, their families, and allies marched, boycotted, and rallied across the United States, a movement that culminated in nationwide mobilizations in hundreds of cities around the country in May 2006, drawing more than three million people. Seemingly spontaneous, these mobilizations were in reality the result of decades of activism and advocacy extending back to the 1960s, but which began to explicitly address border militarization and immigration policy since the passage of the Immigration Reform and Control Act in 1986 (Bada et al. 2006). This moment and others like it across the country in the spring of 2006 established a national platform for a transnational panethnic citizenship rights movement that continues to challenge the politics of immigration and defiantly argues for the right to stay (Pallares and Flores-González 2010, xxiii). Now, perhaps more than ever, recent organizing—around the Dream Act, for instance—is taking on the ferocious anti-immigrant politics that dominates the daily lives of migrants and which tells them that they may exist within the borders of the nation-state only as subjugated labor and not in any other meaningful capacity.

With this swirling political context in mind, we can move beyond, once more, the idea of place as genius loci and toward a view of places as gatherings of intensity, as the coming together of life paths, sometimes durational and ephemeral—as poetic, where a space of desire melds into a cumulative swarming of experience, layered on top of and preceding other moments in which placeness wells up, where sensing bodies respond to a mutually held cohesion of sentiment and desire. Such a state of potentiality bloomed in the spring of 2006, and its impacts continue on in the activism of dreamers and young people across the United States defiantly coming out as undocumented and claiming the United States as home. In what remains, I attend to the placial attachments cultivated through huapango arribeño performance among Mexican migrants as a way of binding lives and geographies across the knotted dissonance of class, race, and politics as key dimensions of transnational mobility.

A music relatively unknown outside its region of origin in the Mexican states of Guanajuato, Querétaro, and San Luis Potosí, huapango arribeño takes its name from the Nahuatl word *cuauhpanco*—signifying the expression "atop of the wood," which is a reference to the *tarima* (wooden platform) atop which people dance *zapateado* (patterned footwork) to various styles of vernacular Mexican music. The term *arribeño* (highlander) is a reference to the mountainous region of the states of Guanajuato and Querétaro (known as *La Sierra Gorda*) and also to the mid-region of San Luis Potosí (*La Zona Media*). Typically placed beneath the arch of what is considered *son*—or string-music, in academic circles—the designation, to a degree, distinguishes huapango from other genres of Mexican music: the *corrido* (Mexican ballad), the *canción ranchera* (country song), the accordion-driven *música norteña* of northern Mexico, and the brass and woodwind *banda popular* of the Pacific Coast region. The term *huapango* is also often invoked in reference to the signature galloping 6/8 rhythm typical to the style. This and other features make it familiar and recognizable, for many ethnic Mexicans and appreciators of Mexican music know huapango when they hear it in all of its variations, whether it be via the accordion-based stylings of música norteña or rendered in dramatic *bel canto* style by the immortal stars of the golden era of Mexican cinema. While deemed an emblematic sound of assumed national tradition during this period thanks to the silver screen's stylized representation of the *huasteco* variant of huapango, its broader historical origins (i.e., a regional music parallel to adjacent styles such as the *son jarocho* from Veracruz) must be understood as the product of centuries of culture building between Indigenous, African, and Spanish peoples amid extreme and brutal circumstances.

One of huapango arribeño's most salient features is the use of the Spanish *décima*, or ten-line stanza, as poet-practitioners use the form to assemble poetic narratives. And it is best expressed during *topada* performances, which are organized for any number of celebratory occasions. The name *topada* comes from the verb *topar*—to collide with—and signals the heightened reciprocity and intensity of such encounters. There, two huapango arribeño ensembles face one another, engaging in a musical and poetic marathon duel that lasts for hours. During the performance, both groups—made up of two violins (a lead and second fiddle, or *primer* and *segunda vara*), a *guitarra quinta huapanguera* (a large eight-stringed guitar) and *vihuela* or *jarana* (small five-stringed chordophones)—tower above the audience atop *tablados* (or raised benches), one at each end of the dance floor, physically facing each other while a sea of people dance zapateado below them. An elaborate code of etiquette guides this performative encounter, such that both ensembles are responsible for bringing to bear an array of musical and poetic resources. Accordingly, audiences expect to be fully engaged, taking on an evaluative role, and practitioners thus adhere to this responsibility, for people desire (and thus make real and necessary) laborious bursts of musical and discursive energy.

In 1985 huapango arribeño crossed into the United States for the first time. A Houston-based hometown association (hta) invited two huapango arribeño ensembles to perform at a topada benefit dance organized to raise funds for a church construction project back in San Luis Potosí. At that time, htas were not as commonplace as they are today. Yet, even in the mid-1980s, these then-nascent migrant organizations helped provide disaster relief, fund charitable work, and finance infrastructure projects for their communities of origin (building roads, churches, clinics, sewage plants, schools), as well as support civic, cultural, and religious events and festivals (Vertovec 2004). On the occasion in question, the Houston-based hta had successfully acquired short-term tourist visas for two ensembles. The first ensemble crossed successfully, while the second was denied entrance at the border, only making it across weeks later. Needless to say, the topada didn't happen, but the groups played independently for a stretch of time on their own in Texas. The first topada in the United States would come a few years later. According to huapango arribeño practitioner Guillermo Velázquez, it occurred in Dallas, Texas at a similar hta-type event in the early 1990s. Guillermo Velázquez and Los Leones de la Sierra de Xichú—his ensemble—were invited to the United States for the first time in 1988 where they performed at a hta benefit dance in San Diego, California, in addition to a Mexican music festival in Los Angeles. They subsequently began traveling to Dallas, Texas, regularly to perform at hta fundraisers, and it was at one such event in the early 1990s where they participated in a topada with another local ensemble whose members were part of a robust community of huapangueros—or huapango arribeño practitioners—that began to emerge at around that time. Through multiple circumstances (work, family, mutual friends, social networks), a number of these musicians came together in central Texas, and by the late 1990s they were joined by subsequent waves of migrant musicians who arrived in search of work in the area.

These individual musicians became the foundation of the huapango arribeño community in the United States, which now boasts ensembles in Austin, Dallas, Houston, northern Mississippi, and, most recently, northern California, Florida, and Tennessee. It is often the case that veteran musicians from Mexico arrive in the United States, work, perform, and take the time to instruct novice musicians, such that young huapangueros have now come of age on the U.S. side of the border, learning the musical trade by performing largely for migrant communities, telling of life lived in these places, out loud.

POSTNATIONAL VOICINGS, OR TRANSMODERN ENACTMENTS

Music making in everyday Mexican migrant life is positioned at the tensive center of a volatile discursive and political terrain, where its sounding both symbolically and materially claims a place in the space of the U.S. nation-state, refiguring the borders of citizenship and alienage as embodied and agentive forms of cultural expression. In other words, for performers, "auditory perception is intimately enmeshed with bodily action" (Berger 2009, 13). Therefore, the corporeality of performative enactments is aesthetic labor, the materiality of which—just like "the subjectivity of migrant labour"—attains a "subversive potential" given that the economic subordination of migrant workers within the space of the U.S. nation-state is inseparable from the structures of immigration law, policy, and the juridical nature of illegality (De Genova 2009, 461). Indeed, attention to huapango arribeño's nexus of music and poetics foregrounds the role aural immediacy plays in articulating selves and subjectivities in relation to others, all of which, as my argument will suggest in the following ethnographic rendering, acquires a postnational politics.

So, consider the tensive center of a story full of multiple movements and arrivals across places, where vulnerable bodies bear witness to the vertigo of a precarious present. Consider the ways in which that story becomes itself storied, voiced publicly in all-night performances in the company of hundreds, thousands, or sometimes only a few dozen friends. Consider how Mexican migrants become caught within this dramatic dispersal of public feelings and personal histories, folding in on themselves, taking hold as a transformative force. Consider, then, how a public comes into being through the aesthetic voicing of shared experiences, connecting to the sobering reality of clandestine border crossings or the sultry conviviality after a hard day's work; the shock of a loved one's death or waiting for the weekly phone call from a relative on the other side of the border. Consider how the work of huapango arribeño practitioners is that of translating/storying this polyphonic connectivity, generating a new shared experience (through performance) where everyone present is bound up together in the same interpretational space of living in that moment (of performance). Consider all of this a type of self-authorization that lives in relation to others no matter where they are and in the face of everyday borders and exclusions that dictate where home is, that tell 'others' that they don't belong in a place. Imagine the sweat trickling down the side of your face, welling at the back of your neck; the heat and humidity are smothering. It's a typical sweltering July evening in Central Texas, close to ten o'clock. The incandescence of city lights in the distance washes over the night sky, an amber glow that crowns the ballroom outside of town where Mexican migrants have gathered to witness a topada.

The multitude sways to and fro, wave after wave of shifting bodies stirring the dust beneath them into a cloud. This gathering of flesh, this uncontained breathing mass, is that which thrives, crisscrossing the U.S.-Mexico border in spite of the low-intensity violence mobilized against it in the post-9/11 ruins of NAFTA (Hardt and Negri 2004; Rosas 2012). Four silhouettes appear on one stage, moving leisurely with their instruments—two violins, a vihuela, and a guitarra quinta huapanguera. They assume their positions, exchange glances, and confer quietly, subtly coaxing the music about to be played. They gaze over at the other stage, now similarly occupied by a matching ensemble, waiting patiently. And suddenly, the strumming of instruments booms out through the sound system; elaborate fiddle melodies erupt, followed by the soaring voice of the troubadour, Graciano, whose unraveling verses proclaim:

> Dándoles las buenas noches
> les brindo la bienvenida
> en esta fiesta florida
> hoy que se abren los broches
>
> Bidding you all a good evening
> I offer you a warm welcome
> in this florid festivity
> now that the space has been opened

Everyone is fully absorbed. Graciano scans the scene before him, his mind weaving in and out of the audience, shaping embryonic thoughts into *moving* verses. And the moment opens up, as he suggests, growing wide and dense with spatiotemporal imaginings binding, stretching, bridging across the stark geographies of transnational life as he and the opposing troubadour, don Lencho Olvera—a transnational migrant who has lived his life between the United States, where he now labors in construction, and his native San Luis Potosí since the 1980s—skillfully layer the present-tense currency of this time and place with that of El Caracol, San Luis Potosí, Mexico. Don Lencho Olvera declares:

> Les honro con mi presencia
> y antemano lo sostengo
> por segunda vez que vengo
> ya que Dios nos dio licencia
> gracias a la omnipotencia
> mi canto ya se quedó
> en el verso se notó
> tierra donde alumbra el sol
> los de allá del caracol:
> DE TODOS SOY SERVIDOR
>
> I honor you with my presence
> and in advance I make known to you
> I've come here for the second time
> by the grace of God
> thanks be to the omnipotent one
> my sonorous voice remains
> it has been noted in the verse
> land where the sun does shine
> to all those from El Caracol:
> YOUR WISH IS MY COMMAND[6]

Don Lencho Olvera's voice maps memory into a place of conflated spatial imaginings, affectually self-authorizing the materiality of his presence in the land he now claims as his own. He poeticizes thus:

> Es el zapote la tierra mía
> tierra florida donde nací
> es mexicana y es potosí
> ALLÁ ES ENCANTO DE MI ALEGRÍA
>
> En ese rancho yo fui nacido
> esa memoria no se me pierde
> porque en el pueblo allí de Rioverde
> allí mi nombre fue escribido
> ciertas personas fueron conmigo
> a dar los datos de mi teoría
> en el juzgado con fecha y día
> quedó archivado mi nacimiento
> bajo las leyes de un reglamento:
> ES EL ZAPOTE LA TIERRA MÍA
>
> Yo de Rioverde soy ciudadano
> mis documentos me acreditaron
> que en aquel templo me bautizaron
> para que fuera yo un buen cristiano
> el señor cura ahí con su mano
> me persignaba y me bendecía
> ahí rezaba y también decía
> "mis bendiciones te harán feliz"
> porque en el estado que es de San Luis:
> ES EL ZAPOTE LA TIERRA MÍA
>
> El Zapote is my native land
> flowery earth where I was born
> it's Mexican and of Potosí
> there lay the enchantment of my happiness
> In that rural hamlet I was born
> that memory does not escape me
> because in the town of Rioverde
> there my name was written
> certain people went with me
> to attest to my existence
> in court, the date and time
> of my birth were archived
> according to the rule of law:
> EL ZAPOTE IS MY NATIVE LAND

> I am a citizen of Rioverde
> my documents confirm this
> that I was baptized in that church
> so that I may be a good Catholic
> at the baptismal font the priest
> with his hand did bless me,
> there he prayed and also said
>
> "God's blessings will make you happy"
> because in the state that is San Luis:
> EL ZAPOTE IS MY NATIVE LAND

Momentarily, Texas and San Luis Potosí become virtually one: The dancers bend long and pivot rapidly, their inertia extending out to different parts of the body only to tumble back to its core. Steps grow louder, building a sonic wake that mirrors the music being vigorously bowed and strummed. Its tones sweep across the skin, and its utterances linger, caught in the air, fading but slowly as Graciano and don Lencho Olvera dynamically maneuver between the warmth of the gathering and distant places, crafting poetics that are close at hand, that drag things into view, tracing the trajectories of transnational migrant life in Texas, where the embodied voicing of "*Yo de Rioverde soy ciudadano, mis documentos me acreditaron*" (I am a citizen of Rioverde, my documents confirm this) exposes the viscosity of illegality—its precarity, its dangers, and the historical density and depth of its material presence.

Claudio Lomnitz (2005) traces how the genealogy of death as a Mexican totem has been woven into nationalist discourse, processes of state formation, and both commercial and public spheres from the colonial period through the post-revolutionary era, including its contemporary transnational pilgrimage into the space of the U.S. nation-state. Similarly, Stanley H. Brandes (2006) observes that such representations have promoted the caricature of the morbid Mexican who is irreverent toward and yet obsessed with death. And, returning to where we began, expressive culture, as Paz indicates, is believed to be the wellspring of this sentiment—a position that edges perilously toward a type of cultural ecology where place, character, nation, and nationalism are indistinguishably inscribed onto an imagined space that yields the myth of the melancholic being as part of a larger project of national awareness—the chrono-trope comes into full relief (Bartra 1992). My position, however, is not intended to suggest that beneath the layers of invented tradition there rests a transcendental premodern cultural substrate à la Guillermo Bonfíl Batalla's (1996) "Deep Mexico." Quite the opposite, this ontological distinction between 'deep' and 'imaginary' is false, as Claudio Lomnitz (1992) explains in his critique of Bonfíl Batalla's formulation:

> Both ideologies are linked to sets of real practices and . . . both ideologies are products of the collective imagination. In other words, they are both 'deep', and they are both 'imaginary'. In attributing 'reality' to one and "illusion" to another, Bonfil is merely returning to the nationalist drawing board of the Mexican Revolution without having fully confronted the reasons why the 'imaginary' Mexico has become so very real (248).

The national looms, yet the décimas above force us to listen to the many and particular worlds that make up Mexico, beyond received notions of a harmonious sphere of national culture in the context of space (Lomnitz 1992). This is to say, we must account for multiple spatialities in localized settings and the frames of interaction among diverse groups of people in those settings; otherwise, we are complicit in the project of "a historical sociology of the silence that has characterized the relationship of certain sectors of the Mexican population and state institutions" (Lomnitz 2001, 284). As opposed to a deep Mexico, this silent Mexico—or "the various populations that live beyond the fractured fault line of Mexico's national public sphere"—exists at the very heart of the project of modernity, the failure of democracy, and the contemporary transnational politics of the neoliberal state. And to mitigate the conditions of their marginalized lives, large portions of this silent Mexico migrate across the U.S.-Mexico border. With this sense of transgression in mind, I return to the analytic undergirding this entire discussion—borderlands.

Indeed, the borderlands analytic poses a material challenge to modernity's master narrative of the separation of space-time, whereby crossing the threshold of bordered geographies entails passing from one temporality to another, an ideological act that essentializes difference at the distal edges of progress (Brady 2000). Bearing in mind this disjunct, huapango arribeño's narrative productions provide another story, one that empties the semiological systems and higher-order social indexicalities that fix the border in place, reinscribe difference, and criminalize those who cross these thresholds clandestinely. These poetics encounter the violent cultural signification—cloaked rhetorically in the semantics of citizenship and democracy—which normalizes migrant death by wielding the seemingly neutral juridical category of illegal alien as a covert racial indexical (Dick 2011). This pragmatics of reification is key to producing the border, border violence, and bordered subjects. And while dominant discourses that rely on the categories of the citizen, alien, and illegality struggle to reduce migrants to less than human others, the multitude who are living out their lives beneath the arch of these strategies of containment invoke their own aural cartographies of lived life—a dynamic and disruptive semiotic display of space-time soundings to which listeners align themselves in articulating their existence across national boundaries.

In his extension of Enrique Dussel's concept of transmodernity, Ramón Grosfoguel (2011) suggests, fulfilling the incomplete project of decolonization involves "a multiplicity of decolonial critical responses to eurocentered modernity from the subaltern cultures and epistemic location of colonized people around the world" (26). One such site of this multiplicity of transcendence is postnational—in thinking, existing, and living. The sonorous atmosphere of huapango arribeño performance, thus, is saturated with desires of transmodern connection, building adjacencies in time and space that fold geographies/locations together through densely layered politics and senses of place that touch suddenly, interrupting physical and essentialist borders and all that they entail. And so, we may position the embodied dimensions of huapango arribeño performance—in contexts where migrant bodies are subject to various forms of structural and cultural violence—as extending beyond: (1) the time-space of illegality, where performance voices a semiotic display of personhood that grates against the nation-state; and (2) the ethos associated with folklorized music making as part of the Mexican state's essentialist bounds of nationalist discourse (mostly melancholic in tone). The poetic echoes of this are perhaps best expressed in these concluding verses, as Graciano defiantly claims in Texas:

> Yo lo digo sin tristezas
> Porque lo miro y lo creo
> Para eso del huapangueo
> ¡Nomás aquí en Dallas, Tejas!

> I say it without lament
> Because I see it and I believe it
> In questions of huapango merry-making
> Dallas, Texas is the place!

NOTES

1. More recently, Robert R. Alvarez Jr. (2012) has offered a model for "bridging" that draws from Cherríe L. Moraga and Gloria Anzaldúa's multilayered, critical approach. In critiquing U.S. state-centric scholarship that has "reinscribed the nation-state on the border" (539) and thus neglected how the border-security framework extends into the "interior range of the state" (552), Alvarez suggests using bridging to emphasize connections and contrasts that might inform new approaches to border studies, including ethnography. While calling for an understanding of bridges as "connectors . . . of the history and meanings of people and places," Alvarez's claim that "the nation state is not tied to its borders" (552) evinces a continued state-centric approach.

The door to what he calls a "refreshing cartography" (545) of borders and bridges for border studies is ultimately left open, the thought half-finished (in part, intentionally).

2. This is a reference to romantic representations of the countryside in contradistinction to the dismantling of the hacienda system due to agrarian reform, *ejido* land redistribution, and the nationalization of the oil industry (Hershfield 1991).

3. In their glossary to *The Dialogic Imagination*, Caryl Emerson and Michael Holquist clarify further and suggest that the chronotope is "an optic for reading texts as x-rays of the forces at work in the culture system from which they spring" (1981, 425–426).

4. This is a reference to the film *Allá en el Rancho Grande* (Out on the Big Ranch), directed by Fernando de Fuentes and released in 1936 and hailed as the film that marks the beginning of what many term the golden age of Mexican cinema. The film's music, as much as its visual lexicon, played a crucial role in authenticating certain ideas concerning Mexican identity through the sounds of tradition located in a pastoral dream world—a formula that would be recreated time and again in the *comedia ranchera*, the most commercially successful genre of Mexican national cinema in the twentieth century, popularized the world over.

5. Centered on illegality and border inventions/inspections/crossings, respectively, the contemporary work of Nicholas De Genova (2005) and Alejandro Lugo (2008) explores how the materiality of U.S.-Mexico border policies extends across the continental United States and subsequently shapes cultural logics that produce and restrict citizenship in everyday life. Modes of surveillance, in this regard, are present in "informal managements" (Rosas 2012), as well as official policy efforts.

6. I represent base quatrains, or plantas, orthographically with all capitalization to indicate their function as syntagmatic and paradigmatic anchors of corresponding décimas that follow.

REFERENCES

Alvarez, Robert R., Jr. "The Mexican-US Border: The Making of an Anthropology of Borderlands." *Annual Review of Anthropology* 24, 1 (1995): 447–470.

Alvarez, Robert R., Jr. "Reconceptualizing the Space of the Mexico–US Borderline." In *A Companion to Border Studies*, edited by Thomas M. Wilson and Hastings Donnan, 538–556. Oxford: Wiley-Blackwell, 2012.

Anderson, Benedict. *Imagined Communities: Reflections on the Origin and Spread of Nationalism*. London: Verso, 1991.

Appadurai, Arjun. *Modernity at Large: Cultural Dimensions of Globalization*. Minneapolis: University of Minnesota Press, 1996.

Bada, Xóchitl, Jonathan Fox, Andrew D. Selee, and Mauricio Sánchez Álvarez. *Invisible No More: Mexican Migrant Civic Participation in the United States*. Washington, DC: Mexico Institute, 2006.

Bakhtin, Mikhail. *The Dialogic Imagination: Four Essays*. Edited by Michael Holquist and translated by Caryl Emerson and Michael Holquist. Austin: University of Texas Press, 1981.

Bartra, Roger. *The Cage of Melancholy: Identity and Metamorphosis in the Mexican Character*. New Brunswick, NJ: Rutgers University Press, 1992.

Berger, Harris M. *Stance: Ideas about Emotion, Style, and Meaning for the Study of Expressive Culture*. Middletown, CT: Wesleyan University Press, 2009.

Brady, Mary Pat. "The Fungibility of Borders." *Nepantla: Views from the South* 1, 1 (2000): 171–190.

Brandes, Stanley H. *Skulls to the Living, Bread to the Dead: The Day of the Dead in Mexico and Beyond*. Malden, MA: Blackwell, 2006.

Bronner, Simon J. *Folk Nation: Folklore in the Creation of American Tradition*. Wilmington, DE: Scholarly Resources Inc., 2002.

Chávez, Alex E. 2017. *Sounds of Crossing: Music, Migration, and the Aural Poetics of Huapango Arribeño*. Durham, NC: Duke University Press, 2017.

———. "So ¿Te Fuiste a Dallas? (So You Went to Dallas?/So You Got Screwed?): Language, Migration, and the Poetics of Transgression." *Journal of Linguistic Anthropology* 25, 2 (2015):15–72.

De Genova, Nicholas. "The Queer Politics of Migration: Reflections on 'Illegality' and Incorrigibility." *Studies in Social Justice* 4, 2 (2010): 101–126.

De Genova, Nicholas. "Conflicts of Mobility, and the Mobility of Conflict: Rightlessness, Presence, Subjectivity, Freedom." *Subjectivity* 29, S1 (2009): 445–466.

De Genova, Nicholas. *Working the Boundaries: Race, Space, and "Illegality" in Mexican Chicago*. Durham, NC: Duke University Press, 2005.

Deleuze, Gilles, and Félix Guattari. *A Thousand Plateaus: Capitalism and Schizophrenia*. Minneapolis: University of Minnesota Press, 1987.

Dick, Hilary Parsons. "Language and Migration to the United States." *Annual Review of Anthropology* 40 (2011): 227–240.

Dussel, Enrique. *Hacia una filosofía política crítica*. Bilbao, España: Desclée de Brouwer, 2001.

Flores, Richard R. *Remembering the Alamo: Memory, Modernity, and the Master Symbol*. Austin: University of Texas Press, 2002.

———. "'Los Pastores' and the Gifting of Performance." *American Ethnologist* 21, 2 (1994): 270–285.

Gonzalez, Anita. *Afro-Mexico: Dancing between Myth and Reality*. Austin: University of Texas Press, 2010.

Gradante, William. "'El Hijo del Pueblo': Jose Alfredo Jimenez and the Mexican 'Cancion Ranchera.'" *Latin American Music Review/Revista de Música Latinoamericana* 3, 1 (1982): 36–59.

Grosfoguel, Ramón. 2011. "Decolonizing Post-Colonial Studies and Paradigms of Political-Economy: Transmodernity, Decolonial Thinking, and Global Coloniality." *TRANSMODERNITY: Journal of Peripheral Cultural Production of the Luso-Hispanic World* 1, 1 (2011): http://dialogoglobal.com/texts/grosfoguel/Grosfoguel-Decolonizing-Pol-Econ-and-Postcolonial.pdf.

Grossberg, Lawrence. "Identity and Cultural Studies: Is That All There Is?" In *Questions of Cultural Identity*, edited by Stuart Hall and Paul Du Gay, 80–107. London: Sage, 1996.

Hershfield, Joanne Leslie. *Mexican Cinema/Mexican Woman, 1940–1950.* Tucson: University of Arizona Press, 1996.
Holquist, Michael. "Glossary" In *The Dialogic Imagination: Four Essays.* Edited by Michael Holquist and translated by Caryl Emerson and Michael Holquist, 423–434. Austin: University of Texas Press, 1981.
Kun, Josh. *Audiotopia: Music, Race, and America.* Berkeley: University of California Press, 2005.
Lomnitz, Claudio. *Death and the Idea of Mexico.* Brooklyn, NY: Zone, 2005.
Lomnitz, Claudio. *Deep Mexico, Silent Mexico: An Anthropology of Nationalism.* Minneapolis: University of Minnesota Press, 2001.
Lomnitz, Claudio. *Exits from the Labyrinth: Culture and Ideology in the Mexican National Space.* Berkeley: University of California Press, 1992.
Lugo, Alejandro. *Fragmented Lives, Assembled Parts: Culture, Capitalism, and Conquest at the U.S.-Mexico Border.* Austin: University of Texas Press, 2008.
Madrid, Alejandro L. "Transnational Musical Encounters at the U.S.-Mexico Border: An Introduction." In *Transnational Encounters: Music and Performance at the U.S.-Mexico Border*, edited by Alejandro L. Madrid, 1–16 New York: Oxford University Press, 2011.
Nájera-Ramírez, Olga. "Engendering Nationalism: Identity, Discourse and the Mexican Charro." Working Paper no. 3, Chicano/Latino Research Center, University of California at Santa Cruz, 1997.
Pallares, Amalia and Nilda Flores-González. "Introduction." In *Marcha! Latino Chicago and the Immigrant Rights Movement*, edited by Amalia Pallares and Nilda Flores-González, xv–xxviii. Chicago: University of Illinois Press, 2010.
Paredes, Américo. *"With His Pistol in His Hand": A Border Ballad and Its Hero.* Austin: University of Texas Press, 1958.
Paz, Octavio. *The Labyrinth of Solitude: Life and Thought in Mexico.* New York: Grove, [1961] 1985.
Peña, Manuel H. *The Texas-Mexican Conjunto: History of a Working-Class Music.* Austin: University of Texas Press, 1985.
Rosa, Jonathan and Yarimar Bonilla. "Deprovincializing Trump, Decolonizing Diversity, and Unsettling Anthropology" *American Ethnologist* 44, 2 (2017): 201–208.
Rosas, Gilberto. *Barrio Libre: Criminalizing States and Delinquent Refusals of the New Frontier.* Durham, NC: Duke University Press, 2012.
Trouillot, Michel-Rolph. *Global Transformations: Anthropology and the Modern World.* New York: Palgrave Macmillan, 2003.
Turino, Thomas. "Nationalism and Latin American Music: Selected Case Studies and Theoretical Considerations." *Latin American Music Review* 24, 2 (2003): 169–209.
Vertovec, Steven. 2004. "Migrant Transnationalism and Modes of Transformation." *International Migration Review* 38, 3 (2004): 970–1001.
Woodward, Keith, and John Paul Jones III. "On the Border with Deleuze and Guattari." In *B/ordering Space*, edited by Henk Van Houtum, Olivier Thomas Kramsch, and Wolfgang Zierhofer, 235–248. Aldershot, UK: Ashgate, 2005.

Chapter 7

Reclaiming 'the Border' in Texas-Mexican Conjunto Heritage and Cultural Memory†

Cathy Ragland

> We are a border culture—Indigenous, Spanish, Mestizo, Mexican, Texan, and American—and all of our cultural expressions are a synthesis of these social,cultural, economic, and political elements that has produced unique and original forms of art, such as Tejano music.
>
> —Juan Tejeda, from "Tejano: Local Music, Global Identity" (2014)

On a late summer afternoon in 2016, a small group of mostly late middle-aged Texas-Mexican (Tejano) residents in the small deep South Texas town of San Benito settled in at the Narciso Martínez Cultural Arts Center for a screening of a thirty-minute documentary, *For a Quarter a Song* (Manuel Medrano, 2013) about Tejano accordionist and conjunto music pioneer, Valerio Longoria (1924–2000).[1] Tejano (also Tex-Mex) conjunto is anchored by the diatonic button accordion and Mexican *bajo sexto* (a twelve-stringed bass/guitar hybrid), and supported by electric bass and drums. Longoria has long been recognized by Tejano music historians, folklorists, and culture brokers as an important 'pioneer' of the music, and this summer afternoon a group people gathered to celebrate his legacy and to hear some of his songs played by his son, Flavio. While Longoria is remembered for his significant contributions to the development of Tejano music in the mid-twentieth century —retuning his accordion to produce the voluminous and iconic *sonido ronco* (rough voice) sound that now defines the tradition, and for introducing boleros to the genre—his career was, nonetheless, spent in Chicago and, later, San Antonio, both hundreds of miles from San Benito.

After the film and music performance, attendees reminisced about listening to Longoria and other local Tejano accordionists and musicians who had remained in the region. They recalled personal experiences growing up in and around San Benito, attending open-air dances with families and friends after working in the agriculture fields that once dominated the region and local way of life. As urban development began to remap this geography, many of these fields became suburban-style housing divisions, shopping centers, and business parks. The region's transition from rural area to cross-border trade and distribution hub was a byproduct of NAFTA (North American Free Trade Agreement), which caused regional record growth in the last decade of the twentieth century.[2] Still, many admitted to making quiet pilgrimages to these sites and the memories they experienced: from learning to dance to falling in love to growing old with family and neighbors. Memory becomes the narrative that binds this community, and routine gatherings such as this have been central to the longevity of their musical tradition as part of these imaginings, thus grounding it in irrefutable authenticity (Hobsbawm and Ranger, 1983; Viejo-Rose, 2015). However, globalization, rapid urban development and an institutionalized push toward heritage management (and its focus on objects, museums, and the attraction of tourism) has, in the minds of some community actors, privileged artifact over memory, staging tradition over lived experience. For some, this disconnect from memory and emotion has placed the personal and the communal in danger of becoming trivialized or overtly commercialized amid the "flattening effects of globalization" (Mikula 2015, 241).

Always in the background of San Benito is the Texas-Mexico border (approximately ten miles to the south of the town), a constant reminder of the cultural politics and policy debates between the two nations on a variety of topics such as immigration, trade policies, border security, and economic disparity. For the most part, this region is largely unknown to most U.S.-Americans—most Texans too—until there is a 'crisis.' The most recent being President Donald J. Trump's "zero tolerance" policy that included separating children from their mostly Central American parents seeking asylum from April 2018 until the policy ended in June 2018, although the practice continued well into 2019. The region has several immigrant detention centers (some for holding children who have been separated from parents and others for adults and/or families) located mostly near Brownsville. In McAllen, the largest city in the region, the bus station was dubbed "America's New Ellis Island" in a *New York Times* article focusing on the thousands of detained refugees wearing ankle monitoring devices who were being bussed to locations across the U.S., as their cases are processed through the immigration court system.[3] However, as Alejandro L. Madrid reminds us, border dwellers "live in a borderland for which *la línea* [the line] is undoubtedly an important component of everyday life, but [it's] not what defines emotional or cultural loyalties and networks of identification and belonging" (2011, 8). Whether one identifies as Hispanic, Mexican American, Tejano/a or Chicano/a, the emergence of a hybrid music tradition (conjunto) amid oppression, discrimination, and second-class citizenship (Castillo, Socorro, and Córdoba 2002) can elicit sentiments that waft between nostalgia, pride, and entitlement in its assent to becoming the crown jewel of Tejano (and Texas) artistic expression. In the mythology of Tejano music, the 'border' where different narratives coexist in the same locale, an imagining of border culture has found full expression in a type of middle-to-upper-class Tejano ethno-nationalism (inspired by the Chicano movement and a more exclusive notion of Texas nationalism), as observed by José Limón (2011), and a robust form of border regionalism that is unique to South Texas and the Rio Grande Valley. Being a border citizen "encompasses the subjectified experience of the region" that is so much more than the 'crossing' metaphor predominantly ascribed to the experience, but also the connective elements—proximity, asymmetry, and interaction—that have historically defined this experience (Velasco Ortiz and Contreras 2014, 37).

By focusing on this micro-level case study, I hope to offer a critique of institutionalized ideas of border culture and border life as perpetually in conflict with dominant U.S. (read Anglo-Texan nationalist) culture and a subordinate Mexican/Mexican-American minority that is constantly in flux (Klein 1997; Vila 2000; Grimson and Vila, 2002; Castillo, Socorro, and Córdoba 2002). While many in the region are deeply entrenched in familial roots—some tracing this lineage back to Spanish colonial and Mexican land grant settlements dating to the eighteenth and nineteenth centuries—they also have ambivalent attitudes toward recent immigrants and those who cross daily for work and to conduct business from 'the other side.'

RIO GRANDE VALLEY OF TEXAS AND THE 'BIRTH' OF TEJANO MUSIC

The Rio Grande Valley of Texas (locally known as the RGV or simply "the Valley") lies at the southernmost region of South Texas. It is made up of several small towns linked by the two larger cities: Brownsville, at the state's southernmost tip and along the Gulf Coast, and McAllen, about an hour's drive west on U.S. Hwy 83 (also Interstate 2), which runs parallel to the Rio Grande. The spoils of urbanization are on display all along the state highway in the form of big-box stores, gas stations, car dealerships, and the like, which give the region the look of a full-fledged metropolis. The only way to know which of the many towns you are passing through are the signs that indicate where to exit. The casual tourist might mistake the town names for streets and likely not venture out beyond their destination—most likely the resort towns near Port Isabel dominated by mostly Midwestern retirees referred to locally as "Winter Texans" and "Snowbirds." Those who do find their way to the town centers would likely have traveled on one of the 'old' farm-to-market roads, such as Business 83 and U.S. Hwy 281, that run on either side of Hwy 83. In the 'historic' town centers of San Benito, Harlingen, Mercedes, Donna, and Weslaco, visitors will encounter decaying relics of once-grand hotels, banks, and other businesses from the boomtown days of the early 1900s.

Much of that prosperity was bolstered by another large migration of people, primarily from the Midwest: the large-scale migration of farmers from the turn of the century to the early 1930s. This was matched by a growing surge of Mexican immigration during the same period (a large boost between 1910 and 1920 during the Mexican Revolution), which led to dramatic population growth in RGV counties and provided the low-wage workforce needed. (Foley 1988, 6–7). The original border citizens (Spanish settlers and land grant families)—a tight-knit community that also straddled the Rio Grande on both sides—regarded both Anglo settlers and Mexican migrant laborers as "transients" or interlopers (gringos and *fuereños*) (Paredes 1958, 13). However, by the early part of the twentieth century, Anglo dominance over Mexican immigrant workers brought an end to cattle ranching, which influenced the dispossession of landowners and left many in poverty (Foley 1988, 66–67; Montejano 1987, 110).

Conjunto music grew out of this social, economic, and increasingly politicized border region, becoming a dynamic cultural force that connected descendents of Spanish settlers and Mexican immigrant communities. Today, the music's origin among the RGV's working class farming community is a source of pride for largely middle- and upper-class fans who refer to themselves as Mexican American and Chicano/a or Tejano/a in San Antonio and other Texas cities to the north. Today it is Mexican migrants, mostly undocumented, who toil in the fields (though there are fewer of them) and who have increased the popularity of *música norteña* (also known as *norteño*), which features the same instrumentation but with more emphasis on narrative ballads, less accordion, and somewhat erratic rhythmic accents. By comparison, it is less suited to the region's more intimate dancehalls dominated by conjuntos. Conjunto's popularity was intimately tied to social life, dancing, and the lively accordion that came to define it both musically and culturally. Extremely portable and loud, it required few accompanying instruments and represented the hybrid nature of the Mexican American experience in Texas. San Benito was the site of the manufacturing, sales, and distribution base of the nation's first record label, IDEAL Records, owned by Armando Marroquin, a former jukebox entrepreneur from Alice, a town about two hours north. IDEAL began production in 1946, inspiring numerous independent labels and studios established throughout the border region beginning roughly two decades later when recording technology became more accessible. Inspired by Marroquin's DIY (Do It Yourself) model, these labels had names that reflected the region's flora and fauna as well as its unique position on the Texas-Mexico border: Falcón, Río, Zarape, Corona, Nopal, Del Valle, Bronco, and so on. By the early 1980s, all had gone out of business and much of the working-class population and local music industry relocated to urban centers, most notably San Antonio, Corpus Christi, and Houston. In these cities, the conjunto sound has been transformed into radio-friendly popular genres that reflect contemporary middle-class tastes and experiences such as *conjunto progressive*, *música tejana* (or simply tejano), and *tejano cumbia*, all influenced in one way or another by rock, blues, jazz, country, and Colombian tropical music by way of Monterrey, Mexico (see Ramos-Kittrell's chapter in this volume).

Yet, the border imaginary continues to be invoked in the inclusion of songs written about places and experiences on the border, performed in the 'style' of pioneering conjunto musicians, particularly on the accordion, and evoking tropes of the region's working-class past—either left behind or progressed from. Conjunto, as Manuel Peña, author of books on contemporary Tejano and conjunto music, writes, "represents a clear musical and ideological alternative to the Americanized forms that more acculturated, upwardly-mobile Mexican-Americans [Chicanos and Tejanos] have come to embrace."[4] In conjunto music, the working-class ethos remains symbolically embedded ready to be conjured up—as in the gathering at the documentary screening described earlier in this chapter—and as a marker of belonging in a self-defined community and place-based cultural citizenship (Flores 2003, 76).

NARCISO MARTÍNEZ AND FREDDY FENDER: SAN BENITO'S HOMETOWN LEGACIES

San Benito, as the focus of this chapter, is deeply tied to how memory and legacy operate within a community of cultural brokers (fans and self-appointed *cronistas*) and a local municipality inspired by capitalist notions of urban development, economic growth, and cultural tourism. Through their efforts, this once insignificant border town could be remapped and reimagined as economically viable, ready to be reclaimed and made new again in the present by the past. The legacy of two of the city's 'native sons'—Mexican-born Narciso Martínez, the celebrated "father of conjunto music," who died in 1992 poor and nearly forgotten until he was 'rediscovered' in the final two years of his life by Juan Tejeda, a noted San Antonio culture broker and founder of the Tejano Conjunto Festival; and, Baldemar Huerta (aka Freddy Fender), who changed his name, left San Benito in 1959, and became a Billboard-charting country rock musician and Grammy recipient before his death in 2006—have been memorialized in two opposing positions to reclaim border music history in a context of globalization and hypermediacy that seeks to counter representations of a U.S.-Mexico border perpetually 'in crisis.' What appears to be at stake for all of these actors is how to shape, preserve, and promote a border culture that is based on multiple metaphors and narratives, all of which share some aspects with Mexicans on 'the other side,' but are defiantly regional and celebrated as uniquely Tejano (Vila 2000).

The three San Benito actors who claim to be advocating on behalf of these legacies and represent the focus of this chapter reveal the complexity of this type of enterprise, which has become entwined with politicized visions of urban renewal, and with what Barbara Kirshenblatt-Gimblett has described as "adding value to an oppressive and colonialized past through memory, collection, exhibition, and difference" (1995, 374). In this case, such valorization refers to the canonization of a Tejano musical past born out of struggle, discrimination, and exclusion. Two of these actors have operated initially as 'self-authorized' culture brokers, having acted upon their own compulsive and nostalgic desires to give substance to the ritualized and performative dimensions of cultural memory. In the process, the hope is for San Benito to become the site of conjunto music legacy and heritage, as an (in)tangible place of importance and pilgrimage (Roberts and Sara Cohen 2014, 8–9). Both actors procured minimal support in the mid-1990s from the city

Figure 7.1. Mural depicting Narisco Martinez and Freddy Fender in downtown San Benito. Photo by Carlos R. de Souza, 2017.

in the form of office and exhibition space, both badly in need of repair and from which they worked independently of one another to create a makeshift museum (The Tejano Conjunto Music Hall of Fame and Museum) and a literary-community center-music performance space (The Narciso Martínez Cultural Arts Center).

The third actor is the local municipality itself, led by the mayor, who imagines San Benito as an "urban utopia" that she hopes can be realized through an ambitious regeneration plan that involves a "cultural clustering" of museums—the Narciso Martínez Cultural Arts Center, the San Benito Historical Museum, the Tejano Conjunto Music Hall of Fame and Museum, and possibly the Freddy Fender Museum (a separate permanent exhibit belonging to Fender's family)—a few miles away from the dilapidated historic city center where they currently reside. The municipality hoped that this vision will bolster the city's image and will connect with statewide efforts to promote what the Texas Historical Commission is calling "Hispanic Heritage Tourism," an initiative that identifies and promotes important sites in the state that have creatively fused history, place, and modern design to attract mostly middle-class Tejanos and newly enlightened aficionados. In a promotional article on the Hispanic Heritage Tourism Guide titled "Hispanic Texans: Journey from Empire to Democracy" that the Commission produced in 2015, the author, Mitch Goulding wrote, "Heritage tourism is a big moneymaker, raking in $2.2 billion in spending and making up about 10% of all travel in the state each year."[5] While the transnational nature of Texas-Mexico border culture and border life that existed, particularly during the first part of the twentieth century, gave birth to the hybrid culture and musical tradition we now celebrate on the Texas side as Mexican-American—and in modern (and some might say nationalist) terms Tejano—such culture was never concentrated in one place, town, or city. However, the legacies noted above and the role of San Benito entrepreneurs in the recording, packaging, and dissemination of the music's pioneering recordings (first to regional and later national and international listeners) has motivated these actors to concentrate their efforts in the city.

The different actors involved in this effort represent a variety of legitimizing discourses of popular music as heritage, ranging from personal and collective attachment to memory and commercial endeavors. In a paradoxically globalized and isolated border region, often characterized by stereotypical notions of poverty, illegal border crossing, and drug cartel violence, their artful manipulation of the mythology of musical legacy is a powerful claim of inclusion against the grain in both Tejano and Mexican-American notions of *mexicanidad* and cultural heritage. It is not so much the raw past that is the object of their obsession, but rather legacy, that is, the way that past, tradition, collective memory, cultural heritage, and even biography are reshaped and made operational in different, and often conflicting, ways. Ironically, the gentrification and commercialism necessary for economic growth and renewal that San Benito so desperately needs is deeply tied to its claim over the legacy and memory of two of Tejano music's most iconic, albeit, contradictory pioneers. "San Benito has never found its footing," Meg Jorn, a prominent local architect who designed and built the town's new Tejano music and history museum and has worked in developments in the nearby and more prosperous city of Harlingen, told me. "But it has those legacies that can turn it around, that is, if the city and other preservationists can agree."

Narciso Martínez and Freddy Fender are represented in this effort by the two organizations operating in their name. On the one hand, there is the Narciso Martínez Cultural Arts Center, directed by longtime Chicano rights activist and writer Rogelio Núñez. The Center is aligned with historic perceptions of the region as rural- and working-class, and advocates for community activism, much of which is woven into weekly poetry readings, writer's forums, dances at a local historic dance hall, and an annual festival. The festival is the only event that openly invites tourists or casual listeners, and it receives the bulk of the small amount of funding that Núñez receives. Throughout the year, most of the Center's activities are participatory: individual memories and experiences are of paramount importance since they bring together past and present in the representation of self as part of the cultural identity of border Tejanos, to which the Center aims to bring attention.

The Tejano Conjunto Music Hall of Fame and Museum, on the other hand, is headed up by a devoted fan and music cronista, Rey Avila, and evokes middle-class perceptions of cultural preservation that embrace mainstream American popular music and fandom. Unlike the Cultural Center, the Hall of Fame and Museum are driven by a commercial and tourism potential that celebrates Tejano music as local music with a global identity. Both exhibit distinct representations of Limón's Tejano ethno-nationalism, where pride has morphed into privileging Tejano identity (and music) over that of Mexican immigrants. In the RGV, as in other parts of Texas, Tejanos have raised concerns about music associated with Mexican immigrants (predominantly *música norteña, banda,* and *cumbia norteña*), which currently dominates local radio airwaves and larger and more prominent dance halls. "There's been a lot of very nasty anti-immigrant rhetoric from the Texas Mexicans," notes Cristina Ballí, a Brownsville native and current Executive Director at the Guadalupe Cultural Arts Center in San Antonio. "The debate about music brings out a lot of intra-ethnic tension."[6]

CULTURE AS INTERVENTION: SALVAGING WHAT WAS LEFT BEHIND

By the late 1970s, San Antonio was emerging as the hub of the Tejano music industry thanks in large part to having received the bulk of the post–WWII population exodus from the RGV. San Antonio is also ground zero for all things Tejano, whether it be music, culture, art, or politics. Avila got the idea for the Tejano Conjunto Music Hall of Fame and Museum while visiting San Antonio for the annual Tejano Music Hall of Fame awards show. After attending the event, he went in search of a museum dedicated to pioneering musicians with photographs and memorabilia. "They didn't have any physical location for the Hall of Fame in San Antonio," he said. At that moment, he decided that San Benito would be that place.

I first met Avila in 2010 when I came to San Benito with some students to look at uncatalogued items of his memorabilia collection. We found piles of dusty vintage 78, 45, and 33$\frac{1}{3}$ single discs and long-playing albums, many still in shrink-wrap along with remains of recording equipment, master discs made of steel for printing records, presses, large reel-to-reel tape recorders and other artifacts from well before the digital age. Avila acquired these physical remains of musical tradition in 1999 from the Rio Grande Music Company, which handled distribution and pressing of all IDEAL Records until it closed in 1981. The owner's son, longtime businessman Lionel Betancourt, sold the building and let Avila take what was left before he threw it out—it was as if he'd struck gold. Betancourt told me he could not understand why Avila wanted "all that junk." What's at work here is the self-conscious act of preservation—the creation of the archive—at the moment of the structural breakdown of memory, which happens over time (Derrida and Prenowitz 1995, 14), and the importance of marking the ways in which a once-repressed community significantly impacted the artistic and cultural trajectory of the region and, eventually, the state. This passionate pursuit of collecting gives meaning to these objects as they become a "triumphant unconscious discourse"; what gives them most value is what is missing (Baudrillard 1968, 2).

Avila's acquisition came nineteen years after Chris Strachwitz, owner of the California-based Arhoolie Records, had (in Avila's words) "picked through everything" in the Betancourt warehouse. Strachwitz came looking to license some recordings and ended up purchasing the entire IDEAL catalog of master tapes and rare publicity photos. In 1991, Strachwitz began reissuing recordings of many border-music pioneers, including accordionists Narciso Martínez, Tony de la Rosa, orquesta tejana bandleader Beto Villa, sister singing duo Carmen y Laura, Lydia Mendoza, and many others already well known across the state, thanks in large part to Manuel Peña's seminal book. Avila boasted that he "saved these artifacts of our Tejano music history" before they met their fate in the garbage bin and were lost forever. "Chris Strachwitz took most of the good stuff to California," Avila said. "This is the home of conjunto music. This is its birthplace. I had to save them." His actions indicate the inherent value of memorabilia and the importance of intervention by local actors, which makes the category of legacy more tangible, all the while indicating its worth as a commodity. What is also significant about Avila's effort is the notion of creating something out of what was left over or left behind (Baker and Huber, 2015: 114–115); that which was deemed worthless by Strachwitz, a German-Polish immigrant who wanted to preserve border music in order to reboot his then struggling American roots music label at the time. Both express similar concerns but with different motivations and outcomes.

In Avila's museum, Freddy Fender's motorcycle, 'Elvis-inspired' stage costumes, photographs, and gold records are on display in one tiny room and the Hall of Fame inductee's photographs are in another. Fender left San Benito at age twenty-two and returned late in his career to receive local honors and finally, to be buried in the San Benito Memorial Park. He was born Baldemar Huerta in San Benito in 1937 to a Mexican immigrant father and Tejana mother. Many of the city's elders tell stories about seeing him sweeping up outside of the Rio Grande Music Company where he worked as a janitor after he returned from serving a three-year prison sentence in Louisiana's Angola State Prison due to his arrest in Baton Rouge for possession of marijuana. At the Company, he graduated to record packer and then sound engineer in the early 1950s. Before traveling north, he changed his name in honor of the Fender Telecaster guitar, the most important cultural icon of the rock 'n' roll era, and is quoted in interviews with the press stating that he thought that name might better appeal to "the gringos." It was clear, Fender had a plan and it meant leaving San Benito.

Eventually, his first two singles "Before The Next Teardrop Falls" and "Wasted Days and Wasted Nights" shot to the top of Billboard country and pop music charts, earning him the Academy of Country Music's Best New Artist award in 1975 and the distinction of being the first with a bilingual song. Somewhere along the way he earned the moniker "Bebop Kid," and while his success as a Mexican American was unheard of at the time, what was even more remarkable was his ability to appeal to fans across musical genres. Country and pop/rock music rarely crossed paths as they often do today. Tejanos and Chicanos from San Antonio to Los Angeles believed his Spanish-language verses to be shout-outs to 'la raza,' and a nod to the very active Chicano movement of the time. While many in the country music world in the 1970s and early 1980s may have viewed Fender's tendency to switch to Spanish in his songs as a novelty, locals like Avila liked to think he put the RGV on the map, even if it was just for a while. "We speak Spanglish here, some English mixed in with Spanish," he said. "It comes natural to us here in the Valley. Freddy never forgot his roots, even though he left to make it with the gringos." Fender spoke about his hometown often in interviews with the press and on television shows, though he described the difficulties overcoming poverty, discrimination, and his long and bumpy road to stardom.

Perhaps the most striking homage to Fender's legacy in the region is San Benito's water tower, easily the tallest structure in the lower RGV. It is a $1.4 million monument built in 2004 with a larger-than-life portrait of Fender along with the words "Hometown of Freddy Fender." Fender is depicted in his trademark leather jacket, moustache, and what locals call his 'Chicano fro' smiling over the comings and goings of travelers on Hwy 83. The water tower locates the town, as do many in rural America, but this one locates legacy and the return of the prodigal son who accomplished the unthinkable: acceptance (at least for a time) in U.S.-American mainstream country and popular music (see Figure 7.2).

Figure 7.2. San Benito's water tower memorializing the image of Freddy Fender. Photo by Carlos R. deSouza, 2017.

NARCISO MARTÍNEZ CENTER: HERITAGE AS COLLABORATION AND COMMUNITY ENGAGEMENT

Known as *el huracán del valle* (The Hurricane of the Valley), accordionist Narciso Martínez is the 'other' part of San Benito's legacy and an important cultural icon. While Fender might be best known for 'making it' in the Anglo world (bringing national attention to San Benito and, by extension, to the RGV), Martínez's contribution is his musical innovations: his distinctive 'staccato' playing style, his emphasis on playing buttons on the treble side while leaving the bass accompaniment to his bajo sexto player, and his original instrumental polkas, waltzes, mazurkas, schottisches, and huapangos, which gave birth to this unique homegrown sound. He emigrated with his parents as an infant from Mexico in 1911 after the Mexican Revolution broke out in Reynosa, Tamaulipas, just across the border from McAllen. His parents worked in the fields and he did the same. He became the house accordionist at IDEAL Records until the mid-1950s, when he left for more steady work as a laborer outside of the region, and later, as a caretaker at the Brownsville Zoo. He enjoyed a resurgence in popularity—in Texas and among audiophiles across the U.S. and Europe—only in the last few years of his life, thanks in large part to the IDEAL masters that Strachwitz purchased and released on his Arhoolie Records label. Martínez never learned much English, never became a U.S. citizen, never went to school, and remained in the San Benito area—only leaving for short periods to do farm work. He told Manuel Peña that he did not become a naturalized American citizen because he didn't want to. His parents were Mexican and, therefore, he considered himself to be "*mexico-americano*" (as opposed to Mexican American or simply American), which Peña believes represents a clearly stated "allegiance to his Mexican heritage" (1985, 54). Martínez is not the only border musician to articulate a 'méxico-americano' identity. In the early 1970s, musician, songwriter, activist, and school teacher Rumel Fuentes (1944–1986) who lived in the border town of Eagle Pass, Texas (about five hours northwest from San Benito) wrote "México-Americano," his popular ode to the progressive Chicano nationalism championed by young activists across the Southwest. In order to convey the movement's sentiment to his community in colloquial terms, Fuentes opens the song with: *Por mi madre yo soy mexicano / Por déstino soy americano / Yo soy de la raza de oro / Yo soy méxico americano* (From my mother I am Mexican / By fortune I am American / I am from the race of gold / I am Mexican American).[8] Though Fuentes wrote several songs inspired by the movement, it is "México Americano" that resonates most among his numerous songs and for this reason was recorded by several noted artists, including Alejandro Escovedo (2002), Los Lobos (2005), Los

Texmaniacs (2018), and La Santa Cecilia (2017), whose members are from Mexico and the U.S. Recently, the group described the song as a "Chicano pride anthem" and, they claim, renders the border culturally "obsolete and meaningless."[9] Ironically, this is a sentiment with which many border residents would likely concur.

Martínez's legacy is associated with having made the first recordings, in 1936 (La chicharronera b/w El Troconal) for Bluebird Records, an imprint of RCA Victor. Peña notes that it is this recording that established the core instrumentation of the new hybrid ensemble, the Texas-Mexican conjunto: accordion and *bajo sexto* (56). He was pronounced the "father of Texas-Mexican conjunto music," in Peña's seminal book *The Texas-Mexican Conjunto: History of a Working-Class People*, and this led to the initial recognition of Martínez as a cultural icon for Tejanos and Mexican Americans throughout the Southwest. In essence, Peña's book was viewed by many as documented proof that conjunto (and Tejano music) was a cultural treasure in need of preservation and documentation. It also gave the RGV its bragging rights as being the place of origin for this music. Martínez and bajo sexto player Santiago Almeida (1911–1999) are responsible for establishing the core instrumentation of the Texas-Mexican conjunto sound. However, in spite of these achievements, Martínez never gained financial success for his efforts, and his life mirrors perceptions of the region as rural and working-class.

The Narciso Martínez Center was founded in 1991 by two local businessmen and Núñez, who is also Executive Director of Casa de Proyecto Libertad in Harlingen, which among many things, provides legal services in defense of human rights for immigrant families in the RGV. In fact, Núñez was at the forefront of the cause to provide legal support and advocacy to detained Central American immigrants in 1981 and has continued to advocate for refugees and immigrants seeking asylum in the U.S. The organization also helps undocumented women and their children—who are mostly from Mexico—to apply for permanent residency and citizenship under the Violence Against Women Act (VAWA) and the U non-immigrant status (U visa), among other laws. Even though Núñez 'officially' retired in 2014, he continues to work at the Proyecto as a volunteer.

"When I was in college, I got influenced by, and became part of the Chicano movement," Núñez recalled in an interview. "So that movement began to tell me that it was important that we do things to better our community of Chicanos. One of the leaders of the Chicano Movement was a guy named José Angel Gutiérrez, who was the founder of the La Raza Unida (political) party. He used to say things like, 'We need to create institutions by us, for us, and about us.' Because it wasn't being done by the institutions that existed then." Núñez's vision was not a place for artifacts and memorabilia, but for community and collaboration. The cultural memory that is evoked here is not stagnant, but ongoing. It is heritage with a small "h" (or heritage-as-praxis), a process of engagement with a musical past that is imagined as authentic, devoid of commercial trappings, and a source of pride in its innovation and creativity (Roberts and Cohen 2014, 14). According to Roberts and Cohen, heritage-as-praxis is informed by "individual and collective memory," "everyday practice," and "cultural bricolage," which operates in opposition to "heritage as object" or 'Big H' Heritage (2014, 14–15).

Núñez and Avila represent two self-authorized approaches to preserving heritage and cultural memory. Each created their grassroots organizations out of a personal desire to preserve and protect cultural values, traditions, and customs of their Mexican heritage that for years had been suppressed, undervalued, and, more recently, exploited by dominant Anglo culture and its actors. By focusing on music, the most visible and inclusive of the expressive arts, the hope is that though the recovery, preservation, presentation, and honoring of artifacts of conjunto's past (Avila) and enlisting the memory-work through performance and activism (Núñez) will enhance cultural identity, help heal personal and community conflict and provide a stimulus for creativity among those who experience it today (Kirshenblatt-Gimblett, 1995; Clavir, 2002).

SAN BENITO MUSEUM COMPLEX AND RESACA DREAMS

In July of 2016, the San Benito city manager released plans to build a large museum complex that would house all of the museums and the Narisco Martínez Cultural Arts Center together. They were granted $1.7 million in 2006 to build a museum complex "in the shape of a guitar on the front entrance (honoring Fender) and the back part of the complex will be in the shape of a colorful accordion (honoring Martínez)." However, by 2016 the complex had not yet been built, and they needed to begin construction soon or lose the funding. The city's then mayor, Celeste Z. Sánchez, and council came up with a new plan: to build the museum complex as part of a planned development on the banks of the city's *resaca* (a dry river bed that was once inlet channels of the Río Grande). At the beginning of the twentieth century, resacas were used for irrigation of crops and then left to dry up. However, as the region has urbanized, many smaller resacas are being pumped with water and developed as parks or centerpieces for new residential communities. San Benito's resaca is larger than those in nearby Harlingen (a popular destination for Anglo retirees) and Brownsville. It has been the center of a campaign to rebrand San Benito as "The Resaca City," and a destination for Anglo retirees as well as middle-class Tejano families. In the city's new plan, the museum complex would be joined on the resaca by a performance arena, new restaurants and shops, and a boardwalk. However, one question looms heavily regarding the execution of this project. Currently, there are modest residential homes belonging to working-class families who have deep ties to the neighborhood that stretches along parts of the resaca. How would the gentrification and development of planned communities affect these residents? I was not able to obtain a clear answer. As Sara Cohen observes, "city planners execute plans about how cities should be, which create contradictions, anomalies and gaps: people and places that do not fit the plan" (Cohen 2012, 155). For the mayor and city planners in San Benito, the relationship between community life and the creation of a global urban environment that is shaped by the creativity and memory of its two most important musical legacies should be of primary consideration.

Avila enthusiastically supported the city's plan, as it suited his rendering of Fender's legacy at his museum—a middle-class perception of integration into the American dream that embraces mainstream popular music, fandom, and seeks to imagine San Benito as a place where ranchero meets pop. Like Núñez, Avila often references Tejano music's emergence in the region as a response to its working-class and border-crossing past. However, his plan to preserve and display the Rio Grande Music Company's disc-engraving and -pressing equipment and create a replica of the IDEAL recording studio, among others, celebrates individual entrepreneurship, individuality, and style—all accoutrements of success, self-fulfillment, and fulfillment of the 'American Dream.' Quite probably, Freddy Fender would have approved.

Núñez and supporters of the Narciso Martínez Cultural Arts Center, however, were not interested in the city's new plan. They argued that the building in which the Center has been housed for over twenty years should be preserved since it was the city's first library, constructed in 1942 under FDR's Works Progress Administration. The city plan originally called for the old library to be destroyed when the Center moves to the new complex. Núñez and his supporters mobilized and fought back, noting that the Center had garnered nationwide attention for San Benito by bringing in tourists for its popular annual conjunto festival. Of course, they argued, the old library would best honor its community-based mission and outreach efforts. This form of 'heritage-as-practice' centers on individual and collective memory and is driven by the sociality and culture of everyday life (Roberts and Cohen 2014, 15). Surely, this is how Narciso Martínez would have wanted his contributions to the music's humble beginnings to be remembered.

After examining the original grant, the city manager realized that in order to receive the funds to build the museum complex, it had to be built on the original property, where it stands now. They could not use this money to relocate to the resaca after all. Mayor Sánchez explained that she and the city council were not giving up on the move. "It's only a matter of time," she said. "We will build the museums near the resaca one day. Those legacies represent our people, our music, our history. We can't let anyone forget that." As of this writing, Mayor Sanchez lost her reelection bid and it is not clear what the city's next move will be regarding the resaca project. The new seven thousand square-foot museum complex (complete with the guitar and accordion design intended for the resaca site) is now called the San Benito Cultural Heritage Center. It was built on the downtown location indicated in the grant and next door to the dilapidated buildings where the museums and the Cultural Center were originally located. The museums have yet to occupy the space, as of this writing.

Meanwhile, the Narciso Martínez Center successfully reached an agreement in 2016 to remain in the old library. A year later, however, with a new mayor installed, Núñez learned that he did not receive funding from the city for his twenty-sixth annual conjunto festival. Instead, the city staged its own music festival on the banks of the resaca and on the very weekend in October that the conjunto festival was originally—and has always been—scheduled. Rather than focusing exclusively on Tejano conjunto music, the San Benito city festival also featured country, rock, and blues bands in an obvious attempt to lure seasonal, mostly white winter Texans, to the event.

A FINAL ACT

Núñez and the Center have since left the old library space and managed to rustle up sponsorship from local businesses, fundraisers, and a grant from the Community Development Council in the town of Los Fresnos, just twelve miles away. He and his small staff hosted the event in the Los Fresnos Memorial Park on October 19, 20, and 21 of 2018, featuring artists from across South Texas, including a high school conjunto band, 2010 Grammy Award winner Max Baca and Los Texmaniacs from San Antonio, several longtime regional pioneering artists, and a few up-and-coming groups. Núñez says he is now doing the Center's work out of the First Presbyterian Church in San Benito, and that there are regular gatherings for other musical and cultural events at La Villita, a recently restored 1940s dance hall that is also in the city.

While Núñez still maintains his San Benito roots where he lives and continues the organization's work, moving the popular festival out of the city challenges the notion that the performance and embodiment of its musical memory and history be tied to this place. Likewise, the memory of Fender and Martínez is liberated, and judgement of Núñez's act as 'anti-heritage,' described by Roberts and Cohen as a rather "more progressive form of cultural engagement," is ultimately up to the people to decide as they build their own map to create and experience heritage (2014, 16). Speaking (oddly enough) to the *San Benito News*, Núñez is clearly aware that the festival is a key symbolic event of the Center's work, "to preserve, develop, and promote the conjunto musical genre born on the Texas-Mexican Border and to ensure that Los Fresnos, Texas is a major cultural tourist destination."[10] After all, Narciso Martínez's gift to Tejano culture and identity is much larger and grander than San Benito or even the Rio Grande Valley. It appears that while the long-awaited and much maligned San Benito museum complex idea (whether remaining downtown or on the resaca) seems hung up in bureaucracy, local politics, and economic limbo, Núñez has set about to practice a form of anti-heritage" or perhaps even better, heritage as resistance, that advocates honoring the music's roots which reflects the experiences of Mexican Americans and México Americanos from across the border region, and not just in one city. Perhaps the best way to honor the memory of San Benito's legacies is heritage management through social action.

NOTES

† In memory of Meg Jorn, lead architect of the San Benito Heritage and Culture Museum.

1. The *For a Quarter a Song* documentary was produced by Dr. Manuel Medrano, Professor Emeritus, University of Texas, Brownsville and UT-RGV, and it is part of the "Los del valle" series.

2. The North American Free Trade Agreement (NAFTA) was a bill signed in 1992 by President George H. W. Bush, and implemented on January 1, 1994 by President Clinton. NAFTA introduced free unrestricted trade between the three countries on the North American continent (U.S, Canada, and Mexico) to eliminate trade taxes and increase trade. The agreement was recently renegotiated and is now called the U.S.-Mexico-Canada Agreement (USMCA). To read more about NAFTA's impact on the Rio Grande Valley, visit: http://citeseerx.ist.psu.edu/viewdoc/download?doi=10.1.1.146.4964&rep=rep1&type=pdf

3. Fernandez et al., "See America's New Ellis Island: A South Texas Bus Terminal," *The New York Times* (July 27, 2018), https://www.nytimes.com/interactive/2018/07/27/us/immigration-mcallen-bus-terminal-texas.html.

4. Peña, Manuel. "The Texas-Mexican Conjunto." *Borders/Fronteras* (Smithsonian Online Exhibition), Smithsonian Center for Folklife and Cultural Heritage, 1996. https://folklife.si.edu/resources/frontera/pena.htm.

5. Mitch Goulding, "State Rolls Out Hispanic Heritage Tourism Guide," *Spectrum News Austin,* (May 6, 2015), http://spectrumlocalnews.com/tx/austin/news/2015/05/6/state-rolls-out-hispanic-heritage-tourism-guide. See guide at: http://www.thc.texas.gov/public/upload/publications/hispanic-heritage-travel-guide.pdf.

6. Saul Elbein, "Get Your Norteño out of My Conjunto," *The Texas Observer* (May 20, 2011), https://www.texasobserver.org/get-your-norteno-out-of-my-conjunto/.

7. "México-Americano" and other original corridos written by Rumel Fuentes were recorded between 1972 and 1975. They appear on Rumel Fuentes, *Corridos of the Chicano Movement*, ARH00507, Arhoolie Records, 2009, Compact Disc: 507.

8. Cantor-Navas, Judy. "La Santa Cecilia's Rockabilly-Norteño 'México Americano': Watch the Video." *Billboard*. https://www.billboard.com/articles/columns/latin/7849391/la-santa-cecilia-mexico-americano-cover-video (accessed February 16, 2019)

9. Editor, San Benito News, "Conjunto Fest to Move to Los Fresnos," *San Benito News* (February 20, 2018), https://www.sbnewspaper.com/2018/02/20/conjunto-fest-to-move-to-los-fresnos/

REFERENCES

Aparna, Kolar. "Re-mapping the U.S.-Mexico Border: High Agency, Everyday Region-making, and Lived Spaces of The U.S.-Mexico Border in Tijuana." Thesis, Radboud University, Nijmegen, Netherlands, 2013.

Appadurai, Arjun. *Modernity at Large: Cultural Dimensions of Globalization*. Minneapolis: University of Minnesota Press, 1996.

Avila, Rey. Director/Curator of the Texas Conjunto Music Hall of Fame and Museum. Personal Communication. San Benito, TX. July 20, 2016.

Baker, Sarah and Alison Huber. "Saving 'Rubbish': Preserving Popular Music's Material Culture in Amateur Archives and Museums." In *Sites of Popular Music Heritage Memories, Histories, Places*, eds. Cohen, Sara, Robert Knifton, Marion Leonard and Les Roberts, 112–124. New York: Routledge, 2015.

Baudrillard, Jean. "The System of Collecting." In *The Cultures of Collecting*, ed. John Elsner and Roger Cardinal, 7–24. London: Reaktion 1994.

Betancourt, Lionel. Retired San Benito Businessman and son of Paco Betancourt, co-founder of IDEAL Records (with Armando Marroquin) and owner/operator of Rio Grande Music Company. Personal Communication. San Benito, TX. July 27, 2016.

Bourdieu, Pierre. *Distinction: A Social Critique of the Judgement of Taste.* London: Routledge, 1984.

Bowles, David. *Ghosts of the Rio Grande Valley.* Haunted America. Mt. Pleasant, SC: The History Press/Arcadia Publishing, 2016.

Clavir, Miriam. *Preserving What Is Valued: Museums, Conservation, and First Nations.* Vancouver, University of British Columbia Press, 2002.

Cohen, Sara. "Sounding Out the City: Music and the Sensuous Production of Place." *Transactions of the Institute of British Geographers*, New Series, vol. 20, no. 4 (1995): 434–446.

_____. "Bubbles, Tracks, Borders and Lines: Mapping Music and Urban Landscape." *Journal of the Royal Musical Association*, vol. 137, no. 1 (2012): 135–170.

Corona, Ignacio and Alejandro L. Madrid. "Introduction: The Postnational Turn in Music Scholarship and Music-Making." In *Postnational Musical Identities: Cultural Production, Distribution, and Consumption in a Globalized Scenario*, eds. Ignacio Corona and Alejandro L. Madrid, 3–22. Lanham, MD: Lexington Books, 2008.

Derrida, Jacques and Eric Prenowitz. "Archive Fever: A Freudian Impression." *Diacritics*, vol. 25, no. 2 (Summer, 1995): 9–63.

Elbein, Saul. "Get Your Norteño out of My Conjunto." *The Texas Observer* (May 20, 2011). https://www.texasobserver.org/get-your-norteno-out-of-my-conjunto/.

Fernandez, Manny et al. "See America's New Ellis Island: A South Texas Bus Terminal." *The New York Times* (July 27, 2018). https://www.nytimes.com/interactive/2018/07/27/us/immigration-mcallen-bus-terminal-texas.html.

Flores, William V. "New Citizens, New Rights: Undocumented Immigrants and Latino Cultural Citizenship" in *Latin American Perspectives* 30, no. 2 (March 2003): 87–100.

Foley, Douglas. *From Peones to Politicos: Class and Ethnicity in a South Texas Town 1900–1987*. Austin: University of Texas Press, 1988.

García Canclini, Nestor. *Consumers and Citizens: Globalization and Multicultural Conflicts*. Minneapolis: The University of Minnesota Press, 2001.

Goulding, Mitch. "State Rolls Out Hispanic Heritage Tourism Guide." *Spectrum News Austin* (May 6, 2015). http://spectrumlocalnews.com/tx/austin/news/2015/05/6/state-rolls-out-hispanic-heritage-tourism-guide.

Grimson, Alejandro and Pablo Vila. "Forgotten Border Actors: The Border Reinforcers. A Comparison Between the U.S.-Mexico Border and South American Borders." In *Journal of Political Ecology*, vol. 9 (2002): 69–88.

Hobsbawm, Eric and Terence Ranger (eds.). *The Invention of Tradition*. Cambridge: University of Cambridge Press, 1983.

Jameson, Fredric. *Postmodernism, or, The Cultural Logic of Late Capitalism*. Durham: DukeUniversity Press, 1991.

Jorn, Meg. Founder/Owner/Director of Megamorphosis Architecture and Design. Personal Communication. Harlingen, TX. August 3, 2016 (deceased, September 2017).

Kirshenblatt-Gimlett, Barbara. *Destination Culture: Tourism, Museums and Heritage*. Berkeley: University of California Press, 1998.

———. "Theorizing Heritage" *Ethnomusicology*, vol. 39, no. 3 (Autumn, 1995): 367–380.

Klein, Alan M. *Baseball on the Border. A Tale of Two Laredos*. Princeton, N.J.: Princeton University Press, 1997.

Kun, Josh. *Audiotopia: Music, Race, and America*. Berkeley: University of California Press, 2005.

Limón, José. "This is our Música Guy! Tejanos and Ethno/Regional Musical Nationalism." In *Transnational Encounters: Music and Performance at the U.S.-Mexico Border*, ed. Alejandro L. Madrid, 111–126. New York: Oxford University Press, 2011.

Madrid, Alejandro L. "Transnational Musical Encounters at the U.S.-Mexico Border: An Introduction." In *Transnational Encounters: Music and Performance at the U.S.-Mexico Border*, ed. Alejandro L. Madrid, 1–16. New York: Oxford University Press, 2011.

Mikula, Maja. "Vernacular Museum: Communal Bonding and Ritual Memory Transfer Among Displaced Communities." *International Journal of Heritage Studies*, vol. 20, no. 3 (2015): 241–261.

Montejano, David. *Anglos and Mexicans in the Making of Texas, 1836–1986.* Austin: University of Texas Press, 1987.

Nora, Pierre. "Between Memory and History." *Representations,* vol. 26 (Spring, 1989): 7–24.

Núñez, Rogelio. Executive Director of The Narciso Martínez Cultural Arts Center. Personal Communication. San Benito, TX. March 14, 2016 and September 1, 2017.

Paredes, Américo. *"With His Pistol in His Hand": A Border Ballad and Its Hero.* Austin: University of Texas Press, 1958.

Peña, Manuel H. "The Texas-Mexican Conjunto." *Borders/Fronteras* (Smithsonian Online Exhibition), Smithsonian Center for Folklife and Cultural Heritage, 1996. https://folklife.si.edu/resources/frontera/pena.htm.

———. *The Texas-Mexican Conjunto: History of a Working-Class Music.* Austin: University of Texas Press, 1985.

Ragland, Cathy. "Tejano and Proud": Regional Accordion Traditions of South Texas and the Border Region." In *The Accordion in the Americas: Klezmer, Polka, Tango, Zydeco, and More!*, ed. Helena Simonett, 87–111. Urbana, IL: University of Illinois Press, 2012.

———. *Música Norteña: Mexican Migrants Creating a Nation between Nations*, Philadelphia: Temple University Press, 2009.

Roberts, Les and Sara Cohen. "Unauthorizing Popular Music Heritage: Outline of a Critical Framework." *International Journal of Heritage Studies*, vol. 20, no. 3 (2014): 241–261.

San Benito Historical Society. *Images of America: San Benito.* San Francisco: Arcadia Publishing, 2010.

San Benito News (Editor). "Conjunto Fest to Move to Los Fresnos." *San Benito News* (February 20, 2018). https://www.sbnewspaper.com/2018/02/20/conjunto-fest-to-move-to-los-fresnos/.

Sánchez, Celeste Z. Mayor of San Benito (in office 2014–2017). Personal Communication. San Benito, TX. August 4, 2016.

Tejeda, Juan. "Tejano: Local Music, Global Identity." *GIA Reader (A Journal of Arts Philanthropy)*, vol. 25, no. 3 (2014). https://www.giarts.org/article/tejano-local-music-global-identity.

Velasco Ortiz, Laura and Oscar F. Contreras. "The Border as a Life Experience: Identities, Asymmetry and Border Crossing between Mexico and the United States." *Frontera Norte*, vol. 26, no. 3 (2014): 37–56.

Viejo-Rose, Dacia. "Cultural Heritage and Memory: Untangling the Ties that Bind." *Culture & History Digital Journal*, vol. 4, no. 2 (2015). http://cultureandhistory.revistas.csic.es/index.php/cultureandhistory/article/view/83.

Vila, Pablo. *Ethnography at the Border.* Minneapolis: University of Minnesota Press, 2003.

———. *Crossing Borders, Reinforcing Borders: Social Categories, Metaphors and Narrative Identities on the U.S.-Mexico Frontier.* Austin: University of Texas Press, 2000.

Chapter 8

Sounding Cumbia

Past and Present in a Globalized Mexican Periphery

Jesús A. Ramos-Kittrell

> Test, test, yes, hello . . . remember, friend, that this invitation is for you to come and enjoy of this grand tropical party. Remember that *Sonido Duéñez y Hermanos* will be enlivening for you tonight. Remember that your date is at the crossroads of Antiguo San Agustín and Castelar [streets]. Remember, enlivened by *Duéñez y Hermanos* (Bárcenas and Cryma 2010).
>
> —Gabriel Duéñez, from *Sonido Duéñez y Hermanos*

Voiced over the sound of "Tampico" (performed by Mike Laure), Gabriel Duéñez's invitation is similar to many I heard as a child in the flea market beneath the *Puente San Luisito* (also known as *Puente del Papa*, a bridge that connects *Colonia Independencia* with Monterrey's business and tourist district; where Pope John Paul II gathered thousands of people in the dry basin of the Santa Catarina river below the bridge in 1979). Along with the song, Duéñez's voice evokes the memory of the sound of the market, mixed with the city traffic, and the music that *sonideros*[1] like him and Mario Murillo (the two pioneers of sonidero activity in Monterrey) advertised and sold there. "[My wife] would sit with a boom box and a little table on the bridge to sell tapes, and I had another table by the staircase going down," Duéñez recalls. "Later, after six years, they [the authorities] put us down in the river" (Campuzano 2009). At the flea market Duéñez and Murillo sold mixtapes of songs from their coveted vinyl record collection of Colombian music, "from import" (*importados*), as Duéñez proudly observes. But they also enlivened dances and private parties on the weekends (*quinceañeras*, weddings, birthdays, and baptisms), which they advertised over the microphone from their market stalls. In the middle of the city's sonic havoc, Duéñez cranked up the volume of his Radson sound system and Colombian music would come blasting out of the speaker (*la trompeta*, as it is commonly called) to set the reminder. Putting the microphone down, Duéñez's words took effect as his voice reverberated in the listener's mind, carried over by the music. The EQ band in his Radson console is worn and missing knobs today. Yet, he has made sure to add an extra-big-sized knob to the middle potentiometer, the one he has always used the most. This is because the low fidelity of the speaker made it necessary to boost the mid-range in the EQ to make the song's vocal tracks (and his own voice) pierce through the low end of the LP recording. It is hard to tell how many times I listened to and danced to songs like Mike Laure's "Tampico" at dance halls enlivened by young tape jockeys, where middle-class teenagers danced to Colombian music—to cumbia, more specifically—at quinceañera parties. In these rituals, cumbia acquired clearer definition through high-tech JBL speakers (the most coveted brand in Monterrey back in the 1980s), which turned the low-brow sound of this music into a performative site of bourgeois leisure. The dark hue and low fidelity of the Radson speaker, however, was encrypted with the memory of the urban aural mayhem of the flea market at Colonia Independencia. By boosting the middle frequencies Duéñez created a sonic smudge that expanded through the space below the bridge, colliding with the sound of the city traffic running above: car horns, police whistle, and running engines dissipated as the light turned green on the street, and the music remained, and with it, the echo of Duéñez's words: remember, friend . . .

Recently, scholars have brought attention to the capacity of sound for symbolic representation. This capacity, it has been mentioned, urges us to rethink "the largely visuocentric epistemology that has dominated western intellectual inquiry in order to account for alternative sensorial ways to knowledge" (Madrid 2016, 127). There seems to be consensus in sound studies literature about how the study of the aural can "enrich our understanding of perception and its role in situating oneself, forming beliefs, and acting upon the environment" (O'Callaghan 2007, 3). Technological, economic, and structural changes in how sound has circulated throughout the twentieth and twenty-first centuries have made it an increasingly important component in the ways people make sense out of the natural, social, and cultural world in which they live. Ana María Ochoa Gautier has referred to this phenomenon as the "intensification of the aural," given that "under contemporary processes of globalization and regionalization, coupled with the transformation in technologies of sound, the public sphere [has been] increasingly mediated by the aural" (2012, 392). It is due to this intensification, and the way it permeates experience, that the field of sound studies has problematized the very act of listening in relation to sensation as a process through which people produce knowledge. The concept of episteme has accompanied this notion, alluding to sound as an index of sensation, "an instance for making sense of the world and produce knowledge" (Madrid 2016, 128).

The current epistemological quandary transpiring in sound studies is too complex to address here. Concerns over the experience of sound, nonetheless, suggest that the imbrication of perception with sensation informs ideas about knowledge in this field: a byproduct of a process of empirical (experiential) synthesis from our perception of reality, which we use to act upon the world (see O'Callaghan above). For David W. Samuels and others this implies re-approaching the body and the senses as sources of knowledge. By focusing on the senses (on the ear, specifically), Samuels, Louise Meintjes, Ochoa Gautier, and Thomas Porcello attend to practices of signification that take place through mediation, given that mediating technologies have made sound a more democratically accessible locus to inscribe experience, thereby pointing to the ear as central in the constitution of knowledge (Samuels et al. 2010, 331–332). This suggests that the phenomenology of aurality and aural knowledge can be symbolically referenced. Such reference to the aural-signified involves the inscription of sound(ed) memory: the (re)cognition of aural experience that, encoded and mediated, (re)presents a kind of knowledge through recall. It is thus that the aural query over the structure of signification has nuanced the logocentric concern for presence, advocating for the "felt nature of memory, time, and place" (Samuels et al. 2010, 333).

Interests in the aural inscription of memory and its preservation as a type of heritage date back to the nineteenth century and are still prevalent today. The early development of recording technologies produced sound documents that became important historical registers, to the extent that in 1999 the United Nations Educational, Scientific and Cultural Organization (UNESCO) incorporated sound to its initiative to preserve the documentary heritage of humanity. UNESCO's Memory of the World Programme lies at the center of this initiative. The vision of the Programme is that "the world's documentary heritage belongs to all, should be fully preserved and protected for all and, with due recognition of cultural mores and practicalities, should be permanently accessible to all without hindrance."[2] Thus, UNESCO's Jikji Memory of the World Prize recognizes institutional contributions to the preservation of and accessibility to a vast array of documental sources, which in 2007 included the *Phonogrammarchiv* of Austria's Academy of Sciences.[3] The Fonoteca Nacional in Mexico City (Mexico's national sonic archive devoted to the research, registry, preservation, and diffusion of the country's aural (*sonoro*) patrimony) was created in 2001 following precisely UNESCO's concern for heritage preservation. Seemingly, the Fonoteca was a response by federal authorities to the fear that the nation's aural past was in danger of disappearing due to the fragile state of some of the formats in which historical recordings were initially made (Madrid 2016, 4; Rodríguez Reséndiz 2012, 195). The Fonoteca today "safeguards the sonic patrimony of the country through methodologies aimed to gather, preserve, and give access . . . to Mexico's sonic heritage" (see Fonoteca Nacional in references).

If sound is memory and listening is remembering, mediation, therefore, frames the affectual traces that permeate the experience of sound, and the recollection of such experience. Media engages the ear in an act of symbolic listening to recognize elements that have been sonically inscribed. Recording and listening, therefore, are also political acts with stakes in processes of inscription. In this regard, Alejandro L. Madrid has mentioned that the mediation of sound projects by artists and/or institutions can involve relations of power that undermine the social inclusiveness of sound as a source of knowledge accessed and experienced in the public sphere (Madrid 2010, 129). It is perhaps for this reason that Ana María Ochoa Gautier considers the aural an important locus of cultural analysis, given that its seemingly democratic characters make it a potential site for political struggle (2012, 392).

The account of Gabriel Duéñez at the opening of this chapter serves as a backdrop to tease out these politics. Specifically, this chapter addresses how the activity of sonideros like Duéñez made Colombian music in Monterrey, Mexico (particularly cumbia) the basis of an index of local culture traversed by class tensions. The chapter also explores why such activity inspired new recording projects through which modern artists reimagined the past to reposition themselves in a globalized cosmopolitan present. The longevity of Colombian music in Monterrey relates to the transnational circulation, performance, and consumption of this music since the 1960s. The anchorage of this activity in a specific part of the city—Colonia Independencia—made the music a referent to this place and to the aesthetic sensibilities of those who lived there. For the middle class of the 1970s, 1980s and 1990s, cumbia represented an expressive discharge of working-class affect, the patterns of behavior of *nacos* (i.e., socially ill-mannered people), and their marginality; in short, the bottom-end of a hierarchical social ladder. For Duéñez and others, however (who due to their working class condition were alien to the image of the 'ideal' citizen in Monterrey—someone from the middle class, with a good job, and focused on earning money), Colombian music was a means to map and make sense out of their environment:

> I mean, understand this, we live in a neighborhood neglected by the government, we live in the middle of wild nature (*vivimos en el monte*), and you see these huge wild plants, eight feet tall, taking over sidewalks; you see palm trees, trails that go into the wild and into the hills (*brechas que van al monte y al cerro*). Then you see the cover of *música tropical* records, you listen to the

lyrics talking about nature, and you associate it, you know what I mean? (*lo asocias, ¿me explico?*) (López Carrera, personal communication).

More than a register of lived material experience, Colombian music eventually became a platform of corporate visibility amid the city's dominant ideology of economic progress. During the 1990s, the pressures of neoliberal capitalism challenged notions of cultural self-reference among middle-class youths. The liberalization of trade, the opening of economic borders between Mexico and the U.S., and the democratization of media opened markets for the promotion and consumption of music by the working class, but also spaces for the consumption of new products from the U.S. These changes pushed for a socio-economic and cultural restructuring of the public sphere, fueling desires for globalized cosmopolitanism and reframing ideas about cultural origins among the middle class, but also cultural channels for the representation of working-class sensibility. In light of this context, the present chapter traces the process by which Colombian music became a register of local cultural memory: a referent encrypted with a class-informed perception of 'roots' grounded in a particular time and place; a cultural ground zero from which to derive new cultural imaginings to situate oneself in globalization. Recorded Colombian music (songs circulating in mixtapes from the collection of vinyl records of sonideros) was central to this process, since it mediated a signifier (cumbia) through which middle-class artists 'read'—(re)cognized aurally—an urban 'other.' The chapter argues that if new recording projects involve the reproduction of class tensions it is because the 'sounding' of otherness (its aurally signified—'written'—presence, perceived and legible as peripheral) is a condition to render the middle-class subject 'visible.'

SOUNDING COLONIA INDEPENDENCIA

For Gabriel Duéñez, his public advertisement of *bailes sonideros* (dance parties at a local venue enlivened by a sonidero) is part of an aggregate of music practices that has mapped aurally Colonia Independencia. Invitations to *bailes* at the heart of the Colonia (like the one at the opening of this chapter), either from his flea market stall or from another private party that Duéñez might be enlivening, have charted the performance of Colombian music in this place. Music played from his record collection (which Duéñez has accumulated since the 1960s) has been the material for such mapping. Over the course of five decades of activity Duéñez developed a canonic set of songs and artists that he selected for the events in which he played, and that people now recognize as the aural memory of the neighborhood.

> Now for a dance people get a band or a tape-jockey (*cintas*) with lots of equipment. No, man! [Back in the days] we just took a small sound system with a tiny speaker and we would carry them uphill with a bunch of LPs; 80, 90 LPs in a small box, every time you played you took them (Campuzano 2009).

Colonia Independencia is one of Monterrey's oldest neighborhoods, and since approximately the 1970s, one of the most marginalized. "This is Colonia Independencia," says Duéñez from a balcony on the roof of his house, pointing his finger to a section of the *Cerro de la Loma Larga*, a long hill accurately named in the sixteenth century by Spanish cartographers. In here, low-income families made their homes, either buying land or simply taking it and building their houses without purchase since the 1960s. Bailes sonideros were a common source of income for Duéñez, in addition to weddings, quinceañeras, birthdays, or sudden gatherings in the neighborhood. "I always needed help, so one guy would carry a box with the records, another one the Radson [sound system], someone else la trompeta, and there we went uphill in the trails, because they used to be trails," not paved streets (Canal 22 2017). For decades the city government neglected the incorporation of a large sector of Loma Larga to its labor in urban planning and upkeep—in terms of providing basic services, such as paving streets, landscaping, sanitation, water, and electricity—as the hill was overtaken by the increasing immigration of people from other states who joined the city's working class as cab or bus drivers, servers, merchants, domestic servants, or laborers in one of the factories in the metropolitan area. Thus, the sonic map that sonidero activity charted in different sections of the Colonia eventually became an aural symbol of the aesthetic tastes and patterns of sociability of the working class that lived there in the public imagination.

LPs of Colombian music began circulating via a transnational network that included Bogota, Mexico City, and Houston, and that through the efforts of Duéñez and others, eventually incorporated Monterrey.

> It was very hard [because] before there was no Colombian music in the city. We would find one or two records in local stores, but the good ones we brought from Houston . . . sometimes we would go to Mexico City [to get] records of $300 or $400 pesos each. It was very rare music and not just anyone could get it (Torres 2011).

At sixty-eight, Duéñez has amassed over 3,500 records, which he keeps in mint condition. His record collection is a historical account of the transnationally circulating sounds that found anchorage in Colonia Independencia. Local favor for this music also inspired artists to record and perform it actively in this neighborhood during the 1970s and 1980s, thereby strengthening the associations of

Colombian music with this place. "All of this music [pointing to a section in one of his record shelves] is from the oldies (*de la antigüita*)," Duéñez explains.

> We sold from our collection; look (showing a record), by Lucho Bermúdez. Here is another one by Los Corraleros [del Majagual]. It was music to dance cheek-to-cheek. Now dudes like to dance alone and jump up and down. No, this was yummy music to dance really close, like this, with your woman [*era música rica, para bailar pegadito, así, con su mujer*] (Campuzano 2009).

The distribution of the oldies to which Duéñez refers was largely the endeavor of Discos Fuentes, a Colombian record label founded in 1934 that sought to capitalize on the market of *música tropical*. Peter Wade, Toño Carrizosa, and Alejandro L. Madrid have addressed the changes in performance and production practices that music from Colombia underwent during the 1960s and 1970s as it became increasingly popular in Mexico. According to Wade, the 1950s represented the golden era for the exportation of music from the Colombian Caribbean coast, which predominantly encompassed porro, cumbia, vallenato, and gaitas (a term used for music performed by traditional gaita flute ensembles. See Ramos-Kittrell 2014, 190–201). Being music from the warm region between the Equator and the Tropic of Cancer, it was marketed with the label of música tropical (also called *música costeña* or from the coast, *música bailable* or danceable, and *música guapachosa* or festive, boisterous, a term used for music with a certain degree of Afro-Caribbean or Afro-Colombian influence. See Madrid 2013, 118). For Wade, the popularity of música tropical during the 1950s was due to the international appeal of Afro-Caribbean music, which was headed by Cuban rhythms such as mambo and guaracha (Wade 2000, 145). By the end of the 1950s all of these genres were internationally marketed as 'Latin music,' and música tropical was distributed under this label as well.

The influence of música tropical began with the promotion of artists such as Lucho Bermúdez by Discos Fuentes, who became a key figure in the dissemination of cumbia. But more important was the influence of Bermúdez's orchestral sound. The record *Vamos a la playa* is an example of the Afro-Cuban tinge and orchestration permeating music of the late 1950s, featuring saxophones, trumpets, piano, drum set, maracas, bass, and clarinet. Yet, the one-two, one-two rhythm of the shekere is what drove and organized the orchestral mix. *Música rica, para bailar pegadito*, as Duéñez mentioned. Or as the song "Vamos a la playa" says, juntos, pero muy "juntitos, como dos palomitas dándose piquitos" (together, very close together, like two little doves, beaking each other tenderly). During the 1960s Discos Fuentes moved towards rhythmic simplification, and the ensemble Los Corraleros del Majagual was responsible for an innovation that stamped the sound of música tropical: the incorporation of accordions to play along with the orchestra's brass section. This addition brought two Colombian music practices together: on the one hand, the orchestra, which mostly focused on playing porros, gaitas, and cumbias; and on the other, the accordion ensemble known for playing paseos and sones (two out of the four rhythms that characterize vallenato music, namely son, merengue, paseo, and puya. See Ramos-Kittrell 2013).

Duéñez's *música antigüita* (music by Lucho Bermúdez, Los Corraleros del Majagual, Pedro Salcedo, and Ismael Rivera) is an aural register of the Colonia's past, not only because Duéñez sold and promoted this music, but also because it was actively performed there by artists outside the roster of Discos Fuentes. "Here is where Carmen Rivero, Mike Laure, and Sonia López started [their careers] in those years; over there, in the hill (pointing with his finger), you could hear them play," Duéñez recalls (Canal 22 2017). Artists such as La Sonora Santanera, Chelo y su Conjunto Tropical, Carmen Rivero, and Mike Laure y sus Cometas replaced the mambo and guaracha rhythms that dominated Mexico in the 1950s. Yet, resonant elements in their music—such as big band orchestrations, clarinet and saxophone duets (referencing the sound of gaita ensembles), and the consistency of the one-two, one-two driving rhythm—made songs like "La pollera colorá" (performed by Carmen Rivero and written by Pedro Salcedo), "La rajita de canela" (Mike Laure), and "Maquinolandera" (performed by Chelo y su Conjunto Tropical and written by Ismael Rivera) long-standing hits. The increasing number of música tropical ensembles in Mexico during the 1960s was due to the lack of opportunities that Mexican rock musicians had in the mainstream. Instead, they found steady work in the proliferating dances among the working class, where música tropical had become widespread (Madrid 2008, 9–10).

The marketing and consumption of música tropical in Monterrey was not restricted to the flea market where Duéñez worked. As a matter of fact, other places could be found in different sectors of the city known for their "stalls" (*tianguis* or *puestos*, literally, stalls), where people could find a plethora of merchandize from the U.S., Taiwan, Hong Kong, or Japan that included clothing, electronics, toys, groceries, auto parts, and bootlegged music and video. Nevertheless, in the minds of people, Colonia Independencia remained the root place of Colombian music, a notion that has been re-emphasized by emerging scholarly literature on this topic (see Blanco Arboldea 2014, and Olvera Gudiño 2005, 2010). According to Luis Alberto Méndez, Director of Development of Popular Cultures (i.e., low-brow) at CONARTE (Consejo para la Cultura y las Artes de Nuevo León; Nuevo León state's council for arts and culture), this might be either because "for decades, sonideros sold records and mixtapes of this music at the flea market, or because musicians from that area, who play this music, became famous in the late 90s–early 2000s and got GRAMMY nominations. Either way, that's how people conceptualize it" (Méndez, personal interview). This awareness—in part informed by the mainstream attention that Mexican artists playing Colombian music received in the late 1990s—created a nostalgic aura around this neighborhood. Increasing recognition of sonideros like Duéñez and Mario Murillo, but also of local artists like Celso Piña and La Tropa Colombiana, gave corporate visibility to the working class in the public sphere, mainly due to the widespread marketing and consumption of Colombian music (See Ramos-Kittrell 2011).

This moved the state government to incorporate Colombian music and Colonia Independencia to new initiatives in cultural policy. In 2011, the Colonia was declared cultural patrimony of Monterrey, along with the music that characterizes it as a site of the historical and cultural origins of the city. The rhetoric of heritage became even more acute when Celso Piña—Monterrey's quintessential Colombian cumbia artist, who after twenty years of performing at local dances, ill-reputed bars, and other venues and events geared towards the working class, reached the mainstream by partnering with famed DJ Toy Selectah—became cultural ambassador for Mundo Fest 2005, the first international music festival hosted in the city. These cultural initiatives also secured state subsidies for two local festivals showcasing vallenato, Colombia's quintessential folk music. By 2011, both festivals had become quite popular, which propelled the decision to recognize Colombian music as aural patrimony of Monterrey following UNESCO's narrative of "sound as intangible patrimony of the people" (Contreras Delgado 2010, 151–152). The festival *Somos Indepe* (We Are Indepe[ndencia]) was organized specifically to highlight this initiative: it celebrated Colonia Independencia as a "historical, cultural, and architectonic landmark of the city of Monterrey. Its streets, trades and knowledge, gastronomy, music, and dance speak of the richness of the cultural traditions of our community, which show the rooted identity of its inhabitants."[4] *Somos Indepe* was strategically programmed as part of the celebrations for the bicentennial anniversary of Mexican independence, thereby legitimizing Colombian music as a local 'Mexican' expressive form.

Today, Duéñez is much sought after to play his records across the city and in the U.S. (he often advertises upcoming engagements in Houston, Los Angeles, and other American cities through social media). More often, he performs at *Salón Morelos*, a club in Monterrey's *barrio antiguo*, the city's burgeoning night entertainment district. Here, he continues to spin the oldies, although now for working-class and middle-class fans, tourists, and actors and actresses who want to listen to the memory of the "internationally known Colonia Independencia" (Montes de Oca Films 2018). The reimagining of the city's local history in relation to the Colonia stemmed from the way in which its sound became eventually referenced and mediated by modern artists. As it will be discussed below, their search for roots made them approach Colombian music as a locus of cultural memory to signify a sense of origins. Today, this notion is what makes people visit *Salón Morelos* to recollect and imagine the city's history, by experiencing the 'sounding' of the Colonia.

SOUNDING CUMBIA, RE-MAPPING ORIGINS

It would be a mistake to say that the practice of foreign musics such as hip-hop and electronic dance music (EDM) did not exist in Monterrey prior to the socio-economic changes produced by the North American Free Trade Agreement in 1993 (NAFTA). It is possible to say, however, that the accelerated flow of American products and services made the public more receptive to local versions of American music practices because of their cosmopolitan appeal. Control Machete became arguably the most prolific Mexican hip-hop band of the 1990s, and Genitallica, Plastilina Mosh, and Kinki (among others) gave momentum to the wave of rock and pop music production from Monterrey that became known as the *Avanzada Regia*. This music gave a desired exposure to the local sensibility of Mexican middle-class youth. For Toy Selectah, however (the creative DJ force behind Control Machete), such desire related to a concern for representation.

After four years of intense hip-hop production—which included songs featured in super bowl commercials and award-winning motion pictures—and reaching platinum album sales with his band Control Machete, the twenty-six-year-old DJ felt the need to come to terms with himself. This activity was important to Selectah in that it made him realize that his aesthetic outlet (hip-hop) lacked a point of self-reference. He traveled to different cities looking for sounds that could reflect (or accommodate, perhaps) a sense of Mexicanness. However, in New York Selectah realized that music was more about Puerto Rico than Mexico. And in California he found the music of Ozomatli (a band from Los Angeles that blends Latin—salsa, reggae, jazz, but also funk—with hip-hop and rock) to be a bit schizophrenic (Sattley 2002). It was in East Los Angeles, while seeing Mexican immigrants cross a bridge on their way to work downtown, that Selectah remembered the Puente del Papa that connected Colonia Independencia with Monterrey's business and tourist district. The scene reminded him of the sound of Gabriel Duéñez's Radson trompeta speaker and the cumbia music that spread through the flea market, right below the bridge. He also remembered that the music from this place had been a part of his life while growing up. Toy Selectah recalled that "in Monterrey everybody was exposed to cumbia, no matter what your [social] class [was]. I realized I was proud of Monterrey and I started to appreciate the magic of my city" (Sattley 2002). As reporter Melissa Sattley once said, rarely do the words Monterrey and magic come together in the same sentence, given the city's fame for its rampant consumerism and its industrial past. Selectah's magic, however, referred to the expressive and representational possibilities that cumbia opened to him. Cumbia offered the possibility of finding a cultural marker of local urban 'roots.' This idea allowed Selectah to identify a part of himself beyond the city's well-known bourgeois corporate work ethics of just producing money, which was the cultural paradigm that he experienced growing up in Monterrey's middle class (cervezaindio 2015).

Selectah became interested in exploring the intersection of the traditional with the globally eclectic, and not so much with remaining true to Colombian cumbia style. Therefore, his aesthetic interest was less about finding a 'musical calling' (i.e., becoming a cumbia sonidero) and more about flowing with the splicing of sounds that would let him express a global, yet urban Mexican outlook. "The deal about remixing is a bit complex," he says. "There is implicit creativity in the fact of reconstructing, of rearranging [the components] of a song, (and sometimes you even end up adding melodies to it)" (andamosarmadosvideo 2009). Initially, Selectah came up with a mix sound that he called cumbia dub. He first used it in 2001 for the production of Celso Piña's single "Cumbia sobre el río" (featured in the album *Barrio bravo*). With cumbia dub Selectah approached cumbia rhythms through hip-hop techniques, "a procedure of cutting and pasting . . . conceptualizing, deconceptualizing. That allows me to understand a lot of things related to rhythm and cadence" (Zertuche 2015, 21). While Selectah's hip-hop practice reflected his interest in global eclecticism, this practice also informed his approximation to cumbia as a means to locate a point of cultural self-reference in the flow of his creative process (i.e., to include elements that could reflect his cultural origins, as he imagined them). Nevertheless, a power imbalance lies at the core of this intersection—the global meeting tradition—pointing to a politics of representation in Selectah's middle-class idea of origins. "Cumbia sobre el río" is an example highlighting this tension.

Celso Piña, proclaimed the "king of Colombian cumbia" in Monterrey, joined Selectah's aesthetic project in 2001 with the production of *Barrio bravo*. The album also included collaborations with younger artists, such as El Gran Silencio, whose albums *Libres y locos* (1998) and *Chuntaros radio poder* (2001) were also important to the mainstream circulation of cumbia music in Mexico. "I took a chance. We flipped a coin and it worked—we came up with something new," said Piña after releasing the album (Sattley 2002). For Selectah, the collaboration was not necessarily about glorifying Monterrey's quintessential Colombian music artist (although the album did just that) as it was about tracing self-history.

> I have been a DJ since I was a little kid; instead of finding the piano I found the turntable and LP records. Later, as a teenager, I started to build relationships with tape jockeys and with record stores. I was never a virtuoso playing an instrument (or the type of person who would sit for eight hours to practice, as it should be). But I did use to sit for eight hours listening to records, messing around with the EQ band of the stereo, the volume knob, and mixing stuff. And then I realized that I really liked mixing, and started doing just that. What is really important [to me] is to listen to a lot of music, to read, study genres, to find out why one thing led to another. It is not enough to say "ok, I want to do this or mix that." [Music carries] a lot of stuff behind, from issues about which record label produced what music, to where an artist is from. You have to track, to do that tracing of things and make a map in order to understand your ideas and instincts; to know why a beat or an idea sounds good to you. That's what's important, to know where you are standing (andamosarmadosvideo 2009).

Although adhering to Colombian cumbia style was not central to Selectah, the issue was, nonetheless, important to Piña (which is why Piña became important to Selectah in the first place). Along with other local musicians, Piña started his career playing cumbia in small working-class cantinas, dance clubs, and private parties in the 1980s. During this time, artists like Rigo Tovar y su Costa Azul had begun to popularize cumbia under the label of música tropical. Rigo Tovar's music, however, mixed cumbia with rock, bolero, ranchera music, and Spanish pop ballads through arrangements that featured electric guitars, drum sets, and synthesizers. These instrumental and stylistic modifications later characterized the 'Mexicanization' (or Mexican appropriation) of cumbia, and created an aesthetic standard that gained popularity with the *onda grupera* movement, from the 1970s to the late 1990s. The unprecedented stardom of Rigo Tovar in the 1980s helped fuel the momentum of onda grupera, which led to the opening of spaces for the consumption of this music through Mexican media (Madrid 2013, 111 and 116). For Piña, however, cumbia sounded great as it came from Colombia, and he could not understand why other people did not play it "as it should be." Sometimes he even lost performance opportunities for refusing to play in a more onda grupera style.

> One time I played, and a damn girl (*una pinche vieja*) came to me and said "hey, hey, hey, excuse me, when are you going to play cumbia?" She wanted a cumbia like the ones by Rigo Tovar. So I told her "look girl, since I arrived I have been playing Colombian cumbia, the mother of all cumbias, not bullshit (*no mamadas*)." "Ugh, well those songs are very ugly. I want a song like Rigo Tovar's." And I said "oh no, no, no, baby. Excuse me, but I don't know that guy. Who is he? What does he sell, or what?" And forget it. There I went kicked out from the gig with the band (Olvera Gudiño 2005, 79–80).

Cumbia audiences in Monterrey were not aloof to the national market of música tropical or the onda grupera movement (and were indeed receptive to Rigo Tovar's music). Piña's Colombian zealousness, however, started a trend followed by local bands and supported by the activity of sonideros like Gabriel Duéñez (Olvera Gudiño 2005, 81). The Colombianness of the cumbia sound from Colonia Independencia (usually in the minor mode, featuring accordion, güiro, bass, congas or bongos—although nowadays Piña's band also features electric guitar and drum set) was an aural referent to this geography and its working-class inhabitants, in whose marginalization Selectah recognized an invigorating cultural individuality and local character; the true socio-economic 'roots' of Monterrey's urban culture. Selectah considered cumbia an aural source of knowledge of the city's social and cultural base. Such socio-cultural imaginary acquired density in his music, metaphorically referenced by thickening the bass and rhythmic tracks at the bottom of the mix. Thus, Selectah made cumbia a platform to position himself historically, deploying an imagined idea of cultural 'roots' through hip-hop aesthetics.

For Selectah, DJ urban music culture is a site where the historical socio-economic tensions that inform this imaginary can be aesthetically synthesized. In this sense, his music acts as a contact zone. According to Mary Louise Pratt, a contact zone is a space in which people who are geographically and historically separated come into contact to establish ongoing relations that are not free of conflict. In this zone, both peoples are co-present, and both are constituted in and by their relations to each other (Pratt 1992, 8). Selectah's music acts in such a way, given that his reference to cumbia is a nod to his 'Mexicanness,' defined in terms of the socio-political marginality that the sound of cumbia recalls as necessary to represent his (middle-class) origins: the club or the lounge (sites for the aural experience of sounds like rave, house, or techno, signifying 'the global') meeting 'base culture' (marginality, sonically referenced and aurally imagined), a point of contact that constructs bourgeois ideas of 'roots' in the midst of global cosmopolitanism. It was through this contact zone that Selectah embarked on a process of self-searching, which led him to dive into the bootleg market of Colombian music in the flea market of Colonia Independencia, looking for the best-known local sonideros. Allegedly, it was here that he bought armloads of cumbia records, which he played for friends and collaborators. "He is like a mad scientist," said Adrian Quesada, former guitarist of Grupo Fantasma, a GRAMMY Award-winning Latin music American band. "He is always pulling old records out, putting them out and saying 'check this out.' He is going deeper into the history of music . . . reviving the careers of older musicians" (Sattley 2002). Revival eventually became part of Selectah's project of self-discovery: his cumbia dub sound was not only an outlet into the mainstream for Celso Piña; it was also a tribute to sonideros like Duéñez. *Barrio bravo* reached the top of the charts, earned Piña a Latin GRAMMY nomination, and catapulted his career to music stardom. According to Piña, this has been his most successful record, the one that opened Latin American and European markets to his music (Ramos-Kittrell 2011, 203). In the twelve years that followed after *Barrio bravo,* Piña released twelve more records, collaborated with artists such as Alex Lora (from Mexican rock band El Tri), Eugenia León, and Benny Ibarra. He also got to perform in Mexico's Auditorio Nacional, and became known as the *maestro de la cumbia, desde México* (the cumbia master from Mexico).

Uprooted from the low-life cantinas of central Monterrey, the AM radio frequency, and the flea market of Colonia Independencia, Piña's accordion entered Toy Selectah's musical utopia. In here, Piña's concern for Colombianness spreads beneath an aural map that mythologizes class and territory. Selectah's cumbia dub sound becomes a simulacrum that makes Piña's accordion riffs the basis of the DJ's working-class aesthetics, visually mapped in the video of the hit single "Cumbia sobre el río." This song is framed by a sonic and visual collage of references to local marginality: the video displays dislocated snapshots of Loma Larga's rough, non-urbanized space (i.e., unpaved streets and dirt trails used as sidewalks), fading in and out on different parts of the screen. Meanwhile, the looping of riffs from the famous song "Cumbia sampuesana" merge with *rebajada*[5] voice-calls to reference this geography, which Selectah imagines as the socioeconomic ground zero of his sociocultural experience of the city. Thus, Selectah's cumbia dub sound in "Cumbia sobre el río"—and in his rearrangement of the ubiquitous "Cumbia de la paz," also featured in the record—functions as a contact zone where the marginal is part of a hip-hop logic of cutting and splicing the traditional with the cosmopolitan (roots and the modern) to articulate the past and the present in Selectah's historical imagination.

According to Selectah, this process was part of a trend among DJs working in different parts of the world fascinated with cultural peripheries. Ten years after *Barrio bravo* Selectah's sound metamorphosed into a freer style that he called raverton. In raverton he mixed cumbia and reggae with house, hip-hop, and rave. With this new sound Selectah participated in an EDM trend called global ghettotech. According to him, global ghettotech initiatives transpired mostly in cosmopolitan cities such as London, New York, Mexico City, Paris, San Francisco, and Buenos Aires, where base-culture dance events celebrated music from the peripheries. The continued interest in sounds across the EDM spectrum in these places—from the most underground to the most mainstream, in Selectah's words—is what inspired the creation of a sonic periphery in global ghettotech (DJsounds 2010). Raverton eventually led Selectah to develop more complex projects based on this idea, where cumbia remained a consistent element. His latest collaboration turned out to be a significant commercial opportunity for him, not least because a craving for globalized Latin American rhythms had expanded throughout the entire continent—from Argentina to the Bay Area in the U.S.—and beyond (Silicon Valley De-Bug 2009). With the support of Red Bull, Selectah embarked on a recording trip to studios in New York, Los Angeles, London, São Paulo, Tokyo, and New Delhi to work with artists such as Boy George, Maluca Mala, Kool A.D., MC Lyte, Rulo, Sly and Robbie, and the legendary Maytals, among others. Yet, the eclecticism of these collaborations was part of a recording project that, in Selectah's words, had true "denomination of origin." In *Compass* (2016), Selectah and co-producer Camilo Lara (founder of Instituto Mexicano del Sonido, an electronica project also focused on mixing folk and traditional musics with EDM sounds) strategically drop "a trumpet, a guacharaca, a tuba, a rhythm, a Spanish hook" in some of the tracks, in order to round up a sound that otherwise would come across as just urban and foreign. "[These were] different ways of showing why we are here," explained Selectah (Zertuche 2015, 25).

It is interesting to note that all of the aural referents that Selectah uses in his music have a geographical dimension to them. The notion of 'place' (*lugar* or *lugares*), constant in his rhetoric, shows to have a complex character. For him, the cosmopolitanism of 'places' like Ibiza, London, or Buenos Aires, alludes not to the modern EDM sounds that one might find at a lounge or club (e.g., house, rave, techno). Rather, such cosmopolitanism refers to the *place* that the periphery finds in the work of DJs in these venues. In these cities, the urban is a site where the marginal and the modern engage in conversation, which is what ultimately gives the urban a globalized cosmopolitan character. This suggests that the signification of a sonic periphery is a necessary condition to articulate the cosmopolitan urban, and that its aesthetics emerge from the encryption of tensions between these two fields. DJ urban sound practices, therefore, function as aural texts that position the cosmopolitan subject by referencing cultural memory: the reproduction and affectual recall of the historical power relations (between the marginal and the modern) that constitute bourgeois subjectivity. This phenomenon brings up important questions about the conflicts inherent in processes of representation stemming out of contact zones, especially as they pertain to the (re)cognition of marginalized people and their practices.

MEXICANIDAD AS CONTINGENCY

Selectah's aural signification of the urban 'other' suggests the (im)possibility of agency, since in his symbolism (articulated through the aesthetic logic of middle-class nostalgia) the 'other' can only be historically (re)cognized as long as it remains peripheral. The records that Celso Piña released prior to his collaboration with Selectah (*Dile* 1996, *Una aventura más* 1999, and *Antología de un rebelde* 2000) cannot compare to *Barrio bravo*, neither in sales nor in the influence that the 2001 album had on his career. Furthermore, it was only after the mainstream commercial success of *Barrio bravo* (and of bands like El Gran Silencio in 1998) that the aurally imagined culture of Colonia Independencia got the attention of the academic community, the film industry (Villarreal 2007, Bárcenas 2010), state institutions, and newspapers. This attention inspired Selectah and Camilo Lara to embark on yet another revival venture now involving Los Ángeles Azules (a band from Mexico City that has played cumbia music for over thirty-five years). In 2014 the two DJs produced *Cómo te voy a olvidar ¡Edición de super lujo!* The album (featuring collaborations with Lila Downs, Carla Morrison, and Kinki, as well as symphonic arrangements of some of their songs performed by the *Orquesta Sinfónica de la Ciudad de México*) was a compilation of some of the band's best-known songs. Yet, nothing prepared Los Ángeles Azules for the unprecedented, groundbreaking sale of more than 600,000 copies, which earned the band a double diamond record, and made them the first cumbia act in 2018 to appear in the Coachella Music Festival (Notimex 2015, Aguila 2018). The decades of performance activity by Los Ángeles Azules and Celso Piña, and of sonidero Gabriel Duéñez notwithstanding, it seems that Selectah's magic touch is all that was needed for this music to enter middle-class consciousness. As a matter of fact, it seems that the visibility of cumbia artists (and the places they ultimately symbolized) would not have been possible otherwise.

Given that in his music Selectah unfolds a process of self-representation, the issue of visibility for the working class becomes politically important. By deploying his cosmopolitan 'Mexicanness' in his recording projects, Selectah acts as a historical agent with an imagined cultural past that enables him to find a place in the present. However, Selectah's Mexicanness is encoded in an aural signifier that signifies cumbia—and those who have sounded cumbia historically—as peripheral. For although the activity and visibility of Gabriel Duéñez has increased, and the careers of Celso Piña and Los Ángeles Azules have reached new heights, their working-class status has remained a condition for their ongoing popularity. Alejandro L. Madrid has analyzed this phenomenon in discourses of representation that arise from the consumption of music associated with the working class. Such discourses, Madrid observes, point to the visibility that marginalized constituencies gain in the public sphere as alterities in relation to sanctioned narratives of culture.

In his chapter about cumbia star Rigo Tovar, Madrid points out that, while the democratization of the Mexican media in the 1980s and 1990s (after NAFTA) opened a large market for the circulation and consumption of cumbia, such opening was also a site through which working-class audiences (for whom the "Mexican Miracle" rhetoric of economic development was an empty promise) saw their desire for cosmopolitan representation reflected in Tovar's stardom. Self-described as a naco (an ill-mannered person), Rigo Tovar became a popular idol because of his appeal to working-class social sensibility: the singer's unpretentious demeanor, unpolished mannerisms, and his apprehensive distance from the middle class resonated heavily with his audience. According to Madrid, working-class audiences identified in Rigo Tovar's humble charisma their sense of grassroots origins and aesthetic taste, which until then mainstream media had ignored. Thus, the development of a working-class market through Rigo Tovar's music opened a site of cultural identification and validation (Madrid 2013, 109–110 and 116). Borrowing from Toby Miller's work, Madrid uses the concept of cultural citizenship to frame his analysis. For Miller, cultural citizenship entails a process concerned with the maintenance and development of cultural lineage through education, customs, language, and religion, and the positive acknowledgment of difference in and by the mainstream (Miller 2001, 2). For Madrid, this form of citizenship—articulated through the consumption of music resonant with social customs, values, and sensibilities—afforded working-class audiences a right to belong in ways that recognized their difference. Music played an important dialectical role in this case, Madrid points out, because it provided an image of the past (tradition, class belonging) that could be recognized in the present. Such recognition provided an avenue into a *possible* new future (i.e., being culturally visible through the market). In this way, music acted as a "dialectical sounding": a way of making visible the invisible through a specific type of process in the present (Madrid 2013, 114–115).

Madrid's case study touches on important points that broaden our inquiry about the dialectical logic of such soundings. In Madrid's analysis, citizenship does not refer to the zero degree of collective relationships among individuals, all equal to one another before the law (as it is usually understood in a liberal sense). Rather, citizenship emerges from consumption practices that are culturally situated in the dynamics of social exchange of the working class. This conceptualization resonates with Claudio Lomnitz's analysis of Mexican citizenship and its values in how both are culturally situated and produced (Lomnitz 2001, 58–61). Madrid, however, goes a step further in making cultural citizenship a discursive site in terms of how representation through the market opens up the possibility to imagine the future, and therefore, for historical discourse. Lomnitz's theorization of contact frames locates these types of discourses in the reworking of the balance between modernity and tradition. When the balance between what is considered tradition and roots and the modern is disrupted, a contact frame of tension emerges, which exposes the ugly flipside produced by the latter's progressivist agenda. Contact frames, Lomnitz observes, are sites where identity is imagined historically in the working out and rebalancing of this tension. Here, tradition is perceived to have a collective 'spiritual' dimension, "which is incorporated as an aesthetic into a unique modernity that is the country's present, and above all, its future" (2001, 133). By focusing on the 'boom' of Rigo Tovar as a discursive phenomenon steeped in the tension between modernity (the logics that characterized the socio-economic project of the 'Mexican Miracle' that the Plan Nacional de Desarrollo aimed for) and tradition (the opening of a market for working-class sensibility; the visible flipside of national modernization) Madrid uses cultural citizenship as a contact frame through which the working class can claim corporate visibility in the public sphere.[6] According to him, citizenship thus articulates forms of cultural representation through consumption that are dialectical.

Madrid's insightful analysis raises points that deserve further attention. In his case study, he concludes that, although the recognition of working-class sensibility through the market opened a space for validation and inclusion, the fact that such recognition did not necessarily translate into more positive material changes for the working class highlights the very dialectical character of this process (Madrid 2013, 117). This form of validation (the "positive acknowledgment of difference," as Toby Miller proposes in his definition of citizenship, which Madrid uses), raises questions about its historical discursive potential given that representation operates rather as a strategy for social containment.[7] I would argue that the cultural reintegration of the working class into the public corporate body does open possibilities for historical change that are out of the state's control, notwithstanding its involvement. I would like to borrow Claudio Lomnitz's expansive analysis of Pratt's "contact zone" concept to elaborate this argument further. Lomnitz sees a contact zone as a site where contact frames meet and articulate a broader region of identity production. Contact zones, Lomnitz observes, comprise institutions and their images and narratives of identity, for which class-identity production is important (2001, 130 and 137). I am proposing that the imbalances and relational asymmetries addressed by Pratt (in which groups constitute each other through a logic of power) are part of larger institutional processes that sanction ideas of heritage and belonging. Contact zones act as public front stages for identity images produced by necessarily inter-relational exchanges between class-based imaginaries. For Monterrey cumbia artists, promoters, and audiences, as well as for Toy Selectah—but also state institutions—the renewal of the 'Mexican' image of the middle class (disrupted by the logics of transnational circulation of services and commodities, and the liberalization of trade that characterized the cultural experience of global capitalism in the late 1990s) was contingent upon the visibility of the working class to materialize new ideas about tradition and roots, and to make them historically significant (the material recognition of Monterrey's urban 'spirit,' to use Lomnitz's terminology).

In this particular case, the contact zone involves two frames of cultural action informed by class-based imaginaries. On the one hand, cumbia audiences and musicians in Monterrey's Colonia Independencia sought to find in the transnational circulation of music records, symbols to make sense out of their experience of the physical environment of the city. In their invisibility to the state, and their marginalization as undesired subjects that did not conform to the ideal image of the middle-class, bourgeois citizen, the working class made this music a site for self-recognition. On the other hand, the activity of middle-class youths who did not find in the city's corporate materialistic culture expressive spaces that reflected their new socioeconomic cultural experience after NAFTA triggered concerns for cultural origins. While on their own efforts artists such as Celso Piña, La Tropa Colombiana, and Los Príncipes del Vallenato, but also Los Ángeles Azules, and even star Rigo Tovar, did not break across class markets, their symbolic presence in the public sphere made it possible to create a point of contact with middle-class audiences to address their concerns. Far from democratic, dialogue between these two frames of cultural action is necessarily uneven, for such asymmetry makes ideas about roots and urban 'base culture' viable. Thus, contact zones produce ideas of heritage and belonging steeped in conflict and narrativized by the state, which enable the positioning of both class subjects through mutual interrelation. This, I argue, is the aporia of the dialectical, the double bind of history's (im)possibility. For the historical positioning of one is contingent upon the positioning of the other.

CONCLUSION

The conflict inherent in contact zones and the historical discourses they produce do not pertain to those whose ideas of roots are ultimately validated through the logics of consumption (i.e., the one who sells more wins). Rigo Tovar's unprecedented stardom surely validated the desires for recognition of the working class, but his fame (sustained by record sales and his exposure in poorly produced cinema) did not reframe ideas about tradition and cultural heritage. The tension permeating dialogues among groups in contact zones pertains to the articulation of historical discourse, not in terms of whose memories are ultimately recollected, but in terms of the material process that produces cultural memory. The constitution of memory involves a symbolic referencing of tradition as the basis of new ideas of heritage steeped in conflict. In this chapter, the class tensions that sustain the marketability of Selectah's dominant contact frame is what articulates a historical discourse that remaps ideas of heritage and belonging, which through state involvement become narrativized.

This analysis urges us to consider processes of aural signification in terms of the conflicts that arise from historical processes of representation. In this case, the marginal 'other', aurally signified in the middle-class imagination, is shown to be the true modernity of a bourgeois desire for cosmopolitanism. These types of phenomena remind us of the necessary presence of the marginal subject for the existence of power, and even society (Pandey 2006, 4736). It is not an entity produced in tandem with normativity, but rather productive of it. This means that we ought to rethink patterns of historical development in order to grasp the contradictions that lie at its core, and that outline political possibilities that have been lost in our purview, where the marginal subject can be recognized only as the underdeveloped figure of history. The present chapter problematized this notion in light of the subject-object characterization that the signified marginal shows: it is a subject of history, but also one being acted upon. While this might suggest that Mexicanidad—as difference—involves the objectification of a subaltern subject, one must not forget that such objectification is only realized when the subaltern renders the mainstream (the 'ideal' norm) historically visible.

NOTES

1. Sonidero is the name usually given to DJs who, in addition to providing music for private and public events (such as weddings, birthday parties, or public dances), also sold mixtapes and burnt CDs compiling some of the most popular songs of *música tropical* (although they handled other genres too) from their personal record collection. See Ragland, "Mexican Deejays," 2003, and "Mediating between Two Worlds," 2000.

2. United Nations Educational, Scientific and Cultural Organization (UNESCO), "Memory of the World Programme: Programme Objectives," http://www.unesco.org/new/en/communication-and-information/memory-of-the-world/about-the-programme/objectives/.

3. Founded in 1899, the Historical Collections of the Vienna *Phonogrammarchiv* was the first sound archive in the world. Upon recommendation by the Austrian

government, the *Phonogrammarchiv* was included in the Memory of the World Register in 1999. United Nations Educational, Scientific and Cultural Organization (UNESCO), "Memory of the World Programme: The Historical Collections (1899–1950) of the Vienna Phonogrammarchiv," http://www.unesco.org/new/en/communication-and-information/memory-of-the-world/register/full-list-of-registered-heritage/registered-heritage-page-8/the-historical-collections-1899-1950-of-the-vienna-phonogrammarchiv/#c191394. See also UNESCO, "Memory of the World Programme: Previous laureates of the UNESCO/Jikji Memory of the World Prize," http://www.unesco.org/new/en/communication-and-information/memory-of-the-world/unesco jikji-prize/previous-laureates/.

4. From *Somos Indepe*, a pamphlet guide to the *Somos Indepe* cultural festival, published by CONARTE, the state's arts council. The pamphlet titled "Colonia Independencia, an architectonic patrimony to discover," was also published by CONARTE in 2011 for the festival.

5. *Cumbia rebajada* or simply *rebajada* (i.e., reduced) is a term referring to cumbia music recorded on tape from LP vinyl records at a less number of revolutions per minute to make it sound slower and lower in pitch. This is something that sonideros discovered by accident. After making dozens of bootleg tapes from records, the needle of the turntable would wear out and the recording would come out 'defective.' However, music buyers liked this sound and started to ask sonideros to "reduce" cumbia songs by their favorite artists. See Campuzano 2009. Also, Ramos-Kittrell 2011, 201.

6. A consequence of the political and economic project behind the "Mexican Miracle," was a break in the connection between the state and the Mexican citizenry. The inability of the state to account for the needs of citizens (due to the fiscal crisis of the 1980s and the collapse of the economy in the 1990s, which left more than 30% of the productive sector of the population without stable or legally sanctioned work, and without public security and welfare) made obvious the fact that civil society had become unencompassable. The emergence of spaces for democratic participation (rallies, demonstrations) exposed this 'ugly' flipside of national modernization, where the state's inability to respond to the needs and rights of its constituency led to a crisis in citizenship—a system of representation in which individuals are anonymous members of corporate groups. It was through such corporate structure that the working class had once become part of the polity (because there was a doubt about whether the lower sector actually could be assimilated through public education). Thus, the *naco* (working-class social subject) was organized as part of a faceless collective mass that, by engaging in a series of exchanges with state and corporate agencies, was represented as a massified citizen. See Lomnitz 2001, 76–78.

7. Discontent over the failure of the "Mexican Miracle" rhetoric to improve the socio-economic condition of the working class was dispersed by rendering this group corporately visible in the market of Mexican cultural industries. The relational position of the working class with the public corporate body, however, remained the same.

REFERENCES

Aguila, Justino. "Los Angeles Azules Conquer Coachella, Prepare for Chella Show with Cuco & More." *Billboard* (April 16, 2018). https://www.billboard.com/articles/columns/latin/8342168/los-angeles-azules-coachella-chella.

"An Interview with DJ Toy Selectah." YouTube video, 8:15. Posted by "Silicon Valley De-Bug," January 21, 2009. https://www.youtube.com/watch?v=ee1CIOB2UaY.

Associated Press. "Ángeles Azules hacen bailar a Bosé y Fito Paéz." *Chicago Tribune* (September 29, 2016). http://www.chicagotribune.com/hoy/ct-hoy-8720001-angeles-azules-hacen-bailar-a-bose-y-fito-paez-story.html.

Bárcenas, Ana. *Regiocolombia*. DVD. Casa de Piedra, Universidad Regiomontana. 2010.

Blanco Arboleda, Darío. *Los colombias y la cumbia en Monterrey: Identidad, subalternidad y mundos de vida entre inmigrantes urbanos populares*. Monterrey, Mexico: Universidad Autónoma de Nuevo León, 2014.

Celso Piña, *Barrio bravo*. Metro Casa Musical. CBBR–174

Consejo para la Cultura y las Artes de Nuevo León. *Colonia Independencia, un patrimonio por descubrir*. Monterrey, Mexico: CONARTE, 2011.

Consejo para la Cultura y Las Artes de Nuevo León. *Somo Indepe* (a guide to the *Somos Indepe* cultural festival). Monterrey, Mexico: CONARTE, Dirección de Desarrollo y Patrimonio Cultural, 2011.

Contreras Delgado, Camilo. "Paisajes sonoros." In *Colores y ecos de la Colonia Independencia*, edited by Camilo Contreras, 151–158. Monterrey, Mexico: COLEF, CONARTE, Municipio de Monterrey, 2010.

"Entrevista Toy Selectah." YouTube video, 7:33. Posted by "andamosarmadosvideo," November 12, 2009. https://www.youtube.com/watch?v=JJBpcqj0v7o&index=32&list=PL0362374815173E1E.

Fonoteca Nacional. "Misión y Visión." Fonoteca Nacional (2018). http://www.unesco.org/new/en/communication-and-information/memory-of-the-world/unescojikji-prize/previous-laureates/.

Jaramillo Torres, Guillermo. "Tras el sonido de la gaita: El sonidero Gabriel Duéñez." *El Norte* (January 3, 2011). https://raizdelglifo.wordpress.com/2011/01/03/tras-el-sonido-de-la-gaita/.

Lomnitz, Claudio. *Deep Mexico, Silent Mexico: An Anthropology of Nationalism*. Minneapolis, MN: University of Minnesota Press, 2001.

López Carrera, Luis Manuel. Founder and Director of Festival Voz de Acordeones. Personal Communication. Monterrey, Mexico. June 1, 2011.

Los Ángeles Azules, *Cómo te voy a olvidar ¡Edición de super lujo!* Sony Music. 888837224123

Lucho Bermúdez, *Vamos a la playa*. Discos Fuentes. D10131

Madrid, Alejandro L. "Landscapes and gimmicks from 'the sounded city': Listening for the nation at the sound archive." *Sound Studies* 2, vol. 2 (August 2016): 119–136.

———. "Rigo Tovar, Cumbia, and the Transnational *Grupero* Boom." In *Cumbia! Scenes of a Migrant Latin American Music Genre*, edited by Héctor Fernández L'Hoeste and Pablo Vila, 105–118. Durham: Duke University Press, 2013.

———. *Nor-tec Rifa! Electronic Dance Music from Tijuana to the World*. New York: Oxford University Press, 2008.

Méndez, Luis Alberto. Director of Development of Popular Cultures, CONARTE. Personal Communication. Monterrey, Mexico. June 19, 2015.

Mexican Institute of Sound and Toy Selectah, *Compass*. Six Degree Records. 657036-124127

Mike Laure, *Boleros con Mike Laure*. Musart. 1167

"Monterrey, ese vato sí es colombia." YouTube video, 56:34. Posted by "canal22," September 12, 2017. https://www.youtube.com/watch?v=Bws66yVd_u8.

Notimex. "Los Ángeles Azules reciben doble disco diamante." *Excelsior* (April 27, 2016). https://www.excelsior.com.mx/funcion/2016/04/27/1089214.

Ochoa Gautier, Ana María. "Social Transculturation, Epistemologies of Purification and the Aural Public Sphere in Latin America." In *The Sound Studies Reader*, edited by Jonathan Sterne, 388–404. New York: Routledge, 2012.

Olvera Gudiño, José Juan. "Los caminos de la vida en la Independencia son de migración y diversidad, además de la Colombia." In *Colores y ecos de la Colonia Independencia*, edited by Camilo Contreras, 135–147. Monterrey, Mexico: COLEF, CONARTE, Municipio de Monterrey, 2010.

———. *Colombianos en Monterrey: Origen de un gusto musical y su papel en la construcción de una identidad social*. Monterrey, Mexico: Consejo para la Cultura y las Artes de Nuevo León, 2005.

Pandey, Gyanendra. "The Subaltern as Subaltern Citizen." *Economic and Political Weekly* 41, no. 46 (November 18–24, 2006): 4735–4741.

Pratt, Mary Louise. *Imperial Eyes: Travel Writing and Transculturation*. New York: Routledge, 1992.

"Promo Sonido Duéñez 2018." YouTube video, 1:12. Posted by "Montes de Oca Films," February 9, 2018. https://www.youtube.com/watch?v=yTY-xvFZkAk.

Ragland, Cathy. "Mediating between Two Worlds: The Sonideros of Mexican Youth Dances." In *New York State Folklife Reader: Diverse Voices*, edited by Elizabeth Tucker and Ellen McHale, 133–144. Jackson, MS: University Press of Mississippi, 2013.

———. "Mexican Deejays and the Transnational Space of Youth Dances in New York and New Jersey." *Ethnomusicology* 47, no. 3 (Fall 2003): 338–354.

Ramos-Kittrell, Jesús A. "Cumbia". In *Latin Music: Musicians, Genres, and Themes*, edited by Ilan Stavans, 190–201. Santa Barbara, CA: Greenwood, 2014.

———. "Vallenato". In *The Grove Dictionary of American Music*, second edition, edited by Charles Hiroshi Garrett (November 26, 2013). https://doi.org/10.1093/gmo/9781561592630.article.A2263300.

———. "Transnational Cultural Constructions: Cumbia Music and the Making of Locality in Monterrey." In *Transnational Encounters: Music and Performance at the U.S.-Mexico Border*, edited by Alejandro L. Madrid, 191–206. New York: Oxford University Press, 2011.

Samuels, David W., Louise Meintjes, Ana María Ochoa, and Thomas Porcello. "Soundscapes: Toward a Sounded Anthropology." *Annual Review of Anthropology* 39 (2010): 329–345.

Sattley, Melissa. "Cumbia Sobre El Rio: Celso Piña Exports New Cumbia Dub." *The Austin Chronicle* (October 18, 2002). https://www.austinchronicle.com/music/2002-10-18/106216/.

"Sonidero Duéñez." YouTube video, 8:24. Posted by "Alberto Campuzano," May 19, 2009. https://www.youtube.com/watch?v=JLJHzYguzpk.

"Toy Selectah from Mexico." YouTube video, 5:55. Posted by "DJsounds," March 15, 2010. https://www.youtube.com/watch?v=WVPnAuK90dI.

United Nations Educational, Scientific and Cultural Organization (UNESCO). "Memory of the World Programme: Programme Objectives." UNESCO (2017). http://www.unesco.org/new/en/communication-and-information/memory-of-the-world/about-the-programme/objectives/.

———. "Memory of the World Programme: The Historical Collections (1899–1950) of the Vienna Phonogrammarchiv." UNESCO (2017). http://www.unesco.org/new/en/communication-and-information/memory-of-the-world/register/full-list-of-registered-heritage/registered-heritage-page-8/the-historical-collections-1899-1950-of-the-vienna-phonogrammarchiv/#c191394.

———. Memory of the World Programme: Previous laureates of the UNESCO/Jikji Memory of the World Prize." UNESCO (2017). http://www.unesco.org/new/en/communication-and-information/memory-of-the-world/unescojikji-prize/previous-laureates/.

"Uno en un millón: Toy Selectah." YouTube video, 7:07. Posted by "cervezaindio," January 15, 2015. https://www.youtube.com/watch?v=JXQTaLjuFN8.

Villarreal, René U. *Cumbia callera*. DVD. Venevision International, 2007.

Wade, Peter. *Music, Race, and Nation: Música Tropical in Colombia*. Chicago: The University of Chicago Press, 2000.

Zertuche, Juan Antonio. "Toy Selectah: Desde Tampiquito, un ritmo global." *Residente Monterrey: Acciones para una ciudad mejor* (January 2015): 19–25.

Chapter 9

Southern California Chicanx Music and Culture

Affective Strategies Within a Browning Temporal System of Global Contradictions

Peter J. García

The long-standing popularity of the Eastside Los Angeles music and dance scene reflects a multinational, multilingual and multicultural consumer Latinx market. Latinx make up over a third of California's population and comprise nearly the majority of residents of Los Angeles County. Local artists, fans, and audiences that make up the Eastside L.A. music scene comprise bilingual Mexicans (spanning several generations of Mexican-American and Chicanx people), Latinx, and people of mixed descent, all musically organized into diverse groups that voice particular popular and political movements. These cultural formations emerge from a global, transnational, and cosmopolitan population, subjects of their lyrical voices, but also potential consumers and cultural producers (Viesca 2004, 720).

Within this context, José Esteban Muñoz (2006) has defined 'feeling brown' as a way of recognizing the affective particularities of specific historical subjects. The 'x' currently used in categories of representation (such as Chicanx and Latinx) has emerged to represent instances of such feeling as an insistence on the here-ness of the diverse Latinx population in the United States. However, scholars have questioned whether the 'x' reflects a generational evolution in Latinidad. Is this a passing trend or the reification of an identity politics arguably in flux and imprecise, and a move forward to sites that Latinx create and narrate (Milian 2013)? This chapter examines this question in relation to postnational movements of MeXicanidad in Los Angeles. Resurgent forms of neo-*chicanismo* and neo-*mexicanidad* have gained strength via social media alongside traditional, local community-based ritualistic observances, street festivals, and music ceremonies. In these movements MeXicanidad is frequently produced within browning musical soundscapes: urban beats, and Latin/o sonic mixtures resulting in a cosmopolitan fusion that overlaps and affects Greater Mexican urban aesthetics, historical memory, popular nostalgia, borderlands, and identity consciousness. It is here that the X in MeXicanidad becomes an important cultural referent. According to Rosa Linda Fregoso, the X serves to locate the historical, material, and discursive effects of contact zones.[1] As a marker of these zones, the X points to 'feeling brown' as the phenomenological intersection of Mexican aesthetics, memory, and nostalgia with the global, transnational, and cosmopolitan character of Latinx sound fusions. Thus, MeXicanidad operates as a historical instance where the X marks the spot of a discursive space in which identity is produced and contested.

For Nancy D. Munn, "when time is a focus, it may be subject to oversimplified, single-stranded descriptions or typifications, rather than to a theoretical examination of basic sociocultural processes through which temporality is constructed" (Munn, 1995, 93). East Los Angeles is a glocal center in a flourishing cosmopolitan music network and urban cultural scene with a renewed Chicanx aesthetic circuit, connected to an enduring Mexican ethnic imaginary. The music of this urban scene emerged in the 1990s and is currently led by a collective of socially conscious and politically active Latin fusion bands that include Aztlán Underground, Blues Experiment, Lysa Flores, Ozomatli, Ollin, Quetzal, Quinto Sol, Slowrider, and Yeska. "Along with visual artists, activists, and audiences, the musicians of the Eastside scene comprise an emergent cultural movement that is grounded in the new spatial and social relations generated in Los Angeles in the transnational era" (Viesca 2004, 719). At the core of this urban sound and musical movement is a particular Mexican ethnic pride and solidarity expressed through several open temporalities that overlap shifting identities (Mexican-American, Chicanx, Latinx) in community celebrations and browning mediascapes. Ethnomusicologists tend to agree that regional musics today are difficult to define cogently, as 'the local' is not a precise bounded community site for ethnographic study. Mark Slobin explains how even "within regional musics, traditional local styles coexist alongside trans-regional musics crossing ethnic, class, and racialized boundaries, even becoming continental, world, or global musics" (1992, 15). Furthermore, a more flexible sense of region and musical mapping is needed nowadays because of the reach of social media, network broacasting, and online recordings and video streaming. Slobin shows how the concept of ethnoscape (the viewpoint of "tourists, immigrants, refugees, exiles, guestworkers, and other *moving groups* and persons rather than of the more traditional stable populations that ethnographers and economists use as standard units") alludes to such fluidity (1992, 15). For Slobin, "ethnoscapes are deeply significant mediascapes, sites produced by private or state interests that tend to be image-centered, narrative-based accounts of strips of reality from which people make their own life-scripts" (1992, 9). 'Feeling brown,' thus, points to neo-chicano discourses of MeXicanidad as affectual, transtemporal instances that such ethnoscapes produce.

QUERENCIA: MARIACHI MUSIC AND CHICANX HERITAGE MAPPING

Lisa Lowe and David Lloyd point out how according to some analysts of transnationalism, "global capitalism has penetrated and saturated all social terrains, exhausting the possibilities for challenges or resistance" (Lowe and Lloyd 2008, 140). However, re-readings of U.S. history problematize such a thesis in light of a history of resistance that has not been properly considered in terms of its enduring social effects. The civil rights movement of the 1950s and 1960s, specifically, represented "the apogee of the civic-national perspective in the twentieth century, because this movement, founded in large part on the principle of equality of all citizens before the law, gave rise to laws (the Civil Rights Act of 1964, the Voting Rights Act of 1965, and all their ramifications)" (Cohen 2005, 176). This point in history, argues James Cohen, "began 'a minority rights revolution'" but "paradoxically at the same moment there began a movement in the opposite direction; that is, the emergence of a range of currents that rejected any vision involving a civic reunification of the nation" (2005, 176). Cohen suggests that several ethnonational movements (e.g., Black Power, Chicano, Puerto Rican Power) and multiculturalist currents tended to justify these movements as expressions of an irreducible diversity that carried more weight than the idea of national unity" (2005, 176). For Cohen, "although multiculturalists and ethnonationalists of different stripes constitute a small minority, they succeeded, (. . .) in shatter[ing] a broad consensus on the virtue of the American nation, the beneficence of its civic ideals, and the imperative of fighting community where it reared its head" (Cohen 2005, 176). The possibility of cultural resistance, therefore, has been historically at the core of this activity. And respecting mexicanidad, it has never been more publicly pertinent than today in light of the current presidential policies toward the Mexican population at large.

On July 15, 2018, NBCNews.com journalist Dennis Romero announced a "Chicano Renaissance" occurring in Southern California as Mexican-American millennials embraced the term 'Chicano' without fully understanding the long-standing history of political struggle and interethnic conflict that often confounds its shifting cultural meanings. Romero reported how "on streets and college campuses, in fashion and in art, there's renewed energy around a term associated with 1960s Civil Rights and farm worker activism" (Romero 2018). According to Romero, "the recharged movement is a metaphorical safe space for young Mexican Americans and Latinos who feel battered not only by President Donald Trump's politics and rhetoric regarding south-of-the-border immigrants but also by a far right emboldened by his rhetoric." Not since 1970, the year of the East Los Angeles Vietnam Moratorium and the Chicano high school blowouts, has political unrest and cultural reawakening been so strongly manifested through music expression and as a rediscovery of Mexican heritage.

In the 1980s, an important Mexican music explosion shifted the aesthetic focus of the Latin music industry away from Latin fusion with increased popular interest in and promotion of traditional mariachi music, which had also begun during the Chicano movement era. In 1987 Elektra/Asylum Records, a division of Warner Communications, released *Canciones de mi padre*, which was followed by the sequel, *Más canciones,* in 1991. These two albums were produced by American popular rock and country music singer Linda Ronstadt with the collaboration of several Mexican, Mexican-American, and non-Mexican U.S. musicians, promoters, and producers. *Canciones de mi padre* consists of a traditional mariachi repertoire of the golden age of Mexican popular music, a period that lasted from the 1920s through the 1940s in post-revolutionary Mexico. Many Mexican-American children grew up listening to *Canciones de mi padre*, and according to Daniel Sheehy "several years later, the late Mexican-American superstar vocalist from Corpus Christi, Texas, Selena Quintanilla-Pérez, recorded similar arrangements of several of the 'classic' melodies selected from Ronstadt's *Canciones de mi padre* album, taking mariachi music to still greater audiences and inspiring adoring imitators nationwide" (1997, 150).

Chicanx communities connect such history to East L.A. mariachi activity, which is regionally mapped through landmarks in the city such as the iconic Mariachi Plaza and the recently restored Mariachi Hotel in Boyle Heights. Catherine I. Kurland and Enrique R. Lamadrid's *Hotel Mariachi: Urban Space and Cultural Heritage in Los Angeles* (2013) provides a historical and ethnographic investigation of the dynamic mariachi space, community ceremony, and the numerous ensembles connected to Boyle Heights from throughout the East Los Angeles Greater Mexican musical communities. Los Angeles is home to several internationally renowned groups including Los Camperos de Nati Cano, Mariachi Sol de México de José Hernández, and Mariachi Reyna de Los Angeles. Curland and Lamadrid combine cultural history and ethnographic interpretation with artistic photography by Miguel Gandert along with a compact disc recording featuring samples of music from local festivals like Santa Eulalia, Cinco de Mayo, as well as religious processions and special Mass celebrations. The annual *Fiesta de Santa Cecilia*, a community-based and locally organized mariachi music festival, is one such event. The musical space of the festival is a portal through which open temporalities overlap the historical past with the present. In here, 'feeling brown' functions as an arena in which shifting Mexican identities converge with a sense of local cultural belonging. Several local and international mariachi ensembles and individual musical participants gather annually on November 22nd for the day-long ritual observance that includes an outdoor Catholic Mass on the plaza, a ritual procession (see Figure 9.1), and a community street festival that lasts into the evening.

According to Dan Sheehy, mariachi in the U.S. has been an agent for social change (2006, 51). This could be in part because, since the 1960s, migrants' rights, women's rights, and the goals of the Chicano movement have all been articulated through the art of mariachi music. For Lamadrid, "if mariachi in Mexico is the symbol of national pride, in the United States it is a symbol of international pride and the assertion of transnational identity and the human rights on which it is based" (2013, 68). Lamadrid explains how mariachi music practice stems from the famous Plaza Garibaldi in Mexico City, which tops the list of significant mariachi spaces alongside the legendary *Cantina Tenampa*, and the mariachi heartland (Jalisco and Michoacan), where mariachi tourism exploded after World War II (Lamadrid 2013, 67). According to Lamadrid,

> These are all centers where the intangible heritage of mariachi culture converges, and so their importance is not in their stones and mortar, but in the space that they lend where the culture is nourished and thrives. It can be argued that every town in Mexico has such spaces, since mariachi flourishes in the entire nation, and most correspond with that most central of spaces, the plaza. Mariachi Plaza de Los Angeles is in no way peripheral to this network, but is rather an epicenter of its own. What has happened in Boyle Heights and East L.A. changed and expanded mariachi traditions to include new meanings for both Mexico's, the republic south of the border, and the millions of Mexicans who live north of it (2013, 67).

Mariachi performers ranging in ages, nationality, and degrees of celebrity are always well represented from central Mexico to Alta California, including traditional male, female, and mixed-gender ensembles performing throughout the day. However, Mariachi Plaza also serves as a traditional gathering place for local townsfolk, as it resembles the sunlit commons near the central plazas of Mexican villages, towns, and barrios (see Atencio 2009, García 2015, Vigil et al. 2014).

Enrique Lamadrid invited me to observe and participate in the early morning *mañanitas* and witness the *misa*, a music procession and festival, in 2010. Over the years, my own California State University Northridge students, who perform in Mariachi Matador, have also been participating. The portrait of

Figure 9.1. Mariachi procession celebrating the *Fiesta de Santa Cecilia* at Boyle Heights. Photo by Miguel Gandert, used with permission.

Santa Cecilia is adorned with flowers and carried by a mariachi honor guard reclaiming space and reterritorializing the streets, neighborhoods, and suburban routes as part of the Mexican observance and musical celebration, as several mariachi groups dressed in their finest *trajes* accompany the image (see Figure 9.2). According to Lamadrid, this cultural process is a way of producing collective cultural knowledge as part of a phenomenon that New Mexico and Chicanx scholars are calling *querencia*. The term combines the words *querer* (to love) with *herencia* (heritage) to reflect a 'love of heritage' with a deep-rooted attachment to place.

Figure 9.2. Mariachi performance during the *Misa de Santa Cecilia*. Photo by Miguel Gandert, used with permission.

Chicanismo and MeXicanidad: Querencia, 'Feeling Brown,' and Cultural Schizophrenia

In *The Country and the City*, Raymond Williams referred to an accrual of sentiment, emotion, and ideology as a structure of feeling (1973). The study of public feelings considers how and why feelings and emotions (assumed to be a private and personal experience) influence politics and notions of social belonging in intimacy. As neurologically prompted reactions developed over human generations, an affective citizenship is a "feeling and a state of being" according to María Elena Cepeda, whose unique spelling of "imagiNation" highlights "both noun and verb", as a "collective activity embedded in a definite sense of place(less-ness)" (Cepeda 1997, 27–38). With increasing angst over Donald Trump's travel bans and his "anti-migratory epistle,"[2] the United States finds itself decentered and divided in political tribalism and an endless and ongoing culture war that has produced disorienting temporalities. This disorientation is itself the result of conflicts among a plurality of social rhythms, and between individual and collective experiences over the uncertainty that lies ahead. For Alicia Gaspar de Alba, cultural schizophrenia relates to these conflicts in the sense that they point to "antagonistic beliefs, social forms, and material traits in any group whose racial, religious, or social components are a hybrid of two or more cultures (also known as *mestizaje*)" (2003, 199). For Gaspar de Alba, "that state of cognitive disorientation—a psychological side effect of 150 years of Anglo colonization" is the predominant form of cultural schizophrenia among Chicanx, Latinx, and Mexican communities across the United States" (2003, 199).

A notion of 'temporalization' that views time as a symbolic process continually being produced in everyday practices is useful to tease out MeXicanidad as an accrual of sentiment, emotion, and ideology that through 'feeling brown' emerges as a structure of feeling and as a phenomenological instance of belonging. As such, MeXicanidad is steeped in cultural schizophrenia, as it is a discursive space produced at a cultural intersection.[3] Georgina Born proposes a materialist framework for the analysis of these interactive and partially open temporalities in terms of "distinctive scales, speeds, rhythms, and shapes of change opened up and exacted by cultural objects and events that, through our complex interactions, participate in the emergent processes we identify as history" (Born 2015, 381). This theorization opens a productive discursive ground to understand how the symbolic performativity of rituals such as Santa Cecilia position MeXicanidad as one of such temporal instances that articulate contemporary Chicano identity in relation to 'feeling brown'. Russel Rodríguez, has mentioned that "Mexican identity is just one of several identities U.S. musicians maintain, knowing they also go to a U.S. educational system, have engaged political and social spaces, and have most likely experienced the popular culture that U.S. society provides" (2009, 348). In this regard, NBC journalist Dennis Romero reported that chicanismo "is having its day in the sun perhaps most luminously through youth culture, art and fashion." Referring specifically to Los Angeles indie band Chicano Batman, Romero noticed that the band "has put the word out that there is something not only political but something that's hip and edgy" about chicanismo. According to NPR Music, "Southern California's Chicano Batman sent waves of velvet-sounding Chicano soul out—think 1970s-era guitar and organ funk played by a band outfitted in *quinceañera* tuxedos" (2016). Chicano Batman is arguably the most recent popular Latin alternative band reaching diverse audiences through their 'brown' soul and lyrical verse, reclaiming and rearticulating a refashioned neo-chicanismo with references to Indigenous signifiers.

Chicano Batman reassembles the fragmented mestizo soul of young Chicanx and Latinx hipsters across the West Coast. As an affectual schizophrenic temporalization, Chicano Batman is part of what scholars call *La Resolana*,[4] a dialogic 'learning society' based on respectful, critical listening, exchange of information, and a belief that people coming together can figure out their own lives (see García 2015, Vigil 2014, Montiel et al. 2009, Romero 2001). Chicano Batman expresses its strong cultural attachment and sense of belonging to East Los Angeles through music regarded as *el oro del barrio*—the collective customs and wisdom of the people that articulate *querencia*. Thus, Chicano Batman's glocal sound reveals hidden transcripts in their nostalgic beat and attachment to place and people. The band offers musical catharsis, political nostalgia, and musical rediscovery by "closing the gap between the Mexican and American in order to validate the ongoing mestizaje taking place across the United States" (see Davis-Undiano 2017).

Whereas conflict has indeed preserved cultural differences in East Los Angeles, it has also created a deep and complex musical mestizaje that serves as a register of cultural, symbolic, performative, and historical expressions, and blended musical aesthetics. Among younger Angelinos, Chicanx identity and brown feeling is not the result of reflection or contemplation of where things come from as much as vigorous musical enactments that reflect meaningful and memorable temporal experiences through social participation in music festivals, city art walks, diverse ethnic food, urban farmer's markets, nightclubs, and community dances, which continue to promote the recognition and celebration of the historic survival of East Los Angeles. According to Rubén Funkahuatl Guevara,

> One night in late 2012, I experienced a cultural landscape shift that possibly foreshadowed the future of Boyle Heights. I had just performed a spoken-word set (with Quetzal Flores on guitar and Martha Gonzalez on *cajón*) for a benefit

for Liliflor at Little Casa and Corazón del Pueblo, and decided to stop by the Eastside Luv for a glass of wine. Then I went across the street to the MBar to say hi to a friend, before moving on to the Salón de la Plaza on First and State for a concert by a new buzz band, Chicano Batman. I expected to see the usual Eastside denizens but was surprised to see the place packed with mostly downtown wannabes, mostly white hipsters having the time of their lives. I felt mixed emotions. Although I was glad to see a successful turnout for the new talent, I wasn't so sure what it would mean for the future of my neighborhood (2018, 324).

Social geographers define homeland as the relationship between people, place, and identity. Within this neo-chicanismo, Guevara's reaction might allude to a binary identity politics that calls for attention. In 2013, a Telemundo segment titled "Los Chipsters" (see Forestieri 2013) was reblogged by Pocho.com, arguing that Chipster and hipster are synonymous and occupy the same location within the Los Angeles urban political spaces and mediascapes.[5] Such homology, however, neutralizes and conceals the blighted racial history of economic and political inequality experienced by Mexicanx, Chicanx and mixed brown (i.e., Mexipin/x, Blatin/x and Blaxican), white, and Asian hipsters. More than just a Chicano hipster, Chipster points to the tensions between the white norms of corporate marketing and increased purchasing power among Latinx and brown youth who live in and outside East Los Angeles. Rather than a benevolent attempt to create a trendy identity, the term Chipster alludes to an assimilationist paradigm that reconstructs temporal movement through select memory and nostalgia, too often erasing or omitting important details along with vital musical and historical voices. The appropriation of the trademarked United Farm Workers of America logo on shirts by Urban Outfitters in August, 2013 without permission is one example that raised consciousness and resulted in Chicanx outrage and protest demanding action. A company spokesperson with Urban Outfitters notified *The Huffington Post* that it would immediately be removing the item from its stores and website stating "It was never our intention to infringe on a culture or trademark."

Likewise, Pixar's animated blockbuster movie *Coco* (2017) was also criticized by angry fans who found the film too close in comparison with *The Book of Life* (2014) written and directed by Jorge Gutiérrez. Earlier in 2013, Disney attempted to trademark the iconic traditional Mexican Day of the Dead imagery as a corporate attempt to brand and market their forthcoming animated movie but instead fueled more angry online protests. For Renato Rosaldo, the "Chicano warrior hero has seen better days. No longer can he serve as the 'unified subject' around which Chicano sagas of masculine heroics revolve" (Rosaldo 1993, 165). Likewise, for Gloria Anzaldúa, "being

Chicana is not enough—nor is being queer a word or any identity label I choose or others impose on me." Conventional, traditional identity labels, she writes, "are stuck in binaries, trapped in *jaulas* (cages) that limit the growth of our individual and collective lives" (1989). Thus, while Chicano Batman aligns with other Latinxs and Latin American musicians singing about undocumented migration alongside La Santa Cecilia, Calle 13, Los Tigres del Norte, Las Cafeteras, Willie Colón, Winsin & Yadel, Rebel Diaz, Molotov, and Ana Tijoux (Vargas 2017, 51 fn39), it does so by opening uncomfortable spaces of complex temporalized interactions (to use Georgina Born's term) that disrupt the historical binaries that have informed Chicano identity politics.

Seeking fresh and open-ended tags that portray the complexities and potentialities of emergent mixed brown feeling and identity, "certain musics," writes Rafael Pérez-Torres, "may go as far as invoking a simulacrum of Latino music." However, "with the growing success of *Rock en Español*, the increased exchange of musical commodities across national and cultural borders, the proliferation and diversification of music and music video programming in all countries and continents, the term 'Chicano music' itself seems somewhat antiquated" (2006, 332). With a neo-chicanismo renaissance underway, a new phase of Latin reckoning seems to be in the works, as popular fashion magazine *Vogue* declared: "whatever the period, retro references are an assertion of pride and an act of hope . . . going back in time to let the new generation know: 'We existed. We were here'" (2017). The magazine's 125th anniversary featured an online photo-exposé with high quality photography by Stefan Ruiz entitled "Latinas in Los Angeles" (see Aguirre 2017). Abbey Aguirre writes,

> Across the Southwest and especially in L.A., retro references have long been a vital element of Latina style. But throwback looks are not merely data points in fashion's larger recycling of eras, cuts, and proportions. 'A lot of young Chicanos want to connect to their history,' explained John Carlos De Luna, a vintage clothing dealer and the owner of Barrio Dandy Vintage, a showroom in Boyle Heights. 'Inherently they're connecting to an America that didn't really accept them, an America that looked down on them. There's such power in that—to own that history' (Aguirre 2017).

In his historical theorization of this cultural tension, Nestor García Canclini observes that "a very dynamic cultural production is also growing [in the U.S.] . . . due to the fact that the so-called Latin cultures produce films like *Zoot Suit* and *La Bamba*, the songs of Rubén Blades and Los Lobos, the aesthetically and culturally advanced theater of Luis Valdes, and visual artists [who] . . . interact with modern and postmodern symbolism [and] incorporate them into North American mainstream" (1995, 231). *Vogue*'s "Latinas in Los Angeles" might very well refer to such incorporation. Yet, Canclini's assessment, as well as Rafael Pérez-Torres' problematization of the term "Chicano music," point to the way in which Mexican Americans have historically negotiated the essentialisms embedded in power asymmetries characteristic of how minorities are represented by U.S. mediascapes and culture industries (such as *Vogue*). Anthony Macias states:

> From the 1950s through the 1960s, many Mexican-Americans took a 'holiday' or vacation from their designated place in the social structure, and in the city, by participating in a sophisticated Spanish-language cosmopolitanism . . . rather than claim to be 'Latin' or 'Latin American,' most Mexican-American Angelinos simply referred to themselves as 'Mexican'. Yet in the tradition of California's mythical Spanish fantasy heritage, the film and television industries disseminated a generalized image of 'Latins', along with a bland, deracinated Latin music, into the nations's culture and consciousness. Meanwhile, actual Mexican-Americans maintained individual and group ties to Mexican culture, even as they dabbled in Latin music (2008, 230).

Renato Rosaldo notes that in such mediated spaces (which he calls "multiple border zones") previous notions of homogenous community are displaced. The "unified subjects" who once resided securely within their cultural boundaries and groups acquire "a multiple personal identity" (1993, 16). Individuals belong to various communities whose borders cross and mix, confounding the dividing lines of group and culture. Chicano Batman is such an example of cultural and historical border crossing. For *LA Weekly* reporter Chris Kissel, Chicano Batman is indeed "a sign—reassurance that a band, whose music distills this city's cultural heritage, could step forward— a band that straddles the classic and the new, the nostalgic and the identity shifting" (2017). Chicano Batman is a multi-sounding brown blend of smooth Brazilian pop, urban soul, and local Mexican cultural musical codes and progressive politics that transgresses temporal lines. Kissel describes their latest album, *Freedom Is Free* as "a step forward and a record that finds the band growing fully into their sound, and harnessing it to make a statement for disorienting times" (Kissel 2017). The band's music, and its reception by this current generation of Chicanx and Latinx articulate an affectual site in which people map and make sense out of their temporal interactive complications. Georgia Born further explains how a continuum of musical practices:

> foregrounds novel aesthetic treatments of the very historicity of sonic or musical media, as well as of the sounds they afford. Critics have dubbed this continuum "retromania" or (with reference to Derrida) "hauntology". The genres at issue— hauntology, hypnagogic pop, chill wave, and others—knowingly recycle former

musical, cultural, and mediatic materials, along with their associations, in order to remediate the past disturbingly, nostalgically, affectionately, or ironically, invariably as an exercise in transtemporal invention (2015, 378).

Chicano Batman's trans-temporality contributes to our understanding of the postnationalist impulse that defines mexicanidad as a strategic essentialism with deeper hidden transcripts that reveal multiple connections and musical codes, which are meaningful to several communities and their shifting identity politics. Based on the diversity of sociological profiles among U.S. Latinx, James Cohen finds it particularly questionable to refer to them, as it is often done in an automatic and untheorized way, as forming a "community" (Cohen 2005, 176). Mexicans constitute such a large and varied group in California that a singular notion of community falls short of the multiple temporal possibilities stretching beyond a panoramic ethnographic gaze or concentric Chicano cultural abstraction. For Rafael Pérez-Torres, there emerges in the music a recognition that a broad conceptualization of mestizaje can be both a liberating process and one inscribed by tremendous political, social, and cultural conflict. "The music that highlights this double movement of connection to a troubled history and affirmation of liberatory inspiration displaces the easy musical stylings of pop musicians profiting from the growth of a Latino presence in the United States" (2006, 334).

Like their predecessors in the Chicano movement, younger Angelinos continue experiencing the cultural expressions of Mexico as a process of rediscovery in the same way that Stuart Hall's notion of "imagined re-discovery" (see 1998, 1989) allows us to challenge static and singular notions of mexicanidad and chicanismo. However, and as Manuel Peña reminds us, while the cultural economy of late capitalism has transformed the post-Chicano generation into a fragmented, heterogenous mass with a 'decentered' sense of ideological purpose (1999, 189), Juan Velasco avoids the dangerous ahistorical and subject-less celebration of 'difference' by reintroducing older mexicanist theories that go beyond the male-gendered and assimilationist limitations imposed by earlier theories of mexicanidad developed during the 1920s and 1940s by early modern writers Alfonso Reyes and José Vasconcelos. George Lipsitz argues that the Chicano movement "was an effort to convince people to draw their identity from their politics rather than drawing their politics from their identity" (1991, 79). Because Chicanos are themselves collages—an amalgam of Indian, Spanish, Mexican, Latin/o and Anglo elements, Curtis Márez claims, "their cultural products are also mixtures and fragments from diverse traditions" (Marez 1996, 122). Thus, without rejecting the past, the concept of MeXicanidad references the political task of Rosa Linda Fregoso, but also that of anthropologist Manuel Gamio in reevaluating the role of artists as that of cultural ethnographers (see Paredes 1977, 9; cited in Velasco

2006, 207). As cultural schizophrenia, 'feeling brown' in current Chicanx cultural discourse shows MeXicanidad to be a collage and a stylistic corollary of the 'impure,' estranged status of racial and decentered national mixture.

NOTES

1. See Rosa Linda Fregoso in *MeXicana Encounters: The Making of Social Identities on the Borderlands*, xiv.

2. In 2018, it is no longer just the outcry of a culture that wants to turn back the clock so that it can pretend that gay people do not exist. Now, it is the outcry of a culture that wants to Make America Great Again, to turn back the clock so that no one outside a monolith can exist within its borders: not gay people, and not black and brown people either. Amanda Lawrence, who plays the Angel in the current Broadway production *Angels in America*, has related such racial exclusionism to gendered and sexual readings of the body: "This whole anti-migratory kind of thing is just fantastic to say . . . Marianne [Elliott, the director] said in rehearsal, 'The Angel and Roy Cohn are very similar. This disgust, this racism'" (Grady 2018). Indeed, it is via Roy Cohn that the shadow of Trumpism looms largest.

3. MeXicanidad, therefore, is different from the cultural discourse of mexicanidad articulated by the Mexican nation-state, a construct that has remained historically monolithic in relation to 'Mexico,' understood as a geopolitically well-defined cultural location until very recently—the contribution of *neozapatista* discursivity towards the pluralization of 'Mexico' or 'mexicanidad,' for that matter, notwithstanding (Joysmith 2003, 148). For a further problematization of this construction see Alex E. Chávez and Lizette Alegre González in this volume.

4. Tomás Atencio describes *la resolana* as "a place where the sun reverberates off a wall creating a place of light, warmth, and tranquility" (Atencio 2005, Montiel et al. 2009); "a local tradition of congregating in a public place where the sun reflects its warmth off a southern-facing wall in a plaza or courtyard" (Atencio 2009). Cipriano Vigil calls this way of learning "*música de la resolana*" (2014, 239). David Floyd García argues that "The resolana (. . .) is known traditionally as a place where people gather on the plaza in the warmth of the sun during the cold season. In the turn of events, both women and men have reworked the idea of resolana to include new practices in new informal spaces such as having coffee at McDonald's or meeting people serendipitously at other commercial places such as Wal-Mart" (2015, 14).

5. "On the Chipster Question," ahuante explains how, "Chipster assures and secures the neoliberal project by ensuring the foregrounding of a consumer identity and assuming a safe racial identity—white (or whitening) identity—equating whiteness "vis-à-vis the aforementioned consumer identity" (2013). That Chipsters or Chicano hipsters connote a visual potential for critical whiteness or creolization, brown feeling as musical affect blurs color lines and mends sonic splits offering novel potential for more radical political action, social change, musical creativity, and border consciousness taking place through mexicanidad as resurgent citizen-activism. ahuante further

questions: Why their disassociation from Chicano in the first place? Why not identify as Chicano or Xicano and leave it at that? It may speak to other issues regarding the term Chicano, however it's still worth noting that, as of yet, Chipster is predicated on a primarily consumer identity and a (real or perceived) upwardly mobile aspiration (ahuante 2013).

REFERENCES

Aguirre, Abby. "Latinas in Los Angeles." *Vogue* (March 8, 2017). https://www.vogue.com/projects/13528517/mexican-american-women-east-los-angeles-chicano-fashion-latina-style/.

ahuante. "On the Chipster Question." *The Glove Project: Exploring the Urban Geography of Race and Racism* (August 8, 2013). https://ahuante.wordpress.com/2013/08/08/on-the-chipster-question/.

Anzaldúa, Gloria. *Borderlands/La Frontera: The New Mestiza*. San Francisco: Aunt Lute Books. 1989.

Born, Georgina. "Making Time: Temporality, History and the Cultural Object." *New Literary History* vol. 46, no. 3 (Summer 2015): 361–386.

Cepeda, María Elena. *Musical ImagiNation: U.S. Colombian Identity and the Latin Music Boom*. New York: New York University Press, 2010

Cohen, James. "Sociopolitical Logics and Conflicting Interpretations of 'Latinization'." In *Latin@s in the World-System: Decolonization Struggles in the 21st Century U.S. Empire*, edited by Ramón Grosfoguel, Nelson Maldonado-Torres, and José David Saldivar, 165–182. Boulder: Paradigm Publishers, 2005.

Davis-Undiano, Robert Con. *Mestizos Come Home! Making and Claiming Mexican American Identity*. Norman, OK: University of Oklahoma Press, 2017.

de la Torre Castellanos, Renée. "The Zapopan Dancers: Reinventing an Indigenous Line of Descent." In *Dancing Across Borders: Danzas y Bailes Mexicanos*, edited by Olga Nájera, Norma E. Cantú, and Bernda M. Romero, 19–47. Urbana and Chicago: University of Illinois Press, 2009.

Fregoso, Rosa Linda. *MeXicana Encounters: The Making of Social Identities on the Borderlands*. Berkeley: University of California Press, 2003.

García Canclini, Néstor. *Imagined Globalization*. Durham: Duke University Press. 2014.

———. *Hybrid Cultures: Strategies for Entering and Leaving Modernity*. Minneapolis: University of Minnesota Press, 1995.

García, David Floyd. *La Resolana: Tracing the Communicative Cartographies of Gathering Spaces in North Central New Mexico*. Ph.D. diss., The University of Texas at Austin, 2015.

Gaspar de Alba, Alicia. "Rights of Passage: From Cultural Schizophrenia to Border Consciousness in Cheech Marin's Born in East LA." In *Velvet Barrios: Popular Culture and Chicana/o Sexualities*, edited by Alicia Gaspar de Alba, 199–214. New York: Palgrave Macmillan, 2003.

Grady, Constance. "How 2018 Reshaped Angels in America: The Ghost of Trump is Always Next to Roy Cohn in the New Production of *Angels in America.*" *Vox* (June 10, 2018). https://www.vox.com/culture/2018/4/30/17199540/angels-in-america-2018-broadway-nyc-tony-kushner.

Guevara, Rubén Funkahuatl. *Confessions of a Radical Chicano Doo-Wop Singer.* Berkeley: University of California Press, 2018.

Hall, Stuart. "Introduction: Who Needs Identity?" In *Questions of Cultural Identity*, edited by Stuart Hall and Paul du Gay, 1–17. London: SAGE, 1998.

———. "Cultural Identity and Cinematic Representation." *Framework: The Journal of Cinema and Media* 36 (1989): 68–81.

Joysmith, Claire. "Response (Re)mapping Mexicanidades: (Re)Locating Chicana Writings and Translation Politics." In *A Critical Reader: Chicana feminisms*, edited by Gabriela F. Arrendondo et al., 148–154. Durham: Duke University Press, 2003.

Kissel, Chris. "Chicano Batman Brings the Sounds of Latino L.A. to the Rest of America." *LA Weekly* (February 27, 2017). https://www.laweekly.com/music/chicano-batman-bring-the-sounds-of-latino-la-to-the-rest-of-america-7970140.

Lamadrid, Enrique. "A Paean to Santa Cecilia, Her Fiesta, and Her Mariachis: Mariachi Plaza/Pueblo de Nuestra Señora de los Ángeles Alta California, Greater México/U.S.A." In *Hotel Mariachi: Urban Space and Cultural Heritage in Los Angeles*, edited by Catherine L. Kurland and Enrique R. Lamadrid, 61–94. Albuquerque: University of New Mexico Press, 2013.

———. *Hermanitos Comanchitos: Indo-Hispano Rituals of Captivity and Redemption.* Albuquerque: University of New Mexico Press, 2003.

Lipsitz, George. "Not Just Another Social Movement: Poster and Art of the Movimiento Chicano." In *Just Another Poster? Chicano Graphic Arts in California*, edited by Chon Noriega, 71–87. Seattle: University of Washington Press, 1991.

"LOS CHIPSTERS." YouTube video, 3:02. Posted by "Claudia Forestieri," January 24, 2013. https://www.youtube.com/watch?v=uCkw-9xzUN4.

Lowe, Lisa. and David Lloyd. "Introduction." In *The Politics of Culture in the Shadow of Late Capital*, edited by Lisa Lowe and David Lloyd, 1–32. Durham: Duke University Press, 1997.

Macias, Anthony. *Mexican American Mojo: Popular Music, Dance, and Urban Culture in Los Angeles, 1935–1968.* Durham: Duke University Press, 2008.

Marez, Curtis. "Brown: The Politics of Working-Class Chicano Style." *Social Text* 48, no. 3 (Fall 1996): 109–132.

Milian, Claudia. *Latining America: Black-Brown Passages and the Coloring of Latino/a Studies.* Atlanta: University of Georgia Press, 2013.

Montiel, Miguel, Tomás Atencio, and E.A. "Tony" Mares. *Resolana: Emerging Chicano Dialogues on Community and Globalization.* Tucson: University of Arizona Press, 2009. Munn, Nance D. "The Cultural Anthropology of Time: A Critical Essay." *Annual Review of Anthropology* vol. 21 (1992): 93–123.

Muñoz, José Esteban. "Feeling Brown, Feeling Down: Latina Affect, the Performativity of Race, and the Depressive Position" *Journal of Women in Culture and Society* vol. 31, no. 3 (Spring 2006): 675–688.

Paredes, Américo. "On Ethnographic Work among Minority Groups: A Folklorist's Perspective." *New Scholar* vol. 6 (1977). Reprint in *New Directions in Chicano Scholars*, edited by Ricardo Romo and Raymund Paredes, 1–32. Santa Barbara: UCSB Chicano Studies, 1984.

Pérez-Torres, Rafael. "Chicano Hip Hop and Postmodern Mestizaje." In *The Chicana/o Cultural Studies Reader*, edited by Angie Chabram-Dernersesian, 324–339. New York: Routledge. 2006.

Rodríguez, Richard T. *Next of Kin: The Family in Chicano/a Cultural Politics*. Durham: Duke University Press, 2009.

Rodríguez, Russell. 2009. "Folklórico in the United States: Cultural Preservation and Diffusion." In *Dancing Across Borders: Danzas y Bailes Mexicanos*, edited by Olga Nájera-Ramírez, Norma E. Cantú, and Brenda M. Romero, 335–358. Urbana and Chicago: University of Illinois Press, 2009.

Romero, Dennis. "A Chicano Renaissance? A New Mexican-American Generation Embraces the Term." *NBC News.com* (July 15, 2018). https://www.nbcnews.com/news/latino/chicano-renaissance-new-mexican-american-generation-embraces-term-n869846.

Rosaldo, Renato. *Truth and Culture: The Remaking of Social Analysis*. Boston: Beacon Press, 1993.

Sheehy, Daniel. *Mariachi Music in America: Experiencing Music, Expressing Culture*. New York: Oxford University Press, 2006.

———. "Mexican Music: Made in the U.S.A." In *Musics of Multicultural Americas*, edited by Kip Lornell and Anne Rasmussen, 131–154. New York: Macmillan, 1997.

Slobin, Mark. "Micromusics of the West: A Comparative Approach." *Ethnomusicology* vol. 36, no. 1 (Winter 1992): 1–88.

Vargas, Jennifer Harford. "The Undocumented Subjects of El Hueco: Theorizing a Colombian Metaphor for Migration." In *Symbolism: An International Annual of Critical Aesthetics* vol. 17, edited by Rüdiger Ahrens, Florian Kläger and Klaus Stierstorfer, 31–54. Berlin: Walter de Gruyter GmbH, 2017.

Velasco, Juan. "The X in Race and Gender." In *The Chicana/o Cultural Studies Reader*, edited by Angie Chabram-Dernersesian, 203–210. New York: Routledge, 2006.

Viesca, Victor Hugo. "The Battle of Los Angeles: The Cultural Politics of Chicana/o Music in the Greater East Side." *American Quarterly* vol. 56, no. 3 (September 2004): 719–739.

———. "Straight Out the Barrio: Ozomatli and the Importance of Place in the Formation of Chicana/o Popular Culture in Los Angeles." *Cultural Values* vol. 4, no. 4 (October 2000): 445–473.

Chapter 10

Listening from 'The Other Side'
Music, Border Studies, and the Limits of Identity Politics

Alejandro L. Madrid

Ethnomusicologists have been in conversation with border studies almost since the inception of these fields as proper scholarly endeavors in the 1950s.[1] One could almost trace the trajectories of ethnomusicology and border studies as unfolding in a parallel fashion through the end of the 1990s, when questions about mestizaje, hybridity, and transculturation at the core of border studies became common among ethnomusicologists.[2] However, music historians focusing on western art music noticed and started taking border studies seriously only in the early twenty-first century. The fall of 2012 appears to be a particularly important moment in that process of recognition, with *Transnational Encounters. Music and Performance at the U.S.-Border*, a multi-disciplinary volume centered around issues at the U.S.-Mexico border, receiving the American Musicological Society's Ruth A. Solie Award, and Tamara Levitz's curated colloquy "Musicology beyond Borders?" being published in the *Journal of the American Musicological Society*.[3] This coincidence puts in evidence that there was a sense of novelty and anticipation among musicologists about the intellectual possibilities of border studies in approaching the study of music. Seen in retrospect, it seems that, regardless of the multiple approaches to border studies, hybridity, and diaspora, investigating and dwelling on borders opened the possibility of moving new, original, and important intellectual questions into the mainstream of musicological inquiry at the time.[4]

This optimistic take among musicologists notwithstanding, by the time their field became interested in borders, border studies scholars had become aware of its shortcomings. In the closing chapter of *Ethnography at the Border*, sociologist Pablo Vila warned his readers of the tendency to construct the border subject "into a new privileged subject of history" (Vila 2003, 307) that had characterized the field. By trying to expand the concept of border to address the epistemic and political flows that define the body and the body politics in my earlier work, especially in *Nor-tec Rifa!* and *Postnational Musical Identities,* I had also become aware of the limitations of the border as an interpretative lens and epistemological model.[5] This concern also informs Tamara Levitz's suggestion that "rather than euphorically celebrate metaphorical border crossings, it might be time for musicologists to turn their attention to the material reality of borders themselves and the violence they perpetuate" in the introduction to the *JAMS* colloquy mentioned earlier (Levitz 2012, 823). The recent relevance of borders, border crossers, and border walls at the center of the polarized political debate that brought the Donald Trump administration to the United States, Brexit to the United Kingdom, and ultra nationalist and xenophobic regimes to Poland, Hungary, Croatia, and Brazil at the end of the second decade of the twenty-first century reminds us of Levitz's admonishment and forces us to look back and reevaluate the real power of borders, or talk about borders in shaping senses of belonging and otherness, as well as setting political agendas in motion. In doing that, we may also question again how listening to a variety of musical practices from the liminality of the border may help us move back and forth between contradicting individual and collective desires and between old fashion discourses about academic objectivity and scholarship as a practice that could have a political impact on our everyday lives.[6] I explore these issues in the spirit of healthy skepticism, always keeping in mind the following question: whom do we empower when we speak of borders?

One of the borders that I am interested in exploring here is the boundary between scholarship as a report of events and practices and scholarship as an intellectual activity that seeks to critique and question the performative power of those events and practices. This intellectual paradox is one that I had to face early in my academic career when my intellectual concerns forced me to move away from traditional musicology into the field of cultural studies and especially performance studies. The subjectivity and political valence of any academic project has always been at the center of performance studies as a discipline; however, musicologists have only recently welcomed applied musicology as a legitimate academic pursuit—nonetheless, still separated by its own borders from other forms of more mainstream musicological work still thought of as 'uncorrupted' by everyday politics. I argue that by looking at the boundaries between these two forms of intellectual inquiry one may also elucidate the current relevance of border studies as well as its possible shortcomings for the humanities in general and music studies in particular. I explore these issues through the screen performance of Mexican singer and songwriter Juan Gabriel, a liminal figure who crosses a wide variety of geographic, epistemic, and imagined borders, and also one of the most striking, against-all-odds cases of commercial success, for he was an artist universally perceived as homosexual in the largely homophobic societies of 1970s Latin America. In doing this, I take as point of departure Juan Gabriel's performance of diasporic self in the 1979 film *Del otro lado del puente* [*From the Other Side of the Bridge*] to explore the potential of the idea of being from 'the other side' to investigate the relationship between the geographic borders of the nation-state and the imagined borders of heteronormativity. I suggest that asking what does it mean to look at oneself from the estranged perspective of the Other enables one to take Juan Gabriel's paternalistic and even moralistic musical and performatic commentaries about Mexican-American culture—enunciated from the singer's perceived homosexuality—to speak about the reproduction of problematic notions of fixed national, ethnic, and gender identity that the transborder experience questions on an everyday basis. By focusing on Juan Gabriel's performance, with its successful queering of gender but unsuccessful queering of nationalism in terms of border policing, the first part of this chapter addresses the problematic outcome of traditional border studies that Tamara Levitz and Pablo Vila have criticized. The second part of the chapter branches out of Juan Gabriel's case study to theorize about the potential and shortcomings from border studies within larger discourses of identity politics and to explore their implications on musicology as a discipline.

DEL OTRO LADO DEL PUENTE: JUAN GABRIEL AND THE MEXICAN-AMERICAN EXPERIENCE

The song "Nada, nada, nada" in the film's soundtrack features a funky synthesizer line on the downbeat, following a short melodic ascending line in the violins. The brief harmonic chain seems to hint towards a modal cadence on C-sharp minor; however, the repeat of the introductory instrumental section quickly rectifies the harmonic motion, establishing E major as the song's harmonic center. Here, the violins playing long accompanying harmonies join the driving synthesizer countermelody, a jumpy bass line, and a drum set and conga obsessed with the upbeat, to set up a catchy groove upon which Juan Gabriel sings a syncopated melody, "*Yo ya no quiero nada, nada, nada más de ti.*" While the soundtrack offers this Mexican take on the typical sound of disco music from the end of the 1970s, the screen shows a choreographed scene in which Juan Gabriel is followed and almost stalked by a young American woman through a number of iconic places in Los Angeles: the UCLA campus, Tower Records on Sunset Strip, and the historical Mexican-American square, Placita Olvera. Her pursuit ends at the Sixth Street Bridge, where Juan Gabriel, who has stoically ignored her dancing for several miles, waves goodbye and, leaving her weeping in sadness and disbelief, crosses to the other side, East Los Angeles (see Figure 10.1).

This scene marks the dramatic turning point in the plot of *Del otro lado del puente*, a movie in which Juan Gabriel stars as Alberto, a young and sassy Mexican American who, after having been raised in Mexico returns to the United States to study urban planning at UCLA and pursue an unlikely career as singer and performer. There, he learns about the systematic discrimination experienced by Mexican Americans but also about the crime and internal leadership divisions that afflict this community. At first, Alberto is fascinated and bedazzled by mainstream American culture, to which he is introduced by Doris, the Bel Air American girl he fancies but who does not take him seriously and for whom he seems to be an exotic curiosity (the girl he leaves behind when crossing the bridge to East L.A.). Alberto's brother, Danny, played by Billy Cardenas, the legendary East L.A. music manager and producer from the 1960s, is a former gangster turned community activist who struggles to keep young Chicanos away from drugs and crime. The scene discussed above represents Alberto's recognition of his marginality in mainstream American culture and, by crossing over to 'the other side of the

Figure 10.1. Screen shot of Doris at the Sixth Street Bridge in the film *Del otro lado del puente* (1979).

bridge' a metaphorical return to his Mexican-American roots in East L.A., the legendary Mexican-American side of town.

Ser del otro lado [being from the other side] implies being different. If one uses the term in Mexico it would mean being from the United States—thus, being American or, if one is from Mexican descent, being *pocho,* as Mexican nationals often refer to Mexican Americans disdainfully. If one uses the term in the United States it would mean being Mexican; but regardless of where one uses it, colloquially, the term always has the potential of indexing homosexuality. I would like to dwell precisely on this identitarian ambiguity of the term to explore the relationship between the geographic borders of the nation-state and the imagined borders of Mexican masculinity; the real and imaginary boundaries of identity in relation to the gendered experience of the body and the ethnicized experience of the body politics.

Del otro lado del puente presents a series of ambivalences at different levels; from superficial aspects of style in specific actions that give the movie its unique color, to more structural aspects at the level of representation in the performances of the characters within the movie, to discursive aspects that the movie performs in everyday life, to uncertainties between Juan Gabriel's fictional character, his public persona as a songwriter, and his private persona as imagined by his audiences, which often seem to collapse into one another. I argue that these ambiguities could be productively read in terms of estrangement in order to better understand the scope of Juan Gabriel as a performance complex that allows us to read quotidian and normalized gender, race, and ethnicity practices from new perspectives. In other words, I am interested in seeing how Juan Gabriel as a performance complex gives us a chance to look at the familiar from an unfamiliar point of view. I suggest looking at a few ambiguous moments in the movie as instances that allow us to move to the other side and see things from an estranged perspective. I argue that these moments could help us understand the potential of border studies as a liberating project but also as a restrictive lens that may prevent us to see beyond the limits it helps create or reproduce.

The first of these ambiguous moments takes place when Juan Gabriel/Alberto bumps into a group of American students at the UCLA campus. They invite him to join them for a football game. Juan Gabriel quickly turns the motions and gestures of the game into a disco choreography that effectively queers the gender overtones of the sport that better symbolizes American masculinity (see Figure 10.2).

Looking at football from the other side—from the side of a foreigner who does not belong to the culture for which football has become a space where masculinity is negotiated—expands the cultural horizon of the game. An estranged version of the game that takes its codified motions to make them

Figure 10.2. Screen shot of the football choreography in the film *Del otro lado del puente* (1979).

into a queer choreography works as a window into what queer instances of estrangement may be able to produce within mainstream American culture. As such, football is not just a game that takes place on the pitch, it is a ludic choreography of movements, gestures, and performatic corporeal plots that transcend the boundaries of the field to metaphorically become the performative moves that give meaning to the body politics. Juan Gabriel's liminal gender performance sets in motion a type of libidinal friction between the normative expectations of the game's standard ludic encounter of bodies and the queer subliminal identifications in these bodies' playful dance.

The second moment I would like to discuss is the choreography at the end of the movie. Here, Juan Gabriel and his girlfriend walk on a street in East L.A. when a group of lowriders approach them. The *cholos* (Mexican-American gang members) slowly get out of their cars but instead of the expected gang fight, what ensues is a dance choreography to Juan Gabriel's pop song "Me gusta bailar contigo." Within the plot of the movie, this is a moment of harmony between Chicano gangs that may have been at odds, but that come together under the leadership of Juan Gabriel, the "Mexican without inferiority complexes," as his UCLA professor describes him earlier in the movie. Here, the choreography looks at stereotypical Chicano culture from the other side, as in the case of the football scene, to queer the overtones of violent masculinity that mainstream culture ascribes to this specific American subculture. By replacing the violent encounter of fighting gangsters' bodies with the queer choreography of dancing bodies, Juan Gabriel's performance of difference transcends the boundaries of normative masculinity, setting in motion once again a libidinal encounter between expectation and identification.

The meanings of the music choreographies in the football and gangster scenes are determined not only by the specific queer dancing moves and the intersubjective relations these dance moves allow; their meaning is unavoidably mediated by the presence of Juan Gabriel's performing body and the homoerotic overtones it brings to the movie. This is particularly poignant as the movie seems to constantly blur the boundaries between fiction, public life, and private life. For example, Alberto, the character is also the real name of Juan Gabriel; moreover, the continuous shift between footage shot for the movie and material taken from Juan Gabriel's actual concerts seems to further reinforce the porosity between movie character, artist, and public persona. Regardless of the fact that the movie is not a biopic, for an audience captivated by Juan Gabriel the public figure, Juan, Alberto the character, and Alberto Aguilera the person are one and the same; and their gender identities are also one and the same. Borders are continually crossed and made meaningless at many levels of performance in the film and the habitus that makes its reception culturally and socially meaningful. I believe the two choreographies from the movie are examples of the type of productive estrangement that Juan Gabriel's performance of queerness entails and that resonates with his overall performance and its reception.[7]

However, as much as I am fascinated by the productive potential of Juan Gabriel's performance to estrange mainstream cultural practices and experiences I am also concerned with the fact that such challenges fail to translate into the field of nationalism and nationalist discourse, as exemplified in the singer's take on *mexicanidad* not only in this film but throughout his artistic career. This is evident in some of the songwriter's later productions, especially "Canción 187" and "El México que se nos fue" from the 1995 album of the same title. As we will see later, these songs show that instead of providing a platform for the critique of the shortcomings of Mexican discourses of national identity, Juan Gabriel's look at Mexico and Mexican culture from the estranged point of view of the other side of the Rio Grande actually ends up reinforcing those very nationalistic ideas. This is already evident in his problematic and often patronizing take on Chicano culture, which informs the main argument in the plot of *Del otro lado del puente*. Alberto, hailed by his UCLA professor as the "Mexican without inferiority complexes," represents a type of dystopian messianic figure that comes to emancipate Mexican Americans. The underlying discourse in the movie's awkward plot seems to be that Mexican Americans need the presence of an 'authentic' Mexican to lift them from their psychological and cultural oppression and offer a path towards liberation—a path that involves more than the metaphorical return to Aztlán that Chicano culture has mythologized since the 1960s; an actual return to Mexico as the 'authentic' source of collective identity that will give meaning to the lives and struggles of individual Mexican Americans.

The problem with this narrative and with Juan Gabriel's representation is that it fails to recognize Chicano culture as a surplus in relation to Mexican ideas of national identity. Chicanos are not failed Mexicans, as Octavio Paz argues in *El laberinto de la soledad*.[8] Their bicultural condition and binational experience surpasses the condition of mexicanidad that the Mexican gaze attempts to ascribe on them. Juan Gabriel's take on Chicano culture ends up reproducing the mistaken Mexican stereotypes that look at Chicanos as lacking something; his estranged gaze unproductively reproduces these stereotypes precisely because it reinforces the essentialist ideas about authenticity that inform traditional discourses about Mexican national identity. So, in the specific case of border crossings, of looking at his own culture from the other side, Juan Gabriel's estrangement results in a missed opportunity. The very borders that inform Juan Gabriel's novel queer gaze on U.S. culture prevent him from understanding a Chicano reality that those borders not only cannot contain but they also completely fail to explain. These geographic and epistemological borders predetermine how Alberto the character, Alberto Aguilera the person, and Juan Gabriel the artist, understand, channel, and express mexicanidad, preventing them from challenging the risky exceptionalist overtones of such identitarian discourse at the performative, personal, as well as aesthetic levels.

The unfamiliarity provided by estrangement would seem like a logical moment to expose the flipside of normativity. However, not every experience with the unfamiliar results in productive estrangement; it is not just the disconnect between expectation and experience that is central to productive estrangement but the challenge to expectations and the defiance of norms. Moments of unsuccessful cognitive estrangement, like Juan Gabriel's take on Chicano culture or Mexican national identity, show this very clearly because they happen as a result of the strangeness of the experience failing to articulate or engage aesthetic discourses and challenge cultural expectations already instilled in both audience and artist. The dynamics that inform the unproductive or successful processes of cognitive estrangement in Juan Gabriel's performance are good indicators to measure the potential as well as the limitations of border studies as interpretative framework and epistemological model.

THE OTHER SIDE AND BORDER STUDIES IN THE TWENTY-FIRST CENTURY: AGAINST EXCEPTIONALISM

In his critique of the potential of Latin American cultural studies in challenging neoliberal utopias and transnational capital, Alberto Moreiras warns us of the dangers of conceptualizing identity politics and hybridity as constructions working against neoliberalism and late capitalism. He argues that as such, "identity politics, whether hybrid or not, becomes in effect all there is in the realm of the political—a simplifying counterpart to capitalism's world simplification, unable, in spite of itself, to move beyond tautology" (Moreiras 2001, 275). I believe that a critical take on the contradictory processes of cognitive estrangement in Juan Gabriel's liminal performance in *Del otro lado del puente* and beyond expose a similar tautological feature of border studies.

Cultural breaks that offer radical reconceptualizations of ossified or naturalized aspects of identity are difficult to assimilate. In order to be successful, they often need to be balanced by leaving untouched other similarly questionable aspects of the identity project at stake. In order to survive as viable subjects, individuals need to latch onto something that provides a sense of stability; revolutionary breaks that challenge the wholeness of the identitarian project at once would result in the negation of the discursive subject. Thus, I would argue that the success of Juan Gabriel's gender project as a transborder endeavor and its paving of important changes in quotidian behavior, social norms, and eventually legislative normativity in Mexico could not be possible without the sedimentation of values and beliefs that reinforce other borders; in this case, the borders of ethnic difference that strengthen questionable essentialisms about Mexican national identity. The reinforcement of these ethnic identity models provides the sense of identitarian stability needed for Juan Gabriel's questioning of sexual and gender norms to be accepted. While the singer's performance transcends gender borders, it also polices ethnic boundaries in terms of exclusion, containment, and belonging. Nothing provides a better example of this than the scene when Juan Gabriel crosses the Sixth Street Bridge to East L.A. in *Del otro lado del puente*: such a move shows the singer as a privileged character that is able to navigate the porosity of a border that is at the same time conclusively closed for Doris.

These dynamics put in evidence a central epistemic problem of border studies. By focusing on liminal regimes of seeing, listening, and understanding, border studies may provide a critique of mainstream culture; however, it may also reproduce the discourse of difference and identity politics that such borders entail. In that way, the field could be critiqued as an exceptionalist project, since it is the exceptionalism of the marginal subject that defines him/her as the privileged subject in history that border studies often celebrates.

Sheldon Wolin has identified this as a problem with nationalist cultural politics by stating that "in insisting upon boundaries that establish differences . . . but proclaim identities as well . . . the political becomes associated with purification or, more precisely, a reversal in which the stigma of impurity as well as the badge of purity are switched so that the pariah or victimized group is now pure, even innocent, while the dominant group is impure" (Wolin 1996, 32). Juan Gabriel's crossing the Sixth Street Bridge may be a reversal of the traumatic dynamics behind the U.S. discourse that attempts to keep the Mexican body away, on the other side of the border; however, it also reinforces the very idea upon which such discourse is based: that only some privileged bodies are meant to cross borders. Thus, Juan Gabriel crossing to the other side is a metaphor that could be interpreted as the climactic moment in a cleansing process that ends up reproducing the oppressive ideology that defines the boundaries of difference. From that perspective, border studies appears as a redemptionist project, a vicious circle that fails to critique the power structures that actually provide its interpretative gaze with a critical potential.

If border studies could become a reifying project it is precisely because the collective dichotomic identities it reproduces lie at the core of the larger project of modernity and thus it is central in the establishment of the neoliberal utopia that globalized capitalism has engendered. As a sibling project of cultural studies, border studies has proposed the ideas of hybridity and mestizaje as ways out of the problematic identitarian dichotomic dead alley that borders may entail. Thus, since the publication of Néstor García Canclini's influential *Culturas híbridas* in 1990, hybridity has been celebrated for the potential of residual traditions to shape new poly-vocal critiques of Enlightened modernity.[9] Nevertheless, as Moreira points out, "hybridity cannot go beyond the horizon of identitarian representation" because its tactical game of identification and disidentification "cannot position itself beyond the ideological interpellation of transnational capital" (Moreiras 2001, 275). Thus, as an exceptionalist project, border studies has the potential to simply reproduce the cultural, social, and economical asymmetries that allow for the blossoming of the neoliberal dystopia.

An ironic example of how these dynamics work can be found in Juan Gabriel's 1995 album *El México que se nos fue* (see Figure 10.3).

As mentioned earlier, the album features "Canción 187," a song written in response to the anti-immigration climate that led to the passing of Proposition 187 in California in 1994. Here, Juan Gabriel impersonates Juan, an imaginary undocumented migrant who has returned to Mexico and sings: "*Ahora trabajo en los campos / trabajo de sol a sol / ahora estoy con mi familia / y cada vez mucho mejor*" ("Now I work in the fields / I work from

Figure 10.3. *El México que se nos fue* (1995), album cover.

sun to sun / now I am with my family / and it's getting better all the time"), chauvinistically emphasizing the wonders of return migration and living in his own country. The song ends with a forceful identitarian statement: "*Adiós gringos peleoneros / buenos pa' las guerras son / Ellos creen que dios es blanco / y es más moreno que yo*" ("Bye American bullies / they are good for wars / they think god is white / but he is darker than me"). In an overtly chauvinistic tone, Juan Gabriel calls for Mexican migrants to avoid the humiliations and racial discrimination they experience in the United States and return to Mexico instead. The song's lyrics paint an idealistic and unrealistic picture of the Mexican countryside (towns full with colorful decorations and people wearing stylish Indigenous clothing and charro attires) and how welcoming Mexicans would be toward migrants upon their return (see Figure 10.4).

Figure 10.4. Screen shot of Juan Gabriel talking to Juan, the fictional return migrant in the video of "Canción 187" (1995).

Ironically, "El México que se nos fue," the following track in the CD, originated as a critique of the neoliberal policies that, since their systematic implementation in the country beginning in the mid-1980s, have led to the disappearance of the romantic and nostalgic Mexico Juan Gabriel dreams about in the previous song. I do not want to dwell on the problems of the nostalgic gaze on the past in Juan Gabriel's song; instead, I want to focus on how the singer tries to rhetorically argue his critique. Superficially, lyrics such as "Now people no longer work in the fields, they went to start a new adventure ... knowing they have lost the sugarmill, the mill, and their common sense"[10] seem to put forward a critique of the neoliberal-triggered economic and social conditions that led to the radical changes in the Mexican countryside that the singer despises (see Alegre in this volume). On the surface, the song sounds like a critique of neoliberalism. However, from a more critical standpoint, these statements clearly reinforce the false dichotomy of tradition/modernization and argue for a return to an imagined pre-industrial past that not only does not exist but that has in fact never existed. It is at this discursive juncture that nostalgia, the values naturalized in the tradition/modernity dichotomy, and the celebration of difference (reversed in the bold reterritorializing power of the lyrics at the end of the song, "They think god is white / but he is darker than me") pave the way to rendering invisible the true experience of exploitation of those who lived in a past that has been questionably transformed into an object of desire.

Thus, I would argue that Juan Gabriel's apparent critique of the shortcomings of neoliberalism is instead a nostalgic cry for a return to the asymmetrical conditions that lie at the very core of this economic and philosophical model. Expanding on Walter Mignolo's ideas, I argue that this type of "border thinking" is not only possible by the re-establishment of colonial difference, it in fact reproduces modernist difference (both colonial and imperial) in the asymmetries of neoliberal difference.[11] Looked at from a proleptic perspective, the rhetoric in the singer's critique of both U.S. racism and anti-immigration policies, and the neoliberal politics that have decimated the Mexican countryside in the last forty years seem to foreshadow the kind of protectionist talk that has dominated U.S. politics since Trump's presidential campaign as well as the rhetoric behind Brexit in the U.K. In fact, this emphasis on racial, cultural, and even spiritual difference stands as a nationalist call that takes the border as a *point de capiton* that gives meaning to a field of floating signifiers within a discourse of difference. It is the very invocation of the border that allows difference to become a viable political option. Neither Juan Gabriel's nationalist call nor Trump's or Brexit's protectionist discourse are real critiques of the neoliberal dystopia; they all fail to escape it as their premises acquire meaning precisely within the structures of modernist and eventually neoliberal difference.

Recent music scholarship about borders has continued to celebrate hybridity as a relevant analytical tool. In his recent work about music and dance in Arica, at the triple border between Peru, Bolivia, and Chile, Juan Eduardo Wolf appeals to hybridity when he asks: "How else to explain the situation of listening to Peruvian *chicha* while eating Bolivian *fricasé* in a *ramada*—the entertainment tents set up during national Chilean celebrations?"[12] Although I understand Wolf's to be a rhetorical strategy I would like to take the opportunity to propose an anti-exceptionalist perspective that closely considers the historical transnational fluxes that characterize border regions. Regardless of the essentialist claims of white supremacists and other racially motivated conservative activists, everything is a hybrid, everything is mestizo; therefore, I find no incongruity in the practices Wolf describes. But this brings us to an important epistemic conundrum: strategic essentialism has been a powerful tool of the subaltern and the marginalized, and multiculturalism has provided spaces of power for those who had none. However, we should not lose sight of a very important and somehow obviated aspect of subaltern theory: strategic essentialism is that—strategic—it is a move to benefit from mainstream oppressive configurations that it nevertheless continues to reproduce.

Is it possible to maintain the estranging power of border studies while avoiding the dangers of its potential to reproduce hegemonic structures? I argue in favor of an anti-essentialist and decolonial take on borders too. It is not that borders are unique spaces of continuous cultural contact; in a larger geographic and temporal scale this has been the history of humanity. Renato Rosaldo was very emphatic about that when, in his preface to the English translation of García Canclini's *Culturas híbridas*, he wrote: "hybridity can be understood as the ongoing condition of all human cultures, which contain no zones of purity because they undergo continuous processes of transculturation . . . Instead of hybridity versus purity, this view suggests that it is hybridity all the way down."[13] If Rosaldo is right, then the interpretative and political power of concepts like hybridity, mestizaje, or creolization is weakened. The very idea of mexicanidad was probably one of the more visible political projects validated on the idea of mestizaje or hybridity; an idea that, as Ignacio Sánchez Prado argues, regardless of the rhetorical shortcomings as well as its palpable eugenic overtones, continues to inspire hemispheric critical and decolonial projects (Sánchez Prado 2009, 381). Nevertheless, even the political valence of the mestizaje project as a tool for the homogenous discursive imagination of mexicanidad has waned following the limitations of the Mexican state in guaranteeing a more ethnically and economically egalitarian society. Before this dystopian post-mestizaje landscape, Pedro Ángel Palou states that for the particular case of Mexico, "the post-identitarian project is still unresolved and remains an urgent political act" (2014, 37). I would argue that, beyond the Mexican case, such is the task at hand when assessing the political and intellectual relevance of academic projects that have systematically invoked identity politics for decades.

Nevertheless, in calling attention to these problems I do not intend to dismiss border studies altogether; instead, I am arguing we should cherish the estranging potential of border studies while avoiding falling into the hegemonic trap that an uncritical walk into the field may lead us into. I still believe that looking from the margins provides a unique power to estrange mainstream practices and epistemologies. However, we must also be very cautious with the performative power of borders; we must keep an eye on what happens when borders happen because, as much as invoking them may allow us to make the familiar unfamiliar, such invocation also does very dangerously real things in the real world. My argument is for a type of cultural critique (border studies or otherwise) that provides estrangement without Orientalism. I propose that a productive way out of this epistemic labyrinth would be to use the border to identify and refocus on the surpluses that I mentioned earlier; those excesses that Octavio Paz missed in his attempt to characterize Mexican Americans as failed Mexicans and that may also mark them as deficient Americans in the overtly polarized rhetoric of today's politics. These types of failures of identification, of fitting in the box, of meeting standards, are precisely the kinds of failures that Judith Halberstam argues for as moments "to poke holes in the toxic positivity of contemporary life" (2011, 3); and following on that, I would add, to challenge the neoliberal model of apparent efficacy, efficiency, and standardization that thrives on clear-cut difference. So, using borders to refocus on surpluses as that which discourses of difference fail to explain, in order to move on to that which transcends both the particularities of identity politics and the ambiguity of hybridity and mestizaje discourses, may allow us to break the epistemic impasse that border studies entails. But the challenge remains in that focusing on these surpluses should not be an excuse to continue reproducing difference. Instead, I argue for a move to take these border surpluses as indexes of shared histories of marginalization and exploitation. I believe it is in this move towards critical sameness instead of difference that we can find a productive space for engaging people on both sides of the aisle in conversation who, feeling left out of the benefits of globalization and neoliberalism, take identity politics as an excuse to blame each other for their marginalization and exploitation.

In 2000, Paul Gilroy published *Against Race*, a critique of identity politics motivated by the relationship between race theories and fascism that, unfortunately, was not as academically influential as his previous work on race and double consciousness in *The Black Atlantic* (1993). The advent of fascist or fascist-like regimes worldwide in the second decade of the new millennium may be a good moment to revisit some of the polemical ideas he proposes in *Against Race*. Here, Gilroy argued for a move away from 'race' towards an emphasis on 'diaspora' as an interpretative and political reagent to overcome the essentialist and absolutist identitarian concepts at the core of both identity politics and fascist ideology. His main concern was that "political and cultural identity might be understood via the analogy of indistinguishable peas lodged in the protective pods of closed kinships and subspecies being" (2000, 125). In proposing to focus on the temporal and geographic tensions and the translocal solidarities that the notion of diaspora entails, Gilroy offers a critique of "pure sameness" as a fascist mechanism that symbolically materializes the identitarian fantasies at the core of this ideology. My call for an emphasis on critical sameness in my assessment of border studies and the identity politics the field sponsors takes Gilroy's concerns as a point of departure; however, instead of emphasizing difference—as I believe the notion of diaspora still does since, like border studies, it favors the experiences of certain individuals over others, making them into the "privileged subject[s] of history"[14] that Vila warns us about—it seeks to establish an anti-privilege common ground upon which to develop trans-experiential alliances among apparently opposite, dichotomic political constituencies—for example, "conservatives" vs. "progressives." Critical sameness promotes a move away from identity and spectacles of identity into processes of identification. But by that I do not mean the identification with someone else (individuals or groups) entailed in identity politics; instead, I refer to the processes of identifying shared conditions of oppression beyond our own identity groups. As such, critical sameness would strive for the postnational recognition of neoliberal capitalism and its operative elites as the marginalizing force and the real beneficiaries of these constituencies' sidelining, exploitation, and precarization. In other words, critical sameness would not simply be a critique of difference and the artificial polarization that identity politics often instigate, its final utopian goal would be the complete reconfiguration and reimagination of the current political scenario.

MUSIC SCHOLARSHIP: A LOOK FROM THE FENCE?

With the development of popular music studies as a serious academic endeavor and the arrival of sociologists and cultural theorists into the field of music studies in the 1970s and 1980s, policing the borders of their discipline became a constant endeavor among musicologists. This attitude was often defensive and, as it happens in all border policing, it was meant as a marker of difference. First, expressed in a rhetoric that emphasized the unique technical character of music, it was used to discredit the work of scholars who approached music studies without having been trained in music.[15] This type of move attempted to demarcate the object of study of musicology from an exceptionalist perspective in order to keep perceived outsiders away from it. However, as the music scholarship produced by those non-musicologists became intellectually relevant beyond the borders of musicology, musicologists began to open themselves to transdisciplinarity. Trained within a field that one could describe as interdisciplinary by nature but that for decades remained trapped in the borders of a narrowly defined object of study, musicologists have begun to cross the ontological borders they had fought so hard to defend and have begun asking questions that engage intellectual concerns beyond their discipline. This type of transdisciplinary inquiry may have prompted conservative scholars to question whether musicology still exists as a discipline (since they claim these turns have moved musicology away from music); nevertheless, it has opened the door not only to tackle truly relevant intellectual questions but also to reimagine how we define the borders of music and the musical.

Yet, regardless of all the borders that musicology has crossed in the last forty years a last disciplinary frontier lies ahead. Performance studies, a field that has nurtured a number of important music scholars in the last decade has defined itself as an activist project since its inception.[16] Performance studies scholars have never been afraid of being critical of and take a stance against the inequalities reproduced by the practices they study. Instead, they have fully embraced the subjectivity of their interpretative gaze and the political valence that a rigorous cultural critique may produce. Nevertheless, this border between activism and scholarship seems to still be drastically enforced within the field of musicology. It is as if this border demarcates the last bastion of positivism and the idea of objective knowledge for a discipline born out of strictly positivist concerns. The implications of taking such a stand in a project like the one about Juan Gabriel I have discussed here would be the uncritical reification of difference, borders, and ethnic imaginaries that reproduce political and social asymmetries. Reinforcing these principles has been central to musicology as a scholarly validation of colonialism, imperialism, nationalism, and white supremacy. Given the political events and cultural wars unfolding in the last twenty years, musicology cannot afford to remain at the fence of its disciplinary constraints and observe from the apparent safety of the Other side. Instead, musicologists should become aware of the profound political performativity in the alleged objectivity of their academic gaze. It is time for musicologists to see that by naturalizing these imaginary lines we call borders we create the structures that limit our modes of understanding and listening. It is time to listen beyond those structures, to listen to the cultural surpluses that fail to be inscribed within the boundaries of the discipline or of our listening training and take them as points of departure to build a decolonial musicological project. It is time to ask ourselves whom do we empower when we speak of borders; given their currency in politics worldwide during the last two decades, it is evident who benefits from talking about them.

NOTES

1. Probably there is no better work to show these parallel developments than Américo Paredes's foundational *"With His Pistol in His Hand": A Border Ballad and its Hero* (Austin: University of Texas Press, 1958).

2. See among others Frances R. Aparicio and Candida F. Jaquez, *Musical Migrations: Transnationalism and Cultural Hybridity in Latin/o America* (New York: Macmillan, 2003); Gerard Béhague, "Boundaries and Borders in the Study of Music in Latin America: A Conceptual Re-Mapping," *Latin American Music Review* 21, No. 1 (2000), 16–30; John Hutnyk, *Critique of Exotica. Music, Politics, and the Culture Industry* (London: Pluto Press, 2000); José E. Limón, *Dancing with the Devil:*

Society and Cultural Poetics in Mexican-American South Texas (Madison: University of Wisconsin Press, 1994;) Peter Manuel, *East Indian Music in the West Indies: Tān-singing, Chutney, and the Making of Indo-Caribbean Culture* (Philadelphia: Temple University Press, 2000); Manuel Peña, *The Texas-Mexican Conjunto, History of a Working-Class Music* (Austin: University of Texas Press, 1985); Cathy Ragland, "Mexican Deejays and the Transnational Space of Youth Dances in New York and New Jersey," *Ethnomusicology* 47, No. 3 (2003), 338–354; Helena Simonett, *Banda. Mexican-American Life across Borders* (Middletown, CT: Wesleyan University Press, 2001); Martin Stokes, "Imagining 'The South': Hybridity, Heterotopias and Arabesk on the Turkish-Syrian Border," in Border Identities: Nation and State at the International Frontiers, ed. by Thomas M. Wilson, Hastings Donnan (Cambridge: Cambridge University Press, 1998), 263–288; and José Manuel Valenzuela Arce, *Jefe de jefes. Corridos y narcocultura en México* (Havana: Casa de las Américas, 2003).

3. See Tamara Levitz, ed., "Musicology Beyond Borders?" *Journal of the American Musicological Society* 65, No. 3 (2012), 821–861; and Alejandro L. Madrid, ed., *Transnational Encounters. Music and Performance at the U.S.-Mexico Border* (New York: Oxford University Press, 2012). See also, among others, Georgina Born and David Hesmondhalgh, "Introduction: On Difference, Representation, and Appropriation in Music," in *Western Music and Its Others. Difference, Representation, and Appropriation in Music*, ed. by Georgina Born and David Hesmondhalgh (Berkeley and Los Angeles: University of California Press, 2000), 1–58; Brigid Cohen, "Diasporic Dialogues in Mid-Century New York: Stefan Wolpe, George Russell, Hannah Arendt, and the Historiography of Displacement," *Journal of the Society for American Music* 6, (2012), 143–173; Brigid Cohen, *Stefan Wolpe and the Avant-Garde Diaspora* (Cambridge: Cambridge University Press. 2012); Timothy D. Taylor, *Beyond Exoticism. Western Music and the World* (Durham, NC: Duke University Press, 2007); and *Global Pop. World Music, World Markets* (New York: Routledge, 2014).

4. A renewed interest in borders, diaspora, crossing borders, and hybridity has also been evident among ethnomusicologists in recent years. See Catherine M. Appert, "On Hybridity in African Popular Music: The Case of Senegalese Hip Hop," *Ethnomusicology* 60, No. 2 (2016), 279–299; Philip V. Bohlman, *Focus. Music, Nationalism, and the Making of the New Europe* (London: Routledge, 2011); Alexander M. Cannon, "Virtually Audible Diaspora: The Transnational Negotiation of Vietnamese Traditional Music," *Journal of Vietnamese Studies* 7, No. 3 (2012), 122–156; John Morgan O'Connell, "A Staged Fright: Musical Hybridity and Religious Intolerance in Turkey, 1923–38" *Twentieth Century Music* 7, No. 1 (2011), 3–28; Greg J. Robinson, "Remembering the Borderlands: Traditional Music and the Post-Frontier in Aisén, Chile," *Ethnomusicology* 57, No. 3 (2013), 455–484; Nolan Warden, "Crossing Diaspora's Borders: Musical Roots Experiences and the Euro-American Presence in Afro-Cuban Music," *African Music* 8, No. 4 (2010), 101–109.

5. Alejandro L. Madrid, *Nor-Tec Rifa! Electronic Music from Tijuana to the World* (New York: Oxford University Press, 2008); and Ignacio Corona and Alejandro L. Madrid, "Introduction: The Postnational Turn in Music Scholarship and Music

Marketing," in *Postnational Musical Identities. Cultural Production, Distribution and Consumption in a Globalized Scenario,* ed. by Ignacio Corona and Alejandro L. Madrid (Lanham, MD: Lexington Books, 2007), 3–22.

6. This in a way branches out of and problematizes the conversation about disciplinary borders that Kay Kaufman Shelemay promoted back in the mid-1990s. See Kay Kaufman Shelemay, "Crossing Boundaries in Music and Music Scholarship: A Perspective from Ethnomusicology," *The Musical Quarterly* 80, No. 1 (1996), 13–30.

7. I have explored this at length in Alejandro L. Madrid, "*Secreto a voces:* Excess, Vocality, and *Jotería* in the Performance of Juan Gabriel," *GLQ: A Journal of Lesbian and Gay Studies* 24, No. 1 (2018), 85–111.

8. Octavio Paz, *El laberinto de la soledad* (Mexico City: Fondo de Cultura Económica, 1959 [1950]).

9. Néstor García Canclini, *Hybrid Cultures: Strategies for Entering and Leaving Modernity* (Minneapolis: University of Minnesota Press, 1995).

10. *Ya la gente del campo se ha ido a emprender una nueva Aventura . . . de saber que en su pueblo han perdido el ingenio, el molino y cordura.*

11. See Walter D. Mignolo, "The Geopolitics of Knowledge and the Colonial Difference," *The South Atlantic Quarterly* 101, No. 1 (2002), 57–96.

12. Juan Eduardo Wolf, "Styling Borders: Mediation of Borderland Relationships through Music-Dance," paper presented at the 2018 National Meeting of the Society for Ethnomusicology. Denver, Colorado (October 27, 2017).

13. Renato Rosaldo, "Foreword" in García Canclini, *Hybrid Cultures,* xv.

14. Vila, *op. cit.*

15. See for example, Jack Westrup's critique of popular music critics in "Editorial," *Music and Letters* (1968), xix.

16. See the work of music-performance studies scholars like Michelle Kisliuk, Alexandra Vazquez, T. Roberts, and Christine Balance.

REFERENCES

Gilroy, Paul. *Against Race. Imagining Political Culture beyond the Color Line.* Cambridge, MA: Harvard University Press, 2000.

Halberstam, Judith. *The Queer Art of Failure.* Durham: Duke University Press, 2011.

Juan Gabriel, *El México que se nos fue.* Ariola International/RCA. 29580

Levitz, Tamara ed. "Musicology Beyond Borders?" *Journal of the American Musicological Society* 65, No. 3 (Fall 2012): 821–861.

Martínez Ortega, Gonzalo. *Del otro lado del puente.* Producciones Del Rey. 1980.

Moreiras, Alberto. *The Exhaustion of Difference. The Politics of Latin American Cultural Studies.* Durham, NC: Duke University Press, 2001.

Palou, Pedro Ángel. *El fracaso del mestizo.* Mexico City: Ariel, 2014.

Sánchez Prado, Ignacio. "El mestizaje en el corazón de la utopia: *La raza cósmica* entre Aztlán y América Latina." *Revista Canadiense de Estudios Hispánicos* 33, No. 2 (Invierno 2009): 381–404.

Vila, Pablo. "Conclusion: The Limits of American Border Theory," in *Ethnography at the Border*, edited by Pablo Vila, 306–342. Minneapolis: University of Minnesota Press, 2003.

Wolin, Sheldon S. "Fugitive Democracy," in *Democracy and Difference. Contesting the Boundaries of the Political*, edited by Seyla Benhabib, 31–45. Princeton: Princeton University Press, 1996.

Index

Adkins, Trace, 92
Accordion, 149, 152, 153, 157, 160–162, 164
Affect, xxv, xxviii-xxxi, 4, 36–38, 128, 130, 141, 172, 183, 193, 195, 200, 201, 204, 206
Afrodiasporic, 3–7, 9, 11–13, 15, 17, 19n3
Aguilar, Angela, 65
Allen, Paula Gunn, xiii
Almodóvar, Pedro, 52, 69, 72
Altered Movement, 104, 105, 110, 115, 116, 118n13
Alterity, xix, 11
Anderson, Benedict, 78
(Los) Ángeles Azules, 184, 187
Anzaldúa, Gloria, xiii–xv, 144n1, 202
Arhoolie Records, 157, 160
Aurality, xi, xiii, xv, xxvii, 104, 127, 129, 130, 133, 139, 143, 170–174, 176, 177, 181–184, 188
Authorization
    Self-, 139, 141
Avila, Rey, 156-159, 162, 163
Aztec, 54

Bajo sexto
    149, 160, 161

banda, 78, 82, 84, 86–89, 95nn10 and 14, 102, 104, 117n2
Bartra, Roger, xix, xxii, xxiii, xxix, xxxvn4
Bermúdez, Lucho, 175, 176
Blackness, 2, 4, 7, 10, 11, 18
Black Power, 195
bolero, 180
Border, xi-xv, xvin6, xxxi, xxxii, 9, 11, 15, 49, 50, 66, 67n8, 81, 84, 88–90, 102, 104, 106, 107, 109, 111, 113, 114, 116, 117n10, 127–130, 132, 133–139, 143, 144, 145nn1 and 5 149–161, 163, 165, 173, 194, 196, 197, 204, 206nn2 and 5, 211–213, 215, 217–220, 223–227, 228n4, 229n6
    Studies, 83, 145n1, 211, 212, 219, 220, 224
Brownsville, TX, 150, 151, 156, 160, 162
Buknas de Culiacán, 109
Butler, Judith, 41n9

Camacho, Ariel, 99, 101, 117nn2 and 5
(Los) Camperos, 199
    de Nati Cano
Campesino, xxiii, 26, 51, 64

231

Capitalism, xx, xxiv, xxxvi, 29, 101, 128, 173, 187, 195, 205, 219, 220, 226
Carrillo, Héctor, 90
(La) Casa Azul, 52
Cash, Johnny, 95n9
Castro, Fidel, 49
Censorship, xxi, 14, 16, 106, 111–114
Chamán, chamana, 56, 60
Chelo y su Conjunto Tropical, 176
Chicanismo, *See* Chicano
Chicano, xvin6, xxxii, 150–153, 156, 158–161, 193, 195, 196, 200–203, 205, 206n5, 214, 216–218
    Movement, xxxii, 151, 159, 161, 166n7, 196, 197, 205
Chicano Batman, xii, 201, 202, 204, 205
Chipsters, 202
Chomsky, Noam, xxxvn4
Cihuacóatl, 54, 70
Citizenship, xii–xiv, xxiv, xviin8, 24, 25, 27, 28, 40, 40nn1, 3, and 6, 47, 64, 66n3, 79, 129, 130, 134, 136, 138, 143, 145n5, 151, 153, 161, 172, 185, 186, 189n6, 200
Civil Rights Movement, 195
Civil society, xxi, xxiii, 189n6
Class, xi, xii, xx, xxii–xxiv, xxvi–xxviii, xxx, xxxi, xxxiv, 5, 54, 78, 79, 82, 91–93, 94n6, 95n10, 103, 108, 132, 136, 151–153, 155, 156, 161, 163, 170, 172–182, 184–188, 189nn6 and 7, 194
Cody, "Buffalo" Bill, 83
Cohen, Sarah, 163
Coloniality, xxiii, xxviii–xxx, 20n17, 23–25, 29, 38, 39, 40nn1 and 4, 47, 48, 55, 65, 66n2, 78–80, 83, 92, 93, 129, 131, 132, 142, 151, 154, 223, 227
Colosio, Luis Donaldo, xx, 112
CONARTE, 176, 189n4
    (Consejo para la Cultura y las Artes de Nuevo León)

Conjunto (music), xii, xxxi, 158, 161–165
Contact frame, 186–188
Contact zone, xii, xiii, xxxiv, 181–183, 186–188
Control Machete, 178
Coqueta (film), 1, 2
Corraleros del Majagual, 175, 176
corrido, 104
Cortés, Hernán, 83
Cosmopolitanism, xxvii, 3, 5, 7, 91, 94n6, 172, 173, 178, 181–185, 188, 193, 194, 204
Costa Rica, 49, 50
country (music), 81–83, 89, 90, 92, 93, 94n3, 95nn9, 10, and 12
Cowboy, 82–83
Critical Sameness, 225, 226
Crossing, 127, 129, 139, 143, 150, 155, 163
Cuevas, Aida, 65
Cuevas, Manuel, 95n9
cumbia, xxx, xxxi, 153, 156, 169, 170, 172, 173, 175–185, 187, 189n5
    rebajada, 182, 189n5
Cyrus, Billy Ray, 93

Dana International, 94n5
(El) Dasa, 88, 89
Décima, 137, 143
Decoloniality, xiii, xv, xxx, xxxiii, 38, 40n5, 47, 49, 50, 63, 65, 77, 78, 91, 92, 144, 224, 227
Difference, xv, xix, xxiii, xxv, xxvi, xxxii–xxxv, 5, 23, 30, 32, 39, 54, 80, 81, 128, 143, 154, 185, 186, 188, 205, 217, 219, 220, 223, 225–227
Discos Fuentes, 175, 176
Disenfranchisement, xx, xxi, xxiii, xxv, xxxii, 29, 116
Displacement, xxvi, xxxiv, 10, 15, 24, 35, 49, 131
Downs, Lila, 65

Duéñez, Gabriel, 169, 170, 172–178, 181, 182, 184
duranguense (music), 78, 84, 86

Enfranchisement,
    See Disenfranchisement
Essentialism, 39, 77-82, 87, 88, 90-93, 130, 131, 144, 204, 218, 219, 223–225
Estrangement, xxxiii, 216–219, 224
Ethnoscape(s), 194, 195
EZLN, xx
    (Ejército Zapatista de Liberación Nacional)

Fanon, Frantz, xiv
Feeling Brown, 193, 194
Fender, Freddy, xxxi, 82, 153–156, 158, 159, 163
Flores, William, 153
Folklore, xxx, 108, 132, 133
Fonoteca Nacional, 171, 172
Fontdevila, Jorge, 90
Foucault, Michel, xxv, xxxvn4, 41n11
Fuentes, Rumel, 160, 166n8

Gabriel, Juan, xxxii, 213–223, 227
Gamio, Manuel, 205
García, Peter J., 96n18
García Canclini, Néstor, 224
Gender, xi, xii, xxvi–xxx, xxxii, xxxiv, 2–5, 13, 18, 19n4, 21n19, 28, 29, 32, 37, 40n4, 41nn9 and 10, 47, 48, 50, 51, 55, 61, 64, 68n22, 77–80, 82, 86–93, 107, 133, 197, 205, 206n2, 213, 215–217, 219
    Trans(gender), 77, 78, 80, 88, 91, 92, 94n5
Genitállica, 178
ghettotech (music), 182, 183
Gilroy, Paul, 225
Globalization, xii, xxi, xxiv, xxvi, xxviii, xxxiv, xxxv, 23, 102, 104, 127, 150, 154, 170, 173, 225

GRAMMY Award, 65, 113, 119n31, 154, 164, 177, 181, 182
(El) Gran Silencio 179, 184
Grupo Fantasma
guaracha, 175, 176
Gutiérrez, Jorge, 202

Halberstam, Judith, 225
Heritage, xxiii, xxxi, 18, 83, 107, 149, 150, 153–156, 158, 160–165, 171, 172, 177, 186–188, 195–197, 199, 204
Hip-hop, xxxi, 178, 179, 181, 182
house (music), 181–183
Huapango, xii, xxxi, 127, 130, 136–138, 143, 144
Huasteca (region), 30, 31, 34, 35
Hughes, Charles, 82
Hybridity, xv, 40, 55, 59, 134, 152, 155, 161, 200, 211, 219, 220, 223–225

IDEAL Records, 152, 157, 160, 163
Identity Politics, xii, xxxii, 16, 105, 193, 202, 203, 205, 211, 213, 219, 224–226
Illegality, 49, 109, 133–135, 138, 142–144, 145n5, 155
Immigrant(s), xx, xxiii, 84, 89–91, 93, 100, 111, 136, 150–152, 156, 158, 161, 178, 194, 196
Indigenismo, xxiii, xxvii, xxviii
Indigenous, xxii, xxiii, xxvii, xxix, 10–12, 24, 26, 29, 39, 40, 41n8, 51, 54, 58, 83, 149, 201, 221
    communities, xii, xx, xxii, xxviii, xxix, 23–26, 37, 39, 40, 40n4, 41n8
    culture, xxvii, xxix
    people, xiii, xxii, xxviii, xxix, 27, 137
Isthmus of Tehuantepec, 54, 55, 59

Jiménez, José Alfredo, 56
Juchitán, 55

Kahlo, Frida, xii, xxx, 47–75
Keith, Toby, 83
kink communities, 77
Kinki, 178, 184
Kirshenblatt-Gimblett, Barbara, 154, 162
(El) Komander, 104, 109, 110, 113, 115
Kulick, Don, 94n5

Lafourcade, Natalia, 65
Lara, Camilo, 183, 184
Laure, Mike, 169, 170, 176
León, Eugenia, 65
Lewis, George H., 94n8
Limerick, Patty, 95n15
Limón, José, 151, 156
(La) Llorona, xxx, 47–75
Lomnitz, Claudio, xxv, xxvii, 185–187
López Obrador, Andrés M., xxii
López, Sonia, 176
Lorde, Audre, xiii, xiv, xv

Madrid, Alejandro L., xxxii, xxxiii, xxxiv, 150, 172, 175, 184–186
(La) Malinche, 54, 70
mambo, 175, 176
Márez, Curtis, 82, 94n8
Marginality, xxvii, xxx–xxxiii, 29, 40n4, 172, 181–183, 185, 187, 188, 214
mariachi, xxvii, 51, 81, 88, 89, 103, 117n10, 195–197, 199
    Reyna de los Angeles, 199
    Sol de México, 199
Marroquin, Armando, 152, 153
Materiality, 138, 141
Martínez, Narciso, xxxi, 150, 153–157, 160, 165
Mediascape(s), 194
Melancholy, 132, 144
Memory, xx, xxiv, xxx–xxxiv, 49, 108, 141, 149, 150, 153–157, 162–165, 169–173, 177, 178, 183, 188, 193, 194, 202
Méndez, Luis Alberto, 176

Mestizaje, xxiii, xxvii, 3, 6, 7, 9, 10, 12, 15, 40n3, 200, 201, 205, 211, 220, 224, 225
Mestizo/a, xxvii, xxviii, 11, 18, 27, 28, 40n3, 83, 104, 149, 201, 223
Mexican-American(s), xxxi, xxxii, 89, 90, 150, 152, 153, 160, 165, 166n8
(The) Mexican Miracle, 185, 186, 189nn6 and 7
Mexicanness, See Mexicanidad
Mexicanidad, xi, xii, xix, xxi, xxvi–xxx, xxxiv, 1, 4, 9, 11, 12, 15, 47, 48, 51, 63–65, 66n1, 77, 78, 81, 87, 88, 90–92, 95n14, 129, 130, 155, 178, 181, 184, 188, 193–195, 200, 205, 206, 206n3, 217, 218, 224
Migrants, See Migration
Migration, xxi, xxx, xxxi, 6, 28, 49, 91, 102, 127, 130, 131, 133–136, 138, 152, 203, 221
Miller, Karl Hagstrom, 82
Miller, Toby, 185, 186
Mirikitani, Janice, xiii
Mulatta/o, 2, 4, 5, 8
Murillo, Mario, 169, 177
música tropical, 172, 175, 176, 180, 181, 188n1

NAFTA, xx, xxi, xxxvn3, 112, 114, 135, 139, 150, 165n2, 178, 185, 187 (North American Free Trade Agreement)
Nahua (Nahuatl), 30, 35, 36
Narco
    corrido, 100–102, 106–108, 115, 116
    music, xii
Nation, 23, 24, 40, 40n1, 104, 114, 171
    -State, xi, xiii, xiv, xx, xxi, xxiv–xxix, 23, 24, 26, 29, 37, 39, 40, 40nn3
    and, 6, 186, 188, 189n6
Nationalism, xiii, xxiv, xxvi, xxx, xxxii, 10, 11, 50, 51, 68n23, 78–80, 83, 88–90, 92, 95n10, 129, 131, 132, 151, 156, 160, 213, 217, 227

Neoliberalism, xxiii–xxv, xxix, 23, 25, 28, 29, 37, 114, 143, 173, 206n5, 219, 220, 222, 223, 225, 226
norteño (music), 78, 84, 86, 95n11, 102, 104, 117n2, 152, 156
North America, xxi
nueva canción, 51
Núñez, Rogelio, 156, 161, 165

Obrerismo, xxiii
Ochoa Gautier, Ana María, 170–172
onda grupera, 84, 86, 93, 95n12, 180, 181
Ortiz, Gerardo, 110
Otherness, xx, xxvii, xxviii, xxxvin5, 4, 24, 40n4, 129, 133, 173, 212
Ozomatli, 178

Palacio de Bellas Artes, 61, 72
Palou, Pedro Angel, 224
Paredes, Américo, 83, 128, 205, 227n1
Parton, Dolly, 95n9
paseo, 176
Paz, Octavio, 132, 218, 225
Pecknold, Diane, 82
Peña, Manuel, 153, 158, 160, 161, 165n5
Performativity, xxvi, xxxi, xxxiii, xxxiv, 7, 23, 30–32, 35, 36, 41n9, 47, 48, 50, 53, 61, 63, 64, 69, 78, 88, 90, 92, 137, 138, 170, 200, 201, 212, 218, 224, 227
Phenomenology, xxv, xxvi, xxviii, xxx, xxxi, 35, 171
Piña, Celso, 177, 179, 180–182, 184, 187
Plan Nacional de Desarrollo, xx, 186
Plastilina Mosh, 178
pop music, 81
Populism, xix, xx, xxii, xxvi, xxix
porro, 175, 176
Postnationalism, xii–xv, xvin6, xix, xxiv, 127, 129, 134, 135, 138, 139, 144, 193, 205, 226
Pratt, Mary Louise, 181, 186

PRI, xx, xxix, 112
Public sphere, 29, 170, 172, 173, 177, 185–187
Puerto Rican Power, 195
punk music, 81

Queerness, xxx, 50, 57, 61, 64, 91, 217
querencia, 199
Quintanilla, Selena, 199

R&B music, 93
Race, xi, xiv, xv, xxiii, xxiv, xxvi–xxviii, xxx, xxxii, xxxiv, xxxvi, 1, 3–6, 10–12, 15, 18, 24, 40n3, 48, 49, 78–82, 92, 93, 128, 129, 132–134, 136, 143, 160, 194, 200, 202, 206, 206nn2 and 5, 215, 221, 223, 225
Ramos-Kittrell, Jesús A., xi, xii, xxxvin6, 24, 66, 91, 153, 175
ranchera (music), xxviii, 50, 51, 55, 81, 84, 86, 180
Rancho, 131, 132, 141
rap, 81, 93
rave (music), 181–183
reggaetón, 81, 93
regional Mexican music, 77, 78, 84, 86, 92, 94n3, 100, 104, 110, 115, 116
Resaca (region), 162–165
Resolana, 201
Reyes, Alfonso, 205
Rio Grande Music Company, 158, 163
Rio Grande Valley, 151, 152, 156, 157, 159, 161, 165
Rivera, Diego, 48, 52, 53, 58
Rivera, Ismael, 176
Rivera, Jenni, 89
Rivero, Carmen, 176
Roberts, Les, 154, 163, 164
rock (music), 180
Rock en español, 203
Rodríguez, Jesusa, 51
Rodriguez, Johnny, 82
Ronstadt, Linda, 196
Rosaldo, Renato, 224
Rumberas, 6, 7, 9–15, 17, 20n9, 20n13

Cine de, xii, 1, 3–7, 9, 10, 13, 15–18, 19nn4 and 6, 20n8

Salcedo, Pedro, 176
Salinas de Gortari, Carlos, xx, 28, 111, 112
Samuels, David W., 171
San Antonio, TX, 149, 152, 153, 156, 158, 164
San Benito, TX, 149, 152–160, 162, 164, 165
Sánchez, Chalino, 100, 102, 103, 117n2
Sánchez Prado, Ignacio, 224
Sariñana, Ximena, 65
Schizophrenia (cultural), 200
Seger, Bob, 95n12
Sevilla, Ninón, 1, 2, 5, 6, 13, 14, 16, 18
Sexuality, xi, xii, xxvi, xxviii–xxx, xxxiv, 4, 9, 12–14, 47, 48, 55–57, 61, 64–66, 77–79, 82, 87, 89–92, 213, 215
Silverblatt, Irene, 78–80, 92
Simonett, Helena, 95n10
Sinaloa, 99, 101–104, 109, 111, 113, 115
ska, 81
Snyder, Michael, 79, 86, 88
son istmeño, 54, 65
Sonidero, xii, 169, 172–174, 176, 177, 179, 181, 189n5
Sonido ronco, 149
(La) Sonora Santanera, 176
South Texas, 149, 151, 164
Spain, 52, 66, 68, 69
Spivak, Gayatri Chakravorty, xxxv, 39, 106
Strachwitz, Chris, 157, 158
Structure of Feeling, 200
Stryker, Susan, 80, 90
Subalternity, xxii, xxx, xxxii, xxxv, 27, 39, 91, 144, 188, 223
Surplus, 218, 224, 225, 227

Taibo II, Paco Ignacio, xxii, xxiii
Teatro-Bar El Hábito, 51, 69
techno, 181–183
tejano (music), xxxi, 82, 84, 150, 153, 156–158, 161, 163, 165
Tejeda, Juan, 149, 153
Texas Rangers, 83
Third World Feminism, xiii

(Los) Tigres del Norte, 107, 111–113
Tourism, xxvii, 150, 151, 153, 155, 156, 197
Tovar, Rigo, 180, 181, 186, 187
Toy Selectah, 177–184, 187, 188
Tradition, xix, xxii, xxiii, xxviii, 24, 25, 39, 179, 182, 185–188
Transnationalism, 6, 78, 81, 84, 88–92, 94n5, 95nn10 and 12, 130, 134, 195
(La) Tropa Colombiana, 177, 187
Trope, xxvi–xxviii, xxxiv, 3, 12, 104, 131–133, 142
Trump, Donald, xvin8, xix, xx, 49, 93, 150, 196, 200, 212, 223

UNESCO, 171, 177
United Farm Workers (UFW), 202
Valdez, Luis, 203
Valerio, Longoria, 149
vallenato, 175–177
Vargas, Chavela, xii, xxx, 47–75
Vasconcelos, José, 205
Virgen de Guadalupe, 49, 54, 59, 63 (Virgin of Guadalupe)
Voice/Voicing, 129, 130, 138, 139, 141, 142, 144

Wade, Peter, 175
Waggoner, Porter, 95n9
War on Drugs, xxi, 106, 109, 110, 114
Weismantel, Mary, 92
Wynter Sylvia, xiv
Yoakam, Dwight, 95n9
Zapotec, 54, 55

About the Contributors

Lizette A. Alegre González is a faculty member of the Escuela Nacional de Música of the Universidad Nacional Autónoma de México (UNAM). Her research focuses on the study of music as part of the body of oral traditions of Indigenous groups in the Mexican Huasteca region. Her thesis, *Viento arremolinado: el toro encalado y la flauta de mirlitón entre los nahuas de la Huasteca hidalguense*, was awarded a publication subvention by the Instituto Veracruzano de la Cultura in 2012. Moreover, she was awarded the Gabino Barreda medal of academic merit by UNAM. Alegre González has presented her research at international congresses and colloquia in México, Spain, France, Finland, Italy, Chile, Portugal, and Cuba. Her publications include "Cuerpo y agencia en la danza de Inditas de la Huasteca" 44–55; (2013) and "La flauta de mirlitón como vehículo de reificación y expulsión del Mal entre los nahuas de la Huasteca hidalguense" (in press).

Ana R. Alonso-Minutti is associate professor of music, faculty affiliate of the Latin American and Iberian Institute, and research associate of the Southwest Hispanic Research Institute at the University of New Mexico. She was born and raised in Puebla, Mexico, and holds a B.A. in music from the Universidad de las Américas, Puebla, and M.A. and Ph.D. degrees in musicology from the University of California, Davis. Her scholarship focuses on experimental and avant-garde expressions, music traditions from Mexico and the U.S.-Mexico border, and music history pedagogy. Her research areas include Latina/Chicana feminist and queer theories, critical race studies, and decolonial methodologies. Her work has appeared in Latin American Music Review, Revista Argentina de Musicología, Journal of Music History Pedagogy, Pauta, and elsewhere. She is coeditor of Experimentalisms in Practice:

Music Perspectives from Latin America (2018), and her book Mario Lavista and Musical Cosmopolitanism in Mexico is under contract with a publisher.

César Jesús Burgos Dávila is Professor at the Department of Psychology of the Universidad Autónoma de Sinaloa in Mexico and is a member of the university's program in social work. He graduated with a Ph.D. in social psychology from the *Universitat Autònoma de Barcelona*. Previously, he held a postdoctoral appointment at the Ethnic Studies Department of the University of California, Berkeley. Professor Burgos Dávila is a member of Mexico's National System of Researchers of the Consejo Nacional de Ciencia y Tecnología (CONACyT). His work focuses on the cultural expressions of drug trafficking, in particular forms of production, appropriation, and consumption of nacro-music in a local and transnational context. His publications include "La censura al narcocorrido en México: Análisis etnográfico de la controversia," (in press); "¡Que truene la tambora y que suene el acordeón!: Composición, difusión y consumo juvenil de narcocorridos en Sinaloa" (2016); and "Narcocorridos: antecedentes de la tradición corridística y del narcotráfico en México" (2013).

Alex E. Chávez is the Nancy O'Neill Assistant Professor of Anthropology at the University of Notre Dame, where he is also a faculty fellow of the Institute for Latino Studies. His work explores Latina/o/x expressive culture in everyday life as manifested through sound, language, and performance. Supported by the National Science Foundation and the Ford Foundation, his book *Sounds of Crossing: Music, Migration, and the Aural Poetics of Huapango Arribeño* (2017) was the recipient of the Alan Merriam Prize from the Society for Ethnomusicology (2018), the Society for Latin American and Caribbean Anthropology's Book Prize (2018), and the Association for Latina and Latino Anthropologists Book Award (2018). Chávez has consistently crossed the boundary between ethnographer and performer with his publicly engaged work as an artist and producer. He has recorded and toured with his own music projects, and has composed documentary scores (most recently Emmy Award-winning *El Despertar* [2016]). In 2016, he produced the Smithsonian Folkways album *Serrano de Corazón* (2016). Currently he serves as a governor for the Chicago Chapter Board of the Recording Academy.

Peter J. García is associate professor of world music studies, Chicana/o folklore, and U.S. Latina/o borderlands anthropology, performance and cultural studies at California State University Northridge. His work on Borderlands music engages decolonial theory and performance ethnography.

In addition to his monograph *Decolonizing Enchantment: Echoes of Nuevo Mexicano Popular Musics* (forthcoming), García's publications include "Decolonial New Mexican@ Travels: Music, Weaving, Melancholia, and Redemption Or, 'This is Where the Peasants Rise Up!'" in *The Un/Making of Latina/o Citizenship: Culture, Politics, and Aesthetics*, edited by Ellie D. Hernández and Eliza Rodriguez y Gibson (2014); and the volume *Performing the U.S. Latina and Latino Borderlands*, co-edited with Arturo Aldama and Chela Sandoval (2012).

Laura G. Gutiérrez is associate professor in the Department of Mexican American and Latina/o Studies at The University of Texas at Austin where she holds affiliations in the Center for Mexican American Studies, the Center for Women's and Gender Studies, and the Teresa Lozano Long Institute of Latin American Studies. A Mexican and Latinx performance and visual cultural studies scholar, Gutiérrez researches and teaches at the intersections of Latinx studies, Mexican studies, performance studies, visual culture studies, gender studies, and queer studies. She is the author of *Performing Mexicanidad: Vendidas y Cabareteras on the Transnational Stage* (University of Texas Press, 2010), an MLA book prizewinner, and articles and chapters on Latinx performance, border art, video art, and Mexican political cabaret. She is completing a monograph on racial and sexual panic in mid-twentieth-century Mexico through a reading of rumbera films and one on contemporary Latinx performance and visual art. Gutiérrez is also on the board of OUTsider, an Austin-based transmedia nonprofit, and curates the Conference on the Couch at its annual festival. She's also on the board of the Tepoztlán Institute for the Transnational History of the Americas, which meets annually in Tepoztlán, Morelos, Mexico.

Nadine Hubbs is a historian, theorist and a musicologist focused on twentieth- and twenty-first-century popular and classical music. Her writings recast social perspectives of people marked by sexuality and gender, class, race, and immigration history. She is the author of many essays and two books, *Rednecks, Queers, and Country Music* (2014) and *The Queer Composition of America's Sound* (2004), and is currently writing a book, *Country Mexicans: Sounding Mexican American Life, Love, and Belonging in Country Music*, and co-editing a journal special issue, *Uncharted Country: New Voices and Perspectives in Country Music Studies*. A publicly engaged scholar, Hubbs collaborates frequently with journalists and media, and her work has been featured in *The Guardian, Los Angeles Times, The Nation, New York Times, Salon,* and *Slate,* and on NPR, Pacifica, and BBC Radio, among other outlets. She is professor of women's and gender studies and music, and faculty affiliate in American culture at the University of Michigan, where she also directs the Lesbian-Gay-Queer Research Initiative.

Alejandro L. Madrid is professor of musicology and ethnomusicology at Cornell University. He is a cultural theorist whose historical, ethnographic, and critical work focuses on music and expressive culture from Latin America and Latinos in the United States. Madrid's work explores questions of transnationalism and diaspora; homophobia, masculinity, and embodied culture; and archives, historiography, and biographical writing through music from the long twentieth century. Madrid is the author of over half a dozen books for which he has received numerous national and international awards, including the Dent Medal given by the Royal Musical Association and the International Musicological Society for "outstanding contributions to musicology." He is the editor of an award-winning series *Currents in Latin American and Iberian Music* and coeditor of the journal *Twentieth-Century Music*.

Cathy Ragland is associate professor of ethnomusicology in the College of Music at the University of North Texas, and editor of the series *Sonic Crossings* for the university. Previously she taught at the University of Texas—Pan American (now the University of Texas Rio Grande Valley) near the Mexican border where she developed a masters program in ethnomusicology. She is also a former music critic for the *San Antonio Express-News, Seattle Times* and *Austin American-Statesman*, and cofounder of the Mariachi Academy of New York. Ragland primarily conducts research in the Texas-Mexican Borderlands, Mexico, the American Southwest, and Northern Spain. Her research centers on music and the politics of migration, transnationalism, music and identity, and applied ethnomusicology. She is the author of the book *Música Norteña: Mexican Migrants Creating a Nation between Nations* (2009); and book chapters such as "Communicating the Collective Imagination: The Sociospatial World of the Mexican Sonidero in Puebla, New York and New Jersey," in *Cumbia! Scenes of a Migrant Latin American Music Genre*, edited by Héctor Fernández L'Hoeste and Pablo Vila (2013), 119–137; and "'Tejano and Proud': Regional Accordion Traditions of South Texas and the Border Region," in *The Accordion in the Americas: Klezmer, Polka, Tango, Zydeco and More!*, edited by Helena Simonett (2012), 87–111, among other journal articles.

Jesús A. Ramos-Kittrell is assistant professor in residence of ethnomusicology and music history at the University of Connecticut. His work approaches sound as a platform to analyze the relationship of cultural phenomena to the socio-political structures organizing the practices that produce them. In such processes, Ramos-Kittrell identifies power asymmetries that inform the way individuals position themselves politically. His published work covers the early modern period (sixteenth through eighteenth centuries) in the Americas and more current cultural analyses of globalization. Previous appointments include visiting scholar at the Lozano Long Institute of Latin American Studies; joint professor of Latin American studies and ethnomusicology at Tulane University; and assistant professor of musicology at Southern Methodist University. Some of his publications include "Transnational Cultural Constructions: Cumbia Music and the Making of Locality in Monterrey," in *Transnational Encounters: Music and Performance at the U.S.-Mexico Border*, edited by Alejandro L. Madrid (2011), 191–206; and *Playing in the Cathedral: Music, Race, and Status in New Spain* (2016).

Chela Sandoval is one of the most influential voices for women of color in de/postcolonial and third-world feminism. Her most important work, *Methodology of the Oppressed*, developed fully the idea of a differential oppositional consciousness, a mode of "ideology-praxis" rooted in the experiences of the U.S. third world that challenges binary categories of identity in favor of a fluidity that moves between them. Sandoval's work made inroads in theoretical work on race, gender, and sexuality through what has been termed "anti-gender feminism," a type of feminism that regards gender as a harmful social construct according to anti-racism discourses. Sandoval is professor of Chicano/a studies at University of California, Santa Barbara.

Helena Simonett is senior research associate at the Lucerne University of Applied Sciences and Arts, CC Music Education Research. She has conducted extensive research on Mexican popular music and its transnational diffusion, as well as the role of Indigenous music and dance in Northwestern Mexico. Her publications include *Banda: Mexican Musical Life across Borders* (2001) and *En Sinaloa nací: historia de la música de banda* (2004). She is the editor of *The Accordion in the Americas: Klezmer, Polka, Tango, Zydeco, and More!* (2012) and served as guest editor of "Music for Being," *The World of Music* (2009), and coeditor of "Indigenous Musical Practices and Politics in Latin America" (2016).

www.ingramcontent.com/pod-product-compliance
Lightning Source LLC
Chambersburg PA
CBHW061708300426
44115CB00014B/2605